Wizardry

WIZARDRY

MICHAEL A. HUMPHREYS

Baseball's
All-Time
Greatest
Fielders
Revealed

OXFORD
UNIVERSITY PRESS

OXFORD
UNIVERSITY PRESS

Oxford University Press, Inc., publishes works that further
Oxford University's objective of excellence
in research, scholarship, and education.

Oxford New York
Auckland   Cape Town   Dar es Salaam   Hong Kong   Karachi
Kuala Lumpur   Madrid   Melbourne   Mexico City   Nairobi
New Delhi   Shanghai   Taipei   Toronto

With offices in
Argentina   Austria   Brazil   Chile   Czech Republic   France   Greece
Guatemala   Hungary   Italy   Japan   Poland   Portugal   Singapore
South Korea   Switzerland   Thailand   Turkey   Ukraine   Vietnam

Copyright © 2011 by Michael A. Humphreys

Published by Oxford University Press, Inc.
198 Madison Avenue, New York, NY 10016
www.oup.com

Oxford is a registered trademark of Oxford University Press

Library of Congress Cataloging-in-Publication Data

Humphreys, Michael A.
Wizardry: baseball's all-time greatest fielders revealed / Michael A. Humphreys.
p. cm.
Includes index.
ISBN 978–0–19–539776–5 (pbk.)
1. Fielding (Baseball) 2. Baseball—Defense. 3. Baseball players—Rating of. 4. Baseball
players—Statistics. 5. Baseball—Statistics. 6. Baseball—History. I. Title.
GV870.H85 2011
796.357'24—dc22 2010020168

---

1 3 5 7 9 8 6 4 2

Printed in the United States of America
on acid-free paper

To Sandra

Fielding records are known to be grossly inaccurate. F. C. Lane (1916).

There is nothing on earth anybody can do with fielding [statistics].
Fielding ... cannot be measured. Branch Rickey (1954).

"[Defense is] the cognoscenti corner of baseball, the poorly lighted room
in the gallery." Tom Boswell, as quoted in George F. Will, *Men at
Work: the Craft of Baseball* 274 (MacMillan 1987).

As late as June 4, 2002, ... there were still big questions about baseball
crying out for answers; a baseball diamond was still a field of
ignorance. ... No one had established to the satisfaction of baseball
intellectuals exactly which part of defense was pitching and which fielding,
and no one could say exactly how important fielding was. No one
had solved the problem of fielding statistics. Michael Lewis,
Moneyball 98 (W. W. Norton & Co. 2003).

[I]n some respects, fielding is baseball statistics' holy grail. Alan Schwarz,
The Numbers Game: Baseball's Lifelong Fascination with Statistics 239
(St. Martin's Press 2004).

To more closely approach the "holy grail" list of best [all-time] *players*
[not just batters], we will need to improve considerably our assessment of
fielding ability and how to rate its importance compared to offensive
and pitching ability. Michael J. Schell, *Baseball's All-Time Best Sluggers*
216 (Princeton University Press 2005).

Perhaps the next major statistical advance [in ranking baseball players] will
be the incorporation of a model that estimates how the talent pool may
have improved or declined on a year-by-year basis. Id.

In my 30-year career in [baseball research], I have spent far, far, far more
hours studying fielding than I have spent studying hitting or pitching.
I just don't have as much to show for it. Bill James, as quoted
in John Dewan, *The Fielding Bible* (ACTA 2007).

Preface

I was born in Brooklyn (Sunset Park), as were my mother (Flatbush) and father (Bay Ridge). Just after my first birthday we left the borough of churches, and I spent almost my entire childhood in two places that resembled the suburb depicted in *The Wonder Years*. But every couple of months or so the family (I soon had a brother and a sister) would go back to Brooklyn for weekend visits with my grandmother, who lived just a few blocks from where she had raised her daughter. One Sunday, while we were watching a football game on the black-and-white Motorola, my father tried to explain how "downs" work in football. I didn't understand for quite some time how a first down could follow a fourth (or third, or first), or why gaining one yard could be worth more than gaining nine. But he also told us then—I don't remember why he mentioned it—that you should always root for the underdog.

The perennial underdog when it has come to winning the big prizes of baseball—MVP awards, huge free agent contracts, commercial endorsements, movie star girlfriends, Hall of Fame membership, what have you—-has been the scrappy "good field, no hit" player. In fact, even the good hitters who are good fielders have always seemed to lose out to players who might have been better hitters but gave it all back—and more—in the field. Here is one example.

My father's favorite player was "Pistol Pete" Reiser. Legendary manager and tough guy Leo Durocher raved about Pistol Pete's power from both sides of the plate and speed, concluding that he might have been better than Mays: "Willie Mays had everything. Pete Reiser had everything but luck." For the majority of you who, for very good reason, have no idea why Durocher said what he did, let's begin by consulting a baseball encyclopedia. There you will find that, during his first full-time major league season, twenty-two-year-old Harold Patrick Reiser (he got the nickname "Pistol Pete" in boyhood) led the 1941 National League in runs scored, doubles, triples, batting average, and slugging percentage, while playing 133 games in centerfield for the Brooklyn Dodgers, who won their first pennant in a generation. Reiser was, quite simply, a sensation.

You will also find, as you scan down Reiser's post-1941 numbers, that he never played a full season again. Why? A baseball encyclopedia is majestically devoid of explanations. But just Google "Reiser" and "baseball," and you'll eventually get the story. In early July 1942, Pistol Pete hit an outfield wall while running at full speed. In those days outfield walls were neither bordered by warning tracks nor padded. Reiser suffered a severe concussion and a separated shoulder. His batting average dropped from .380 to .310, which means he hit below .250 the rest of the season, though he did lead the league in stolen bases while playing in only 125 games. Reiser served in the armed forces during the 1943–45 seasons. When he returned, he returned as well to his heedless pursuit of deeply hit fly balls. Red Smith wrote that Pistol Pete had eleven outfield wall collisions over the course of his career, at least one nearly enough fatal to justify bringing a priest into centerfield to perform the last rites. Reiser played 122 games in 1946, and again led the league in stolen bases, but only 110 games in 1947, which marked the effective end of his career.

I don't think "luck" was Reiser's problem; he just couldn't figure out how to make the tradeoff—for the sake of himself and his team—of allowing a double or two to go uncaught so that he could be healthy enough to continue leading the league in batting, slugging, and base stealing. Yet Pistol Pete Reiser did suffer one injustice: being passed over for the 1941 National League MVP award, which went to his teammate, first baseman Dolf Camilli, who led the league in home runs and runs batted in. Camilli drew almost twice as many MVP votes as Reiser. Somehow the voters thought that Dolf's advantage over Pete in home runs and runs batted in clearly outweighed Pete's advantage in runs scored, singles, doubles, and triples, plus the value of fielding a more difficult position (centerfield versus first base), and fielding it well. If you had asked the 1941 MVP voters why they thought Camilli was more valuable than Reiser, not one would have been able to provide a logical, statistically sound reason. Fans and sportswriters simply *respected* the guys who "drove in" base runners, as if the latter were just along for the ride. One number (runs batted in) effectively stood for the entire process of run production and, usually, overall player value. Fielding? Fuhgeddaboutit.

With rare exceptions, the slugger with a bad or mediocre glove has been overvalued in MVP voting compared with the well-rounded player with a good glove. Ryan Howard over Albert Pujols in 2006. Frank Thomas over John Olerud in 1993. Andre Dawson over Ozzie Smith, and George Bell over Alan Trammell in 1987. Willie Stargell muscling in on half of Keith Hernandez's award in 1979. Jeff Burroughs over Bobby Grich in 1974. Boog Powell over Tony Oliva in 1970. Orlando Cepeda over Ron Santo in 1967. Hank Sauer over Jackie Robinson in 1952. Ducky Medwick over Gabby

Hartnett in 1937. George Burns (not a slugger, but second in the league in runs batted in) over Johnny Mostil in 1926. (Actually, Ruth should have beaten both; before 1930 players were not allowed to win twice. However, Mostil was clearly the second best American League player in 1926.) Larry Doyle over Honus Wagner in 1912. Interestingly, during the Second World War there were two counter-examples, when Marty Marion (1944) and Joe Gordon (1942) won MVP awards they didn't actually deserve, mainly because of their outstanding glove work. Maybe during that one special moment in our history everybody valued the 'little guy', figuratively speaking (actually, Marion was quite tall, but not a big hitter).

Times may be changing for great fielders, but only because the owners now have the data and financial incentives to get fielding evaluation right. The *Sports Illustrated* 2009 baseball preview issue included a lead article about how major league baseball teams are buying proprietary data that tracks, among other things, the approximate trajectory (ground ball, line drive, fly ball, pop up) and location (for example, "left-center, deep") of every batted ball, and whether it was converted into an out or scooted through or dropped in for a hit. We'll be calling this type of information "batted ball data." In theory, this information should enable owners to measure fielding value very accurately, because it measures the total number and relative difficulty of all batted ball fielding opportunities anywhere remotely near a fielder. The *Sports Illustrated* article suggested a couple of cases in which free agents with good bats but poor gloves failed to obtain the contracts they were expecting in 2009 because the owners could tally the cost of their bad fielding, in terms of runs 'allowed' (or if the player is above average, 'saved') relative to the league-average fielder at the position, or "defensive runs," which can be positive or negative.

But what can the fans do? As a practical matter they're shut out. It goes without saying that since batted ball data has only been available for recent seasons, it can't be used to estimate defensive runs for the all-time best fielders. But even fans that just want to know how well current players are performing must buy the data (subject to licensing restrictions) every year for several thousands of dollars and write software programs to convert the data into defensive runs estimates, or take on faith the evaluations others report using this proprietary data. Ninety-nine percent of baseball fans are probably perfectly content to take at face value such defensive runs estimates, some of which are now available for free on public websites.

For me at least, and I believe for many others, one of the magical things about the work of Bill James, the greatest baseball writer and analyst of all time, is that he has never been satisfied merely to report the results of his research, but has always brought his readers into the process of *understanding* a particular problem and his solution. For thirty years he has been taking the same 'ordinary' baseball statistics everybody else has had for over a century, and used his imagination and a little math to show *how* they can make better sense. He has always been completely open about his methods and has usually demonstrated when they have and haven't worked. His fans have felt empowered, indeed compelled, to build on his methods to develop their own insights. I am only one of many.

The methods we'll be using here to discover the greatest fielders of all time and the impact they had on their teams are more complicated than those James introduced in his annual baseball books during the 1980s, but are actually less computationally intensive than the overall player evaluation system he proposed in 2001 (Win Shares). Every number presented in this book can be independently verified (or corrected or improved) by anyone with the patience (admittedly Job-like) to download free data from the web and organize it into Excel spreadsheets (though a true relational database program would be much more appropriate). As we'll show in chapter three, the fielding estimates generated here for recent players match up very well against estimates based on published reports derived from proprietary batted ball data—about as well as the latter match up with each other. I hope that some readers will discover ways to improve on the ideas developed here in order to generate fielder ratings that are good, open-source, easily verified alternatives to ratings based on proprietary data.

ACKNOWLEDGEMENTS

Before we go any further, I'd like to acknowledge several people:

Dick Cramer, who reviewed several early articles I wrote describing the statistical model for defense (pitching and fielding) that is the foundation of this book ("Defensive Regression Analysis," or "DRA"), and found them interesting enough to forward to Michael Lewis while the latter was writing *Moneyball*. Dick was the first person to appreciate the underlying logic of DRA—without his encouragement, I doubt I would have had the patience to keep working on it. As a founder of STATS, Inc., the first company to collect batted ball data, Dick made possible the compilation of data against which DRA could be tested.

David Smith, and everyone who has ever contributed to Retrosheet, all of whom made possible the data for DRA.

The information used here was obtained free of charge from and is copyrighted by Retrosheet. Interested parties may contact Retrosheet at 20 Sunset Road, Newark, DE 19711.

John Jarvis, whose on-line compilation of Retrosheet data enabled me to put together my first version of DRA.

Pete Palmer, the co-author of the *Baseball Encyclopedia*, who has always been there to help my understanding of the quality and scope of statistics throughout baseball history.

Frank King and his son Jeff King, friends and neighbors who showed me many years ago how much fun reading random pages from the MacMillan Baseball Encyclopedia could be.

Steve Pappaterra, who introduced me to the work of Bill James.

Bill James, who wrote a kind and encouraging e-mail when I sent to him an over-long and under-organized letter in which I tried to describe an early version of the DRA method. Although DRA differs significantly from Bill's defensive Win Shares system, I was inspired to work on this project after reading his *Win Shares* book, and some of the most important ideas in DRA came from *Win Shares*.

Allen Barra, who first put me in bookstores by including in his *Brushbacks and Knockdowns* an e-mail dialogue I had with Bill James regarding Barry Bonds.

Michael J. Schell, who proved that a great university publisher could be persuaded to publish not just one, but *two*, baseball statistics books. Michael has also kindly offered many helpful comments regarding DRA and *Wizardry*.

Dave Studenmund, who has long championed DRA, and who published the second and third internet articles about DRA on the hardballtimes.com website. His colleague David Gassko also provided helpful comments on an earlier draft.

David Pinto, who has also posted DRA results on his website, baseball-musings.com.

Mitchel Lichtman, Tom Tango, and Dan Szymborski. Mitchel provided an invaluable service to all baseball fans by acquiring batted ball data, intelligently converting it into estimates of runs "saved" or "allowed" by individual fielders, and publishing his results, which I could use to test DRA. Tom Tango made available to me the complete database of Mitchel's ratings. Dan edited the first, and very long, DRA article for the baseballthinkfactory.org website.

The team of analysts to whom I disclosed the first version of DRA and all the essential ideas of the model described in chapter two, in April 2007, who, in addition to Dick Cramer, John Jarvis, Pete Palmer, Michael Schell, Dave Studenmund, and David Gassko, included Cy Morong, Jan Vecer, Keith Carlson, and Matt Souders.

My editor, Phyllis Cohen, Dan Rosenheck, writer for *The Economist* and *The New York Times*, and Hannah Miklaus, a good friend of mine, who pushed me to make important improvements.

The blind reviewers for the proposal and initial drafts of this book, as well as the provider of the data in appendix D.

My family, for reasons only they will know, who made this book possible.

There is one more absolutely necessary acknowledgement: that of my own fallibility. In creating DRA and tracking the results of other fielding systems, I had to do an inordinate amount of copying and pasting and hand coding of data into a plethora of spreadsheets. I have done my best, but I'm sure I've made mistakes.

Contents

Motivations and Methods

The Big Picture

Who is a better player—Ryan Howard or Chase Utley? Not who slugs the most home runs (Howard), or steals the most bases (Utley), or drives in the most runs (Howard), or plays the more difficult position (Utley), or scores the most runs (Utley). At the end of the day, taking everything into account, how many more games have the Phillies won because they've had Utley as their second baseman rather than an ordinary second baseman, compared to the number of games they've won because they've had Howard as their first baseman, rather than an ordinary first baseman?

Over the past thirty years or so, a lot of folks have developed answers to this question by converting traditional baseball statistics into estimates of a player's overall net value, in 'runs created' above a baseline level, taking into account all of the elements of the player's offense, the amount of time he plays, and the relative difficulty of the position he plays. These runs created estimates can also be translated into 'wins' created.

But we've left something out, haven't we? How many runs did the player 'save' or 'allow' in the field, relative to other fielders at his position? Yes, we have long had pretty good estimates of how much 'extra credit' a player should get because he happens to play a more difficult position (such as second base) rather than an easier one (first base). But that doesn't tell you how well he plays the position. If you don't know how to answer that question, in terms of a reasonably reliable estimate of runs saved or allowed relative to the baseline fielder at that position, then in any remotely close case of overall player evaluation you don't really know which player was better.

The problem of estimating the value of a player's fielding over the course of a season and career using traditional defensive statistics has been the holy grail baseball statistics problem at least since Branch Rickey declared it unsolvable in a famous *Life* magazine article in 1954. Precisely because it was still considered unsolvable even two generations later, despite some insightful attempts we'll be discussing throughout this book, private companies were formed to collect new kinds of statistics to answer this question for baseball teams. And those answers are probably very good. But they're based on proprietary data, and are only available for recent players.

A different approach must be taken to evaluate the all-time greats. It's clear that Barry Bonds has been a more valuable player than Ken Griffey, Jr. But if you had asked before the turn of the millennium which player had been more valuable over the first ten years of his career, it would have been a very close question. Going a little further back, who was the greatest player before the offensive explosion in the 1990s—Joe Morgan or Mike Schmidt? Schmidt had bigger numbers, but Morgan played what was then a much tougher position than Schmidt. From the moment Mickey Mantle retired in 1968, everyone knew that Willie Mays had had the greater career. But some have argued very persuasively that at his peak or in his prime Mantle was not just a greater player, but a much greater player than Mays.

Ted Williams was a proud man, and didn't hesitate to say that he was a better hitter than Joe DiMaggio, but always granted that Joe was the better all-around player. Was Joltin' Joe, in fact, a more valuable player, overall, than The Thumper? Ty Cobb won a lot more batting titles than Tris Speaker, but at the time they played, some thought Speaker a better all-around player, and Speaker often earned more money than Cobb. Back in the 1890s, Ed Delahanty was the greatest slugger in the game. But was he the best player?

None of the questions posed above can be answered unless we have a method of estimating fielding value, in runs, that is as transparent, logical, and at least close-to-reliable as the methods developed to assess the other components of overall value.

If we could find such a method, it would not only change our rankings of the players throughout baseball history we already 'knew' were among the best; it would bring to our attention for the first time many players who've been forgotten because of their modest batting numbers. And resolve one of the big unknowns of major league history: whether the rare players who have garnered fame primarily through their fielding—Rabbit Maranville, Bill Mazeroski, Brooks Robinson, Omar Vizquel, perhaps a few more—actually contributed all that much to the success of their teams.

To answer these questions, this book presents the first method for quantifying fielding value throughout major league history to which professionals who make their living working with mathematical and statistical models might give their approval. And the results produced by that method, along with a new approach introduced for ranking players who played in different eras, will, I believe, eventually result in the biggest changes seen in thirty years in the assessment of the historical statistical record of our nation's most history- and numbers-obsessed pastime.

As the saying goes, extraordinary claims require extraordinary evidence. So we are going to present a lot of evidence. We'll introduce each concept with relatively simple examples, and then refine things step by step. In addition, sufficiently detailed information is presented in the on-line appendices for anyone interested in replicating, testing, or improving upon the methods introduced here.

The level of detail will, nevertheless, be overwhelming in more than a few places. I can readily imagine how many of you will feel when confronted with some of the formulas and data (and analysis of such formulas and data), because I 'chose' to become an English major in college after a very undistinguished three-semester career in calculus. Although I've since had a reasonably positive mid-life encounter with some fairly advanced mathematics, and have managed to organize all the data and devise all the equations presented in this book, I know exactly what it feels like to confront books packed with math, data, and intricate arguments that seem at first glance, and even after many re-readings, incomprehensible and lacking any clear objective.

I hope I've at least made the objective clear: measuring the season-by-season impact, in runs, of fielders throughout major league history, and finding a way to compare them more fairly across time. When things get a little dense or difficult, do what every mathematician or scientist does when they first come to a part of a technical paper or book that they don't understand: skip ahead to something that recaptures your interest. Browse through the player essays in Part II. Go back and re-read something you felt you more or less understood, but would like to understand better. If and when you feel like it, come back to the parts that seemed a bit hard to follow. I hope and believe they'll be clearer the second or third time around. If not, the fault will be mine.

As we set out on our project of quantifying the fielding value of every player in major league history, we need to keep the following in mind at all times:

> Although this may seem a paradox, all exact science is dominated by the idea of approximation. When a man tells you that he knows the exact truth about anything, you are safe in inferring that he is an inexact man.   —A philosopher to be named later.

We will never arrive at a single number for any fielder with anything like the objectivity of a batting average or runs batted in total. But by letting go of the concept of the existence of an exact number for fielding value, and focusing instead on developing better and better approximations, we'll make a lot of progress.

Whenever you're trying to estimate the approximate value of something, you need units of measurement, a reference point, and a sense of materiality and precision. In evaluating fielders, we'll keep asking ourselves the following questions: How much? Compared to what? Does it really matter? How wrong might we be?

The basic unit of measurement in baseball is runs, which translate remarkably well into the ultimate unit of measurement: wins. About every ten extra runs that a player helps his team score on offense or prevent on defense is associated, over the course of a full major league season, with one extra win for his team. This relationship is close to a 'straight line' or 'linear'. If a player contributes ten extra runs produced on offense and ten runs saved on defense, the total net advantage of twenty runs should generally result in two extra wins. If a player contributes forty extra runs on offense but gives back ten runs on defense, the total net advantage of thirty runs should result in three extra wins. And so forth. Good methods for converting a player's individual batting statistics into an estimate of the number of runs he produced on offense have been in the public domain, if not widely known, for at least forty years, and arguably for ninety years.

Our reference point will generally be league-average performance; that is, we'll generally be seeking to estimate how many runs a particular fielder 'saved' or 'allowed' each season compared to what the hypothetical average fielder at that position in that league in that year would have if he played in place of the fielder being evaluated. We'll refer to this net number as "defensive runs," which are positive for runs saved and negative for runs allowed.

Some baseball analysts believe that it is incorrect to compare fielders on the basis of their runs saved or allowed relative to the average fielder; instead they believe it is better to measure the extent to which a fielder exceeds the minimum acceptable level of fielding performance, or the level at which, if you fall below it, you are replaced at that position, what is known as "replacement level" performance. I believe there are at least four good reasons to use average, not replacement level, performance as our reference point, at least for purposes of fielding evaluation. First, replacement level fielding is generally fairly close to average fielding anyway, because it is much easier to find back-up players who can field at an average level than players who can hit at an average level. Second, with really only one exception, all previously published and currently reported estimates of fielder value are made by reference to league-average performance, so using league-average performance as the reference point makes it much easier to compare and contrast fielding evaluation systems. Third, one can always later define replacement level fielding by reference to average fielding.

Fourth, and most importantly, there really isn't such a thing as a replacement level fielder (or a replacement level batter); rather, there are replacement level *players*, because it is overall value that wins or loses ballgames. A very poor fielder might not be replaced in the field because he hits exceptionally well, and vice versa. It is relatively simple to combine offensive runs and defensive runs, each of which is measured by reference to league-average performance, to estimate overall runs above replacement level, though some judgment is inevitably involved, because replacement level is not a mathematical definition, like an average, but a fact to be inferred from different kinds of often conflicting evidence.[1]

Though replacement level is generally the best reference point for measuring overall player value, for all intents and purposes the concept of league-average performance works equally well when you are comparing exceptional players who play full time, in other words, the ones we care about most for all-time ranking purposes.

How many runs above or below league-average performance really matter? An all-star who plays a full season should be at least twenty, perhaps thirty runs above average at his position, on a combined offensive and defensive basis; an MVP at least fifty. These are approximate thresholds. Bill James has said in his book *Win Shares* that there is more than enough randomness and sheer imprecision in baseball statistics, presumably even offensive ones, that a player who is estimated to have been about ten runs worse than another, even when based upon the best quantitative measures, might actually have been just as valuable.

Over the course of a career, a legitimate Hall of Famer is generally at least three hundred runs, or thirty wins, better than league-average performance at his position, offense and defense combined, although, because of the vagaries of Hall of Fame voting, this is only a very rough estimate subject to many exceptions. A Hall of Famer should ideally be a legitimate MVP candidate for two or three seasons, a true all-star for several seasons, and well above average for a few more. Sometimes the very best players are below

---

1. Here's one approach. Add each player's offensive runs (relative to the entire league, not just players at his position) to his defensive runs to derive "net overall runs." (If a player splits time between positions, allocate his offensive runs to those positions in proportion to his playing time and add his defensive runs for each position to that allocated portion.) Do this for every player at every position. Identify the subset of players at each position who played less than two-thirds of a season, even though they were healthy. Take the average net overall runs for that subset of players at each position. That is the "replacement level," which will differ by position. Any net overall runs for a player above the replacement level for his position equals his "runs above replacement." Though there would undoubtedly be some year-to-year variability in the replacement level per position, it probably would not be that great, because it is defined by reference to the average net overall runs of probably no less than twenty bench players per position, even when the leagues have only eight teams. Large sample averages are relatively stable.

average but still above replacement level for a few seasons, especially in the last year or two of their careers.

Our first table will report various estimates leading analysts have made of career defensive runs by a group of players who are often, based on reputation or Gold Gloves awarded, considered to be the best or among the best fielders at their respective positions during the eras in which they played. By comparing the results we'll get at least a few opinions of the potential relative impact on overall career value that fielding can have. We'll also see how difficult it has been for analysts to reach a consensus on fielding value, and how important it might be to arrive at reasonably accurate consensus on fielding value for each player.

The best known sources for defensive runs are: Pete Palmer's "Fielding Runs" system, published in the *ESPN Baseball Encyclopedia* each year ("Palmer"); Sean Smith's estimates, published for seasons since the 1950s at baseball-reference.com based on his "TotalZone" system (which we will see is really three different systems), and for seasons before the 1950s on his own website, baseballprojection.com, based on a less sophisticated system ("Smith"); Clay Davenport's Fielding Runs Above Average (sometimes also known as Fielding Translations), which are available at baseballprospectus. com ("Davenport" or "D'port"); and Bill James' Fielding Wins Shares, reported in his book *Win Shares* ("James").

The players in the table on the next page "Best-Known Estimates of Career Defensive Runs for Certain Famous Fielders," are grouped in positions listed in descending order of relative fielding difficulty—what Bill James termed the "Defensive Spectrum"—which runs from shortstop, the toughest position to field, down to first base, the easiest, with catcher 'off the chart' and therefore listed at the end. For each position, one player is listed from four of the five historical eras we will be frequently referring to. Defining the first era forces us to answer a difficult threshold question.

When did major league baseball begin? The National Association is sometimes considered the first major league; it was formed in 1871 and folded in 1875. Today's National League was formed in 1876. The American Association was formed in 1882 but closed shop after the 1891 season, with some of its teams being absorbed by the National League. Not until 1893 was the pitching rubber moved back from its original position forty-five feet from home plate to sixty feet, six inches. In 1901 the American League (formerly the Western League) declared itself a major league, and the National League instituted the foul strike rule, probably the last fundamental change in the rules, to prevent batters from intentionally fouling off every pitch not to their perfect satisfaction. *The New Bill James Historical Baseball Abstract* (hereinafter, "*The Historical Abstract*") expresses real doubt about the quality of major league play before the 1890s. Forced to pick one year as the first,

I have chosen 1893, because the collapse of the American Association after the 1891 season should have concentrated more talent in the remaining National League, and because 1893 was the first year pitchers pitched from the current distance from home plate.

Our first historical eras will therefore be the "Dead Ball Era," from 1893 through 1919. The other four eras are the "Live Ball Era," from 1920 (when home runs started going up) through 1946; the "Transitional Era," from 1947 (the first season for Jackie Robinson and Larry Doby) through 1968 (when integration was largely complete); the "Modern Era," from 1969 through 1992; and the "Contemporary Era," from 1993 to the present (when offense noticeably jumped). Because results for one of the fielding systems we'll be reporting are not consistently available after 2001, we'll not list any players from the Contemporary Era.

Best-Known Estimates of Career Defensive Runs for Certain Famous Fielders

Pos	Era	First	Last	Palmer	Smith	D'port	James
SS	Dead Ball	Honus	Wagner	80	85	233	101
SS	Live Ball	Rabbit	Maranville	150	130	168	61
SS	Transitional	Roy	McMillan	93	90	142	46
SS	Modern	Ozzie	Smith	279	239	380	96
2B	Dead Ball	Nap	Lajoie	341	83	178	10
2B	Live Ball	Joe	Gordon	51	150	114	29
2B	Transitional	Bill	Mazeroski	362	148	184	98
2B	Modern	Ryne	Sandberg	99	57	70	36
CF	Dead Ball	Tris	Speaker	161	92	170	110
CF	Live Ball	Joe	DiMaggio	0	49	57	23
CF	Transitional	Willie	Mays	50	185	159	47
CF	Modern	Paul	Blair	37	176	82	47
3B	Dead Ball	Jimmy	Collins	122	121	204	91
3B	Live Ball	Pie	Traynor	25	-32	112	29
3B	Transitional	Brooks	Robinson	103	293	194	81
3B	Modern	Mike	Schmidt	237	129	155	79
RF	Dead Ball	Harry	Hooper	68	77	129	39
RF	Live Ball	Paul	Waner	29	23	80	67
RF	Transitional	Roberto	Clemente	116	204	58	58
RF	Modern	Jesse	Barfield	101	149	129	50
LF	Dead Ball	Fred	Clarke	62	91	157	83
LF	Live Ball	Goose	Goslin	44	50	46	35
LF	Transitional	Carl	Yastrzemski	80	135	48	37
LF	Modern	Barry	Bonds	51	179	102	15

(continued)

Best-Known Estimates of Career Defensive Runs for Certain
Famous Fielders *(continued)*

Pos	Era	First	Last	Palmer	Smith	D'port	James
1B	Dead Ball	Fred	Tenney	135	85	64	15
1B	Live Ball	Bill	Terry	72	73	23	27
1B	Transitional	Vic	Power	135	62	161	20
1B	Modern	Keith	Hernandez	133	120	83	18
C	Dead Ball	Ray	Schalk	121	46	115	66
C	Live Ball	Gabby	Hartnett	107	12	118	95
C	Transitional	Roy	Campanella	52	0	59	43
C	Modern	Johnny	Bench	*100*	97	233	50

A few caveats. First, James' estimates are not denominated in defensive runs (which may be negative), but in fielding 'wins' multiplied by three, which are never negative. I've had to make some assumptions to convert these numbers into defensive runs, and perhaps I've erred, but I've done my best. Also, I've italicized estimates that may reflect defensive runs at positions other than the player's primary position. Finally, the Davenport numbers come from the baseballprospectus.com website as of May 2009; the numbers at the website have changed frequently over the years, and may differ substantially when you read this.

Just eyeballing the numbers, there seem to be many large differences in estimated value. But how might we *measure* the extent to which these estimates, considered as a whole, tend to be different from or similar to each other? There are actually many ways to assess how similar multiple sets of estimates of something are to each other. But the three main ones we will use throughout this book are the "average" ("avg"), the "standard deviation" ("std"), and "correlation" ("corr"). First we'll show a table of the averages and standard deviations and explain them a bit, then we'll address correlation.

	Palmer	Smith	D'port	James
avg	112	106	131	53
std	85	70	72	29

If we calculate the average defensive runs for the above sample of players, we find that the average Palmer estimate is +112 defensive runs, the average Smith estimate is +106, the average Davenport estimate is +131, and the average James estimate is +53. So we can see that the overall level of estimated defensive runs for this set of players is broadly similar under the Palmer, Smith, and Davenport systems, but noticeably smaller under James, suggesting that the James system estimates that fielding has a smaller impact. If the Palmer, Smith, and Davenport estimates of the typical scale of career impact for top fielders is correct, then a typical top fielder generates one-third of a Hall of Fame career's worth of value from his fielding. About four players are estimated under one system or another to have generated a Hall of Fame career's worth of value solely from their fielding. This should certainly pique our interest.

"Standard deviation" is simply a commonly used measurement for the 'typical spread' in values. It is the 'standard' amount by which each outcome 'deviates' from (falls short of or exceeds) the average. If outcomes follow a so-called bell curve or "normal" distribution, then about two-thirds of outcomes are within plus or minus one standard deviation of the average, and about ninety-five percent are within plus or minus two standard deviations. The defensive runs estimates above are not technically normally distributed, but they generally follow an approximately symmetric bell-shaped curve, so the standard deviation is still a useful measure of the typical spread in values. And single-season defensive runs estimates for complete samples of full-time players generally follow something close to a normal distribution.

The standard deviation is calculated by subtracting the average value in the sample from each of the individual values (the deviation), squaring each difference (so it's always a positive number), summing up the differences, dividing the sum by the number of items in the sample (sometimes reduced by one), and then taking the square root of the sum so that the resulting measure is in the same units as the data. Any spreadsheet program will calculate it for you.

The standard deviation in the above sample is 85 defensive runs for Palmer, 70 defensive runs for Smith, 72 defensive runs for Davenport, and 29 defensive runs for James. So the typical spread, so to speak, between high and low values for this particular sample is similar under Palmer, Smith, and Davenport, and narrower, or more compressed, for James.

"Correlation" is a convenient measurement of the extent to which two different sets of data tend to move together. It's a way of measuring the extent to which, if Player A is rated outstanding under one system, he's also rated outstanding under the other; if Player B is rated good under one system, he's also rated good by the other; if Player C is rated average under one, he's also rated average by the other; if Player D is rated poor by one, he's rated poor by the other; and so on. The maximum value for correlation is 1.0, which indicates that two sets of data move together in lockstep, so if you plotted them against each other on an 'x–y' graph, the points would line up in a rising, perfectly straight line. A correlation of 0 generally means that there is no pattern, so if you plotted the points you would see a formless 'cloud'. A correlation of –1.0 (the minimum number) would correspond with a perfectly straight plot sloping down, indicating that the two items moved perfectly against each other.

To calculate the sample correlation between two columns of data (let's call them x and y), you first calculate the sample average and sample standard deviation for each column. Then, for each row, you calculate the difference between the value for x in that row and the sample average of all x's, and the difference between the value for y in that row and the sample average of all y's. Then for each row you multiply the two differences you've just calculated. Finally, you sum up the products (which may be positive or negative) and divide that sum by the number of rows in the sample (minus one), multiplied by the product of the standard deviations. Or you ask an Excel spreadsheet to do all that. The table below shows what was produced for the data in the "Best Known Estimates of Career Defensive Runs for Certain Famous Fielders" table.

corr	Palmer	Smith	D'port	James
Palmer	1.00	0.27	0.53	0.30
Smith		1.00	0.40	0.21
D'port			1.00	0.57
James				1.00

Notice how each system correlates perfectly with itself (correlation 1.00). **The correlations between the various defensive runs systems range from .27 to .57.** What might be an acceptable correlation? In other words, how closely do we think these estimates should move together? In his recent book, *A Mathematician at the Ballpark: Odds and Probabilities for Baseball Fans*, Ken Ross provided the following "rough" definition for a "strong" correlation: .70 or higher. The correlations in the above chart would generally be considered weak.

To put the above correlations in perspective, if you collect the career *offensive* runs created above or below average ("offensive runs") for the same group of players under systems developed by Palmer, Smith, and Davenport (the James numbers are not separately reported), **every single correlation of offensive runs estimates, when rounded to two decimals, is 1.00**. In an absolute nutshell, that's the difference between how inconsistent defensive runs estimates are compared to offensive runs estimates.

Looking just at the three systems that appear to be most similar, based on their respective averages, standard deviations, and correlations (Palmer, Smith, and Davenport), we find several instances of remarkably big differences in career fielding assessments: Wagner, LaJoie, Mazeroski, Mays, and Clemente. Palmer estimates Brooks Robinson saved about a hundred runs, Smith estimates he saved about three hundred runs, and Davenport estimates about two hundred.

Another way of putting these differences into perspective is to look at the standard deviation in the per-player difference between each pair of fielding systems. There are six possible one-to-one comparisons possible for the above four systems. The typical standard deviation of the difference between each pair of ratings is about seventy-five runs, or one-fourth of the threshold number of runs a Hall of Fame player should exceed average overall performance. In other words, **in some sense, the 'typical disagreement' among the best-known estimates of career defensive runs for the above set of players, usually considered among the best fielders of all time, amounts to one-fourth of a Hall of Fame career.**

I would call that a material difference. One of the goals of this book is to reach estimates of career fielding value which, when combined with other high-quality information about the player, will enable fans to get comfortable that the 'typical disagreement' or 'noise' in career fielding value measurements is closer to twenty-five runs, rather than seventy-five.

There also appear to be patterns in the differences between the systems. Palmer generally rates the best infielders as far more dominant than the best outfielders, whereas the other systems and current research indicates that is not the case. As noted before, the estimates of defensive runs under James' system are much lower than the Palmer, Smith, or Davenport estimates.

But it's more than the sheer scale of disagreement and possible error that has long bothered me about estimates of fielding value. It's that most of the systems that estimate defensive runs are black boxes, or at best very difficult to replicate and evaluate, in sharp contrast with the systems used to estimate offensive runs, which have been open source for decades.

The system behind the Davenport estimates has never been disclosed in reproducible detail. Pete Palmer has long disclosed his infielder methods, but not certain necessary aspects of the outfielder methods. James, to his credit, disclosed everything necessary to calculate Fielding Win Shares, but even then, not how to put his system into a common scale with the others so that comparisons could readily be made. Nor did James present his results in such a way as to enable his readers to see at a glance the relative fielding impact of different fielders at the same position. Until I calculated the numbers above, I had little idea of the marginal fielding runs (or 'wins') James estimated the players listed above contributed to their teams—in other words, the *practical difference* their fielding made.

Sean Smith revealed in an on-line article at hardballtimes.com the most important calculations used in his system for seasons since the 1950s. As a practical matter, however, it is very difficult to reproduce Smith's results because it is necessary to build and program a vast relational database. Though the underlying data in the database is open source, because of the challenges of putting the relational database together there may be only two or three other such databases in existence, and none that is available for use by other analysts.

The raw data to be downloaded consists of rows of close to 100 variables per major league plate appearance since the 1950s coded by volunteers at retrosheet.org ("Retrosheet") from original scoresheets of major league games. Among the variables are pitching, batting, fielding, and base running outcomes and the identities of each ball player on the field. In very rough numbers, there have been close to 10 million major league plate appearances and probably 10,000 or more major league players since the early 1950s. Organizing such data into a well-structured relational database and writing computer programs to get it to generate ratings was a project that Smith, who is an economist, told me was the "most difficult thing [he] ever had to do in [his] life." I believe Smith's accomplishment will be replicated a few times in the next decade. I hope to do so myself, for any subsequent edition of this book. In which case one of my next challenges will be to learn database programming.

To the extent the methodologies of the better-known fielding systems *have* been disclosed, they have not been grounded in standard statistical methods and have largely been based on guesswork, some of which we will see was surprisingly good, but some of which was not. In contrast, most of the well-known methods for estimating offensive contribution are derived from standard techniques one would learn in entry-level and intermediate college statistics and probability courses.

Finally, and most importantly, the designers of these systems, with the notable exception of Smith, have never tested their results to demonstrate their validity, whereas offensive formulas have usually been tested as soon as developed and many times thereafter. But how can you test estimates of defensive runs?

By comparing how well they match, in terms of correlation and standard deviation, with estimates of defensive runs it is reasonable to believe must be better. As we'll be discussing throughout this book, there are proprietary data sets that have been collected for recent players that track for every batted ball hit into the field of play its approximate trajectory (ground ball, line drive, fly ball, pop up) and location. Location is often coded by reference to distance from home plate and the direction, or thin 'pie slice' of the field (with home plate the center of the pie and the entire field being one quarter of the pie) in which the ball was hit. Sometimes other variables that may impact the likelihood that the batted ball is fielded, such as velocity, are included as well. Finally, the outcome of each batted ball is recorded, that is, whether or not it was converted into an out, and by whom. Since this proprietary data provides multiple items of information about each batted ball, we'll refer to it as "batted ball data."

Assume you're trying to estimate the defensive runs for a particular fielder. Defensive runs estimates from batted ball data, like all defensive runs estimates, essentially follow a four-step procedure: (i) estimate the number of plays you expect the average player would have made that season if he had been fielding in place of the fielder you are rating ("expected plays"), (ii) subtract expected plays from the actual number of successful plays your fielder actually made that year, which is usually a matter of public record, yielding "net plays," (iii) estimate the average value, in runs, of a net play at that fielder's position ("runs per play"), and (iv) multiply runs per play by net plays, to arrive at defensive runs.

With batted ball data, the first step is accomplished as follows, using right field as an example. Let's say that during a major league season, twenty percent of all "line drives hit to the right-center 'slice', medium deep, were caught by right fielders; that is, eighty percent dropped in as hits. If you are rating a particular right fielder, Player X, his expected number of plays made on line drives to right-center, medium deep would be twenty percent of the total number of line drives to right-center, medium deep that were hit when he was on the field. So if fifty line drives to right-center, medium deep were hit while Player X was playing in right, you would assign twenty percent of fifty, or ten, expected plays for Player X.

You would then perform the same calculation for every other combination of trajectory, slice, and depth assigned to right fielders, such as "fly balls hit to straightaway right, very deep," or "pop flies hit to right-center, shallow." The entire field is mapped out with these designated areas. After summing up all of the expected plays for Player X in each designated area of the field in which any plays were made by major league right fielders, you arrive at total expected plays in right field for Player X.

Second, you subtract the total expected plays in right field for Player X from his total right field putouts to arrive at his net plays. Let's say Player X has +10 net plays.

Third, based on the number of singles, doubles, and occasional triples hit in the designated areas assigned to right fielders, estimate the average value, in runs, of allowing a hit in the right field areas. The average value of a net play is equal to the sum of the average value of the hit prevented in right field (say it's .58 runs) plus the average value of the out created (say about .27 runs), resulting in an average value for a net play in right field of .85 runs.

Fourth, defensive runs for X would be just .85 multiplied by +10, or +8.5 defensive runs, rounded to +9.

Accurately recorded batted ball data in theory provides the least biased and most precise means of estimating net plays and runs per play. Since human beings record the data, it generally does contain some imprecision and inconsistency. There are now at least two suppliers of proprietary batted ball data, and we will see that the underlying raw data differs substantially in the outfield. We shall also see that the systems other human beings have designed to convert batted ball data into estimates of defensive runs have introduced additional biases. Therefore, just because a fielding evaluation system is based on batted ball data does not mean it has 'the answer'. And since neither the underlying batted ball data nor the software programs necessary for performing the calculations are publicly available, to some extent batted ball data systems must be taken on faith.

That said, carefully constructed defensive runs estimates based on two or more independently compiled sets of batted ball data can provide a much clearer picture, a much better estimate of the objective 'truth', against which one can test defensive runs systems *not* reliant on such proprietary data. If systems that do not depend on batted ball data generate results for recent major league players that are consistent with results under the best systems based on batted ball data, we have a great deal more evidence that when the former systems are applied throughout the first hundred or so years of baseball history, for which we do not (and never will) have reliable batted ball data, they are probably approaching the right answer. That is, the approximately right answer.

There exists one final test for every defensive system: do the numbers of defensive runs estimated per player on the team, including all the fielders (from fielding plays) and pitchers (from pitching 'plays' such as walks, strikeouts, home runs allowed, etc.), add up to a good estimate of the number of runs the team in fact allowed above or below the league rate? The latter number is the real bottom line. Some batted ball data systems have trouble with this apparently simple test.

Given the multitude of defensive runs systems currently available, what is most needed is one that is

1. **open source** (reliant solely on freely available data and fully disclosed methods),
2. **empirical** (derived to the greatest extent possible from standard techniques of statistical inference, with a minimum of guesswork and assumptions),

3. **accountable** (in the sense that a team's fielding defensive runs add up with its pitching defensive runs to generate a good estimate of the number of total runs that were in fact allowed by that team above or below the league average rate),

4. **adaptable** (for use throughout major league history even as the data deteriorates further back in time),

5. **readily reproducible** (recognizing that there is usually an inevitable trade-off between accuracy and simplicity), and

6. **demonstrably accurate** (based on tests against well-constructed batted ball data systems).

Chapters two and three and appendix A are written with the goal of showing that the defensive system used in this book to rate the greatest fielders of all time satisfies these objectives. The system, in the words of a 2009 *Sports Illustrated* article, has a "clunky" name that sounds like it comes from a "symposium of mechanical engineers": Defensive Regression Analysis ("DRA"). The name comes from the fact that it applies the 200-year-old statistical technique known as "regression analysis" to "defensive" statistics, including pitching and fielding statistics. The acronym DRA conveniently rhymes with ERA, the acronym for earned run average, and can equally stand for a less forbidding name such as "Defensive Runs Analysis," which is also appropriate, because DRA analyzes, or breaks down and puts back together, the components of defensive runs for a team.

Chapter two demonstrates how DRA works using examples: first some simplified examples, and then some actual examples of famous players. **There is no need to know anything about statistics to develop a good intuitive understanding of the defensive runs system (DRA) that is used in this book. Every major concept behind DRA will be illustrated with concrete examples.**

Chapter three discloses DRA test results against batted ball data. In addition, that chapter analyzes other well-known systems and their test results against batted ball data. The tests indicate that DRA has a strong correlation and a nearly exact standard deviation match with defensive runs estimates based on batted ball data, and is the most accurate non-batted ball data system for estimating a player's defensive runs, given the number of batted balls he's turned into outs, throughout major league history.

However, tests in chapter three also indicate that Sean Smith's TotalZone system (and a similar system developed by Dan Fox), which can be used for different parts of the second half of baseball history, are close to being as accurate as DRA, and potentially could be even better. Both the Smith and Fox systems—results under which are or have been published on the web—will be consulted frequently in evaluating fielders from the second half of baseball history, and particularly in the last twenty years or so.

In Part II (chapters five through fourteen) we discuss and evaluate the few hundred or so fielders throughout major league history who are really worth talking about. Each chapter in Part II covers one position. In each chapter we'll move backward in time to discuss fielders at that position whose careers were centered in the Contemporary Era (1993 and later), Modern Era (1969–92), Transitional Era (1947–68), Live Ball Era (1920–46), and Dead Ball Era (1893–1919). We'll focus mainly on the surprises—the (many) Gold Glovers who really weren't so great; the slow and seemingly clumsy sluggers who weren't so bad—and plainly confront the few important cases in which the evidence remains mixed. At the end of each chapter we'll list the top forty fielders of all time at that position, and profile the top ten and a few honorable mentions. Which brings us to our second big problem.

Take any quantitatively based or supported ranking of the greatest pitchers, batters, fielders, or all-around players: the top hundred players in *The Historical Abstract*; Sean Smith's new rankings, based on his estimates of career overall 'wins' above replacement value, found at baseballprojection.com; the top hundred all-time players in the latest edition of the *ESPN Baseball Encyclopedia*; what have you. With the exception of the world's most famous steroid user, the old timers dominate. Utterly.

But players are not getting worse; they're getting better. It is now possible to watch videotapes of complete games played in the 1970s on certain cable stations. Although the best players of the 1970s were certainly great players, when I watch these games right before or after a current one, it seems that nowadays more pitchers throw in the high nineties, fewer banjo hitters tap out weak grounders and soft outfield flies, more fielders make acrobatic diving and sliding plays in the outfield (though that's partly because very few ballparks these days have artificial turf, which would have been very painful to dive on back in the 1970s), more catchers routinely make crisp, accurate throws to second on stolen base attempts, and so forth. Most players today are built like college wrestlers; back in the 1970s, very few were. Thanks to digital video and the computer revolution, batters and pitchers know each other's performance outcomes for every combination of pitch speed, location, and movement. Fielders (or their coaches) know the precise batted ball distribution for each batter. With this kind of information, pitchers, batters, and fielders can (and must) continually refine their game. The competition is simply sharper and more intense than ever.

Historical fielding ratings have the same old timer problem that all other quantitatively based historical ratings have. If you simply rank all shortstops who played at least 3000 innings or estimated innings by their career defensive runs, the three top full-time shortstops played in the Dead Ball era, and two-thirds of the top shortstops (defined as those with a hundred or more career defensive runs) played before integration was complete. Accepting such output as the basis for an all-time ranking is absurd.

The late paleontology professor Stephen J. Gould may have been the first to argue that the perceived drop in quality of more recent star players merely reflects a reduction in the standard deviation of outcomes, which demonstrates an *improvement* in quality. The best players haven't been getting worse; rather, as more and more players have adapted or learned how to play the game better, the replacement level and average players have been getting *better*, which reduces the standard deviation.

One simple example of this is home run hitting. When Ruth 'invented' home run hitting around 1920, he completely dominated for a couple of years. Then a small number of players began to hit nearly as many. Gradually more and more players learned to be power hitters. Because there still remained some sort of upper bound to the number of home runs anyone would physically hit (let's say the limit was about sixty before smaller ballparks, smaller strike zones, lighter and harder bats, steroids, the ban on brush back pitches, and almost certainly the juicing of the ball circa 1993-94 to boost attendance), as more and more players approached that limit, the standard deviation in home run hitting shrunk. Hence, looking at the raw statistical record, Ruth towered over his peers, Mantle not so much, Mike Schmidt even less so.

There are at least two major factors we can statistically model to begin to account for the perceived drop in quality of the best players, that is, the *improvement* in the quality of bench and everyday players: (i) the three-fold growth of baseball's 'constant' talent pool of young adult white North American males over the course of major league history, and (ii) the introduction, since integration, of completely new pools of African-American, Latin American, and Asian talent. Chapter four will focus on dealing with this talent pool issue, and introduce "Talent Pool Adjusted Runs," or "TPAR." In essence, TPAR puts every fielder in history on a contemporary scale, while taking into account how much more competitive baseball is now, due to the vast increase in the total talent pool from which major league baseball players have been drawn. TPAR will reveal scores of hidden fielding stars from the last sixty years, and particularly the last twenty.

One Way to Measure Fielding

As in "This is merely one way to measure fielding; not the only way to measure it." Other methods have been developed recently to provide good defensive runs estimates for the latter half of baseball history, particularly for the last twenty years or so, and we'll explain how they work as well. But before getting into any details of any defensive system, the first thing to realize, and the most important thing to keep in mind, is that all fielding systems, explicitly or implicitly, directly or indirectly, apply the same basic four-step procedure that we summarized when introducing the basic approach of systems based on batted ball data.

First, estimate the expected number of plays the league-average fielder would have made over the course of the season if he had been playing in place of the fielder being rated ("expected plays"), taking into account the best information you have to make this 'prediction'. By "plays," we generally mean plays in which a fielder catches a batted ball and gets the batter out, either simply by catching the ball (outfield putouts) or by fielding a ground ball and throwing or forcing the batter out (infield assists and first base unassisted ground outs). By "best information," we mean other pitching statistics and fielding statistics at certain other positions that can serve to predict expected plays at the position being evaluated.

Second, subtract estimated expected plays from actual plays made by the fielder you're evaluating, to arrive at the fielder's "net plays," which may be positive or negative.

Third, estimate the average value, in runs, of each net play, taking into account how net plays were calculated.

Fourth, multiply net plays by runs per play to arrive at estimated net runs saved or allowed compared to the league-average fielder, or "defensive runs."

By translating all fielding evaluation systems into this common framework of (i) estimating expected plays, (ii) subtracting expected plays from actual plays to get net plays, (iii) estimating runs per net play, and (iv) multiplying net plays by runs per net play, it will be easier to compare and contrast them.

WHY FIELDING HAS BEEN THE 'HOLY GRAIL' PROBLEM

Two shortstops we'll be talking about a lot in chapter thirteen had interesting seasons in 2000. The first ("X") played 1212 innings at short, led his league in errors for the third and last time of his career, with 36, and recorded 456 assists. (For reasons we'll get to later in the chapter, we'll ignore putouts and treat double play assists the same as ground ball assists.) The second ("O") played 1329 innings at short, tied the major league record for fewest errors in a full-time season at shortstop, with 3, and recorded 414 assists. After the season was over, X got demoted to third base and O was given the Gold Glove.

Since at least 1876, fielders have been evaluated by their fielding average, which is defined as putouts plus assists, divided by "total chances," which in turn is defined as putouts, assists, and errors. Since we're ignoring putouts here at shortstop, let's redefine it as assists divided by assists plus errors (and errors at short are almost always on what would otherwise be assists, not putouts). So under our revised calculation X had a .927 fielding average (456 assists divided by the sum of 456 assists and 36 errors) and O had a .993 fielding average (414 assists divided by the sum of 414 assists and 3 errors).

Implicit in evaluating fielders by their fielding average is the fact that avoiding errors prevents opponent base runners from reaching base safely. On average, studies show that errors have nearly exactly the same effect as clean hits. This certainly makes sense in the case of shortstop, because some errors involve just bobbling the ball but still keeping it in the infield, while others involve bad throws, a few of which allow runners to advance an extra base. Therefore, avoiding errors (all else being equal) has the same value as preventing hits.

Also implicit in evaluating fielders by their fielding average is that the number of "chances" a player "accepts" is a fair estimate of the number of opportunities the player actually had to make plays.

If we accept both premises, we can translate the concept of fielding average into our four-step program for estimating defensive runs. We know the plays made. What are the expected plays made? Well, since we've defined "chances" as assists plus errors, and we know the fielding average of all shortstops in the league that X and O played in (again, defined here as assists

(6,878) divided by the sum of assists (6,878) plus errors (291), or .959), the estimate for expected plays, given the chances each player had, would be the percentage of each player's chances that the average player in his league would have successfully converted into outs: 95.9 percent.

Here goes our first calculation of defensive runs for X and O.

First we estimate expected plays made. That would be the league-average rate of converting "chances" into outs, in other words, the league-average fielding average as we've defined it above, which was 95.9 percent in 2000 for the league X and O played in, multiplied by the number of "chances" X had (456 plus 36, or 492) and O had (414 plus 3, or 417). So expected plays for X are .959 multiplied by 492, or 472, and expected plays for O are .959 multiplied by 417, or 400.

Second, we subtract expected plays from actual plays made to determine net plays. That would be 456 minus 472, or −16 net plays for X, and 414 minus 400, or +14 net plays for O.

Third, we estimate runs per net play. Well-known models of offense that have been around for about forty years indicate that, on average, a single increases a team's expected runs by a little under half a run, and an out decreases its expected runs by a little more than a quarter of a run compared to the league-average team. When a shortstop records an assist instead of an error, he reduces the number of times his opponent reaches first base by one and increases the number of outs by his opponent by one. So the average value in runs per marginal shortstop play is about .75 runs. This may seem like double counting at first, but the easiest way to see why this is correct is to take the perspective of the *batter*. If the fielder converts his batted ball into an out, a batter's seasonal total of singles is lowered by one and his out total is higher by one than it would have been if the fielder failed to convert the batted ball into an out. If you plug those items into the decades-old and well-known formulas for hitters, the overall effect is a reduction of .75 runs in the batter's estimated runs produced above or below the league average rate.

Fourth, X has .75 multiplied by −16 net plays, or −12 defensive runs. O has .75 runs multiplied by +14 net plays, or +11 defensive runs.

O is about 23 runs better than X. Though Gold Glove voters certainly did not make that calculation, they came to a somewhat similar conclusion about their relative value.

What's the basic problem with this calculation? Expected plays made by fielders are estimated largely by reference to their own "chances," which are defined by the number of plays and (to a much, much smaller extent) the errors they have made. Thus the number of expected plays for a fielder depends on the number of batted balls the fielder gets to. In other words, we're using the player's own ability to get to the ball to establish the baseline against which to assess his performance in turning batted balls into outs.

We're going around in a circle. The *estimator* of expected plays is *biased* by the player's own ability to get to batted balls in the first place. Whenever we try to estimate what an outcome should be, we should strive to minimize bias.

Branch Rickey explained this less abstractly in an article for *Life* magazine in 1954, in which he declared fielding averages "utterly worthless," and "not only misleading, but deceiving," because fielders can amass high fielding averages while letting many so-called clean hits go by, for which they are never charged. Almost three generations later, even some of the smartest analysts in the business, using some of the most sophisticated batted ball data, make mistakes in fielder evaluation because they cannot let go of fielding average or the related concept of an "error" as being anything different than a play not made.

One way our fielding average version of the four-step procedure demonstrates the wisdom of Rickey's observation is that it ascribes an absurdly higher value to each marginal error avoided than to each marginal assist made, even though we know that each clean hit prevented with an assist is in fact worth as much as an error avoided. For example, each error X avoids is worth .75 runs multiplied by .959 of each error, or .72 runs, because it directly reduces expected plays by .959. But if X records one more assist, that assist boosts his plays made by one but *also* boosts his *expected* plays by .959, so he only gets credit for 1 minus .959 plays, or .041 net plays, which, multiplied by .75, is only .03 runs. The ratio of the relative imputed value of each error avoided (.72 runs) to each new hit prevented (.03) is about 24:1. The ratio should be 1:1.

Errors are over-weighted by a factor of twenty-four.

Possibly the first thing Bill James ever published, a March 1976 article in *Baseball Digest*, highlighted precisely this fact. As James put it, since the average major league outfielder then had about a .980 fielding average, "if he makes one extra error, he has to chase down forty-nine extra fly balls to come out even. The one error is equal to the forty-nine great plays." Which is simply and massively wrong.

James therefore proposed evaluating fielders not by their plays made, divided by their plays made and muffed (both of which were largely self-determined), but by their plays made divided by their innings played. Given the number of innings a shortstop is in the field, there is very little he can do to impact the number of ground balls that are hit anywhere near him. James multiplied plays per inning by nine to report the number as plays made per nine innings, which he called "Range Factor." James included both putouts and assists in gross plays. For the sake of our X and O example, we'll once again leave putouts out of the picture.

Let's translate Range Factor into defensive runs using our four-step procedure.

First, estimate expected plays for X and O. That would be the league-average rate of shortstop assists per inning, multiplied by the innings played by X and O, respectively, at shortstop. The league-average rate of assists per inning that year was 6,878 divided by 20,141, or .34. X played 1,212 innings, so his expected plays are .34 multiplied by 1,212, or 412. O played 1,329 innings at short, so his expected plays are .34 multiplied by 1,329, or 452.

Second, subtract actual plays made from expected plays made. Therefore, net plays for X equal 456 − 412, or +44; net plays for O equal 414 − 456, or −42.

Third, ascribe .75 runs per net play, for the reasons we gave above.

Fourth, multiply net plays by expected runs per net play, or .75. Defensive runs for X equal .75 multiplied by +44, or +33 runs. Defensive runs for O equal .75 multiplied by −42, or −32 runs.

X is about sixty-five runs better than O.

Recall that the fielding average version of the four-step defensive runs estimate indicated that O was about twenty-four runs better than X. The difference between the fielding average defensive runs estimate of the relative value of X and O and the Range Factor defensive runs estimate is close to *ninety* runs, which is about the difference in total net value, offense *and* defense, between a playoff bound *team* and the average team. Extreme discrepancies like these have led many to view the evaluation of fielding as a mug's game, unless batted ball data is available.

Though batted ball data would show that a Range Factor version of defensive runs is generally better than a fielding average version of defensive runs, it is prone to some mammoth mistakes. Why? The estimate of expected plays is not biased, as in the case of the fielding average version of defensive runs, by the player's own performance. But whenever we try to estimate what an outcome should be, we strive to minimize bias *and maximize precision*. The Range Factor estimate of expected plays is about as *imprecise* as it could be.

Range Factor effectively assumes that the average shortstop would record the same number of assists regardless of the team he played for, in other words, that every shortstop has the same number and kind of ground ball opportunities per inning. Which is also obviously wrong. Teams with pitchers that don't strike out a lot of batters, and that induce ground balls, will generate far more opportunities at shortstop. If players were randomly assigned to teams each year, these effects would probably eventually cancel out, which is why Range Factor is better than fielding average; the player 'carries around' his own 'fielding average' bias, so 'repeating the same experiment' each year with a randomly selected team would not solve the problem.

Unfortunately for the case of fielding evaluation, fielders have not been assigned randomly each year to new teams, so they may experience very different levels of relative fielding opportunities for extended periods of time. We can't wait for Range Factor to average out for each fielder.

James recognized the limitation of Range Factor almost as soon as he invented it, and quickly proposed what would be the solution going forward: creating new data based on carefully prepared counts of all batted balls hit remotely near a player's position, what we're calling batted ball data. In theory, this data is relatively unbiased and much more precise.

The most obvious advantage of batted ball systems is that they count every single batted ball and what every single fielder did with each one, so that, with a sufficiently large sample, the sample average rate of out-conversion yields the best estimator for expected plays. If twenty-five percent of fly balls hit to Area A of the outfield were caught by all major league left fielders, it's generally fair to expect that the average left fielder would have caught twenty-five percent of fly balls hit to Area A of the outfield while Player Y happens to be standing out there.

Systems that don't use batted ball data must rely on 'fuzzier' *indirect* estimators for expected plays. Even if these estimators were unbiased, they would require larger samples, given their much weaker precision, to converge on a correct estimate. Therefore, if you want to estimate how many plays a shortstop should have made in a half season, you are clearly better off with a batted ball system than without one, though it is questionable whether one should rely even on a batted ball data estimate for a short time frame and, as we shall see, with two years of data, the best non-batted ball system would appear to catch up with batted ball data systems.

The most significant problem with batted ball data is that, with the exception of a data set from 1989 through 1999, it is secret and not directly verifiable. Even selfless analysts such as Mitchel Lichtman, who have purchased the data with their own money and published good defensive runs estimates on the web, are legally prevented from releasing the underlying data. But, in the meantime, we've clarified our first problem to solve: finding and correctly using the least biased, most precise, and *publicly available* estimators of expected plays.

A HYPOTHETICAL EXAMPLE OF ONE SOLUTION

The system we'll be using in this book relies on publicly available statistics of major league teams over long periods of major league history that are less biased estimators of the number of successful plays made at each position than estimators that have been used in the past. I will never claim that they are right, only that they are less wrong. I originally called the system Defensive Regression Analysis, or DRA, because it applies to traditional defensive (pitching and fielding) statistics the standard statistical technique known as "regression analysis" to calculate how *much* these estimators are associated with more or fewer expected plays made.

We'll begin with a simplified version of how DRA works. Our example will feature two new characters, the hypothetical average shortstop ("Average"), and the hypothetical shortstop being evaluated ("John Smith," or simply "Smith"), who is also assumed to play every game. Shortstop assists per team run about 475 per season. To make the example easier to follow, we'll round that up to 500, so we will assume that Average would record 500 assists for the average team and, therefore, under the 'Range Factor' version of defensive runs, the expected number of assists for Smith would also be 500.

Baseball analysts have long recognized at least three factors that tend to increase (decrease) the number of assists at shortstop, and, therefore, increase (decrease) the number of assists Average would be expected to record.

The first factor is simply the relative number of total batted balls in play allowed by a team's pitchers (every plate appearance not resulting in a walk, hit batsman, strikeout or home run results in a batted ball in the field of play).

The second factor is the relative level of left-handed (right-handed) opponent batters, which is influenced by the level of right-handed (left-handed) team pitching.

The third factor is the relative tendency of the team's pitchers to give up ground balls or fly balls.

The higher the number of *total* batted balls a team's pitchers allow to be hit *anywhere* in the field, the higher the number of ground balls that should be hit towards shortstop, and the higher the number of expected shortstop assists, *all else being equal*. It's relatively easy to calculate the total number of batted balls a team's pitchers allow to be hit into the field of play: any plate appearance not resulting in a strikeout, walk, hit batsman, or home run will result in a batted ball being hit somewhere in the field, or a batted ball in play (or just "ball in play").

There are about 11 shortstop assists per 100 balls in play. In other words, the league total of shortstop assists divided by the league total of balls in play is approximately 0.11. Therefore, if the pitchers for Smith's team allowed 100 *fewer* balls in play than the average team, which is not at all uncommon, the *projected* total for Average would *decrease by 11*, from 500 to 489.

Analysts have been aware of this contextual factor influencing fielding opportunities at least since Eric Walker and Bill James began focusing on it sometime around 1980. Best of all, it is an estimator that is only biased to a tiny extent by the player being rated. If Smith 'fails' to make a play, that brings another batter to the plate, but only approximately 70 percent of plate appearances result in a batted ball in play, and only 11 percent of those should result in a shortstop assist, so, by muffing a play, the shortstop increases his expected plays by only .077 if he reverts to average performance thereafter.

Many factors can impact the *distribution* around the playing field of a given total of balls in play.

We'll start with the second most important, because it is the easiest. The second most important factor impacting the distribution of a given total of balls in play is the relative number of balls in play hit by right-handed and left-handed opponent batters. Fielders have virtually no impact on this factor.

Batters tend to pull balls they hit on the ground, so the more right-handed batters, the higher the number of expected plays at short. We don't have opponent batted handedness information for about half of major league history. In other words, we don't know the number of batted balls in play hit by each team's right- and left-handed opponent batters. What have instead are good estimates of the number of balls in play that are *allowed* by each team's *left*-handed *pitchers*, who tend to face more right-handed batters due to platooning and pinch-hitting. Other analysts, including Charles Saeger, Bill James, and Pete Palmer, have explicitly incorporated relative levels of left-handed pitching into their defensive systems, beginning probably with Saeger in the mid-1990s. The calculation of balls in play allowed by left-handed pitchers is the same as for team balls in play, but just restricted to the team's left-handed pitchers.

If the balls in play allowed by a team's *left*-handed *pitchers*, given the *total* number of team balls in play allowed, is positive relative to the league-average team, particularly if it is unusually high, this indicates that the number of batted balls hit by opponent *right*-handed *batters* is probably above average, holding the level of total balls in play constant. Notice that by calculating net or marginal batted balls in play allowed by left-handed pitchers by reference to total batted balls in play allowed by all the team's pitchers, the left-handed pitching adjustment controls for the total ball in play factor we've already taken into account. In other words, it isolates the left-handed pitching factor from the total balls in play factor, so they are less correlated, or closer to being independent, from each other.

If you calculate for a large set of leagues and seasons the net number of team assists at shortstop, given total balls in play, as well as the net number of balls in play allowed by each team's left-handed pitchers, given total balls in play, you can do a "regression analysis" to determine the relationship between the two. Regression analysis shows that if the number of batted balls allowed by a team's left-handed pitchers, given the total number of batted balls allowed by all the team's pitchers, is 100 higher than the league-average rate, one should expect the team's shortstop assists, given total balls in play, to increase by 1. It is not uncommon for teams to be plus or minus 1000 in the relative number of balls in play allowed by left-handed pitchers. So, if Smith's team had a below-average amount of left-handed pitching, so that they had 500 *fewer* balls in play allowed by left-handed pitchers, given total balls in play, we would *reduce* Average's projected total by another 5, from 489 down to 484.

The most important influence on the distribution of balls in play is the relative tendency of a team's pitchers to be ground ball pitchers (e.g., Tommy John or Derek Lowe types who keep the ball down and generate a lot of ground balls) or fly ball pitchers (e.g., Sid Fernandez or Tim Wakefield types who frequently fool batters into popping up or hitting soft outfield flies). Given a *fixed* number of *total* balls in play, a ground ball pitching staff will generate more chances for infielders, including the shortstop; given a fixed number of total balls in play, a fly ball pitching staff will generate fewer chances for infielders, including at shortstop.

The best way to estimate the impact of team-level ground ball or fly ball pitching on expected shortstop assists when you don't have batted ball data (or "play-by-play" data, which is a little different) is to calculate the number of *fly outs* recorded by the team above or below what the league-average team would record, given that team's number of total balls in play allowed. Notice again that by calculating relative fly outs and shortstop assists by reference to balls in play, this calculation controls for the total balls in play factor we've already taken into account. In other words, it isolates the *fly ball versus ground* ball factor from the *total* balls in play factor, so they have less impact on each other. (We'll deal with the potential interaction between left-handed versus right handed pitching and ground ball versus fly ball pitching later in this chapter.)

As far as I know, all other analysts up to now have used *assists* to estimate relative ground ball opportunities, because the overwhelming majority of assists come from fielding ground balls, and most ground balls result in an assist. The advantage of using *fly outs* above or below average, given total balls in play, to estimate the impact of relative levels of *ground balls*, given total balls in play, is that shortstop assists have only a small and indirect impact on the fly out estimator, whereas shortstop assists are included in total team assists.

In other words, the *estimator* of *relative ground ball versus fly ball pitching* (team *fly outs* at all positions relative to the league, given total team balls in play), which impacts expected shortstop assists given total balls in play, has no relationship per se with the number of assists the shortstop actually recorded. We'll elaborate on this important point a little further below.

It's relatively easy to get a rough estimate of total fly outs recorded by a team: innings pitched times three (to get total outs), minus strikeouts and total assists. That is because almost all unassisted outs other than strike-outs come from catching fly balls. The main exception to this rule is the not insignificant and variable number of putouts first basemen record by fielding a ground ball and running to first themselves rather than by toss-ing to the pitcher covering the bag. We'll deal with that complexity in our next example.

If you apply regression analysis to a large sample of single-season team level totals, you'll generally find, depending on the sample studied, that for every extra fly out recorded by a team *above* the league-average rate, given the total number of the team's balls in play, there tend to be about .20 to .25 shortstop assists recorded by the team *below* the league-average rate, also given the total number of the team's balls in play, and vice versa.

In the sample data I used to develop this example, the number was .21. So if Smith's pitchers generated 100 *more* fly outs than the league-average pitch-ing staff would have, given the same number of total balls in play allowed, we *reduce* Average's projected total by *another* 21 plays, from 484 to 463. (If, in contrast, Smith's pitchers allowed 100 fly outs *below* the league-average rate, given their total balls in play, that would indicate above-average ground balls, so we would *increase* Average's projected total by 21 plays.) A total of 100 extra or fewer fly outs given the league-average total balls in play is very common; sometimes teams are plus or minus 200 or more.

Thus we estimate, given our example, that Average would have recorded not 500, but only 463 assists for Smith's team, 37 fewer than a Range Factor expectation. Assuming for the sake of the example that Smith played every game, we'd subtract 463 from Smith's assists total to get his *net* assists.

We then do a similar analysis for every team at every position, determin-ing the number of plays each team made above or below expectation at each position, including pitcher (where pitcher 'net plays' are walks, strikeouts, home runs allowed, etc., above or below the league-average rate, and net fielder plays are net center field putouts, second base assists, etc.).

If we perform a second regression analysis of the *actual net* runs allowed by each team above or below the league-average rate that year, given innings played, 'onto' all of the net plays by pitchers and fielders, we obtain the aver-age value, in runs, of each type of net play at each position. We'll show how this was done in the team example towards the end of the chapter.

This second-stage regression analysis reveals that each assist at shortstop that is higher than the expected number as calculated above is statistically associated with a reduction in team runs allowed, over the course of a season, of between .40 and .50 runs, or about .45 runs. The typical DRA estimate of the marginal value of each skill fielding play is about .45 runs in the infield (where mostly singles are prevented) and about .50 runs in the outfield (where sometimes doubles or triples are prevented).

But didn't we say at the beginning of the chapter that each marginal shortstop assist is worth about .75 runs, the value of the hit prevented *and the out created*? Indeed we did. The short answer as to why the DRA estimate of runs per play is seemingly wrong, though actually 'right' for purposes of the DRA model, is that the DRA estimate of net skill plays (positive or negative) has a relatively slight bias and too much uncertainty, or "noise" in it, so the defensive runs associated with such a slightly biased and noisy estimate are dampened a bit by DRA itself. We'll explain this subtle point in more detail right after our next example, in which we calculate a DRA estimate of runs saved in 1984 by the most famous Smith ever to play shortstop, baseball's "Wizard of Oz," one of the hundreds of fielding wizards we'll get to know better in this book.

A REAL WORLD EXAMPLE

Our Ozzie Smith example will take us through a similar set of calculations, but using real data, starting with the team performance at shortstop and then Ozzie's allocable share of that performance. We'll begin to introduce more explicit formulas, so that we can describe the rest of the system more concisely. Nevertheless, to make the transition to formulas as easy as possible, we'll risk being a little repetitive here in this example.

Recall that the DRA estimate of team defensive runs at shortstop follows our four-step formula as follows. First, we estimate the number of shortstop assists ("A6") the 1984 Cardinals would have been expected to record if they had had a league-average fielding shortstop playing ("*Expected A6*"). Second, we subtract *Expected A6* from A6 to obtain net plays ("*Net A6*"). Then we multiply *Net A6* by expected runs saved per *Net A6* (about .45) to arrive at defensive runs at shortstop ("*A6 Runs*").

We know the number of assists recorded by the 1984 Cardinals at shortstop (597). So what we have to calculate is *Expected A6*. The average number of *A6* recorded per team in the 1984 National League was 515. (The 475 estimate above applied around 2000; there are more strikeouts now, and therefore fewer fielding plays.) DRA treats double play assists the same as ground ball assists, for reasons to be explained shortly below, and relay assists generally represent noise, though they are in fact skill plays that create outs, by definition. Thus, using the Range Factor version of defensive runs, the Cardinals' shortstops saved .75 multiplied by the excess of 597 over 515, or about 62 runs.

As explained in the theoretical example, at least three contextual factors impact *Expected A6*. The first factor is the *total* number of balls in play that Cardinal pitchers allowed to be hit *anywhere* in the field (that is, the number of opponent batters facing pitchers not resulting in a strikeout, walk, hit batsman or homerun, or $BFP - SO - BB - HBP - HR$, that is, batted Balls In Play, or "BIP"). The second factor is the *relative* number of such BIP that were hit by *opponent right-handed batters*, who tend to pull ground balls to the left side of the infield where shortstops play. The third factor is the *relative* number of such BIP that were *ground balls*.

All else being equal, the more BIP, that is, the more batted balls hit into the field, the higher the number of chances at short (and everywhere else in the field); the more of such BIP that are hit by opponent right-handed batters, the higher the number of ground balls that are hit to the left side of the infield, including short; the more of such BIP that are ground balls, the higher the number of chances at short (and throughout the infield). The 1984 Cardinals were clearly above average in the first and third categories, and probably about average in the second.

We'll calculate *Expected A6* for the 1984 Cardinals step by step, beginning with a simple calculation based only on the league-average rate of A6 per BIP and the BIP of the Cardinals. That is, the first rough-cut estimate of *Expected A6* is simply the league's total A6 multiplied by the team's share of total league BIP. Note that this number gets calculated for each season for each league; we don't just apply the 11 percent approximation we used in the prior example for every year. So the first estimate of *Expected A6* is simply total league A6 multiplied by the team's share of league BIP. To save space, we'll denote multiplication with an asterisk ("*"), division by a solidus ("/") and "league" as "*lg*." Also, we'll treat *all variables not labeled as "lg" as team* numbers. Therefore, the first estimate of

$$\text{Expected A6} = lgA6*(BIP/lgBIP).$$

Plugging in the 1984 Cardinals and the 1984 National League numbers:

$$\text{Expected A6} = 6{,}183*(4{,}650 / 55{,}103)$$
$$= 522.$$

Thus, considering only the first factor—the number of BIP allowed by 1984 Cardinals pitchers (4,650)—we estimate that the league-average shortstop playing every inning for the 1984 Cardinals would have recorded a total of 522 assists. Stated another way, the relatively higher number of BIP allowed by the Cardinals' pitchers (who were last in the league in strikeouts) would typically result in 7 'extra' A6 (522 minus 515).

To take into account the effect of an above- or below-average number of BIP hit by opponent right-handed batters, we calculate the number of BIP allowed by 1984 Cardinal *left*-handed *pitchers* above or below what the league-average pitching staff would have allowed *given* the total number of *BIP* allowed by 1984 Cardinal pitchers: net Left-handed *pitcher* Balls In Play, given total Balls In Play ("*LpBIP.bip*").

From now on, whenever we report the number of outcomes by a team *above or below* the league average rate, *given* a *single* 'denominator' of opportunities, or contextual factor impacting the expected number of outcomes, we will use the "*OUTCOMES-dot-contextual factor*" format. For example, a team's "*XY*" above or below the league-average rate, given the number of the team's "*ABC*," is denoted as "*XY.abc*" and calculated as follows:

$$XY.abc = XY - lgXY^*(ABC \, / \, lgABC).$$

1984 Cardinals' left-handed pitchers allowed 1,396 *LpBIP*; National League left-handed pitchers allowed 16,440. Again, *all* Cardinal pitchers allowed 4,650 *total BIP*; *all* National League pitchers allowed 55,103 total *BIP*. Applying our calculation method above:

$$LpBIP.bip = LpBIP - lgLpBIP^*(BIP \, / \, lgBIP).$$
$$LpBIP.bip = 1,396 \; - 16,440^*(4,650 \, / \, 55,103).$$
$$= +9.$$

The Cardinals' left-handed pitchers allowed 9 *more BIP* by than league-average left-handers would have, given the *total BIP* allowed by the Cardinals. This is only very slightly above average, indicating that Cardinal pitchers probably faced about the average level of right-handed opponent hitting. Regression analysis indicates that each extra *LpBIP.bip* is associated with approximately 0.01 *more A6* (given the same total of *BIP*), in other words, $+ .01^*LpBIP.bip$, so our *second* estimate for

$$\textit{Expected A6} = 522 \, [\text{prior calculation}] + .01^*(+ 9)$$
$$= 522 \qquad\qquad\qquad + 0 \, [\text{rounded}]$$
$$= 522.$$

To take into account how ground ball versus fly ball pitching could increase or decrease the first estimate of 533, we measure the relative ground ball versus fly ball tendency of a pitching staff using the relative number of *fly outs* recorded by the team, that is, the number of fly outs *above or below* what the league-average team would have recorded *given* the same number of *total BIP* allowed by 1984 Cardinals' pitchers. Again, we'll discuss this seemingly 'backwards' approach in greater detail right after we finish this Ozzie example.

As noted above, at a first approximation, team fly outs are equal to all unassisted outs that are not strikeouts; that is, inning pitched ("*IP*"), multiplied by three, reduced by total strikeouts ("*SO*") and total team assists ("*A*"). However, as Charles Saeger was probably the first to notice for purposes of evaluating first base fielding, a significant number of unassisted putouts at first base are ground balls fielded by first basemen recording the putout directly without tossing to the pitcher covering the bag. In rough numbers, about eighty percent of assists by the team's pitchers ("*A1*"), second basemen ("*A4*"), shortstops ("*A6*"), and third basemen ("*A5*") are made to first base, so if you subtract eighty percent of those assists from total team first base putouts ("*PO3*"), you usually get a decent estimate of total unassisted putouts at first base ("*UPO3*"). About one-third of *UPO3* are unassisted *ground* outs at first base ("*UGO3*"), which should be subtracted from our first estimate of fly outs. So, in a formula:

$$
\begin{aligned}
FO &= 3{*}IP &&- SO &&- A &&- UGO3 \\
&= 3{*}IP &&- SO &&- A \\
&\quad -.33{*}[PO3 &&- .80{*}(A1 &&+ A4 &&+ A5 &&+ A6)].
\end{aligned}
$$

Plugging these numbers for the 1984 Cardinals and the 1984 National League, we arrive at the following estimate of Cardinal fly outs (*FO*) and National League fly outs (*lgFO*):

$$
\begin{aligned}
FO &= 3{*}1{,}449 &&- 808 &&-1{,}999 \\
&\quad -.33{*}[1{,}616 &&- .80{*}(254 &&+ 528 &&+ 389 &&+ 597)] \\
&= 1{,}473. \\
lgFO &= 3{*}17{,}425 &&- 10{,}929 &&- 21{,}557 \\
&\quad -.33{*}[17{,}768 &&- .80{*}(2{,}579 &&+ 6{,}305 &&+ 3{,}933 &&+ 6{,}183)] \\
&= 18{,}941.
\end{aligned}
$$

The number of *FO* that the 1984 Cardinals recorded above or below what we would expect the league-average team to record, given the total *BIP* allowed by the Cardinals' pitchers, using our *XY.abc* calculation, is:

$$
\begin{aligned}
FO.bip &= FO - lgFO{*}(BIP/ \, lgBIP) \\
&= 1{,}473 - 18{,}941{*}(4{,}650 / 55{,}103) \\
&= -125.
\end{aligned}
$$

The large *negative* number for *FO.bip* indicates that the 1984 Cardinals' pitchers had a strong tendency to generate a high percentage of *ground balls*; when *FO.bip* is *positive*, that means relatively fewer *BIP* were ground balls. Again, what's nice about this approach is that Ozzie's assists have relatively little impact on the estimation of relative ground ball opportunities.

The statistical technique of regression analysis indicates that, on average, each *FO.bip* is associated with 0.21 *fewer A6* (given the same number of *BIP*), so our final estimate for

$$Expected\ A6 = 522\ [prior\ calculation]\ minus\ .21^*FO.bip$$
$$= 522 \qquad\qquad\qquad -.21^*(-125)$$
$$= 522 \qquad\qquad\qquad +26$$
$$= 548.$$

Stated another way, we estimate that the ground ball pitching tendency of the 1984 Cardinals' pitchers (as evidenced by their relatively low number of fly outs) increased the expected number of *A6* by 26, to 548.

We therefore estimate a league-average shortstop playing every inning of every game for the 1984 Cardinals would have recorded 548 *A6*, given the level of *BIP*, *LpBIP.bip*, and *FO.bip*, that is, the higher total number of batted balls the 1984 Cardinal pitchers allowed, the very slightly higher number of such batted balls that were hit against left-handed pitchers, and the relatively very low number of such batted balls that were fly outs. Note that this is 33 *more* assists than average (515). These kinds of differences are very common.

In our calculation of estimated *FO* I've taken the liberty of rounding the weights revealed by regression analysis, that is the "coefficients," to easily remembered fractions (one-half, two-thirds, four-fifths); here we'll use .45 per *A6* above *Expected A6*. The number is sometimes a little lower, sometimes a little higher. Therefore, estimated runs saved by 1984 Cardinal shortstops

$$= .45^*(A6\ -\ Expected\ A6)$$
$$= .45^*(597 - 548)$$
$$= .45^*(49)$$
$$= +22\ defensive\ runs.$$

Quite a drop from +62 defensive runs.

To recap in English, we've accomplished step one of the standard four-step procedure for estimating defensive runs by estimating the expected number of assists the average 1984 National League shortstop would have recorded if he had played for the 1984 Cardinals. We did this by taking into account the contextual factors of the 1984 Cardinals that tend to be associated with more or fewer shortstop assists and that we can measure using only traditional, publicly available pitching and fielding statistics. These factors are (i) the total balls in play allowed by the Cardinals' pitchers, (ii) the number of balls in play allowed by the Cardinals' left-handed pitchers above or below the league-average rate, given the total balls in play allowed by all of the Cardinals' pitchers, and (iii) the estimated number of fly outs allowed by Cardinal pitchers above or below the league-average rate, given the total balls in play allowed by Cardinal pitchers.

Second, we subtracted expected shortstop assists from the actual number recorded by the 1984 Cardinals, to calculate net plays.

Third, we estimated the portion of runs statistically associated with each net play.

Fourth, we multiplied our estimate of runs per net play (.45) by net plays to arrive at estimated defensive runs for the 1984 Cardinals at shortstop.

And all of the adjustments and calculations made above were based on regression analysis performed on a large sample of team-level seasonal totals for each statistic.

Let's change one aspect of the notation we've used so far in order to make it easier to set out DRA formulas. To recap our calculations above:

$$A6 - Expected\ A6\ \text{equals}$$
$$A6 - [lgA6^*(BIP/\ lgBIP) + .01^*LpBIP.bip - .21^*FO.bip].$$

This can be rewritten as

$$[A6 - lgA6^*(BIP/lgBIP)]\ minus\ .01^*LpBIP.bip\ plus\ .21^*FO.bip.$$

The portion in brackets is simply the number of *A6* above or below the league-average rate, given the number of *BIP*, or *A6.bip*.

Therefore, net plays made by a team at shortstop above or below average after taking into account known contextual factors using regression analysis (what statisticians call the "residual" of the regression analysis) ("*rA6*"), that is, estimated net team skill plays at shortstop, can be set out in one line as follows:

$$rA6 = A6.bip - .01^*LpBIP.bip + .21^*FO.bip.$$

Think of the first factor in the formula as net plays taking into account *only* total *BIP* allowed by the team's pitchers, the second factor as a penalty for left-handed pitching (when positive), because it is associated with increased opportunities at short, and the third as an add-back for fly ball pitching (when positive), because it reduces opportunities at short. When the *LpBIP.bip* is *negative*, the formula adds back for negative left-handed—that is, extra right-handed—levels of pitching (because it is associated with decreased chances at short). When *FO.bip* is *negative*, the formula penalizes shortstops for negative fly ball—that is, ground ball—pitching, because it increases chances at short.

To calculate Ozzie Smith's share of the Cardinals' defensive runs in 1984, we multiply the value per play (.45 runs) by the sum of (i) Ozzie's pro-rata allocation of team net, regression-adjusted plays (*rA6*), as if he played at exactly the team rate during the innings he was playing, and (ii) the net number of *A6* Ozzie recorded above or below the *team* rate, given his share of the team's innings played at short. Thus Ozzie's (or any individual shortstop's) defensive runs equal

$$+ .45^*rA6^*(\text{player } IP/\text{team } IP)$$

$$+ .45^*[\text{player } A6 - \text{team } A6^*(\text{player } IP/\text{team } IP)].$$

Again, assuming that plain variables are team totals, and abbreviating the "individual" player as "*i*," the formula for allocating the *rA6* team rating to an individual shortstop is

$$+ .45^*rA6^*(iIP/IP) + .45^*[iA6 - A6^*(iIP/IP)].$$

Let's do the numbers for Ozzie, who played in only 124 of the Cardinals' games at shortstop in 1983. Recall that the calculation above determined that *rA6* equals +49 for the 1984 Cardinals. Inputting the innings played and assists data for Ozzie and all Cardinal shortstops combined, we find

$$
\begin{aligned}
\text{Ozzie's 1984 runs} &= .45^*rA6^*(iIP/IP) &+ .45^*[iA6 - A6^*(iIP/IP)] \\
&= .45^*49^*(1065/1449) + .45^*(437 - 597^*(1065/1449)) \\
&= +15 \text{ defensive runs.}
\end{aligned}
$$

Ozzie spent twenty-one days on the disabled list with a broken wrist that year. The Cardinals immediately acquired Chris Speier and then released him as soon as Ozzie could play again. It seems that Speier played about as well as Ozzie did, because Ozzie's assists rate was just slightly below the team assists rate (see the right side of the above calculation). What happened was that Ozzie performed far better before than after he broke his wrist. As I'll emphasize again and again, fielding ratings based on small sample sizes (such as Speier's quarter-season performance) are very unreliable; even the best proprietary batted ball data systems usually require two full-time seasons of data to get a good read on a player. Nevertheless, if one wants to break out the shortstop performances for a team, this is how to do it.

FOUR QUESTIONS; FOUR ANSWERS

1. Other systems include putouts, errors, and double plays in evaluating infielders. Why does DRA include only assists?

With the rarest of exceptions, which certainly cannot be detected with traditional statistics and have yet to be clearly detected using proprietary batted ball data, putouts are not skill plays for infielders (except for unassisted ground ball putouts at first). Obviously simple force outs are not skill plays—credit for the out should only go to the assisting fielder. I'm not aware that anyone has shown that any middle infielder has any particular skill at getting base stealers out by better tagging. Line drives caught are almost always dumb luck plays. There may be a slight skill aspect to line drive fielding, but the noise in any given season, or even a few seasons, swamps the signal. Ninety-five to ninety-nine percent of the pop ups and soft fly balls caught by infielders, whether literally in the infield or beyond (shallow outfield), could be caught by one or more *other* players in the field, so such outs are really discretionary. Given infielders credit for putouts causes ball hogs on easy fly out plays to be overrated. Indeed, since fly outs caught by infielders are virtually automatic outs for any major league team, they are analogous to strike outs, and should accordingly be credited to *pitchers*.

In some sense, then, crediting infielders for their putouts is *duplicative*, because credit for the putout really belongs to another player—the assisting player if the play is a tag out or force out, and the pitcher if the play is a pop up or short fly out. The tiny number of skill shortstop putouts simply cannot be detected using non-proprietary data, and has not, so far as I have seen, been shown to be a real, repeatable, and material skill even using proprietary batted ball data.

Errors and double plays are also duplicative. Each error is already recorded as a play *not* made, given the number of batted balls in play and other adjustments made for estimating relative fielding opportunities. Extensive studies have shown that an error is, on average, essentially no more harmful than simply allowing a clean hit. Separately counting errors is a very old and bad habit that even some of the most sophisticated analysts using the most sophisticated systems cannot seem to break, as we shall see in chapter three, and it continues to lead to significant mistakes in estimating fielding value.

Each double play is likewise already recorded—as an assist by the fielder fielding the ball in play and an assist by the pivoting fielder. Other systems include credit for putouts and double plays as well as assists. This can cause a double play pivot in some systems to be worth twice or more (depending on the relative weights assigned each event) what an assist from fielding a batted is worth, because it triggers credit for a putout, a double play, and an assist. The most sophisticated models for offense show that the second out in a double play is actually slightly less valuable to the defense than the first. Therefore, if one had a choice between a second baseman who each year successfully fielded twenty more ground balls but made twenty fewer double play pivots, he would actually be worth slightly more than a player who had the opposite skill set. It is true that the the relative number of runners at first base, which obviously impacts double play opportunities, is not fully captured in this basic DRA formula, but the most important factor influencing double play opportunities—the total number of balls in play and the ground ball or fly ball tendency of the pitching staff—is in fact already taken into account. Later in this chapter we'll discuss certain additional refinements for adjusting for double play opportunities under DRA.

By intentionally and properly omitting putouts, errors, and double plays, the above shortstop formula actually requires fewer calculations than the corresponding formulas shown in the *ESPN Baseball Encyclopedia* for Pete Palmer's system, and many fewer calculations than those required for Bill James' Win Shares system. Although Clay Davenport's system has never been disclosed in reproducible detail, I would imagine the Davenport shortstop formula is also more complicated than the formula above.

2. Why do shortstops get credit for all their *rA6*? Don't pitchers impact out-conversion rates on batted balls?

DRA takes into account how pitchers *shift* ball in play opportunities around the field by generating ground balls or fly balls, or by facing disproportionately more right- or left-handed opponent batters, but then credits fielders for all defensive runs on batted balls (other than infield fly outs and pitcher assists). This is broadly consistent with current research findings, based on both traditional data and batted ball data.

Voros McCracken earned a shout-out in *The Historical Abstract* for research that showed virtually zero correlation from year to year in ball in play out conversion rates for contemporary full-time pitchers. McCracken concluded that pitchers therefore don't control the probability that a batted ball will be converted into an out by his fielders. After all, if they did control that rate, they would be able to do it somewhat consistently from year to year.

Bill James studied the issue a bit and concluded that this was not exactly true, but largely true. Other studies have tended to show that out-conversion rates on balls in play are somewhat higher for power pitchers, who tend to be fly ball pitchers, and for knuckleball pitchers, but that in general, at a team level over the course of a season, the team's fielders tend to control overall batted all out conversion. Research of my own, discussed in appendices A and F suggests that pitchers may have had more control over batted ball out conversions before a truly striking jump in strikeout rates in the early-to-mid-1950s.

By allocating credit to pitchers for infield fly outs (as well as pitcher assists), DRA further qualifies McCracken's approach, but effectively assigns complete responsibility to infielders for ground balls and to outfielders for balls hit in the air to outfield. The ultimate validation that this is correct is the test results previously published on the internet, as well as those provided in chapter three comparing DRA defensive runs with estimates based on batted ball data, which *does* capture the extent to which a team's pitchers generate balls in play that are easier or harder to field. It's a simplifying, arguably simplistic, assumption, but various tests show that it is generally a reasonable one.

3. Why are *fly outs* used to estimate the impact of relative *ground ball* opportunities for infielders?

As this question addresses a somewhat counter-intuitive idea, the answer will be somewhat longer than the prior two.

We must begin by acknowledging that, strictly speaking, it's impossible to measure a pitching staff's true tendency to generate ground *balls* or fly *balls* from ground *out* and fly *out* data, for the simple reason that the fielding quality of the team impacts the number of *outs*, or successful plays, given the total number of ground balls and fly balls (including any balls hit into the air, such as line drives and pop ups) allowed by the team's pitchers. What you would prefer to know is the total number of ground *balls* (both those that were fielded and converted into ground outs and those that were booted or got through for hits) and the total number of fly *balls* (both those that were converted into fly outs and those that dropped in for hits). The problem is that we don't have these counts for almost a hundred seasons of major league history since 1893, whereas we can count, or at least estimate, fly outs and ground outs throughout major league history.

It turns out, however, that the relative level of ground outs and fly outs per team is predominantly controlled by pitchers, not the relative fielding prowess of a team's infielders and outfielders, and thus in some sense is a decent proxy for fly ball and ground ball pitching. Here's one reason why we know this is true. The number of fly outs relative to the league average, given total balls in play (again, *FO.bip*), has a very strong *negative* correlation ($-.80$) with, and almost exactly the same standard deviation (about a hundred per season) as, the number of *ground* outs above or below the league average rate, given total balls in play ("*GO.bip*"). Thus, if you knew a team had +100 *FO.bip*, you would expect the number of *GO.bip* to be close to -100 *GO.bip* (actually, closer to -80 or -70, based on a regression analysis).

If both statistics reflected solely the fielding quality of the fielders, we would expect the correlation to be virtually zero, because there is no reason to think that the fielding skill of team outfields and infields should be correlated one way or the other. Some teams have good outfields and bad infields, others bad outfields and good infields, others good outfields and good infields, and, yes, bad outfields and bad infields.

Because both *FO.bip* and *GO.bip* use *BIP* as the 'denominator' of opportunities, there is no *arithmetic* reason that they should be so negatively correlated. For example, if the infielders are below average and allow more *BIP* to go through for hits, so that *GO.bip* goes *negative*, that leads to more batters coming to the plate and eventually more *BIP*; but if the outfield is average, and the pitchers are average at generating infield fly outs, they will still convert those extra *BIP* into *FO* at an average rate, and *FO.bip* will *still* remain zero. And while it's true that a good outfield with more total *BIP* to field because of a bad infield will see its *FO.bip* go up, it is equally true that a bad outfield forced to handle more *BIP* will see its *FO.bip* go down; so, again, there is no necessary relationship between *GO.bip* and *FO.bip*.

By contrast, if marginal *FO* and *GO* were 'denominated' in terms of *outs excluding strikeouts* (as some prior systems have done) they would be *perfectly* negatively correlated *by definition*, because all batting *outs* that are not strike outs are *either* fly outs or ground outs: given a fixed number of non-strikeout outs, an increase in fly outs 'results in' a decrease in exactly the same number of ground outs. The fact that *FO.bip* and *GO.bip*, which are *not* subject to this rule, are nevertheless so strongly negatively correlated suggests that they reflect much more the aggregate tendency of team pitching staff to induce relatively more ground balls or fly balls than the aggregate fielding skill of the team's outfielders and infielders.

But if *FO.bip* is correlated (negatively) so well with *GO.bip*, that is, 'predicts' *GO.bip* so well, why not just use *GO.bip* directly to adjust for *A6.bip* for relative ground ball opportunities?

Prior non-batted ball fielding evaluation systems, almost by default, did pretty much the same thing, by using the number of assists to estimate ground ball opportunities for infielders and, sometimes, the number of outfield putouts to estimate fly ball opportunities for outfielders. The main problem with that approach is that it is *self-referential*: a good shortstop will record more assists, which will increase the team total, which will cause one to conclude the team had ground ball pitchers, which will cause one to discount the shortstop's performance as largely attributable to ground ball pitching. A good center fielder will record more putouts, which will increase the team's total of outfield putouts, which will cause one to conclude the team had a fly ball pitching staff, which will cause one to discount the center fielder's performance as largely attributable to fly ball pitching. The adjustments are going around in a circle.

Let's be a little more precise about the degree to which these non-DRA estimators have been more self-referential than the DRA estimators. If you test the correlation between *GO.bip* and *A6.bip*, you'll find a strong correlation (about .70). This suggests that *GO.bip* explains most of the variation in shortstop assists. However, if you *subtract A6.bip* from *GO.bip*, you'll find that the resulting net number correlates with shortstop assists at a much weaker level (only about .20, depending on the sample). In other words, *most* of the correlation between *GO.bip* and *A6.bip*, that is, **most of the ability of relative team assists to estimate relative shortstop opportunities, is due to the correlation between shortstop assists and … shortstop assists.**

In contrast, *FO.bip* has nearly the same power to predict relative short-stop opportunities (only in a negative direction, with correlations of about −.60 or so with *A6.bip*), but very little of that correlation has to do with shortstop assists. In other words, *FO.bip* is a much less self-referential predictor of *A6.bip*, because *A6* are not included in *FO*, whereas they are included in *GO*.

The other advantage of using fly outs given balls in play to estimate the relative fly ball (if positive) or ground ball (if negative) tendency of the team's pitchers for purposes of evaluating infielder ground ball opportunities, is that the sum total of fly outs reflects the fielding of *all* the players on the field at all *nine* positions, including what are usually non-skill plays (*IFO.bip*), thus increasing the chance that the impact of good or bad fielders will even out, or revert to the mean, no longer have as strong an impact, and allow the true relative ground ball tendency of the team's pitching staff to emerge.

The same dynamic is not quite so strong when using *GO.bip*, which we will use to estimate the relative *fly ball* opportunities for *outfielders*, as only six positions record ground outs, though fortunately there are usually some part time fielders, and no pitcher accounts for even one-fifth of pitcher assists. But this approach is still far better than using outfield putouts, which, apart from the pitchers' tendency to induce fly balls, reflect primarily the fielding abilities of players at only *three* positions, to estimate the fly ball chances each *one* of them had. In theory and in fact, an exceptional infield will help the outfield look slightly better under DRA, and vice versa, and we will be alert to this potential source of bias throughout Part II when we discuss player ratings. That said—

It is better for the assists by a great shortstop, such as Ozzie Smith, along with those of *all* of his fellow infielders, to be used to estimate expected fly outs and net plays for *each* Cardinals outfielder, than it is for Ozzie's assists to be used mainly to estimate expected assists and net plays for Ozzie.

Likewise, it is better for the putouts by a great center fielder, such as Mays, along with the fly outs recorded by his teammates at *all* other positions, to be used to estimate expected assists for *each* Giants infielder, than it is for Mays' putouts to be used mainly to estimate expected center field putouts and net plays for Mays.

4. **Why is the estimate of defensive runs per *rA6* only approximately .45 runs, rather than the true value of a marginal play made at shortstop, which is approximately .75 runs?**

The DRA estimate of the number of successful plays that the league-average shortstop would have made is imperfect, because it is based on a limited amount of data, not an actual count of total grounders inside shortstop 'territory'. Therefore, the estimate of marginal plays made by Smith (and other fielders on other teams) vis-à-vis what an average shortstop would record still tends to have a little too much noise in it.

More specifically, the standard deviation in team marginal plays above or below average at shortstop remains too high, even after we take into account the factors described above, because there are other *unknown* factors *not* taken into account—what statisticians would call "omitted variables." Since some of those marginal plays really do not reflect above- or below-average skill, but reflect untracked contextual factors, the second-stage regression analysis of *actual team runs allowed* above or below the league average rate, given innings played, onto such marginal plays at *all* positions tends to associate a weaker level of team runs saved per marginal play.

In addition, as we've just mentioned, shortstop assists are included in an estimate of team ground outs above or below the league-average rate, given total balls in play, and this number is used to estimate the impact of relative ground ball versus fly ball pitching on the number of putouts each average outfielder on the team would make. Therefore, a portion of each shortstop's assists are treated, on average, as merely evidence of ground ball pitching that *shifts* total outs from the outfield to the infield, rather than as evidence of a skill play made that *creates* a net out. Likewise, since the level of outfield putouts is partly attributable to outfield skill plays, the estimate of expected plays made at shortstop is slightly biased, though much less biased than other estimators that have been proposed thus far. This bias in turn causes the per-play run estimate to be decreased.

However, as we shall see in the next chapter, the estimate of defensive runs provided by DRA comes in at almost precisely the right standard deviation, based on best proprietary batted ball data, because the understatement of net run value per play offsets the overstatement of skill plays made above or below average and takes into account the average extent to which shortstop assists reflect out-shifting rather than out-creation.

To be clear: I have not simply haircut the value of each marginal DRA play to make it match with results under batted ball systems; rather, the DRA model independently derives an estimate of the marginal defensive runs associated with its own noisy estimates of marginal plays made above or below expectation. This estimate is based solely on the standard technique of regression analysis applied to standard baseball statistics, not a comparison of standard baseball statistics to proprietary batted ball data. The resulting estimate for runs per marginal play results in estimates for defensive runs for recent players that nevertheless match very well with defensive runs estimates for the same players under batted ball systems, as we shall see in chapter three.

Also, for readers already familiar with alternative systems that seem to use the correct run weights, we will find in the next chapter that they actually haircut the average value of net plays as much or more than the second-stage regression analysis under DRA does.

LEFTY GROUND BALL PITCHING AND RIGHTY FLY BALL PITCHING … AND VICE VERSA

We promised above to address the possible interaction between fly ball versus ground ball pitching and right-handed versus left-handed pitching (which influences right-handed versus left-handed opponent batting).

Let's say that a team had a typical proportion of left- and right-handed pitchers, and a typical proportion of ground outs and fly outs given total balls in play. One would generally expect a very ordinary distribution of batted ball fielding opportunities around the field, and expected plays per position would be simply the league-average rate of plays per batted ball in play multiplied by total balls in play allowed by the team's pitchers.

But the handedness of a pitcher and his tendency to induce ground balls or fly balls are largely independent of each other (though lefties historically have tended to be more ground ball pitchers). What if the left-handed pitchers on a team tended to be ground ball pitchers, while the team's right-handed pitchers tended to be fly ball pitchers? The left-handed pitchers would tend to face more right-handed batters, who would hit more ground outs to the left side of the infield. The right-handed pitchers would tend to face more left-handed batters, who would tend to hit more fly outs to the left side of the outfield. (When a batter flies out, he has probably gotten under and behind a hard fastball, which will tend to be hit to the opposite field.)

Conversely, if the left-handed pitchers were fly ball pitchers and the righties ground ball pitchers, there would be more right-handed opponent batters hitting fly outs to right field and more left-handed opponent batters hitting ground outs to the right side of the infield.

Though recent studies based on batted ball data show that batters tend to control the *left versus right* direction of batted balls, it is probably the case that, per at-bat, batters and pitchers equally influence whether batted balls are hit on the ground or into the air. However, over the course of a season, the difference in fly ball versus ground ball tendencies of a team's pitching staff has a far greater impact on fielding opportunities for the team's fielders than the tendency of their opponent batters, simply because every team of fielders faces a much more similar set of opponent batters, basically everyone except themselves (though this is less true in recent seasons, due to the greater imbalance in schedules).

Therefore, at a first approximation, one can think of pitchers as controlling the relative level of ground balls and fly balls, and opponent

hitters as controlling the direction (left or right) of ground balls and fly balls.

Thanks to the organization retrosheet.org, we now have free, publicly available information going back to the early 1950s that permits us to introduce an improvement that handles this interaction with a minimum of complexity. The necessary information is the *total* number of *BIP* hit by right- and left-handed opponent *batters* (so we no longer have to use the imperfect proxy of balls in play allowed by left- and right-handed *pitchers*), as well as exact counts of *ground outs* and *fly outs* (the latter including line outs, fly outs, and pop outs) hit by *right-* handed opponent batters, as well as exact counts of *ground outs* and *fly outs* hit by *left*-handed opponent batters.

We first calculate, instead of *LpBIP.bip*, the total number of balls in play hit by opponent *right*-handed batters ("*RBIP*") above or below the league average rate, given total balls in play, or *RBIP.bip* (using the "*XY.abc*" arithmetic shown above).

Next, we calculate the number of fly outs hit by opponent right-handed batters (*right*-handed opponent *FO*, "*RFO*") given, *not total BIP*, but *only RBIP*, or *RFO.rbip*. In general, this number reflects the relative tendency of the team's left-handed pitchers, who would tend to face more right-handed batters, to be fly ball (if positive) or ground ball (if negative) pitchers. Of course, because there is nothing close to perfect platooning, the team's right-handed pitchers can also impact this number. Note that this number controls for, or takes into account, the *BIP* and *RBIP* calculations we've *already* made.

Next, we calculate the same thing for opponent *left*-handed batters (who would disproportionately face right-handed pitchers), that is, the relative number of fly outs hit by opponent left-handed batters (*left*-handed opponent batter *FO*, "*LFO*") *given* the total number of *BIP* hit by opponent *left*-handed batters (*left*-handed opponent batter *BIP*, or "*LBIP*"), or *LFO.lbip*. In general, this number reflects the relative tendency of the team's right-handed pitchers to be fly ball (if positive) or ground ball (if negative) pitchers, though, again, left-handed pitchers do face left-handed batters, so the effect of the team's left-handed pitchers bleeds into this number. This is the correct approach, however; as with the case of *RFO.rbip*, *LFO.lbip* focuses attention on the variable having the most impact on the left-versus-right distribution of fly outs: opponent *batter*-handedness.

Note again that this number controls for, or takes into account, the *BIP* and *RBIP* calculations we've *already* made. In other words, *RBIP.bip*, *RFO.rbip*, and *LFO.lbip* are each at least *arithmetically 'independent'* of each other (though not technically independent of each other probabilistically), so that it will be easier to estimate the impact of each of these factors 'independently' of the others.

Here is how these new variables are used in the second base formula, which is basically the same type of formula we showed in our Ozzie example, but with the fly out variable separated by opponent batter-handedness:

$$rA4 = A4.bip + .08*RBIP.bip + .15*RFO.rbip + .32*LFO.lbip.$$

Let's take this one step at a time, in English. Regression-adjusted (or residual) assists at second base ("*rA4*") mean

1. team assists at second base ("*A4*") above or below the league average rate, given *total* balls in play (see the dot-*bip*),
2. increased by .08 (decreased by .08) for every ball in play hit by opponent *right*-handed *batters* ("*RBIP*") above (below) the league-average rate, given *total* balls in play (dot-*bip*) (*negative RBIP.bip* means the same thing as higher opponent *left*-handed batter balls in play),
3. increased by .15 (decreased by .15) for every fly out hit by an opponent *right*-handed batter ("*RFO*") above (below) the league-average rate, given total batted balls in play hit by opponent *right*-handed batters (dot-*rbip*), and
4. increased by .32 (decreased by .32) for every fly out hit by an opponent *left*-handed batter ("*LFO*") above (below) the league-average rate, given total batted balls in play hit by opponent *left*-handed batters (dot-*lbip*).

Notice that the fourth factor is more important than the third, which makes sense. The fourth factor will tend to be positive if the team's right-handed pitchers are fly ball pitchers. These pitchers will tend to face more left-handed hitters and cause them to hit the ball in the air, thus drastically reducing ground out opportunities on the right side of the infield. So we essentially credit the second basemen to take into account this negative factor. Of course, if the fourth factor is *negative*, then the right-handed pitchers will be causing the left-handed batters to hit lots of *ground* balls to the right side of the infield, in which case we debit second base assists for the extra chances given.

The third factor will also be positive if the team's left-handed pitchers are fly ball pitchers. However, notice that the effect is weaker. That's because left-handed pitchers tend to face more right-handed batters, who tend not to hit that many ground balls towards the right side of the infield, whether or not the pitcher is a ground ball ball pitcher. Nevertheless, it does matter somewhat whether left-handed pitchers are ground ball or fly ball pitchers.

Now let's apply the second base formula to a real team, the 1960 Pittsburgh Pirates. Their full-time second baseman was Bill Mazeroski, who won the

World Series that year against the Yankees by hitting a homerun in the bottom of the ninth of the seventh game. For the 1960 Pirates,

$$
\begin{aligned}
rA4 &= A4.bip + .08^*RBIP.bip + .15^*RFO.rbip + .32^*LFO.lbip \\
&= 20 \quad\quad + .08^*(11) \quad\quad + .15^*(-61) \quad\quad + .32^*(-20) \\
&= 20 \quad\quad + 1 \quad\quad\quad\quad + (-9) \quad\quad\quad\quad + (-9) \\
&= +3.
\end{aligned}
$$

Note that the *A4.bip*, *RBIP.bip*, *RFO.rbip*, and *LFO.lbip* numbers were all calculated using the *XY.abc* method described on page 00. The run value for plays at second is about half a run. So, with rounding, we show only +2 defensive runs. Maz played virtually every inning of every game. As we'll see when we get to the historical ratings of second basemen, a lot of Maz's astounding assists totals can be attributed to the fact that his teams tended to have ground ball pitchers (again, measured *without* reference to Maz's *own* performance). Here, it appears that the Pirate left-handers were extreme ground ball pitchers, based on the third factor, while the right-handers were only moderate ground ball pitchers, based on the fourth factor.

As it happens, there are three additional factors in the complete DRA formula for second base, mainly related to double play assist opportunities: sacrifice hits, wild pitches, and home runs, each of which reduce double play opportunities. Sacrifice hits and wild pitches move runners from first to second, and home runs eliminate base runners. Therefore we boost *rA4* (if these factors are above the league-average rate) and reduce *rA4* (if they are below).

These final three adjustments (which are shown in full detail in appendix A) bring the team second base rating for the 1960 Pittsburgh Pirates from +2 defensive runs to +9 defensive runs, which is an unsurprising result, given that Maz is generally acknowledged as the greatest double play pivot man of all time. A good season, but nothing like the +30 defensive runs that *The ESPN Baseball Encyclopedia* reports using Palmer Fielding Runs. The Palmer rating is too high because no adjustment is made for ground ball versus fly ball pitching, and because double play assists (Maz's specialty) are counted twice as much as regular assists, when they are worth approximately the same. Maz was a wonderful fielder, but he typically saved 10 to 15 runs a season, not 20 to 30.

Here is the formula for third base, which works the same way as the formula at second, but with coefficients, shown in **bold**, that reflect the fact that third base is on the opposite side of the field from second base:

$$
rA5 = A5.bip - \mathbf{.10}^*RBIP.bip + \mathbf{.21}^*RFO.rbip + \mathbf{.10}^*LFO.lbip.
$$

We need to *debit* plays for extra *RBIP* because right-handed batters pull ground balls, resulting in extra chances for the left side of the infield that must be clawed back (and vice versa). The third factor is *more* important than the fourth, because the ground ball versus fly ball tendency of opponent right-handed batters (impacted by a team's opponent left-handed pitchers) drastically impact chances at third. The ground ball versus fly ball tendency of the opponent left-handed batters is less important because they are less likely to hit ground balls to the left side of the infield, regardless of the ground ball versus fly ball tendency of the team's pitchers, though the latter effect is not zero.

Let's take an example at third base where there appears to have been a big difference in the ground ball versus fly ball tendencies of a team's left- and right-handed pitchers, while the relative levels of total left- and right-handed pitching were about at the league norm. For the 1983 Texas Rangers, whose full-time third baseman was all-time great Buddy Bell,

$$
\begin{aligned}
rA5 &= A5.bip - .10{*}RBIP.bip + .21{*}RFO.rbip + .10{*}LFO.lbip \\
&= 50 \quad\quad - .10{*}(8) \quad\quad + .21{*}(-99) \quad\quad + .10{*}(+18) \\
&= 50 \quad\quad - 1 \quad\quad\quad\quad + (-21) \quad\quad\quad + (+2) \\
&= 30.
\end{aligned}
$$

Notice how the nearly zero *RBIP.bip* variable indicates that the relative number of total *BIP* hit by opposing right- and left-handed batters was about league-average, thus suggesting that the Rangers probably had an approximately league-average level of left- and right-handed pitching. Also, the slightly positive *LFO.lbip* variable suggests that the relative number of fly outs hit by opponent left-handed batters was only slightly above average, thus indicating that the Rangers' right-handed pitchers probably had only a slight tendency to be fly ball pitchers.

But the *RFO.rbip* variable indicates that the relative number of fly outs hit by opponent right-handed pitchers was very, very low, which indicates that the Ranger left-handed pitchers, who would have faced a disproportionate number of right-handed batters, had an extreme ground ball tendency, thus giving the third basemen about twenty extra plays that we claw back to estimate the true net skill plays at third base. The primary left-handed pitches for the Rangers were Rick Honeycutt and Frank Tanana, neither of whom had high strikeout rates in 1983. *The Neyer/James Guide to Pitchers* says that Honeycutt's primary pitches were a slider, forkball, curve and change, which does seem to suggest he was a groundball pitcher. The same authority says that Tanana relied mostly on a slow curve and change after he lost his fastball.

The run value for *rA5* is about .45 runs. So that leaves about +14 defensive runs by 1983 Texas Ranger third basemen. Just as there are a few extra variables at second base to adjust for double play opportunities, there are a few extra variables at third base to handle bunt opportunities, as shown in appendix A. These last adjustments bring the 1983 Texas Ranger rating up to +17 defensive runs. As Buddy Bell played 154 games at third, just about all of the team rating belongs to him.

AN OUTFIELD EXAMPLE

The basic formula for centerfield, with new components denoted in **bold**, is:

$$rPO8 = PO8.bip - .01^*RBIP.bip + .27^*\textbf{RGO.rbip} + .24^*\textbf{LGO.lbip}.$$

Two key ideas here. First, we use *ground* outs to adjust *outfield* plays made for ground ball versus fly ball pitching for the same reason we use fly outs to adjust infield plays made for ground ball versus fly ball pitching: as discussed above, they're not nearly as self-referential. Second, you'll notice that the effect of extra right-handed batters (i.e., fewer left-handed batters) is quite weak, and the third and fourth factors are approximately equal. This make sense, because a center fielder is, well, in the center of the field, where the impact of left- and right-handed batters (and pitchers) on total fielding opportunities is approximately equal.

Let's calculate net plays for the 1958 Yankees, again using the *XY.abc* method to calculate *PO8.bip, RBIP.bip, RGO.rbip,* and *LGO.lbip*:

$$
\begin{aligned}
rPO8 &= PO8.bip &- .01^*RBIP.bip &+ .27^*RGO.rbip &+ .24^*LGO.lbip \\
&= -44 &- .01^*(+89) &+ .27^*(+64) &+ .24^*(-2) \\
&= -44 &- 1 &+ (+17) &+ (-0) \\
&= -28.
\end{aligned}
$$

Each regression-adjusted, or residual, putout in center ("*rPO8*") is statistically associated with about half a run, so the 1958 Yankees' centerfield defensive runs estimate is −14 runs. As with our infield positions, there are one or two minor additional adjustments in the outfield, this time for ball hogging of short high flies that may also be caught by infielders, and for sacrifice bunts, which by definition can't be fielded by outfielders. These bring the team rating to −15 defensive runs, of which Mantle's share (based on the same calculation we showed for Ozzie Smith above) is −13 defensive runs. That was one of his worst seasons; when reasonably healthy (basically through 1961), Mantle was about an average fielding center fielder.

DEFENSE INCLUDES PITCHING

DRA is a complete model of team defense, which naturally includes pitching. The 'plays' for which pitchers are responsible are strikeouts ("*SO*"), walks and hit batsmen (collectively, "*BB*"), home runs ("*HR*"), and pitcher assists ("*A1*"). In addition, we allocate infield fly outs ("*IFO*") to pitchers because they are almost automatic outs not requiring fielder skill, as discussed above in our Ozzie example. Finally, pitchers are responsible for wild pitches and primarily responsible for passed balls (collectively, "*WP*"). Extreme passed ball totals almost always reflect knuckleball pitching; since the extremes are controlled by pitchers, we assign pitchers responsibility for the variable. However, differences in rates between catchers on the same team get credited (charged) to the individual catchers. Pitchers do have an influence on stolen bases, but catchers even more, so, at least at the team level and on a year-by-year basis, so we allocate to catchers the responsibility for the team outcome.

Recall that for fielding plays, the first fundamental contextual factor is balls in play, or *BIP*, which is why formulas for regression-adjusted (or residual) plays, *rPO8*, begin with the *BIP* factor, for example, *PO8.bip*. The fundamental contextual factor for pitcher assists (*A1*) and infield fly outs (*IFO*) is also *BIP*, thus yielding *A1.bip* and *IFO.bip*, calculated as we did above for *A6.bip*, but instead using *A1* and *FO minus outfield* putouts (which we know) to calculate *IFO*. Since pitchers create their own *A1* opportunities and generated *IFO* by being ground ball or fly ball pitchers, there is no need to regression-adjust either variable.

Thus, if a pitcher induces a ground ball and he fields it, he gets full credit for the out; if he induces an infield or very shallow outfield fly ball that virtually any major league team would convert into an out, he also gets full credit. I believe the latter point, and possibly both points, are new ways of evaluating pitchers. The article that first described DRA, which appeared on the baseballthinkfactory.org website in 2003, proposed crediting pitchers with *IFO*, I believe for the first time, and other analysts have begun tracking individual pitcher *IFO.bip* rates. Now it is true that some analysts have previously credited pitcher fielding, but they *added* it to *overall* pitching results, which *already* reflect those outs, which caused pitcher fielding to be double counted. By all means, credit a good fielding pitcher for the hits he prevents by inducing ground balls and fielding so well—just don't add those runs to his runs saved as measured by his ERA relative to the league, because they are already included.

We don't need to regression-adjust any of the other pitching variables, but we do need to assign them 'denominators', or contexts of opportunities, different from *BIP*, *RBIP*, or *LBIP*.

The context of opportunities for *SO* and *BB* is "batters facing pitcher" ("*BFP*"). This is because each time a batter faces a pitcher, he can be struck out (*SO*), walked or hit-by-pitch (either, "*BB*") by the team's pitchers. Therefore, team *SO* and *BB* are reported as *SO* and *BB* above or below the league average rate, given *BFP*, or *SO.bfp* and *BB.bfp*. Arguably, one could render *BB* and *SO* more arithmetically 'independent' of each other by using *BFP* as the context of opportunities for *BB*, and *BFP* minus *BB* as the context of opportunities for *SO* (or vice versa), but it isn't necessary to add this complexity.

However, it is in fact necessary to render *HR* less correlated with *SO* and *BB* by defining the context of opportunities for *HR* as *BFP* minus *SO* and *BB*, or "balls hit" ("*BH*"). In other words, how many home runs did the team's pitchers allow above or below the league-average rate, given the *BH* against the team's pitchers? We denote this as *HR.bh*.

The correct context for *WP* would be runners on base ("*ROB*"), which can be estimated at the team level a number of ways, but it is not worth the extra complexity. Therefore, we simply use innings pitched ("*IP*") and calculate *WP.ip*.

Therefore, instead of one net plays statistic, such as *rA6*, *rA4*, *rA5*, or *rPO8*, with each net play worth about half a run, there are six net plays made per pitcher, each with its own distinct run value, so that total defensive runs per pitcher equals

$$+ .27^*SO.bfp - .34^*BB.bfp - 1.49^*HR.bh$$
$$+ .42^*A1.bip + .44^*IFO.bip - .56^*WP.ip.$$

The run weights for *A1.bip* and *IFO.bip* are between .40 and .50, just as the weights for *rA6*, *rA4*, and *rA5* were, as discussed above. The run value that is clearly wrong is the run value for *WP.ip*, which should be about half that level. As the impact on pitcher evaluation and team results is very modest, we'll discuss the rather technical reason why the run weight is too high in appendix A.

A PITCHER EXAMPLE

Roger Clemens had his greatest season, and his second best strikeout season (as measured by *SO.bfp*), during the year in which he turned thirty-five years of age (1997). Here are his estimated defensive runs, independent of his fielders:

$$.27^*SO.bfp - .34^*BB.bfp - 1.49^*HR.bh$$
$$+ .42^*A1.bip + .44^*IFO.bip - .56^*WP.ip$$

$$= .27^*(+120) - .34^*(-16) - 1.49^*(-16)$$
$$+ .42^*(+12) + .44^*(+4) - .56^*(-8)$$

$$= +34 \qquad +5 \qquad +25$$
$$+5 \qquad\quad +2 \qquad +4$$

$$= +75 \text{ defensive runs.}$$

In other words, DRA estimates he should have allowed seventy-five fewer runs, given the total number of innings he pitched, relative to the league-average pitcher that year. In fact, The Rocket allowed eighty-one fewer runs. His fielders were just about exactly average, overall. The six-run difference is just noise.

One thing I like about the DRA approach to pitcher evaluation is that is shows the components of pitcher performance in terms of runs, not just overall runs allowed above or below the league-average rate. Nolan Ryan, for example, was about equally effective in his late thirties and early forties as he had been in his mid-to-late twenties. But that was not because he maintained his same level of dominance as a strikeout pitcher—he experienced something close to a normal age-related decline in that area. However, he did succeed in bringing his walk rate way down, counteracting his relative decline in strikeouts.

DRA estimates *total* defensive runs for pitchers, *not* so-called "earned" defensive runs. A pitcher on a poor fielding team might have an unfairly high "earned" run average ("ERA") because the team made relatively few errors but had poor range, thus allowing a lot of clean hits to drop in, while a pitcher on a strong fielding team might have an unfairly low ERA because the team made more errors but had good range. But the problem is even worse than that. Error rates are much higher on ground balls than on fly balls. Therefore, ground ball pitchers, who induce more errors, *benefit* by doing so, as a higher percentage of the base runners they allow reach base on errors, resulting in a lower ERA given the same number of base runners allowed. The opposite applies for fly ball pitchers. This is yet another reason to banish "errors" from defensive evaluations.

HOW THOSE RUN WEIGHTS WERE DETERMINED

Now we're ready to discuss in more detail than we have so far the "second stage" of the "two-stage" regression analysis that generates the average run value per net play. First we need to review all the net plays variables in team defense.

Recall that for the fielding formulas we conducted "first-stage" regression analyses to arrive at the formulas for net plays made at short, second, third, and center: *rA6*, *rA4*, *rA5*, and *rPO8*. The same approach is used to generate formulas for regression-adjusted, or residual, ground outs (including estimated unassisted ground outs) at first base ("*rGO3*"), and balls caught in left field ("*rPO7*") and right field ("*rPO9*").

Then we showed immediately above the relevant variables for pitchers, which don't require a "first-stage" regression analysis but only arithmetic centering by reference to the appropriate 'denominator' of opportunities for each event: $SO.bfp$, $BB.bfp$, $HR.bh$, $A1.bip$, $IFO.bip$, and $WP.ip$.

Here are the remaining skill plays to include in the total model of team defense: runners caught stealing ("CS"), catcher ground outs ($A2$ minus CS, or "$GO2$"), and outfield assists ("$A789$"). For CS, the context of opportunities is simply stolen base attempts ("SBA"), so our stolen base variable is runners caught stealing above or below the league rate, given team stolen base attempts, or $CS.sba$. Catcher assists other than for runners caught stealing are almost always ground outs, for which the simple BIP adjustment is sufficient ("$GO2.bip$"). Finally, as there is no simple context of opportunities for outfield assists, and regression analysis doesn't substantially change the result, we collect all outfield assists and determine the number above or below the league average, given total innings ("$A789.ip$").

So here are all of our team defensive variables:

Pitching plays : $SO.bfp$, $BB.bfp$, $HR.bh$, $A1.bip$, $IFO.bip$ and $WP.ip$
Catching plays : $CS.sba$ and $GO2.bip$
Infield plays   : $rGO3$, $rA4$, $rA5$ and $rA6$
Outfield plays : $rPO7$, $rPO8$, $rPO9$ and $A789.ip$

Recall that they are all centered net plays—they estimate the number of plays the team made above or below what the league-average team would be expected to make at each position, given the same estimated context of opportunities.

To determine the average value in runs of each of these net plays, all we have to do is calculate these numbers for a large sample of major league seasons (including every team in the sample), and then do a "second-stage" regression analysis of the *actual runs allowed* ("RA") by these teams *above or below* the league-average rate, given innings played ("$RA.ip$"), onto the above variables. Note that we are regressing a centered variable onto other centered variables, where all of the central values are zero. Professional statisticians would call this a "forced zero intercept" regression analysis. An Excel spreadsheet program can do this for you, or any statistical package. Here is the result, based on all major league teams from 1957 through 2006, yielding the complete DRA model for team defense for that time period.

Estimated Team Defensive Runs equals the sum of:

Pitching runs = $.27^*SO.bfp - .34^*BB.bfp - 1.49^*HR.bh$.
$.42^*A1.bip + .44^*IFO.bip - .56^*WP.ip$.
Catcher runs = $.59^*CS.sba + .59^*GO2.bip$.
Infield runs   = $.52^*rGO3 + .53^*rA4 + .45^*rA5 + .44^*rA6$.
Outfield runs = $.53^*rPO7 + .46^*rPO8 + .44^*rPO9 + .61^*A789.ip$.

Each of the above run weights estimates the amount of runs the team would save (allow) compared to the average team if the team was one above (one below) in that variable (excluding *BB.bfp*, *HR.bh*, and *WP.ip*, where the signs are reversed). Again, to be clear, this reflects a statistical "association" and is not always the 'true' value, though the first three pitcher variables and *CS.sba* have almost precisely the correct value.

For example, if the team was exactly *zero* in every *other* variable, but was

+10 in *IFO.bip*, we would expect the team to allow 4.4 fewer runs, or
+10 in *rPO7*, we would expect the team to allow 5.3 fewer runs, or
−100 in *SO.bfp*, we would expect the team to allow 27 more runs, or
−10 in *HR.bh*, we would expect the team to allow 14.9 fewer runs.

The DRA estimate of the number of runs a team should have allowed relative to the league-average team, given its pitching and fielding statistics, is simply the sum of pitching runs, catcher runs, infield runs, and outfield runs. Regression analysis assigns run weights to each of the variables so as to minimize the standard deviation of the error in estimated total defensive runs per team.

One indication that DRA models team defense well is that the standard deviation of the error in the DRA estimate for team defensive runs in a season (twenty-two runs for 1957–2006 data) is about the same as the standard deviation of the errors under best-known formulas for estimating team runs *scored*. As John Jarvis has reported, there are about twenty formulas for estimating how many runs a team should score based on the team's offensive statistics. The estimate of team runs scored compared to the league-average team based on these formulas is off by less than twenty to twenty-five runs about two-thirds of the time, though there are occasional errors of fifty or more runs.[1] Likewise, the estimate under DRA of the number of runs a team should *allow* based on the team's *defensive* statistics, compared to the league-average team, is also off by less than twenty-two runs about two-thirds of the time, though there are occasional errors of fifty runs or more. However, it should be said that the correlation between DRA and actual team runs allowed is more like .95, whereas the correlation between offensive runs models and actual team runs scored is virtually 1.00 with rounding.

A TEAM EXAMPLE

The 1973 Baltimore Orioles were probably the greatest fielding team ever, featuring all-time great fielders such as Brooks Robinson at third,

---

1. http://knology.net/~johnfjarvis/runs_survey.html.

Mark Belanger at short, Bobby Grich at second, and Paul Blair in center. Here is how the team as a whole stacked up. First, the pitching staff:

$$
\begin{aligned}
\text{Pitching Runs} &= .27^*SO.bfp - .34^*BB.bfp - 1.49^*HR.bh. \\
&\quad .42^*A1.bip + .44^*IFO.bip - .56^*WP.ip. \\
\text{BAL AL 1973} &= .27^*(-78) - .34^*(-73) - 1.49^*(-5) \\
&\quad .42^*(+5) - .44^*(-11) - .56^*(-22) \\
&= -21 \quad\quad +25 \quad\quad +7 \\
&\quad +2 \quad\quad\quad +5 \quad\quad\quad +12 \\
&= +30 \text{ runs.}
\end{aligned}
$$

Earl Weaver felt very strongly that pitchers should stay ahead in the count and avoid walks, which is just what this team did. Their control also reduced wild pitches and passed balls. Nevertheless, this was hardly a dominant pitching staff.

Now let's look at the team's catching:

$$
\begin{aligned}
\text{Catcher runs} &= .59^*CS.sba + .59^*GO2.bip. \\
\text{1973 AL BAL} &= .59(6) \quad\quad + .59(-22) \\
&= +4 \quad\quad\quad -13 \\
&= -9 \text{ runs.}
\end{aligned}
$$

The primary catcher was Earl Williams, who had a good arm but not a lot of mobility—he did not steal a single base until his eighth and final season. Even the slowest player in baseball history, Ernie Lombardi, stole several bases in the first eight years of his career. I wouldn't pay that much attention to the $GO2.bip$ runs for any one year, however, as they can be affected by sacrifice attempts.

And now the infield, certainly the greatest fielding one of all time:

$$
\begin{aligned}
\text{Infield runs} &= .52^*rGO3 + .53^*rA4 + .45^*rA5 + .44^*rA6. \\
\text{1973 AL BAL} &= .52^*(-28) + .53^*(+68) + .45^*(+36) + .44^*(+39) \\
&= -15 \quad\quad +36 \quad\quad +16 \quad\quad +17 \\
&= +54 \text{ runs.}
\end{aligned}
$$

Boog Powell played most of the team's innings at first. Boog was not nimble at this stage of his career. The primary fielders at second, third, and short were Grich, Brooksie, and Belanger, respectively. All three had stellar seasons, though I would wager that Grich's defensive runs at second base probably overstate whatever his real value was, to some extent. DRA provides well-supported approximations, not irrefutable facts.

The outfield yields a surprise.:

$$\text{Outfield runs} = .53^*rPO7 + .46^*rPO8 + .44^*rPO9 + .61^*A789.ip.$$
$$1973 \text{ AL BAL} = .53^*(+18) + .46^*(+41) + .44^*(+54) + .61^*(-2)$$
$$= +10 \qquad + 19 \qquad + 24 \qquad -1$$
$$= +52.$$

Most serious fans in the 1960s and 1970s would have considered Paul Blair the best fielding center fielder since Mays, and the estimate of +19 defensive runs on center field putouts is consistent with his other single-season defensive runs estimates. The surprises are in left and right. Don Baylor played about two-thirds of the team's innings in left, which would not have helped, but the remaining third were played by Al Bumbry, a speedster and career center fielder. Bumbry also played a bit in right, along with Merv Rettenmund, a good fielder, and Rich Coggins, who played a lot of center field in his career, though not as much as Bumbry.

This team's fielders, collectively, had +97 defensive runs; the team's pitchers, +30 defensive runs. Thus we estimate the 1973 Baltimore Orioles should have allowed 127 fewer runs than the league-average team that year, given the number of innings they played. The actual total was 137 runs, or 10 more runs saved than estimated. Again, the standard error under the main DRA model, covering seasons since the mid-1950s, is 22 defensive runs per team season.

CORE PRINCIPLES: 'INDEPENDENCE', SIGNIFICANCE, RUNS, AND SIMPLICITY

Now that we've walked through examples of how DRA works at short, second, third, center, pitcher, and on an overall team level, let's step back and summarize the core principles of the system.

The first is 'independence'. The first stage of the construction of the model attempts to make each estimate of expected team plays per position as independent of the quality of the team's fielders at the position being evaluated as possible and as little correlated with the quality of their fellow fielders at the other positions as possible. The second stage of the construction of the model attempts to find the most accurate association, in runs, per estimated net play at each position, including pitcher, 'independent' of the net plays at all the *other* positions. The single quotation marks are there because it is not possible to make each expected plays estimate, or estimated runs per net play estimate, independent in the mathematically precise sense.

By doing our best to strip away the impact that various factors have on expected plays made, we obtain a good estimate of net plays that are likely attributable to the skill of the team's fielders at that position, rather than pitching factors (such as ground ball versus fly ball pitching) and batting factors (handedness of opponent batters) beyond their control. In addition, the various arithmetic transformations (for example, from $A4$ to $A4.bip$) and "first-stage" regression analyses (for example, taking $A4.bip$ to $rA6$, achieved by backing out the impact of $RBIP.bip$, $RFO.rbip$, and $LFO.lbip$ on $A4.bip$) limit the cross-correlations of the various net plays estimates to about .10 or −.10; without these adjustments, many pitching and fielding statistics would have correlations above .60 and below −.60.

The technical term for this is "multi-collinearity." When multi-collinearity is present, the coefficients for each variable being used to predict net runs allowed in the "second-stage" regression are highly susceptible to being grossly incorrect. One intuitive way of seeing this is that the second-stage regression analysis can't reveal the impact of a *particular* variable on net runs allowed when everything is cross-correlated, because the other variables are moving with or against the variable at the same time, and thereby could be impacting net runs allowed as well.

In a less technical sense, DRA is 'independent' in that it is not reliant in any way on proprietary batted ball data. DRA was *not* created by using regression analysis to match up traditional statistics to batted ball data defensive runs estimates. Rather—

DRA uses arithmetic transformations and regression analysis to disentangle the relationships between and among publicly available team-level pitching and fielding statistics, so that net skill plays at each position, and their respective marginal impacts in runs, may emerge.

The second principle of DRA is "significance," both statistical and practical. Almost every single variable you will see in any formula at any level in the model is there because it has a so-called "p-value" of .05, which is often misunderstood to mean that the probability the variable could have had an impact by random chance is generally less than five percent. This may be true when a regression analysis is conducted on truly randomized data. But historical baseball statistics are merely observational data that has not been systematically randomized. (Though I would imagine most statisticians would consider it much closer to randomized data than what is typically dealt with in the social sciences.) In such cases, the p-value has the commonly understood meaning only if we are sure the rest of the model has been properly specified, which in some sense begs the question. Nevertheless, economists and other social scientists who run regressions on observational data should, I believe, be comfortable with DRA as a reasonably reliable two-stage, forced-zero-intercept, multivariable least-squares regression model.

Of course, a variable could have statistical significance (or at least have a nice p-value) but have very little *practical* significance. The variables discussed in this chapter all have practical significance, meaning that they tend to have an impact of more than a few runs per season. Some of the minor variables described in appendix A arguably could have been dropped due to their having only a borderline practical significance.

Third, DRA is ultimately about estimating the *runs* fielders save. One reader of an early on-line article about DRA dismissed DRA as merely another version of "Adjusted Range Factor," that is, net plays made after making certain adjustments for the total number of balls in play allowed by the team's pitchers, ground ball versus fly ball pitching, and so forth. However, the adjustments under DRA are probably significantly more accurate than those found in any prior "Adjusted Range Factor" devised to work throughout major league history. In particular, the use of $FO.bip$ to adjust infield chances and $GO.bip$ to adjust outfield chances, and the splitting of both by batter handedness when possible, are new approaches to "adjusting" plays made.

But the bigger difference is that DRA *then* goes on to estimate the average impact in runs of each net play made above average, which no Adjusted Range Factor has done or really could do, because no other Adjusted Range Factor system has been as well constructed or organized to relate itself to ultimate team runs allowed. And the resulting run-weights results in bottom line estimate of defensive runs, given total plays made, that appear to match better with current state-of-the-art batted ball systems than any non-batted ball system, and about as well as the batted ball data systems match up with each other, as we will see in the next chapter.

Finally, DRA is about simplicity, or at least relative simplicity. I would easily forgive any first-time reader for disagreeing, with some exasperation. But hear me out.

Starting from the top down, the DRA team model includes only sixteen team variables. Officially, each position has four counting statistics (putouts, assists, double plays, and errors), which would make thirty-six. Pitchers also have strikeouts, walks, hit batsmen, and wild pitches. Catchers have also had passed balls and (at least for seasons since the 1950s for which Retrosheet has compiled the data) runners caught stealing, opponent stolen base attempts, and passed balls. Which would take us to forty-three variables, nearly three times as many as in DRA. DRA drops unnecessary variables (putouts, assists, and double plays per infield position) and consolidates other variables that involve the same position and have the same effect within a game (walks and hit batsmen into one "*BB*" variable; wild pitches and passed balls into one "*WP*" variable). As discussed above in the Ozzie Smith example, the basic DRA formula is simpler than any other defensive runs formula I have seen published, other than fielding average and Range Factor. And though the complete formulas have more variables, they are still essentially one-line formulas with intuitively clear elements. As can be seen in appendix A, available on-line, it is possible to present the entire DRA model for team defense, position by position, in less than one uncluttered page. No other comprehensive pitching and fielding evaluation system remotely as accurate as DRA can be presented as concisely.

Probably the main reason this chapter seems so dense is that it actually goes to the trouble of disclosing the most important things going on under the hood and explaining why they should work. Of all fielding analysts, only Bill James has done the same in complete reproducible detail, and I believe that anyone who has studied his system, Fielding Win Shares, and then DRA, would agree that DRA is simpler.

A NEAT COINCIDENCE

Speaking of simple formulas, most of the following baseball formula has been in the public domain, if not always widely known, for about ninety years:

$$\text{Offensive runs} = -.27^*(AB{-}H) + .33^*BB + .47^*1B \\ + .78^*2B + 1.09^*3B + 1.40^*HR.$$

When seasonal team or individual batter totals are plugged in, this formula provides an estimate of the number of runs a team or batter creates above or below the league-average team or batter during that season, by charging .27 runs for each at-bat not resulting in a hit (i.e., batting outs) and crediting .33 runs for each walk, 1.40 runs for each home run, etc.

F. C. Lane began developing very similar run values for home runs, triples, doubles, and singles in 1917, yes, *over ninety years ago*, based initially on some reasonable assumptions and intuitive arguments about runner advancement on various types of hits. He refined his estimates over the years as he acquired and analyzed more game data. Lane also provided an estimate of the run value of walks, indeed was one of the first analysts to recognize that batters should be credited for drawing walks, though the run weight he estimated was about half of what it should have been. Further work by analysts over the next fifty years made the modeling more mathematically rigorous and derived the correct walk value and the correct value for outs.

Let's make two slight changes to this classic batting formula. First, let's denote $(AB - H)$, or batting outs, as "*BO*." Second, let's combine triples, doubles, and singles into one category, hits ("*H*"). Based on the relative frequency of singles, doubles, and triples in the major leagues from 1957 to 2006, the weighted average run value of H using Palmer's methods would be approximately .55, resulting in the following version of our batting formula:

$$\text{Offensive runs} = -.27*BO + .33*BB + .55*H + 1.40*HR.$$

The corresponding DRA formula for team batted ball defense, if we combine all batted ball fielding variables (*A1.bip*, *IFO.bip*, *GO2.bip*, *rGO3*, *rA4*, *rA5*, *rA6*, *rPO7*, *rPO8*, and *rPO9*) and average their 1957–2006 run weights (weighted by the standard deviation of each variable) to create one hits *allowed* variable ("*rHA*"), is

$$\text{Defensive runs} = +.28*SO.bfp - .34*BB.bfp - .47*rHA - 1.49*HR.bh.$$

DRA doesn't mirror our classic batting formula perfectly, but the similarity is unmistakable.

TAKING THINGS TO THE NEXT LEVEL

Although simplicity is one goal of DRA, an even more important one is reproducibility. The appendices provide all of the details necessary to reproduce DRA going back throughout major league history: what kind of data to download from retrosheet.org, how to cope with the deterioration in the amount and accuracy of defensive statistics as one goes back in history. Any anomalies, and there are a few, are addressed directly.

There are basically two versions of DRA used in this book. The primary one, which is applied going back to 1952, uses the *RBIP*, *RFO*, *LFO*, *RGO*, and *LGO* data mentioned in the Mazeroski, Bell, and Mantle examples. This data is lacking for prior seasons, which requires us to develop another model.

The second model, which runs from 1893 through 1951, could be seen as one model, or more than one model. It is one model in the sense that the team level equation coefficients from the second-stage regression are the same for all years, to keep things as simple as possible. However, because we don't have separate putout totals in left, center, or right field for seasons before 1920 and, when this was written, any seasons in the 1940s, we have to use two fundamentally different methodologies for estimating net plays for each outfielder. Though the outfielder calculations for 1893–1920 and 1940–51, what I call the Dead Ball DRA calculations, turned out to be quite a bit more complicated, they may represent one of the best contributions of this book, as they are much better than any alternatives, whereas decent infielder evaluations are not too difficult to obtain, provided putouts and errors are ignored.

Dead Ball DRA presents the solution to the problem of fielding evaluation as it was originally posed, based on the original statistics established by the National League in 1876, without the benefit of new statistics (such as separate putout and innings played totals in left, center, and right) compiled by Retrosheet volunteers going through original score sheets or box scores of games. The complete explanation, which is admittedly pretty tricky (and pretty nifty as well), is available on-line in appendix A. Here is an overview.

To break this problem down into manageable pieces, let us first assume that we can estimate each outfielder's approximate percentage of the team's total innings played at each outfield position: the percentage ("P") of total team innings that year played in left ("$P7$"), center, ("$P8$"), and right ("$P9$"). We will summarize how this is done at the end.

Next, we calculate the number of *total* outfield putouts the *team would* have recorded, given its total batted balls in play, if it were league *average*. That is simply the league total of putouts multiplied by the team's percentage of league batted balls in play. We'll call this variable estimated Outfield Put Outs, or "*eOPO*."

For every outfielder for every team in the league *each* year, we multiply his *P7*, *P8*, and/or *P9* by his team's *eOPO*. Then we do a forced zero intercept regression of the *actual total* putouts of all the *individual outfielders* for *each* season onto their respective *P7*eOPO*, *P8*eOPO*, and *P9*eOPO*.

The regression *coefficients* reveal the likely percentage distribution of putouts at each position during that year. They result in an almost perfect match for 1911, the one year for the Dead Ball Era for which we do have the separate putout totals. They also reveal the trends in the distribution of outfield putouts.[2] There were many more putouts in left field than in right field in the 1890s, and this pattern changed to the more modern equal balance gradually, sporadically, and at different rates in each league.

The *residuals* of the regression are the *individual outfielders'* estimated outfield putouts above or below the league-average rate, taking into account *only* their estimated percentage of playing time at each outfield position and

---

2. After this book was written, but before it went to press, Retrosheet published outfield putouts in left, center, and right field for the missing years in the 1940s. The standard deviation of the Dead Ball DRA estimated-versus-actual league-average putouts per outfield position for those years was only two putouts per season, and the worst error was five putouts in center field for one season. In other words, the typical error attributable to a failure to model shifts in outfield putout distributions league by league and year by year would be about one run per season for a full-time outfielder.

the total number of *BIP* allowed by their team's pitchers: we call this *iPO789. bip*. (If you add up the *iPO789.bip* for all the team's outfielders, it does in fact (I've checked) equal the actual outfield putouts for the team, above or below the league-average rate, given total balls in play, which *can* be explicitly calculated, or *PO789.bip*.)

This is analogous to knowing *A6.bip* for a *team* in a given year, harkening back to our Ozzie example. In the Ozzie example, we regressed *team A6.bip*, for example, onto *LpBIP.bip* and *FO.bip* over many seasons to see the impact of the latter. Here, we regress the *iPO789.bip* for *every individual* outfielder-season onto *their respective* estimated percentages of *LpBIP.bip*, *GOE.bip* (which includes infield errors, which are also evidence of a ground ball), and *IFO.bip* (to factor in ball-hogging) when playing in each respective position, resulting in the following formula for regression-adjusted (or *residual*) *individual* net putouts in the outfield ("*riPO789*") for 1940–51 equals

$$iPO789.bip \quad + (\quad\quad\quad\quad\quad\quad + .14^*P7^*GOE.bip \ + .05^*P7^*IFO.bip$$
$$+ .01^*P8^*LpBIP.bip \ + .26^*P8^*GOE.bip \ + .15^*P8^*IFO.bip$$
$$+ .09^*P9^*GOE.bip \ + .04^*P9^*IFO.bip).$$

The *coefficients* reflect the impact that the known team *LpBIP.bip*, *GOE. bip*, and *IFO.bip* each year have on expected plays in left, center, and right. The coefficients show a nice symmetry across the outfield.

The *residuals* reflect the estimated net outfield putouts made by each outfielder, after taking into account the impact of left-handed pitching (only significant in this sample for center fielders) *LpBIP.bip*, ground ball (or fly ball) pitching, as indicated by positive (or negative) *GOE.bip*, and *IFO.bip* to discount ball hogging of fly outs that could likely be equally caught by infielders. The *sum* of *riPO789* for all the outfielders on a team each year equals *rPO789* for the *team* each year and *that* number is what is included in the second-stage regression analysis to determine the average value, in runs, of each marginal outfield putout.

In conclusion, we use the estimated playing time at each position by each player of the league to help us discover indirectly (i) the average distribution of outs at each position, year-by-year and league-by-league, and (ii) the typical impact of left-handed pitching, ground ball pitching, and infield fly out ball hogging on each outfield position. In the process of making these discoveries, we derive an estimate of the net plays made by each outfielder, *riPO789*, taking into account the total *PO789* we know he recorded, his estimated percentage playing time at all three position, the typical league distribution of outs at each position, and his team's *LpBIP.bip*, *GOE.bip*, and *IFO.bip*, which are also known. The team's *rPO789* is then just the sum of its players' *riPO789*.

This raises the question of how we estimate such playing time at each position. I do not claim to have invented the best way to do this, and I am certain improvements can be made. First, we estimate the player's percentage of the team's 'batting' innings, which is his estimated plate appearances (at-bats plus walks) divided by one-ninth of the team's plate appearances (at-bats plus walks). Next, we estimate the player's percentage of total team innings fielded at *non*-outfield positions, based on his percentage of team plays at those positions.

A player's estimated percentage of his team's innings played *anywhere* in the outfield is just the *lesser* of (i) his total games in the outfield, divided by the team's games (as if he played every inning of every outfield game) and (ii) the excess of his 'batting' innings over his 'non-outfield' fielding innings. That way, if a fourth outfielder doesn't get a lot of at bats, his estimated innings go down. If a player plays another position, his estimated outfield innings won't be overestimated.

Now we have to allocate his total estimate outfield playing time among the three outfield positions. If he was a full-time player (greater than seventy percent of estimated outfield innings) who played almost all of his games at one position (no more than three percent at other positions), we fix that percentage for him. Otherwise he goes in the pool of part-time players. Their total estimated outfield innings are initially allocated pro rata to each player on the basis of his percentage of games played at each position. Usually this causes the sum of team estimated innings to exceed the team total for one or more of the outfield positions. In such a case we shrink the part-time players' portions in proportion, so the team estimated innings at each position sums to the total, yielding our final estimate.

This chapter has certainly been a challenge, but it presents all of the most important ideas introduced by DRA for estimating fielder value since 1893. In the next chapter we'll test our output.

Measuring the Many
Measures of Fielding

It is reassuring that the model described in the previous chapter uses objective, open-source information, classic statistical methods, and predicts team defensive runs about as well as the many reliable and decades-old offensive models predict team offensive runs. I would also venture to say that the formulas for estimating defensive runs at each position make sense. And we will see in Part II that the single-season and career fielding assessments based on DRA in almost all cases ring true, or at least appear plausible in light of other sources of evidence.

But if we want to be more confident about the accuracy of individual fielder defensive runs estimates under DRA, as well as those of other systems we will consult in Part II, we should test them somehow against objective reality. The closest thing we have to objective measures of fielding performance are defensive runs estimates derived from batted ball data. Therefore, the way to test DRA and the other systems we'll consult in Part II is to compare their respective estimates for recent players with estimates derived from batted ball data. That is just what we will do in this chapter. But, before getting to the results, we need to spend some time showing how batted ball data systems work in order to understand the reasons for choosing the particular batted ball data system we will use, which we'll call "Test Runs."

As always, the most important principle to keep in mind is that even state-of-the-art batted ball data systems provide only approximations to the truth. We will also find that some of the best-known implementations still have significant biases.

BATTED BALL DATA BASICS

The simplest form of batted ball data systems implements the standard four-step procedure for estimating defensive runs as follows.

Under step one, the expected number of plays is estimated by counting up all of the batted balls hit into each area of the field when a player was playing that season and multiplying that number by the average percentage of plays made by all major league fielders at that position on batted balls hit into each such area.

Starting with a fairly simple example, let's assume that each batted ball is assigned one of four trajectory codes (ground ball, line drive, fly ball, and pop up) and the entire field is divided into five thin 'slices' spreading out from home plate to the outfield (left, left-center, center, right-center, and right). Then draw curves across the slices to demarcate three depths (shallow, medium, and deep) in the outfield. Let's say that during a major league season, twenty percent of all "line drives hit to right-center, medium deep" were caught by right fielders; that is, eighty percent dropped in as hits. If you are rating a particular right fielder, his expected number of plays made on line drives to right-center, medium deep would be twenty percent of the total number of line drives to right-center, medium deep that were hit when he was on the field. So if fifty line drives to right-center, medium deep were hit while he was playing in right, you would assign to him twenty percent of fifty, or ten, expected plays made.

You would then perform the same calculation for every other combination of trajectory, slice, and depth assigned to right fielders. In this simplified example, the combinations would be based on three trajectories (line drives, fly balls, and pop ups), two slices (right and center-right), and three depths (shallow, medium, and deep), thus yielding three multiplied by two multiplied by three, or eighteen separate categories, or 'buckets', of batted balls. After calculating, as we just did, the number of expected plays in each of the eighteen buckets, one would take the simple sum for the eighteen buckets as the total number of plays our right fielder would have made if he were exactly average.

Step two, as before, would be simply to subtract his expected plays from his actual plays, that is, his putouts while playing right field, to obtain his net plays.

Step three would involve calculating the average type of hit allowed by right fielders, in other words, the weighted average type of hit that dropped in. Ignoring triples because they are so rare, if sixty percent of the total hits in right field are singles (worth about half a run) and forty percent are doubles (worth about three-quarters of a run), the expected value of a hit would be about .60 runs. As mentioned in chapter two, when you have a clean unbiased estimate of net plays, the runs per net play are equal to the average value of the hit prevented (about .60 in this example) as well as the out created (about a quarter of a run), or about .85 runs for right fielders.

Step four, of course, would just involve multiplying .85 runs per play by net plays, to obtain defensive runs for the right fielder. (We'll address assists and base runner defense later in this chapter.)

The procedure would work much the same for infielders. At third base, for example, one would track ground balls only, because line drive, fly ball, and pop up out conversions for infielder almost always reflect dumb luck, in the case of line drives, or the tendency of the fielder to be a ball hog who catches soft flies or pop ups that could be caught by two or three or even four other fielders. In a simple batted ball system, third basemen would be assigned two slices of the field (the slice along the third base line, and the hole between third and short) and possibly three depths (shallow, medium, and deep).

BATTED BALL DATA REFINEMENTS

We can improve on steps one and three by refining both our estimate of expected plays and our estimate of expected runs per net play.

To refine our estimate of expected plays, we can take more precise measurements of the trajectory, slice, and depth parameters applied above, as well as add entirely new factors. Instead of assigning each ball hit into the air in the outfield into one of only three trajectories, we could try four (one system codes a ball that is something between a fly ball and a line drive as a "fliner"). Instead of defining five slices in the outfield we could define, say, nine (left field line, straightaway left, left-left-center, center-left-center, straightaway center, center-right-center, right-right-center, straightaway right, right field line). Instead of tracking three depths in the outfield, one could try five or even seven.

In addition to trajectory, slice, and distance, one could track batted balls separately depending on the handedness of the opponent batter, as studies have shown that out conversion rates in many trajectory-slice-distance buckets vary somewhat, depending on the handedness of the batter. Some systems track the handedness of the pitcher as well. In theory, by obtaining a more complete description of the characteristics of each batted ball, one can obtain a more precise estimate of the likelihood that the average major league fielder at a given position would convert it into an out. Finally, in the case of Coors Field or the Green Monster, there are certain outfield positions for which park factors are needed, and batted ball data can pinpoint how best to make such adjustments to determine net plays.

One could also calculate the expected run value per net play separately for each bucket. Presumably "line drives deep down the right field line" more often result in doubles or even triples, while short "fliners" to center are almost always singles, so the right fielder who catches the "line drive deep down the right field line" should get more credit for runs saved than the center fielder who catches the short fliner in shallow straightway center. So one would perform the entire four-step procedure separately for each bucket, to estimate defensive runs just for that bucket, and then add up all the buckets to get total defensive runs.

By relying exclusively on large samples of major league performance, of which only a tiny part is contributed by the player being evaluated, batted ball systems minimize the bias resulting when a player's own plays are largely used to estimate his expected plays. They also avoid biases that result, under DRA for example, when expected ground outs at short are estimated partly by actual fly outs throughout the field, which will be impacted to some degree by the fielding skill of the shortstop's outfield teammates. In general, the quality of the shortstop's teammates has virtually no impact under a properly designed batted ball data system. Furthermore, batted ball data tracks at least three, and sometimes many more, variables that help predict how easy or difficult it is to convert a particular batted ball into an out. Therefore, there is a much smaller chance that we've omitted important factors affecting how difficult it was to field each ball in play when a fielder was on the field, so we can improve precision in estimating the likelihood of the ball being caught or not.

The core concept behind batted ball data systems is actually very simple and perfectly sound. But implementations of this simple and sound concept have at times been faulty. It is necessary to point these faults out because the high tech aura of these systems over-awes fans into thinking 'the experts' have found 'the answer', and that is that. More importantly, by understanding how batted ball systems go wrong, it's possible sometimes to back out implementation mistakes so we can make better use of defensive runs estimates with suboptimal implementations.

Fortunately, since 2003, when the first set of defensive runs estimates based on proprietary batted ball data were published, results under several systems based on data collected by different organizations have been published on the web or in book form. In most cases, even though the underlying data has had to be kept proprietary, the developers of these systems have helpfully provided enough details regarding their calculation methodologies to reveal the major implementation issues.

BATTED BALL DATA INCONSISTENCIES

The most important issue is that there seems to be a surprising degree of inconsistency in the raw data of the two major data providers, STATS LLC

("STATS") and Baseball Info Solutions ("BIS"). In particular, the coding of batted balls hit in the air to the outfield is problematical. For example, employee A working for data provider X might label a particular ball hit into the outfield as a "fly ball, deep right-right-center," while employee B working for data provider Y might label the same batted ball a "line drive, medium right-center." (The people who label batted balls for batted ball data providers are often called "stringers.") Since the actual labels given to each batted ball by each data provider are not a matter of public record, how might we infer that this problem exists?

By seeing how well published defensive runs estimates based on different proprietary data sets match or fail to match with each other. In August 2007, I wrote an article for the hardballtimes.com website (hereinafter "the 2007 article") in which I presented what I believe was the first comparison of defensive runs estimates reported by analysts who used different underlying batted ball data sets. I compared results obtained by the pioneer in the field of converting batted ball data into defensive runs estimates, Mitchel G. Lichtman (who blogs under his initials MGL), with results under a system developed by Shane Jensen. MGL used STATS data; Jensen BIS data. I compared the defensive runs per 1450 innings played of the complete set of outfielders who played at least two full-time seasons for one team (130 or more games) during seasons for which both data sets were available (2003–05).

The MGL and Jensen systems had a correlation of only .65 in the outfield, a frankly shocking result, given the amount of information available and the skill of the respective analysts—MGL was a quantitative consultant for the St. Louis Cardinals and Jensen a Wharton statistics professor with a PhD from Harvard. Each of their systems, I had hoped, was providing a fairly sharp picture of the objective truth that would have a .90 or at least .80 correlation with the other. While a .70 correlation could reasonably be considered a "strong" correlation, so a .65 correlation might appear fairly good, I had reported in an article now available at hardballtimes.com that the 2003 version of DRA, which is similar to the pre-1952 model, had a correlation comfortably above .70 in the outfield with the 2003 version of MGL's system. In fact, the correlation reported in the 2007 article between the pre-1952 version of DRA and Jensen's BIS results, .68, was higher than the correlation between MGL's STATS results and Jensen's BIS results. Oddly, though, the correlation between DRA and MGL's 2007 STATS results was much lower than it had been in 2003: only .42.

Now, in addition to using different data sets, MGL and Jensen used very different calculation methodologies. MGL's system was based on buckets similar to those described above, as well as certain other adjustments; Jensen used highly sophisticated PhD-level statistical methods, subsequently published in the *Annals of Applied Statistics*, which bypass the bucketing methodology. To see if calculation methods were the cause of the inconsistencies, MGL and another well-known fielding analyst, David Pinto, redid the outfielder calculations for my article by applying the basic methodology described at the very beginning of the chapter to both the STATS and BIS data, respectively. Even though this simplified version of STATS outfielder defensive runs estimates had a slightly higher correlation with DRA (.50), the correlation between the simplified version of STATS and BIS outfielder defensive runs estimates was even lower than before: .60.

Since the 2007 article, other analysts have came forward with articles confirming that there are some alarming discrepancies in outfielder defensive runs estimates based on STATS and BIS data.[1] For example, when MGL recently applied his complete methodology to BIS data, his BIS estimate of Andruw Jones' total defensive runs from 2003 through 2008 was +112 runs; using STATS data, –5 runs. That's nearly twenty runs per season—the difference per season between an average and a top flight Gold Glove fielder—over a six-year period—resulting in a cumulative difference equal to the difference between the fielding *career* of an average and an all-time great fielder. The ratings for Carlos Beltran went the other way over the same period: +86 runs using STATS and +9 using BIS.[2] The discrepancies presumably stemmed from the difficulty stringers had in estimating directions and distances on a consistent and unbiased basis in the outfield. The further back the play is made, the harder it is to judge direction and distance. MGL himself recently reported that he had found that the standard deviation in the difference between batted ball locations by BIS and another data provider was ten feet.[3]

I actually think that ten-foot differences in location, especially in the outfield, are not a problem. But there are certainly significant problems in the coding of *trajectory*, that is, in correctly and consistently distinguishing between "fly balls" and "line drives." Harry Pavlidis has recently written an article for hardballtimes.com about the coding of Gameday batted ball data starting in 2009, which, to be clear, is not STATS or BIS data. Gameday hires free-lance stringers to sit in the press box at each ballpark and determine, among other things, whether a batted ball hit in the air was a "fly ball" or "line drive." Pavlidis reported ratios of fly balls to line drives ranging from 1.14 to 2.37, depending on the park. Those were the extremes; the range of outcomes within one standard deviation was about one-third of that spread. It is highly unlikely that even the standard difference can be due to park

1. *See* www.insidethebook.com/ee/index.php/site/comments/uzr_on_fangraphs_using_bis_on_ichiro/#comments.
2. www.insidethebook.com/ee/index.php/site/suzr_v_buzr/.
3. www.insidethebook.com/ee/index.php/site/comments/fielding_bible_excerpt/#19.

effects or even the impact of pitchers on how squarely opponent batters meet the ball: the likely cause is stringer bias.

Due to the sharp difference in out-conversion rates for the average line drive as compared with the average fly ball, such discrepancies in labeling line drives and fly balls can seriously distort outfielder ratings—if a stringer labels too many fly balls as (difficult to field) line drives, expected plays will be understated and the outfielders will be overrated; if a stinger labels too many line drives as (easier to field) fly balls, expected plays will be overstated and the fielder will be underrated.

Brian Cartwright also did a similar study of the coding for "line drives" under the free, open-source, on-line database maintained by Retrosheet. (The Retrosheet database does not, however, include slice-depth location codes, except for the 1989–99 seasons, just trajectory.) By comparing the rates of line drives per batted ball in play by a team and its opponents both at the team's park and at the other parks, he discovered that the line drive rates were eighteen percent above the norm at Arlington (where the Rangers play) and twenty percent below the norm at the Metrodome (where the Twins played). Since Cartwright's test largely controlled for the impact of batters, pitchers, and parks, the reasonable conclusion is that stringers at Arlington tend to code more balls hit in the air as line drives rather than fly balls, and the stringers at the Metrodome did the opposite. A recent study by another analyst showed that the classification of a batted ball as a fly ball or line drive correlates with the height of the press box, which is where stringers usually sit.

When you think about it, it is a little strange that over the years various batted ball data systems have been chopping up the field into a finer and finer grid while allowing the trajectory codes to remain so coarse. The difference in 'fieldability' between even an *accurately* coded "line drive" and "fly ball," or even between an accurately coded "fliner" and a "fly ball," is much more important than a ten or twenty or thirty foot difference in location. Tom Tango has been proposing for years that instead of *assigning* one out of three or four trajectory *codes* to each batted ball hit in the air, it would be far more useful to *record* the actual amount of *time* the ball is in the air, or "hang time." Batted balls could then be bucketed by increments of hang time that would be as precise, as a practical matter, as the increments used for marking off direction and depth. It appears that some such approach may be implemented soon.

In the meantime, I believe the only possible way forward in the outfield is to calculate defensive runs using at least two sets of batted ball data and a correct and consistent methodology, and take the simple average. When MGL and Pinto completed the simplified and standardized calculations for the STATS and BIS data sets, it appeared that the average of the two sets of results generated ratings for the outfielders that matched very well with detailed subjective evaluations in *The Fielding Bible*. These subjective evaluations were based on repeated viewings of video tapes, to assess how well outfielders ran down fly balls, fliners, and line drives in the outfield. Commentary provided about each fielder in *The Fielding Bible* focused many specific fielding attributes, such as jumps, foot speed, the directness of the paths the outfielder generally took, ability to run in and run back on balls, and so forth. The 2007 article quoted from several of these evaluations, and noted only one case in which the subjective evaluation conflicted with the MGL-STATS/Pinto-BIS output. Therefore, the batted ball data system we will use in this chapter to test DRA and other systems will be, in the outfield, based on the systems put together by MGL and Pinto using STATS and BIS data, respectively.

BATTED BALL DATA COMPLEXIFICATION

What follows in the next dozen or so pages may at first seem tedious and without any obvious payoff, but we'll find that the seemingly subtle but actually very simple concepts we work through will help us better understand published ratings of several famous players going back a generation. Furthermore, they will influence how we build the rest of Test Runs and our interpretation of the result of our tests in the chapter.

This will also be our first example of how systems based on richer data sometimes over-complicate things and, when you actually work through the arithmetic, reintroduce biases present under more primitive systems that overvalue errors relative to plays made and cause teammate performance to bias individual fielder estimates. When all is said and done, the first refinements of batted ball data calculations discussed at the very beginning of this chapter, along with proper reporting of batted ball hang time, are all that are needed, provided that the data doesn't get chopped up into buckets that have sample sizes too small to provide good estimates of how the average fielder would handle them, and that location and trajectory is correctly coded. It really should be as simple as that. But unfortunately it hasn't been.

Caring Too Much About Sharing

Recall our hypothetical example of a simple batted ball system, which assigned two slices of the infield to the third baseman—the slice along and inside the third base line, and the hole between third and short. That's actually the grid used for the free batted ball data available from 1989 through

1999 at Retrosheet, which has a diagram on-line showing the slice and depth demarcations in the infield and the outfield: www.retrosheet.org/location.htm.

Ignoring a handful of little areas between the catcher and the pitcher where bunts and nibblers are fielded, the infield grid drawn by Retrosheet has essentially eight slices and three depths. Moving from left to right, the slices emanated from home plate are labeled "5" (along the third base line and the primary third baseman slice), "56" (for the hole between third and short), "6" (the primary shortstop slice), "6M" (for the up-the-middle short-stop side of second base), "4M" (for the second base side of second base), "4" (the primary slice for second basemen), "34" (the hole between second and first), and "3" (along the first base line and the primary first baseman slice). The depths are shallow (denoted by an "S"), medium (no label), and deep (denoted by a "D").

So the slice-distance area of the field for the hole between third and short, deep, is denoted "56D"; the slice-distance area for the same slice, medium depth, is denoted simply as "56"; the slice/distance area for the same slice, shallow, is denoted "56S."

Here's the question. Let's say that based on a sufficiently large sample, perhaps a full major league season, perhaps a multi-year sample, 30 percent of all ground balls ("G") in the 56 area, or "G56," are converted into outs by major league third basemen, 20 percent are converted into outs by short-stops, and 50 percent go through as hits. Imagine that in the 2000 season there were exactly 100 G56 while Scott Brosius and Derek Jeter were on the field, and Brosius converted 40 into outs, Jeter converted 10 into outs, and 50 went through as hits. How should we calculate net plays for Brosius and Jeter on those G56? In other words, **how should we calculate net plays for field-ers who *share* a designated area of the field?**

The simple way is to treat each fielder completely independently, as if the shared location were just like an unshared location. Since the average third baseman would convert 30 percent of G56 into outs, and 100 G56 were hit when Scott Brosius was playing third, this would be to say that expected plays for Brosius are equal to 30 percent of 100, or 30. Brosius actually made 40 plays, so he has +10 net plays. Since the average shortstop would convert 20 percent of G56 into outs, expected plays for Jeter would be equal to 20 percent of 100, or 20. Jeter made only 10 plays, so his net plays would be –10. The team rating would be the simple sum of the Brosius and Jeter rating, or zero net plays, which accurately reflects the fact that Brosius and Jeter com-bined, that is, the team, gave up exactly the expected number of hits, 50.

I believe, and will present arguments in support of such belief, that that is the correct approach, in addition to being by far the simplest. From now on we'll refer to this literally as the "simple method." But others have taken different approaches. The most common alternative approach is inspired by the seemingly benign principle that if there is no harm to the team, there should be no foul charged to any fielder, or the 'no harm, no foul' principle. Since, as we shall see, this method 'mixes together' the performance of the two fielders, we'll call it the "mixed method."

Under the mixed method, if either the third baseman or the shortstop makes the play on a *G56*, the player who did not make the play is neither charged nor credited, in other words, gets booked zero: no harm, no foul. The player making the play gets credit for one minus the probability that neither the average shortstop nor the average third baseman would make the play, in other words, the probability the average team would allow a hit, or .50, which would mean +.50 hits saved. The sum of the two individual ratings (0.00 and +0.50) also equals the team performance for that position, +.50, as the team has made 1.00 plays when only .50 plays were expected.

If neither the third baseman nor the shortstop makes the play, each player gets charged the probability that the average fielder at his position would make the play. So the third baseman is charged –.30 hits allowed, and the shortstop is charged –.20 hits allowed. Once again, the sum of the two individual ratings (–.30 plus –.20) also equals the team performance for that position, –.50, as the team has made 0.00 plays when .50 plays were expected.

Brosius would be credited with +.50 hits prevented for each of his 40 plays, so he's up +20 before we get to the hits that are allowed by the team. Since the team allowed 50 hits, and as the third baseman he is charged –.30 hits allowed per hit the team allows, he is charged –15 under the second step. His net plays are thus 20 minus 15, or +5 net plays, down 5 from the +10 net plays he is credited under the simple method.

What about Jeter? He gets +.50 hits-prevented credit for each of his 10 plays, so he's up +5 after the first calculation; he is charged only –.20 hits allowed for each of the 50 hits the team allowed under the second calculation, or –10, so he's –5 overall, 5 net plays better than under the simple allocation method.

The mixed method shifts credit for five of Brosius's net plays to Jeter— it partially mixes together the high quality fielding of Brosius with the low quality fielding of Jeter.

To disclose a little more precisely what's going on, let's translate this mixed method for calculating net plays into the first two steps of the four-step procedure that all defensive runs systems use, explicitly or implicitly. First we'll show the formula, then explain the net effect of it in English.

In a formula, net plays at shortstop under the mixed method, or *net A6*, given the total number of *G56*, is defined as (i) plays made by the shortstop, multiplied by the probability of *no* play by *either* player, that is, a hit allowed or the event of {a *G56* with *neither* a play at short *nor* a play at third}, with some 'abuse of notation' written as $\Pr(\{G56 - A6 - A5\})$, minus (ii) the number of hits actually allowed by the team, multiplied by the probability of an $A6$. Then *net A6* are equal to:

$$A6^*\Pr(\{G56 - A6 - A5\}) - (G56 - A6 - A5)^*\Pr(A6).$$

With a little algebra,[4] this can be converted into net plays, that is actual plays minus expected plays:

$$= A6 - [G56^*\Pr(A6) - A5^*\Pr(A6) + A6^*\Pr(A5)].$$

The items in brackets in the last line together constitute the mixed method's implicit 'expected $A6$' the first step in the four-step procedure.

In English, we're saying that the expected plays calculation implicit in the mixed method at shortstop on $G56$ equals our usual calculation, which is simply the total number of $G56$ multiplied by the average rate at which shortstops in major league baseball convert $G56$ into outs (that's the first item inside the brackets), as well as two more factors.

The first mixed method adjustment for expected plays subtracts the actual number of plays on $G56$ made by the shortstop's teammate at third, multiplied by the probability that the average shortstop would make a play on $G56$. The second mixed method adjustment for expected plays adds the actual number of plays made on $G56$ by the shortstop being rated, multiplied by the probability that the average third baseman would make a play on a $G56$.

You have every right to feel confused, even when the thing is expressed in English sentences. Here are the practical effects.

First, under the mixed method a player's *own* plays are being used to estimate the number of plays we would *expect* him to make if he were average. That is, the number of expected plays we estimate Jeter would make if he were average is increased by the number of plays *Jeter actually makes*, multiplied by the probability that an average third baseman (yes, that's right) would make a play in that bucket. Once again, the better a player is, the more expected plays are charged to him to calculate his net plays; the worse the player is, the fewer expected plays are charged to calculate his net plays.

This is directly analogous to the distortions created by the fielding average version of defensive runs illustrated in chapter two, which unfairly and irrationally penalize rangy fielders and overrate less mobile fielders. It also means that each *extra A6* a shortstop *does* reach in $G56$ is discounted by the

---

4. Just add the number zero in the form of "$+A6^*[\Pr(A6) + \Pr(A5)] - A6^*[\Pr(A6) + \Pr(A5)]$" and collect and cancel terms, taking into account that the sum of $\Pr(A6) + \Pr(A5) + \Pr(\{G56 - A6 - A5\})$ equals one.

probability that a third baseman will make a play in that bucket. Thus, even though extra plays under the mixed method are purportedly credited .75 runs, if the probability of a play by the third baseman is, say, one-third, the actual runs credited per marginal shortstop play made in *G56* is only two-thirds of .75, or .50 runs. The rangier play made by the shortstop in the hole is discounted. And it is precisely these plays that distinguish the good from the merely adequate shortstops.

Second, now the player's *teammate* can influence his expected plays. Each extra play made by Brosius, multiplied by the probability that the average shortstop (yes, that's right) would make a play in that bucket, is *subtracted* from the number of plays expected at short, thereby lowering the threshold for Jeter to be credited with positive net plays. So if the shortstop's teammate at third is good, the shortstop's rating goes up; if the teammate is bad, the shortstop's rating goes down. This is an example of "teammate bias," which plays a surprisingly large role in fielding systems. (Of course, as we've already pointed out, DRA infielder ratings can be biased by the quality of a team's outfield; and vice versa.)

In other words, the mixed method for shared buckets results in an estimate of expected plays that is biased by the fielder's own performance and by the performance of just one other fielder, who might be exceptionally good or bad. The result is that a rangy fielder is underrated and a player playing next to a poor fielder is underrated; a less mobile shortstop playing next to a good third baseman is overrated. Exactly the same math works for other shared locations, including in the outfield.

There are a couple of reasons for using the mixed method, neither of which I believe is valid: (i) to discount ball-hogging, and (ii) to generate defensive runs estimates with a lower standard deviation, so that fewer of them seem too extreme.

First let's address ball hogging. If balls included in a bucket have a high *total* out probability and *either* fielder can *equally* make the play—in other words, each player can easily get to the other player's 'side' of the location to 'steal' the play from his teammate—you actually *need* the mixed method to keep ball hogs from getting unfair credit for what amount to automatic outs. Before giving an example of this, however, it has to be said that *there are essentially no such ground ball buckets.* In fact, MGL recently commented that in his own studies, based on more granular data, "there is not much overlap in terms of balls that more than one player can actually get to in the infield."[5] And even if the third baseman, say, is so rangy to his left that there are a small number of plays in the hole the shortstop is prevented from

5. www.insidethebook.com/ee/index.php/site/comments/fielding_bible_excerpt/#26.

making, the shortstop should take advantage of this for the sake of his team and shift to his left to get more plays up the middle. Under a batted ball data system, including under the simple method, those plays up the middle will compensate the shortstop for the rare chances 'taken' by the third baseman in the hole.

It's different for high fly balls that can be caught by two infielders and an outfielder, which present the best hypothetical in support of the mixed method. Let's assume there is a bucket for fly balls or pop flies in short center field, where, on average, thirty are caught by the center fielder, thirty are caught by the shortstop, thirty are caught by the second baseman, and only ten drop in for a hit. Now assume that Andruw Jones, who famously played a shallow center field, was a total ball hog on all ten of those short easy pop flies while he was playing, and his middle infielders let him handle every chance he could humanly get to, and yet one dropped in for a hit.

Under the mixed method, Jones would be credited with 9 times .1 hits prevented, or .9 hits prevented, and charged .3 times 1 hit allowed, or −.3 hits allowed, or overall with only +0.6 hits prevented. Under the simple method, Jones would receive credit for 9 plays made minus .3 times 10, or 3 expected plays made, or +6 hits prevented, and the infielders would each be charged −3 hits allowed, which would be a clear distortion of value for all three play-ers, and, if a few similar buckets had the same conditions, would lead to serious distortions in overall fielder ratings.

I am certain that center fielders such as Andruw Jones who play very shallow can be ball hogs on soft fly balls and pop ups vis-à-vis infielders. Chris Dial, who has years of experience working with batted ball data, has confirmed that this is in fact true of Jones. DRA has an adjustment for out-fielder ball-hogging of fly ball chances that could be taken by infielders, and neither credits nor penalizes infielders for pop ups or fly balls. But as long as infield fly outs and shallow outfield pop outs or fly outs are excluded (because they are all outs that belong to the pitcher) it is unnecessary to apply the mixed method to prevent the distortion from the simple method illustrated in our Andruw Jones example. That is the approach Pinto and MGL took when they recalculated outfielder defensive runs using BIS and STATS data for the 2007 article—fly balls and pop ups hit less than 200 feet were simply excluded, because they were virtually automatic outs anyway.

What I am not so certain of is the extent to which outfielders hog balls amongst each other; in other words, whether Andruw Jones consistently takes easy, medium depth, high fly ball chances in the gaps away from his left fielders and right fielders at a higher rate than other centerfielders. From all accounts there is a certain unwritten code among outfielders under which center fielders take all chances they possibly can. If every center fielder is a ball hog vis-à-vis his teammates in left and right, then none can be, relatively speaking, and all the batted ball systems are designed to measure relative performance.

No one has reported separately the impact of ball hogging adjustments for plays between outfielders, or otherwise provided evidence of the practical need for ball-hogging adjustments. Chris Dial has said that Jones's ball hogging is "mainly" of chances from infielders, not of chances by corner outfielders, though "there is some of that."[6] David Pinto has published his own research showing that there does not appear to be any shared slice in the outfield in which it is both highly likely the ball will be caught and the out-conversion rates for neighboring outfielders are at all similar. In other words, there are no slices in which there is a forty-five percent chance the left fielder gets it, a ten percent chance of a hit, and a forty-five percent chance the center fielder gets it. Instead, there might be slices in which there is an eighty percent chance the left fielder gets it, a ten percent chance of a hit, and a ten percent chance the center fielder gets it. So to believe there is a ball-hogging problem requiring the mixed method, you have to believe that there are center fielders out there running over to location where eighty percent of easy fly outs are normally caught by left fielders. It doesn't make sense.

Though we perhaps lack definite evidence that the mixed method is never appropriate for outfielders, it would seem highly unlikely that it is generally appropriate for outfielders, so that the simple method is at least 'less wrong' than the mixed method.

In the infield, we actually have evidence that the mixed approach can seriously distort infielder ratings, because the shared buckets are all places where hits are most likely and the chances of ball hogging are virtually zero. I was involved in an on-line discussion involving a batted ball data system that had first been calculated under the mixed method. The system rated Jeter as essentially average, when all other non-batted ball systems, and even Zone Rating (a primitive version of a batted ball system), rated him well below average. In addition, year-to-year correlations for individual player ratings were quite low, suggesting there was a lot of noise in the system. When the simple method was applied, Jeter re-assumed his rightful place as the worst shortstop and individual ratings suddenly had year-to-year correlations of about .50, suggesting that fielding is a real, repeatable skill. The noise created by the mixed method had been cleared away.

The second reason for the mixed method—reducing the standard deviation in defensive runs estimates—is, I believe, the prime motivation. Analysts who publish defensive runs estimates based on batted ball data are justifiably annoyed by fans who, unaware of the inherent randomness of

---

6. www.insidethebook.com/ee/index.php/site/comments/the_best_defenders_according_to_uzr_of_the_decade/.

baseball outcomes, criticize the estimates because they can vary considerably from year to year. It is not at all uncommon, for example, for a fielder to have +10 defensive runs one year and –10 the next. Some analysts may be seeking, consciously or unconsciously, to dampen the 'noise' in their defensive runs estimates (so that, say, the same player is only +5 runs the first year and –5 runs the second) in order to dampen the 'noise' from the peanut gallery. It is true that one should discount defensive estimates toward the mean when estimating the true talent of a fielder, as opposed to valuing a sample of his performance. And the mixed method does succeed in pulling defensive runs estimates towards the mean, as demonstrated in the Jeter and Brosius example.

The problem with the mixed method is that it is a *biased* method of regressing ratings toward the mean, biased by the fielding quality of both the player and his neighbor. It would be better to report the results under the simple method and then report results regressed (in other words, discounted for random effects) in an unbiased way.

Errors, Yet Again

Another complication introduced by some analysts using batted ball data is a separate calculation designed to identify the defensive runs attributable to a fielder's ranginess and error-avoidance separately ("range runs" and "error runs"). Unfortunately, the calculation results in treating errors much worse than plays not made, which has been shown by a variety of methods, including batted ball data, to be incorrect. So, in a very real sense, the distortions of the most primitive 19th century defensive statistic, fielding average, are finding their way into some of the most computationally intensive defensive runs estimates being made in the 21st century.

The example takes off from our *G56* example, where the player making a play is credited .375 runs (.75 multiplied by .50 hits prevented) and the other fielder in the shared location is not charged anything. The change in the team's expected runs allowed is correct.

If a single goes through, the third baseman is charged –.30 hits allowed, or .75 multiplied by –.30 runs, or –.225 runs. Likewise, the shortstop is charged –.20 hits allowed, or .75 multiplied by –.2, or –.15 runs. The combined effect is -.375 runs. The change in the team's expected runs allowed is correct.

If, however, the shortstop *gets* to the ball, but commits an error, the range runs calculation initially gives him *credit* for the play made, or .375 runs as above. Then, in the error runs calculation the shortstop is charged the *entire* amount of each error, given all the balls he's reached anywhere in the field. Thus –1.00 plays, worth –.75 runs, are charged for each error. The combined effect of range runs and error runs, when an error is committed on a *G56*, is the sum of –.75 runs and +.375 runs, or –.375 runs.

But we just showed above that if the shortstop never reaches a *G56* and it goes through for a hit, he's only charged –.15 runs. Errors are charged –.23 runs more than hits allowed. But errors are essentially no better or worse than a play not made.

So a shortstop who makes 10 more errors but also 10 more successful plays on *G56* is rated 2.3 runs worse than the average shortstop, when he in fact has the same value as the average shortstop. And a shortstop who makes 10 fewer errors but 10 fewer successful plays on G56 is rated 2.3 runs better than average, when he is in fact just average. The net effect is that the rangy error-prone guy is about five runs worse off than the less mobile but sure-handed guy, when they are exactly of the same value.

Now five runs is just noise in the context of one season. But if this distortion is carried through over the course of long careers of certain historically important shortstops, the impact can approach fifty runs or more. As we shall see in Part II.

TEST RUNS

My conclusion, after studying batted ball data systems over the past several years, is that greater efforts must be made to record the underlying data accurately and consistently. Then all that is needed are the very simple calculations described at the very beginning of this chapter, based on buckets of appropriate sample size. If we work hard to get the data right, the data will work hard to give us the right answer.

In the meantime, I needed a form of Test Runs that was as close as possible to being open source, based on reliable data, and free from the distortions of the mixed method and error runs calculations shown. Fortunately, precisely this approach was taken in the 2007 article, which published the outfielder defensive runs calculated separately using STATS and BIS data, and taking the simple average. Those ratings were prepared by two top analysts, published on the web, and never refuted or even questioned by other analysts or data providers.

Unfortunately, there are no such publicly reported defensive runs estimates for infielders—all batted ball systems with published results use the mixed method (one now even uses a variation of the mixed method that does not even result in a correct team defensive runs total), and the most readily available one includes the separate error runs estimate that significantly favors slow but sure-handed infielders over equally valuable rangier but more error-prone infielders.

Here's the compromise. For the same seasons for which we have the public record of properly calculated outfielder defensive runs, we also have very good net plays estimates for infielders, courtesy of John Dewan's "Plus/Minus" system based on BIS data and published in his first fielding book, *The Fielding Bible* (2006). Although Plus/Minus used the mixed method, it also used much finer slices of the infield, so that there were dramatically fewer ground balls in shared slices, thus substantially mitigating the problem.

Imagine the Retrosheet "56" slice being split into three slices, one on the third base side, one in the middle, and one on the shortstop side. All or nearly all of the grounders on the two 'side' sub-slices of 56 would be unshared; only the middle sub-slice of 56 would be subject to the mixed method. Extra plays made by Brosius in his sub-slice of 56 would never be partly credited to Jeter. Although I'm not sure of the precise number of slices used by Plus/Minus, *The Fielding Bible* mentioned that it divided the field into "126 Vectors." In addition, Jensen's article about his system based on BIS data indicated that locations were kept in four-foot increments. It would not surprise me if what is identified as the 56 slice on the Retrosheet grid was divided into at least three and probably more like five slices by BIS when calculating infielder Plus/Minus.

In addition, as reported in the 2007 article, the correlations between infield ratings based on STATS and BIS data were reasonably strong: for middle infielders, the correlation was .81, with a very close standard deviation match. At third base, the correlation was .65, which is actually fairly good, because corner infield positions seem to be more difficult to evaluate. So there did not appear to be a major coding problem in the infield.

Since (i) the Plus/Minus results were presented in a publicly available book that is still in print, (ii) Jensen reported in the *Annals of Applied Statistics* that he and his colleagues considered the BIS data of probably slightly higher quality, and (iii) Plus/Minus did not appear to have nearly as many ground balls in shared locations, or a separate errors calculation, Test Runs is based on Plus/Minus in the infield.

Plus/Minus reported only net plays, not defensive runs. (*The Fielding Bible II* (2009) reports defensive runs, but not for the same sample of players used in the 2007 article.) Based on the net plays reported per player in *The Fielding Bible*, as well as bunt and double play numbers, I converted Plus/Minus net plays into defensive runs by assigning (i) .75 runs per net play (as discussed in the prior chapter, the value of the out created (about .27 runs) and the value of a single saved (about .48 runs), (i) .30 runs for each net extra base saved or allowed, as estimated and reported in *The Fielding Bible*, on doubles hit down the line at first and third (because a double is worth approximately .30 runs more than a single), (iii) .45 runs for each double play pivot above the league-average rate, given pivot opportunities reported in *The Fielding Bible*, and (iv) bunt defense runs based on a sometime intricate but practically insignificant calculation that applies Pete Palmer's offensive linear weights to each of the components of bunt defense reported in the *The Fielding Bible*.

DEFINING SAMPLES BY SAMPLE SIZE

The next issue to consider was the test itself. Even creators and proponents of the most sophisticated batted ball data systems prefer to rate fielders on the basis of at least two full seasons of data. As Tom Tango, co-author with MGL (and astrophysicist Andy Dolphin) of *The Book: Playing the Percentages in Baseball* recently wrote, "Don't talk to me [about batted ball data defensive runs estimates] unless you are talking about at least two years of data."[7] Therefore, I decided to define my sample of players as all players who played at least two full-time seasons (130 or more games at one position for one team) over the 2003–05 time period for which Test Runs are available. That yielded a little over sixty players. The average number of seasons in the sample was a little less than two and a half.

TESTING THE BEST-KNOWN SYSTEMS

The three fielding systems that report results throughout major league history, and that are probably the most widely known, are Pete Palmer's Fielding Runs, available in each year's *ESPN Baseball Encyclopedia* ("Palmer"), Clay Davenport's Fielding Translations (sometimes also shown as Fielding Runs Above Average), available at baseballprospectus.com ("Davenport" or "D'port"), and Bill James's Fielding Win Shares, reported for seasons before 2002 in James's book Win Shares, and for later seasons at hardballtimes.com ("James").

The Palmer system features formulas that have some similarities to the DRA formulas shown in the prior chapter, but the formulas are almost entirely based on intuition, not statistical techniques such as regression analysis. The Davenport and James systems are each roughly based on an idea first published by Charles Saeger in the early 1990s: starting with actual total team runs allowed, do a forced allocation of credit or blame first between the team's pitchers and fielders, and then among the team's fielders on the basis of their respective individual statistics. Some of these allocations

7. www.insidethebook.com/ee/index.php/site/comments/best_fielding_1b_over_the_last_3_years/.

are based on objective factors; others are frankly subjective. Davenport ratings shown below were taken from the baseballprospectus.com website as of August 2007 (the numbers keep changing; we're using the August 2007 numbers for reasons to be explained at the end of this chapter).

The one thing the Palmer, Davenport, James, and DRA systems all have in common is that they are based entirely on seasonal totals of putouts, assists, double plays, total balls in play, etc., by league, team, and individual, not searchable play-by-play data we'll be discussing a little further below.

In the first chart, I compare the ratings for all players with at least two seasons of 130 or more games played at one position for one team (a "full-time season"). For each player, I take the simple average of each rating for each full-time season, which could be two or three, depending on the player. We'll address the omission of first base ratings later in this chapter.

The table below shows average defensive runs per full-time season 2003–05, for all fielders with two or more full-time seasons, excluding first base, as measured under the most well-known fielding systems.

Average Defensive Runs per Full-Time Season 2003–05

Fielder	Pos	Test Runs	DRA	D'port	Palmer	James
Belliard, R	2B	9	11	4	-2	-1
Boone, B	2B	-11	-2	1	-25	-3
Castillo, L	2B	11	9	4	3	3
Giles, M	2B	15	8	14	13	2
Hudson, O	2B	20	20	18	35	10
Kennedy, A	2B	5	3	4	-7	-1
Kent, J	2B	4	1	1	8	1
Loretta, M	2B	3	6	13	-1	0
Roberts, B	2B	8	4	5	-2	-4
Soriano, A	2B	-11	-9	-9	0	-5
Berroa, A	SS	-13	-6	-5	-1	-7
Cabrera, O	SS	3	-6	1	-5	0
Clayton, R	SS	-6	-4	-3	-7	-4
Eckstein, D	SS	-1	-8	-2	4	-3
Furcal, R	SS	10	10	8	17	0
Gonzalez, A	SS	4	-4	-3	2	5
Guzman, C	SS	-4	-3	-1	-15	3
Itzuris, C	SS	8	12	-1	3	4
Jeter, D	SS	-18	-10	3	2	-1
Lugo, J	SS	2	7	11	2	-2
Renteria, E	SS	-1	-10	-10	-14	-9
Rollins, J	SS	13	-4	-6	-14	-4
Tejada, M	SS	3	9	2	16	-2
Vizquel, O	SS	1	-2	7	-8	-4
Wilson, J	SS	14	9	14	19	2
Young, M	SS	-30	-22	-14	-18	-7

(continued)

Average Defensive Runs per Full-Time Season 2003–05 *(continued)*

Fielder	Pos	Test Runs	DRA	D'port	Palmer	James
Batista, T	3B	-4	7	9	2	0
Bell, D	3B	18	23	7	7	1
Beltre, A	3B	17	5	6	4	1
Blalock, H	3B	7	-7	0	-2	-1
Castilla, V	3B	1	-2	6	-1	-2
Chavez, E	3B	8	10	10	16	4
Crede, J	3B	2	5	-7	-3	0
Lowell, M	3B	-3	-9	13	-2	2
Mora, M	3B	-5	-4	-9	6	-4
Mueller, B	3B	4	3	6	-2	2
Rod-A	3B	6	-3	0	-4	-1
Rolen, S	3B	13	9	14	10	2
Beltran, C	CF	9	2	5	4	5
Cameron, M	CF	21	25	9	9	5
Damon, J	CF	-3	2	5	-1	1
Edmonds, J	CF	3	13	15	-4	3
Grissom, M	CF	-10	5	-10	-5	-3
Jones, A	CF	8	9	4	1	3
Kotsay, M	CF	-8	4	8	-5	2
Pierre, J	CF	-1	-11	-7	-5	-10
Wells, V	CF	0	-8	1	-7	-2
Alou, M	LF	-2	-3	-5	-6	0
Burrell, P	LF	2	-6	-1	-4	0
Crawford, C	LF	23	20	7	10	1
Dunn, A	LF	-9	-14	-12	-4	-3
Gonzalez, L	LF	10	-5	7	-5	3
Lee, C	LF	2	5	2	3	2
Ramirez, M	LF	-29	-32	-10	-5	1
Abreu, B	RF	-1	-1	-1	-3	2
Cruz, Jr., J	RF	5	5	2	7	5
Dye, J	RF	4	-2	-2	-8	3
Encarnacion, J	RF	9	-2	-5	-2	-1
Giles, B	RF	4	5	-7	3	1
Green, S	RF	-2	1	5	-6	4
Sheffield, G	RF	-12	1	-2	-3	0
Suzuki, I	RF	13	9	9	10	4
		Test Runs	**DRA**	**D'port**	**Palmer**	**James**
avg		2	1	2	0	0
std		10	10	7	9	4
corr			0.76	0.58	0.55	0.47

DRA is the only non-batted ball data system that crosses the threshold of a .70 correlation. As we've mentioned before, a correlation of .70 or higher is, as a rule of thumb, "strong"—provided, of course, that in some settings it would be weak (particularly in the hard sciences) but in others exceptionally strong (in the social sciences). In fact, the correlation of DRA is closer to .80

than to .70, whereas all of the other systems are below .60. Furthermore, the other systems understate the impact of defense, as shown by their respective standard deviations. DRA is spot on, as the standard deviation of ratings matches exactly with Test Runs.

That being said, I would like to highlight some of the good features of the other systems, though it's difficult to say much about the Davenport system because it was not disclosed in detail or reproducible form.

Palmer defensive runs, as reported in the *ESPN Baseball Encyclopedia*, does not perform that well, but the other main baseball encyclopedia, *Total Baseball*, improved it somewhat for infielders by incorporating certain ideas from James. Unfortunately, there hasn't been an edition of *Total Baseball* published since 2003. If someone (i) applied the current Palmer method, (ii) incorporated the Jamesian adjustments that *Total Baseball* did (such as a suboptimal but still useful ground ball versus fly ball adjustment), (iii) credited the same run-weight for each outfield putout that is granted each infield assist (.4 runs), (iv) ignored infield putouts, errors, and double plays, and (v) credited estimated team infield fly outs to the pitchers, I would imagine you could get a system that would reach close to a .70 correlation and only a slightly-too-compressed standard deviation. It would basically be DRA without regression analysis, but with Pete Palmer's remarkably good guess for infield assist run-weights applied as well to outfield putouts.

James inspired DRA—I can even point to the exact sections in his book *Win Shares* that led me to experiment with regression analysis to estimate the impact of the pitcher-only variables on team runs, as well as a means of factoring out contextual influences on fielder plays. So I am extremely grateful to Bill for developing Fielding Win Shares.

Third base is a difficult position for all systems; DRA clearly outperforms by reaching a .65 correlation. (Recall that was the same correlation at third base between the STATS-based MGL estimates and the BIS-based Plus/Minus estimate.) Right field is also difficult, because the difference in defensive runs between good and bad fielders is narrower there than at any other position: when the spread in actual performance is not much greater than the spread of noise in fielding evaluation, correlations will be low.

PLAY-BY-PLAY SYSTEMS

The ideas behind the DRA model described in chapter two were finalized in April 2007, and I sent an article disclosing the system to a small group of analysts named in the preface in order to solicit their comments. Later that year, three new fielding systems were published by baseball blogger and major league consultant Tom Tango, economist Sean Smith, and Pittsburgh

Pirates consultant Dan Fox. Their respective systems were based on information that is far more detailed than simple seasonal totals, but not as detailed as batted ball data. We'll call it "play-by-play" data, which has been compiled by Retrosheet for all major league seasons since 1952 while this chapter was being written, and which is available at no cost from its website.

With or Without You

Play-by-play data tracks who was on the field at each position for each play. So every time a particular fielder converts a batted ball into an out—for example, every time a shortstop fields a ground ball and throws the runner out, and every time a center fielder records a putout—we know the identity of the pitcher. The trick, first devised by Retrosheet contributor Tom Ruane to estimate the runs catchers save by preventing stolen bases, taking into account the impact of pitchers, is simply to compare a fielder's career success rate when he is fielding for a particular pitcher, with the combined success rate of all other fielders playing that position for that pitcher during the pitcher's career, and summing up the results for a fielder across all his pitchers.

Tango put together a Retrosheet database of play-by-play data going back to 1993. For an article in *The Hardball Times Annual 2008*, he searched the database to calculate the percentage of total batted balls allowed by each pitcher between 1993 and 2007 that were converted into outs by shortstops when each pitcher was pitching *with* the shortstop being rated and *without* the shortstop being rated (i.e., when *other* shortstops were playing behind that pitcher). Tango called the method With Or Without You, or WOWY.

For example, through 2007 Andy Pettite pitched to 3,980 batters *with* Derek Jeter as his shortstop, and Jeter converted 12.7 percent of the resulting batted balls in play into outs; Pettite pitched to 2,411 batters *without* Jeter as his shortstop, and the non-Jeters converted 13.9 percent of the resulting batted balls in play into outs. You would make the same 'with and without Jeter' calculations for all pitchers that Jeter played behind and sum up. The Ruane–Tango idea, translated into our four-step procedure, works as follows.

First, estimate expected plays that Jeter would have made if he were average. Search through the play-by-play database to count all batted balls allowed by Jeter's pitchers when Jeter was *not* fielding behind them and count all resulting shortstop outs. This establishes the rate at which the average shortstop would convert batted balls in play allowed by each of Jeter's pitchers into outs. Apply each respective rate to the number of batted balls that *were* allowed by each of Jeter's pitchers when Jeter was fielding behind that pitcher. This yields an estimate of the total number of batted balls the average shortstop would have converted into ground outs if he played in place of Jeter throughout Jeter's career ("expected career plays").

Tango reported that with 39,544 balls in play when Jeter was on the field through 2007. The other shortstops, when playing behind the same pitchers, and pro-rated on the basis of how frequently Jeter played behind those pitchers, converted 12.5 percent of balls in play into outs. So the expected number of plays Jeter would have made if he were average would be 12.5 percent of 39,544, or 4,943.

Second, subtract Jeter's actual total career plays at short (11.6 percent of 39,544 balls in play, or 4,587) from expected career plays (4,943) to get his career net plays, or –356. Yes, negative three hundred and fifty-six.

Third, though Tango did not convert career net plays into career defensive runs, one would ascribe a value of .75 runs per net play.

Fourth, Jeter's net plays, –356, multiplied by .75, yield –267 defensive runs through 2007. Yes, negative two hundred and sixty-seven runs.

This version of WOWY, effectively controlled for the impact pitchers ("*p*"), can have fielding opportunities, so we'll call it *Tango(p-wowy)*, which I think of as the *Tango(·)* calculation 'function' applied to the pitcher-WOWY ("*p-wowy*") data compiled by Retrosheet. Tango performed other WOWY analyses, but instead of controlling for the pitcher he controlled for the identity of opponent batters, or *Tango(b-wowy)*, the placement of base runners, *Tango(br-wowy)*, and park, or *Tango(pk-wowy)*.

Tango(p-wowy) is probably significantly more accurate than the others, and we will consult it frequently in a couple of key shortstop essays. In general, park factors have minimal impact for infielders and all but a few outfielders. The placement of opponent base runners does have some impact—being forced to play at double play depth or shallow with a runner at third reduces plays made—but generally, particularly over the course of a career, a minor one.

Opponent batters have an impact, but it is more important to control for the identity of the pitcher than the identity of opponent batters, because a fielder is far more likely to have an unusual pitching context than opponent batter context. Tango's article reported that Jeter has fielded behind only 118 pitchers who also pitched in front of other shortstops, while Jeter fielded against 992 batters who also batted in front of other shortstops. One would expect the effect of Jeter's opponent batters to average out more than the effect of Jeter's pitchers. In particular, about *one-fourth* of the batted balls hit into the field while he was playing were hit off just *four* pitchers—if just those four had any unusual tendency to generate ground balls or fly balls, Jeter's fielding opportunities would have been drastically affected. In contrast, no batter accounts for more than two percent of Jeter's opponent batters. Finally, the identity of the pitcher somewhat accounts for at least the handedness of opponent batters (because of platooning). Since that article came out, Tango confirmed that he believes that controlling for the identity of the pitcher is most important. There are methods for aggregating the various measures into one, but this would require very sophisticated statistical techniques.

The best things about *Tango(p-wowy)* are (i) the fielder has literally no impact on the estimator of expected plays—in fact, his performance isn't even included in the data for the league, as it is under batted ball data systems (and all others, for that matter), and (ii) errors are treated no differently than plays not made. There are some potentially complicated issues about how much to weight each pitcher's portion of the calculation, because some pitchers might only or predominantly play in front of just one or two shortstops, who might be very good or bad. But I have to believe that over the course of a career, particularly one as long as Jeter's, a variation of the law of averages must prevail, yielding a much less biased and more accurate career evaluation.

Unfortunately, *Tango(p-wowy)* has two important limitations. First, it counts all batted ball outs by shortstops, not just ground outs, so ball hogs on soft fly balls and pop ups will be overrated. Second, it provides only career, not season-by-season assessments, so it could not be compared against Test Runs. Nevertheless, I think it is a valuable alternative career assessment tool, and we will consult it in Part II.

A Play-by-Play System for the Nineteen Fifties, Sixties, Seventies, and Eighties

Tango(p-wowy) has generated only career net plays estimates for shortstops since 1993. In January 2008, Sean Smith published a play-by-play system somewhat analogous to *Tango(p-wowy)* and *Tango(b-wowy)*, but since he had built a complete Retrosheet play-by-play database going back to the early 1950s, he could apply it to fielders at all positions from the early 1950s through the late 1980s. Smith also has two other versions of his system, which he calls TotalZone ("TZ"), which we'll discuss shortly.

Smith basically relied on two items of information that could be obtained from a complete Retrosheet play-by-play database: (i) the pitcher's *career* ratio, relative to the league he played in, of ground *outs* to total batted ball outs, that is, the *pitcher's ground out ratio* ("*pgor*"), and (ii) the percentage of each batter's *career* batted ball *outs* that opposing fielders caught at each position around the field, in other words, the *batter's out distribution* ("*bod*"). So for *each* batted ball, Smith could assign two variables (*pgor,bod*).

Since Smith decided to base this version of his TotalZone system on *pgor* and *bod*, we'll call it *Smith(pgor,bod)*, as the *Smith(·)* calculations, or 'function', convert the *pgor* and *bod* data into defensive runs. The *pgor* variable essentially provides an approximate probability regarding the trajectory of each batted ball, in other words, the probability of the ball being hit on the ground or in the air. The *bod* variable also provides an approximate probability for trajectory, but also for the direction or slice of the field, that is, whether it is likelier to be fielded by the second baseman or the shortstop, or by the left fielder or the right fielder.

For every non-home run hit allowed by a pitcher, if Batter A gets a hit, and based on his *bod*, 15 percent of his career batting outs are ground outs to shortstop, and the Pitcher Z who gave up the hit has a *pgor* of 1.2, meaning that over the course of his career he has generated up ground outs relative to total batted ball outs at a 20 percent higher rate than his peers, *Smith(pgor,bod)* charges 120 percent of 15 percent, or 18 percent of that hit, or .18 hits, to the shortstop who is on the field. If 10 percent of Batter A's career batting outs are to right field, it is necessary to calculate Pitcher Z's relative fly out rate, which I believe would be 200 minus his *pgor* of 120, or 80. We would then charge 80 percent of 10 percent of the hit, or .08 of a hit, to the right fielder.

Summing up over all balls in play when the player was on the field that year, you would calculate his plays made (for example, putouts in center field), and divide them by his opportunities, which are defined under *Smith(pgor,bod)* as his actual plays made, his errors, and the hits charged to him as shown above. This results in a percentage success rate that can be compared to the league-average player that year at that position. Multiplying that difference by the player's opportunities as just defined yields his net plays, which can then be multiplied by about .75 runs if he is a middle infielder, about .80 runs at third and first (where doubles are sometimes allowed), and about .85 runs per play in the outfield.

The best thing about *Smith(pgor,bod)* is that *pgor* potentially provides an estimate of the expected ground outs versus fly outs for a team in a given year that is much less biased by the fielding quality of the current team than the variables DRA uses. Rather than rely, as DRA does, on the team's fly outs and ground outs recorded in the *current* year, which are impacted to some extent by the fielding quality of *that* year's outfield and infield, respectively, *pgor* could be used to estimate the number of fly outs and ground outs the team's pitchers *would* have generated if they performed at their *career* rates, which would in almost all cases be much less biased by the fielding performance of the particular fielders on the team in the current year.

Numerous studies using batted ball data have shown that one of the most stable characteristics of a pitcher's performance is his rate of generating ground balls and fly balls. Therefore, a pitcher's career ground out and fly outs should be a very good estimator of his expected ground outs and fly outs in the current year, in a way that is generally much less influenced of the quality of the team's current fielders. (Of course, if a pitcher spends his entire career with a Willie Mays or Andruw Jones as his centerfielder, his fly out rate might be too high.) And when you add together several pitchers, the overall team *pgor* is probably a reasonably good predictor of expected fly outs and ground outs, independent of the quality of the team's outfielders and infielders

It would be best, or course, to have the actual counts of total ground *balls* and fly *balls* allowed by a team's pitchers, rather than to estimate the relative level of ground balls and fly balls from ground out or fly out data, whether one uses the DRA or *Smith(pgor,bod)* approach. From 1988 through 1999, and for all seasons since 2003, Retrosheet provides free, open-source data on total counts of ground balls and balls hit into the air. Smith developed an alternative system to exploit this data, and Fox independently developed another.

Play-by-Play Systems Using Trajectory Data Available Since the Nineties

Fox called his system Simple Fielding Runs (or "SFR"); we'll call it *Fox(R(t),f,bh,bo)*, because it (i) is designed by Fox, (ii) relies upon *Retrosheet's* non-proprietary yet inevitably subjective coding of *trajectory* (i.e., whether a ball hit in the air was a line drive, fly ball or pop up) (again, "*R(t)*"), and (iii) also relies upon the identity of the position played by the first fielder ("*f*") that touched each batted ball (either by just picking up a clean hit, allowing an error, or making the play), the opponent batter-handedness ("*bh*"), and the impact the fielding play had on the "base-out" situation, including the advancement of existing base runners and whether the batter got a single, double, or triple (base-out, or "*bo*"). Fox also incorporated some park factors.

Smith called his version of the same system "TotalZone" or "TZ," which is what he also called *Smith(pgor,bod)*. Though he did not disclose its details to the same extent that Fox did, information Smith provided at the baseball-reference.com website, which posts these ratings, indicates that Smith's system may not include base-out (*bo*) variables per batted ball but may provide a blanket seasonal adjustment for the relative number of runners at first, which impacts first base plays and somewhat impacts plays at second and short. However, Smith includes pitcher-handedness ("*ph*") as well as batter handedness (again, "*bh*"), thus yielding *Smith(R(t),f,bh,ph)*. Smith uses true batted ball data provided for the 1989–99 seasons free of charge by Retrosheet for his third version of TotalZone, which uses trajectory ("*t*"), slice ("*s*"), and distance ("*d*") data reported by Retrosheet, so we'll denote that system as $Smith(R(t,s,d))$.

… An Interlude to Explain Our Notation

At this point you may be wondering about what Stephen Colbert might term the 'mathy' names for the systems developed by Tango, Fox, and Smith. Here's how I see it. There are now quite a number of published defensive runs systems for recent players based on batted ball data or play-by-play data, and they all sound alike and fail to convey what they are about. The first quasi-batted ball system was called Zone Rating, which reported a success percentage for each fielder based in part on the batted balls hit in the part of the playing field, or "zone," that was assigned to his position. I call it a quasi-batted ball system because the zones for all of the positions didn't cover the entire field, and balls hit between zones were not counted unless caught. But the word "zone" has been picked up by many analysts and, unfortunately, used inconsistently.

MGL called his system Ultimate Zone Rating ("UZR"). The "Ultimate" conveys that it's better than Zone Rating, because it chops up the single zone for each position into multiple locations, counts all the balls, including balls hit into locations 'between' positions, uses more parameters, and converts ratings into defensive runs. So that makes sense. But John Dewan previously developed, but did not publish, his own version of a system similar to UZR. Can you guess what he called it? Ultimate Zone Rating. Recently MGL published a separate version of UZR, which uses BIS rather than STATS data and a different calculation methodology from the version of UZR he settled on in 2003. That one is called UZR too, so there are now two UZRs (or maybe three). Sean Smith gives his system the one-word name TotalZone, even though it really consists of three very different systems, none of which uses Zone Ratings or is similar to Zone Rating, and only one of which, $Smith(R(t,s,d))$, is similar to Ultimate Zone Rating.

John Dewan has recently begun converting his Plus/Minus net plays estimates into estimates of defensive runs. He calls his new system "Defensive Runs Saved." The trouble is, that is exactly the same name that analyst Chris Dial gave years ago for his system for converting Zone Ratings into defensive runs estimates. Furthermore, every one of these systems estimates defensive runs saved (or allowed, if negative), so that name doesn't convey what's different about Dewan's. Mark Pinto coined a nice new term for his system, Probabilistic Model of Range ("PMR"), but again, in some sense all of these systems (and DRA as well), are "probabilistic models of range." Dan Fox's Simple Fielding Runs, while elegantly simple conceptually, is not significantly less computationally intensive than the others. And so forth.

To avoid confusion and aid understanding of the key features of all these systems, we'll rename each one, so that it will be clear at a glance (i) who designed it (the "*Analyst*"), (ii) where the analyst got any data subject to coding error, for example, the "Data" company, abbreviated by the capitalized first letter of its name (for example, "*D*"), and (iii) which estimators the analyst most relied upon to estimate expected plays made, the key calculation of all fielding systems. Estimator might include, for example, trajectory ("*t*"), slice of the field ("*s*"), and distance ("*d*"), which all combined would be "*(t,s,d)*." All together, the format of the new name for each system would be, based on the above hypothetical, as follows: *Analyst(D(t,s,d))*.

The nested parentheses "(())" are there to highlight the crucial fact that any defensive runs system based on subjective data coded by one human being and converted into defensive runs via formulas or algorithms designed by another human being is in some sense a composite function, analogous to $f(g(x,y))$ ("*f* of *g* of *x* and *y*"). The way a composite function $f(g(x,y))$ works, you first plug in the value of x and y into the function g, which converts those numbers, for example, either into another number, or perhaps a pair of numbers, and then you feed whatever g generates into f, which might in turn convert that single number or pair of numbers into another number. A composite function is really a *two-step procedure* for converting the 'raw facts' x and y into some other value.

The first system we relabeled, *Smith(pgor,bod)*, applicable from the 1950s through 1988, as well as from 2000 through 2002, is not really so much a composite function but a 'plain' function. True, the organization Retrosheet collected the data to permit the calculation of the variables *bod* and *pgor*, but it is objective data not likely subject to human coding bias, so the *Smith(·)* 'calculation function' directly takes in the *pgor* and *bod* data (as well as other items) to generate defensive runs estimates.

In contrast, the trajectories assigned by Retrosheet volunteers for all batted balls since 1989 or so (excluding 2000–02), are subjective items of information subject to human coding error. Retrosheet volunteers labeled the real-world trajectory ("*t*") of each batted ball into one of four trajectory codes (ground ball, line drive, fly out, and pop up). The Retrosheet 'function' $R(·)$ 'takes in' the real world trajectory t and assigns the Retrosheet *code R(t)*, which is G for ground ball, L for line drive, F for fly ball and P for pop up. So when *Smith(R(t),f,bh,ph)* defensive runs are calculated for years since 2003, they are a composite function to the extent they rely on the output of the $R(t)$ function. The *Smith(R(t,s,d))* function uses trajectory, slice, and distance batted ball codes that are *all* generated by the Retrosheet 'function' of volunteer stringers, so all three real world variables are inside the parentheses of the $R(\cdot)$ function, which takes in three 'real world' variables (the exact trajectory, direction, and depth) and generates three codes (trajectory, slice, and distance).

By using notation that highlights the notion of an *Analyst*$(\cdot)$ function, I am trying to keep constantly in view the fact that analysts who use batted ball and play-by-play data make choices about how to use the data, such as how much to chop up the data (that is, whether to collect the data into larger or smaller trajectory-slice-distance buckets), whether to apply the mixed method or calculate error runs, and so forth. There is a lot going on under the hood in these systems that rarely gets disclosed or discussed and can have a surprisingly big impact.

… We Now Return You to Our Survey of Play-by-Play Systems

So *Smith(pgor,bod)* covers 1952–88, *Fox(R(t),f,bh,bo)* and *Smith(R(t,s,d))* cover 1989–99, *Smith(pgor,bod)* covers 2000–02, and *Smith(R(t),f,bh,ph)* and *Fox(R(t),f,bh,bo)* cover seasons since 2003.

Fox(R(t),f,bh,bo) and *Smith(R(t),f,bh,ph)* generate infielder ratings on the basis of an *exact count* of *total* ground balls hit (counted separately by opponent batter-handedness) and an estimator for the *direction* of every ground ball hit. How do they estimate direction without slice data? Well, every ground ball picked up by the left fielder was missed by either the third baseman or the shortstop; every ground ball picked up by the center fielder was missed by either the shortstop or the second baseman; every ground ball picked up by the right fielder was picked up by the right fielders. In other words, the position of the fielder ("f") who first touches a ground ball hit is a simple proxy for the slice ("s") of the field in which ground ball are hit, which is more precisely tracked in batted ball systems.

As explained in a series of articles published at baseballprospectus.com in late 2007 and early 2008, Fox determined the average portion of left fielder ground ball pickups to charge the third baseman and shortstop, the average portion of center fielder ground ball pickups to charge the shortstop and second baseman, and the average portion of right fielder ground ball pickups to charge the second baseman and first baseman. The splits varied but were generally close to fifty-fifty, but closer to sixty-forty for the hole between second base and first base. All ground ball doubles fielded in left were charged to the third baseman; all ground ball doubles fielded in right were charged to the first baseman. Fox tracked this separately by opponent batters handedness ("*bh*").

Fox also tracked for every batted ball the number of outs and placement of base runners (which impacts fielder positioning) before and after the play, what is known as the change in the "base-out" state (*"bo"*). Fox also credited infielders for line drives, fly outs, and pop ups they recorded, even though MGL, Smith, and I do not believe this is appropriate.

In the outfield, *Fox(R(t),f,bh,bo)* tracks how far the batter and base runners advanced on *every* batted ball fielded or picked up by each outfielder, tracked separately by trajectory and opponent batter handedness, whether the outfielder converted the ball into an out *or not*. The good feature of this measure is that it detects how well outfielders limit base runner advancement, not just by catching the ball in the first place or by throwing runners out, but also by cutting off clean hits and getting the ball back into the infield quickly. Johnny Damon, who was a speedy runner circa 2003-05, but a poor thrower, is rated well under *Fox(R(t),f,bh,bo)* for those seasons, which may be measuring an important skill that other systems don't capture.

TESTING DRA AND THE PLAY-BY-PLAY SYSTEMS AGAINST TEST RUNS

Here is how DRA compares with the *Smith(pgor,bod)* and *Fox(R(t),f,bh,bo)*. We can't test *Smith(R(t,s,d))* against contemporary batted ball data systems because the Retrosheet data only runs from 1989 through 1999, and there are no publicly available estimates of defensive runs based on an alternative batted ball data set. Please note that *Smith(pgor,bod)* defensive runs estimates shown here for 2003–05 were posted by him at hardballtimes.com to help analysts get comfortable that it should work for earlier seasons; Smith's TotalZone ratings for 2003–05 at baseball-reference.com are calculated under the *Smith(R(t),f,bh,ph)* methodology. Given the strong similarity between *Fox(R(t),f,bh,bo)* and *Smith(R(t),f,bh,ph)*, test results for the former probably give a good indication of the accuracy of defensive runs estimates by the latter, which are easy to find for seasons since 2003 at baseball-reference.com.

The table on the next page, "Test Runs Compared with DRA and Smith and Fox Play-By-Play Systems" includes all DRA, *Smith(pgor,bod)*, and *Fox(R(t),f,bh,bo)* ratings for players with at least two full-time seasons, including all their playing time during the three-year period, denominated in terms of defensive runs per 1450 innings played at that position during 2003–05. (The reason I did not include partial seasons in the prior test is that I had not collected that data for Davenport ratings back in 2007, and, as discussed below, they have changed since then.)

Neither Test Runs nor DRA is park-adjusted, whereas both the Smith and Fox systems have park factor adjustments. Sean Smith has written at hardballtimes.com that the only park factors that are really necessary are for outfielders at Coors Field and left fielders playing in front of The Green Monster at Fenway Park. My own studies suggest that playing left field for the Red Sox suppresses defensive runs estimates by about ten runs per year (and Fox reported essentially the same result), so I subtracted ten runs from the Smith and Fox ratings (to back out their probable park adjustment) for Manny Ramirez to arrive at the Manny numbers shown above. There are no Coors outfielders in the sample. Without the Manny adjustment the Smith and Fox correlations would be lower, but still above .70.

Test Runs Compared with DRA and Smith and Fox Play-By-Play Systems

First	Last	Pos	Test Runs	DRA	Smith (*pgor,bod*)	Fox (*R(t),f,bh,bo*)
Carlos	Beltran	8	11	10	7	6
Mike	Cameron	8	24	27	18	22
Johnny	Damon	8	-3	5	-7	8
Jim	Edmonds	8	9	19	5	6
Marquis	Grissom	8	-12	1	-19	2
Andruw	Jones	8	9	9	14	6
Mark	Kotsay	8	5	7	-3	3
Juan	Pierre	8	-1	-11	0	-11
Vernon	Wells	8	0	-9	2	-7
Moises	Alou	7	2	-2	-7	-5
Pat	Burrell	7	-4	-6	-5	-4
Carl	Crawford	7	23	22	22	15
Adam	Dunn	7	-6	-8	-4	-11
Luis	Gonzalez	7	6	-4	-5	-4
Carlos	Lee	7	2	6	1	7
Manny	Ramirez	7	-34	-28	-21	-11
Bobby	Abreu	9	-1	-2	-5	3
Jose	Cruz	9	5	6	31	11
Jermaine	Dye	9	5	-3	-3	-6
J.	Encarnacion	9	11	-8	-15	2
Brian	Giles	9	5	3	-9	4
Shawn	Green	9	-3	1	-5	-3
Gary	Sheffield	9	-14	0	-2	-2
Ichiro	Suzuki	9	13	12	19	1
Ronnie	Belliard	4	8	-3	-4	-1
Bret	Boone	4	-19	-5	-7	-1
Luis	Castillo	4	13	13	10	10
Marcus	Giles	4	18	11	11	17
Orlando	Hudson	4	26	27	16	14
Adam	Kennedy	4	10	5	10	8
Jeff	Kent	4	0	3	-1	-4
Mark	Loretta	4	1	-2	1	-1
Brian	Roberts	4	12	4	0	-1
Alfonso	Soriano	4	-12	-10	-15	-7

(continued)

Test Runs Compared with DRA and Smith and Fox Play-By-Play Systems *(continued)*

First	Last	Pos	Test Runs	DRA	Smith (pgor,bod)	Fox (R(t),f,bh,bo)
Angel	Berroa	6	-14	-7	-7	-10
Orlando	Cabrera	6	5	-5	-1	3
Royce	Clayton	6	-7	-1	-4	-5
David	Eckstein	6	0	-6	5	5
Rafael	Furcal	6	11	11	8	7
Alex	Gonzalez	6	3	-2	-5	1
Cristian	Guzman	6	-5	-3	-7	-4
Cesar	Izturis	6	7	14	9	9
Derek	Jeter	6	-18	-21	-9	-9
Julio	Lugo	6	2	13	4	3
Edgar	Renteria	6	-2	-11	-3	-3
Jimmy	Rollins	6	14	-2	11	1
Miguel	Tejada	6	3	10	-2	7
Omar	Vizquel	6	1	-5	8	4
Jack	Wilson	6	15	12	11	15
Michael	Young	6	-32	-25	-24	-16
Tony	Batista	5	-4	4	2	2
David	Bell	5	19	20	8	12
Adrian	Beltre	5	18	8	11	12
Hank	Blalock	5	7	-5	1	-7
Vinnie	Castilla	5	1	-2	8	-1
Eric	Chavez	5	9	11	12	13
Joe	Crede	5	2	2	4	4
Mike	Lowell	5	-5	-8	5	1
Melvin	Mora	5	-6	-1	-2	2
Bill	Mueller	5	3	3	-5	3
Alex	Rodriguez	5	6	-3	-3	-1
Scott	Rolen	5	15	13	18	17

			Test Runs	DRA	Smith (pgor, bod)	Fox (R(t),f,bh,bo)
	Corr. w/Test Runs		1.00	0.80	0.74	0.75
	Standard Deviation		12	11	10	8

DRA has a better correlation and standard deviation match with Test Runs than *Smith(pgor,bod)* and *Fox(R(t),f,bh,bo)*. Though I believe DRA should, for reasons we'll go into shortly, have a slightly better correlation and standard deviation match with well constructed batted ball systems than the current versions of *Smith(pgor,bod)* or even *Fox(R(t),f,bh,bo)*, this is of course just one test. To be clear, this was the first and only test I performed using the 1956-2007 DRA model described in chapter two, for the simple reason that I had already established my sample of fielders for the 2007 hardballtimes.com article and I already had that data. I did not run multiple tests in order to arrive at this favorable result. However, I did subsequently create another version of DRA using just 1977-2008 data, and obtained a correlation for the above sample of only .78, which is barely higher than the *Smith(pgor,bod)* and *Fox(R(t),f,bh,bo)* correlations, though, once again, the standard deviation match was better.

POSSIBLE EXPLANATIONS FOR THESE RESULTS

DRA uses a miniscule portion of the data used by *Smith(pgor,bod)* and *Fox(R(t),f,bh,bo)*. The latter system in particular benefits from using play-by-play counts of total ground balls and total fly balls hit by left- and right-handed opponent batters, as well as the identity of the fielding position that first touched each batted ball, for each ball in play hit while a particular fielder being rated was on the field. This data is available for most seasons since 1989. DRA only uses seasonal team totals of ground outs and fly outs by opponent batter-handedness to *estimate* the relative level of total ground balls and fly balls hit on the left and right side of the field over the course of an entire season. So I would understand anyone's initial skepticism about these results.

However, if we step back and think about all three systems, and in particular translate each of them into the same standard four-step procedure for estimating defensive runs, it will become clear how DRA could slightly outperform *Smith(pgor,bod)* and *Fox(R(t),f,bh,bo)*. In addition, by figuring out the systematic biases in both systems, we can back out estimated effects of some of these biases to derive better second and third opinions for many important fielders from more recent seasons whom we will discuss in Part II.

I wish to emphasize, however, that though I believe DRA is probably a somewhat more accurate methodology than the current versions of *Smith(pgor,bod)* and *Fox(R(t),f,bh,bo)* for evaluating fielders, given the number of successful plays made, any system that fully and properly exploits play-by-play data will eventually outperform the current version of DRA. If there is another edition of this book, which I hope there will be, it will feature a new version of DRA derived from a relational database of Retrosheet data that incorporates the insights of Smith and Fox.

DRA is clearly better in the outfield, and part of this can easily be explained without resorting to any explicit four-step calculations. *Smith(pgor,bod)* charges *hits allowed* to outfielders in part based upon opponent career batter *out* distributions (*bod*). But as Mike Fast showed recently at hardballtimes. com using some batted ball data, hit and out distributions in the outfield are strikingly different—when most batters pull a fly ball or line drive, they are significantly more likely to get a hit than when they hit the ball the opposite way. Many soft fly outs are hit off of high, hard fastballs that batters are swinging under and behind on. So many of the hits charged under *Smith(pgor,bod)* to right fielders should really be charged to left fielders, and vice versa. In other words, *bod* is a biased estimator of the location of hits allowed.

Fox(R(t),f,bh,bo) rates each outfielder based mainly on the relative number of total batted balls he gets to (including hits that drop in) that he converts into an out. But under that approach, an outfielder with poor range will likely be overrated, because the hits he never gets to *at all* are never charged to him, while an outfielder with outstanding range will be under-rated, because the hits he fields when backing up his weaker-fielding outfield teammates are charged to him.

Before going through our four-step calculations, which we'll do for short-stop, let's summarize what they will reveal.

First, *Smith(pgor,bod)* and *Fox(R(t),f,bh,bo)*, which purportedly give full credit for plays made—approximately .75 runs for infielders, a bit more for outfielders—actually discount plays made by about as much, or even more, than DRA. Like DRA, *Fox(R(t),f,bh,bo)* weights skill plays at approximately half a run. *Smith(pgor,bod)* weights them about a third of a run.

Second, *Smith(pgor,bod)* treats errors almost half a run worse, and *Fox(R(t),f,bh,bo)* treats errors about a quarter of a run worse, than not making the play at all, which is incorrect. This also means that a fielder who avoids errors will be overrated compared to a fielder who makes the same number of net plays while committing more errors.

Third, and perhaps most surprisingly, the fielding quality of a player's teammates probably creates more bias under *Smith(pgor,bod)* and *Fox(R(t),f,bh,bo)* systems than under DRA. As we've admitted a few times already, under DRA, an individual infielder's net plays are impacted by the net fielding quality of his team's outfielders, considered as a whole, and an individual outfielder's net plays are impacted by the net fielding quality of his team's infielders (including pitchers), considered as a whole.

Under *Smith(pgor,bod)*, net plays estimates for fielders at every position are distorted by the net fielding quality of the team's fielders at *all* of the other positions, *as well as* the pitching staff's tendency to generate infield fly outs. Net plays estimates under *Fox(R(t),f,bh,bo)* for infielders are distorted by the skill of only the fielders next to them. But the per-player impact of neighboring fielders is so high under *Fox(R(t),f,bh,bo)* that the overall dis-tortion for middle infielders is very likely greater than under DRA, though probably less for corner infielders.

OUR FOUR-STEP, AGAIN

Now let's do the arithmetic to back up the above conclusions, using our basic four-step procedure, which can always be expressed in one line.

Defensive Runs = Estimated Runs per Net Play * (Plays – [Expected Plays]).

After the calculations, we'll summarize the results in a table.

The basic DRA version of defensive runs at shortstop, discussed in chapter two, is

$$.44*(A6 - [lgA6*(BIP/lgBIP) + .06*RBIP.bip - .29*RFO.rbip - .15*LFO.lbip]).$$

If a shortstop records one more *A6*, that *A6* has virtually zero impact on any item in the square brackets, so the net effect is approximately +.44 multiplied by one play, or .44 runs. If he records one less, that would be –.44 runs. Errors, as compared to simply not making the play at all, have no impact, other than the –.44 runs charged for not making the play successfully. If you take the average of the last two items in the bracketed area, even if you weight *RFO.rbip* two-thirds and *LFO.lbip* one-third because there are more right-handed batters, you arrive at a blended coefficient of .25, meaning that for approximately every .25 marginal fly outs, you decrease expected *A6* by one. Now if those extra fly outs are due to the pitchers' tendency to generate fly balls versus ground balls, that is an *unbi-*ased estimate of ground ball versus fly ball pitching. And infield fly outs, especially on a team basis, reflect almost entirely the pitchers' tendency to generate them.

But assume that there is an extra fly out due to the real skill of the team's outfielders. Then the runs that would be 'given' to the shortstops equal .44 multiplied by .25, or .11 runs. So, therefore, each net skill play in the outfield, taken as a whole, biases the runs estimate for the team's shortstops by about .11 runs. Note that there should not be bias if, say, the left fielder is +10 plays, the center fielder is flat, and the right fielder is –10 plays; it's the overall net skill performance of the outfield, not the individuals.

Fox(R(t),f,bh,bo), can be translated into the same type of one-line formula, where "*GB7*" indicates ground ball hits picked up by the left fielder, about half of which are charged to the shortstop, and *GB8* indicates a ground ball hit picked up by the center fielder, also about half of which is charged to the shortstop. So defensive runs at shortstop under *Fox(R(t),f,bh,bo)* is approximately

$$= \text{Runs per Net Play}*(\text{Plays} - [\text{Expected Plays}]), \text{ or}$$
$$= .75*(A6 - [.70*\{A6 + E6 + .50*GB7 + .50*GB8\}]).$$

The ".70" is approximately what Fox reported for the league rate of shortstop ground ball plays made (abbreviated here as *A6*, though Fox also counts the small number of unassisted ground ball putouts at short) per opportunity, where opportunities equal league *A6* plus league *E6* plus .50 multiplied by league *GB7* plus .50 multiplied by league *GB8*. This makes sense, because 70 percent is about the average rate, throughout the field, at which major league teams convert batted balls in play into outs at all positions combined.

The expected plays that an average shortstop if he played in place of the shortstop being rated would make is equal to the league success rate multiplied by the opportunities imputed to the shortstop being rated, which are equal to what is in the curly brackets "{}".

Let's see what happens if the shortstop being rated makes one more *A6* that would otherwise go through as a hit, to be fielded by the left fielder (though it could equally be the center fielder). The numbers that change are in **bold**.

$$=.75*(A6 - [.70*\{A6 + E6 + .50*GB7 + .50*GB8\}])$$
$$=.75*(\mathbf{1.0} - [.70*\{\mathbf{1.0} + 0.0 + .50*(\mathbf{-1.0}) + .50*0.0\}])$$
$$=+.49 \text{ runs.}$$

This run weight is almost the same as under DRA, though I hasten to add that this depends on the league success rate at short, which varies by batter-handedness, etc., and which is only approximately equal to .70. However you slice it, though, the effective run weight for each extra play the shortstop makes is not .75 runs, but closer to .50 runs. And the same applies throughout the infield.

Now let's see what happens if, instead of a ball going through and being picked up by the left fielder, the shortstop gets to a ball but makes an error, which reduces the ground balls first touched by, say, the left fielder, by one:

$$= .75*(A6 - [.70*\{A6 + E6 + .50*GB7 + .50*GB8\}])$$
$$= .75*(0.0 - [.70*\{0.0 + \mathbf{1.0} + .50*(\mathbf{-1.0}) + .50*0.0\}]$$
$$= -.26 \text{ runs.}$$

As we've said many times before, errors must not be treated worse than simply not making a play at all, because they are in fact not more damaging than a play not made, on average. As this is just an approximate example, it would be better to think of the system as penalizing errors by about a quarter run more than simply not making the play, and also over-crediting extra plays made by avoiding errors by the same amount.

Now let's see what happens if the third baseman makes an extra skill play. (The effect is essentially the same if the second baseman does the same.)

$$= .75^*(A6 - [.70^*\{A6 + E6 + .50^*GB7 \quad + .50^*GB8\}])$$
$$= .75^*(0.0 - [.70^*\{0.0 + 0.0 + .50^*(-\mathbf{1.0}). + .50^*0.0\}])$$
$$= +.26 \text{ runs.}$$

Each extra play made, either by the third baseman or the second baseman, boosts the shortstop's defensive runs by .26, or about a quarter of a run.

Now let's look at *Smith(pgor,bod)*. We'll assume the following for the sake of simplicity. The league average shortstop success rate is also 70 percent. The batter's career out distribution, or *bod*, is typical, which would mean that about 15 percent of all batted ball *outs* are recorded as ground outs fielded at short. We'll also assume that the pitcher's career ground out ratio, or *pgor*, is exactly 100, that is, he has an average career rate of ground outs versus fly outs. Therefore, 100 percent of 15 percent, that is, 15 percent, of all team hits allowed ("HA") are charged to the shortstop. The *Smith(pgor,bod)* formula for defensive runs at shortstop is therefore approximately:

$$= \text{Runs per net play}^*(\text{Plays} - [\text{Expected Plays}])$$
$$= .75^*(A6 - [.70^*\{A6 + E6 + .15^*1.00^*HA\}]).$$

If a shortstop makes an extra skill *A6*, thereby preventing a hit, here is the result:

$$= .75^*(\mathbf{1.0} - [.70^*\{\mathbf{1.0} + 0.0 + .15^*1.00^*(-\mathbf{1.0})\}])$$
$$= +.30 \text{ defensive runs.}$$

If a shortstop makes an error instead of simply allowing the ball to go through, he is charged the error but team hits allowed are decreased by one:

$$= .75^*(0.0 - [.70^*\{0.0 + \mathbf{1.0} + .15^*1.00^*(-\mathbf{1.0})\}])$$
$$= -.45 \text{ defensive runs.}$$

If the shortstop does nothing, but the rest of the team converts one more batted ball into an out, given total balls in play, so the team allowed one less hit, the effect at shortstop is

$$= .75^*(0.0 - [.70^*\{0.0 + 0.0 + .15^*1.00^*(-\mathbf{1.0})\}])$$
$$= +.08 \text{ defensive runs.}$$

Let's summarize these results, which estimate the net impact of each system on all three possible shortstop outcomes for a ground ball hit on the left side of the infield or up the middle: (1) shortstop prevents or allows a hit, that is, makes a net play, (2) shortstop commits an error, rather than simply allowing a clean hit, and (3) somebody else on the shortstop's team makes an extra skill play, or allows an extra hit.

System:	DRA	Smith (pgor,bod)	Fox (R(t),f,bh,bo)
(1) Net A6	0.44	0.30	0.49
(2) Error v. No Play	-	(0.45)	(0.26)
(3) Teammate Biases			
(a) net PO7, PO8, & PO9	0.11	0.08	-
(b) net A5 & A4	-	0.08	0.26
(c) net GO3, A1, and IFO	-	0.08	-

Approximate Run Values for Shortstop Plays

In English, the above chart says that if a shortstop makes one more net play, he gets +.44 runs of credit under DRA, approximately +.30 runs of credit under *Smith(pgor,bod)*, and approximately +.49 runs of credit under *Fox(R(t),f,bh,bo)*. All three systems discount net plays; DRA is just more direct about it.

In English, the above chart says that if a shortstop makes one more error rather than allow a clean hit, he is charged zero under DRA (having already been charged for a net play missed), whereas *Smith(pgor,bod)* charges an additional –.46 runs, and *Fox(R(t),f,bh,bo)* charges an additional –.26 runs. Again, the latter two systems incorrectly treat an error worse than a play missed, and an error avoided as better than an extra play made.

In English, the above chart says that, under DRA, if a team's outfielders, on an *overall net* basis, make *one* more net play *not* attributable to the tendency of the team's pitchers to generate fly balls, the shortstop will be incorrectly credited with +.11 defensive runs. Under *Smith(pgor,bod)*, each extra out recorded by a team *anywhere* in the field other than shortstop, including infield fly outs, results in the shortstop being incorrectly credited by approximately +.08 defensive runs. Under *Fox(R(t),f,bh,bo)*, for each net play made at third or second, the shortstop will be incorrectly credited by approximately +.26 defensive runs.

The standard deviation in total net plays made by teams on an overall basis, including infield fly outs, taking into account only the total number of balls in play, is at least twice, and probably more than twice, the standard deviation in net *skill* plays made just in the outfield that are not attributable to fly ball pitching. Therefore, the *Smith(pgor,bod)* teammate distortion, equal to the product of .08 and the sum of *total* net IFO, A1, A3, A4, A5, A6, PO7, PO8, and PO9, is likelier to be bigger than the DRA teammate distortion, equal to the product of .11 and the sum of *net skill PO7*, *PO8*, and *PO9* not attributable to fly ball pitching.

Therefore, even though the database search for *bod* and *pgor* data would seem to have successfully eliminated teammate bias, by predicting where the outs should be distributed around the field without reference to the fielding skill of the current team, the way the other calculations work, bias based on the fielding skill of player's current team is reintroduced to an even greater extent than under DRA.

Under *Fox(R(t),f,bh,bo)*, the bias is concentrated not on the net effect of the skill plays of the three outfield positions, as under DRA, or total net plays made at all positions, as under *Smith(pgor,bod)*, but only at two positions—third base and second, the 'neighbors' of the infielder (shortstop) under consideration. Though the Fox system is distorted only by the net skill plays by the third baseman in the hole and by the second baseman up the middle, that distortion is multiplied by a much greater factor: .26, rather than .11 or .08.

Since the standard deviation in net skill plays at the three outfield positions combined is probably less than three times (.26 divided by .08) the standard deviation in net skill plays at third and second combined, DRA probably introduces less teammate bias at shortstop than *Fox(R(t),f,bh,bo)*. And since the standard deviation in net skill plays at the three outfield positions combined is probably less than three times (.26 divided by .08) the standard deviation in net skill plays at first and short combined, DRA probably introduces less teammate bias at second base than *Fox(R(t),f,bh,bo)*.

Third basemen and first basemen are only impacted under *Fox(R(t),f,bh,bo)* by the fielding skill of *one* player (the shortstop and the second baseman, respectively). At third and first, the Fox approach will be better if the product of the standard deviation in skill plays in the holes by shortstops and second basemen, respectively, is less than .11 divided by .26, or about 42 percent, of the standard deviation in net skill plays made by a team's outfield. I would guess it is, in which case the *Fox(R(t),f,bh,bo)* approach for 1989-99 and the *Fox(R(t),f,bh,bo)* and *Smith(R(t),f,bh,ph)* approaches for 2003 onward would likely be better at third than DRA. In addition, *Fox(R(t),f,bh,bo)* and *Smith(R(t),f,bh,ph)* track doubles allowed down the line, which DRA does not.

Both *Smith(pgor,bod)* and *Fox(R(t),f,bh,bo)* are currently better than DRA at first base, because the current version of DRA lacks the exact number of ground ball out conversions (including unassisted ground ball putouts) per first baseman, whereas Smith and Fox query their respective databases to obtain the exact number. In other words, DRA currently lacks complete information on step two of the four-step procedure for first baseman. If the exact number of groundouts recorded by first basemen were incorporated into the DRA system for accomplishing steps one and three, I'm confident the DRA ratings at first would be about as good as those under the Smith and Fox systems.

KEEPING THINGS IN PERSPECTIVE

I would imagine some readers are slightly under-whelmed by an improvement in correlation that takes us 'only' from correlations between .55 and .60 (Palmer and Davenport) to correlations of between .75 and .80 (DRA, $Smith(pgor,bod)$, and $Fox(R(t),f,bh,bo)$). I believe, however, that most professional statisticians would consider such improvement remarkable. Perhaps more important to keep in mind, however, is that **defensive runs estimates based on batted ball data provided by different suppliers do not correlate any better with *each* *other* than DRA, *Smith(pgor,bod)*, and *Fox(R(t), f,bh,bo)* correlate with Test Runs.** As noted earlier in this chapter, the 2007 article reported that infielder defensive runs estimates based on STATS and BIS data had only a .76 correlation (blending the .81 correlations at short and second with the .65 correlation at third), and the correlations between BIS-based and STATS-based outfielder defensive runs were never higher than .70 and usually closer to .60.

I believe that a system combining some of the elements of DRA, improvements to $Smith(pgor,bod)$ and $Fox(R(t),f,bh,bo)$, and some additional statistical techniques will eventually provide fans with open source (if challenging to replicate) defensive runs estimates that will be, as a practical matter, just as good as those dependent upon proprietary data, in the sense that it is questionable whether major league teams would be willing to bet money (in the form of player contracts and trades) on the differences in reported defensive runs.

AWKWARD DETAILS LEFT TO DEAL WITH

As readers of baseballthinkfactory.org and hardballtimes.com are aware, I have twice tested an earlier version of DRA, which at that time did not rely on Retrosheet counts of fly outs and ground outs separated by opponent batter handedness, against MGL's UZR system, when it was based on STATS data. Our new name for that version of UZR, following our system for naming systems, is $MGL(S(t,s,d,v,bh))$, because it was (i) designed by MGL, (ii) used STATS ("S") data, and (iii) relied upon trajectory, slice, distance, velocity ("v") (useful for ground balls), and batter-handedness data. Both times the correlation between this more primitive version of DRA and $MGL(S(t,s,d,v,bh))$ was at or above .70, with the standard deviation again matching almost exactly both times.[8] On the basis of those results, there is good evidence to suggest that the DRA ratings at second, short, and third are reasonably good, even for seasons before we have the data needed by the version of DRA disclosed in chapter two (1952 when this was written).

There remain a few gaps in the testing record, however. First and foremost, even the earliest versions of DRA developed in 2003 relied on Retrosheet counts of putouts recorded and innings played separately in left, center, and right field. Believe it or not, official baseball statistics for outfielders only included total putouts *anywhere* in the outfield, total games anywhere in the outfield, and total games in left, center, and right.

Thanks to Retrosheet volunteers, we now have outfield putouts recorded in left, center, and right from 1920 through 1939 as of this writing, and the DRA ratings in this book reflect that data and use it in exactly the same way it was used when I tested DRA outfielder results against $MGL(S(t,s,d,v,bh))$ in 2003 and 2005 and achieved correlations above .70, as reported at the hardballtimes.com website. I am confident we'll eventually have it for all seasons since 1920, and perhaps even for all seasons since 1893.[9]

Towards the end of chapter two we described in general terms the approach used for generating defensive runs by outfielders using the much more primitive information available for the Dead Ball Era (1893–1919) and the 1940s. (Appendix A has all the details.) How confident should we be in such outfielder ratings?

With reference to the table on the next page, the correlation of .73 is actually surprisingly good, because the only system we can compare "Dead Ball DRA" to is James, since James's Win Shares is the only system to rate contemporary outfielders using the same primitive original data available throughout major league history, and the Win Shares correlation for the same outfielders in the first chart shown in this chapter was only about .35, and had a much too compressed standard deviation. We can't compare Dead Ball DRA against the Smith or Fox systems, because they can't be applied to those prior periods, and we can't compare the Palmer and Davenport systems, because we don't know how they calculate Dead Ball Era outfielder ratings, so we can't apply that methodology to see how well it would work for today's players. Actually, even if we do compare Dead Ball DRA as applied to recent players to the Smith and Fox systems, Dead Ball DRA actually matches slightly better in the outfield.

---

8. www.hardballtimes.com/main/authors/mhumphreys/2005/.

9. As this went to press, Retrosheet indeed did finish recording outfield putouts separately in left, center, and right for all seasons since 1920.

Outfielder Test Runs Compared with Dead Ball DRA

First	Last	Test Runs	Dead Ball DRA
Bobby	Abreu	-1	-10
Moises	Alou	-2	-8
Carlos	Beltran	9	9
Pat	Burrell	-3	-6
Mike	Cameron	21	34
Carl	Crawford	20	18
Jose	Cruz	5	3
Johnny	Damon	-3	-1
Adam	Dunn	-9	2
Jermaine	Dye	4	-2
Jim	Edmonds	3	20
Juan	Encarnacion	9	-1
Brian	Giles	3	6
Luis	Gonzalez	10	-7
Shawn	Green	-3	-4
Marquis	Grissom	-10	-2
Andruw	Jones	8	16
Mark	Kotsay	-8	3
Carlos	Lee	2	8
Juan	Pierre	-1	-9
Manny	Ramirez	-29	-22
Gary	Sheffield	-12	-7
Ichiro	Suzuki	13	11
Vernon	Wells	0	-9
	Avg	1	2
	Std	11	12
	Corr		0.73

EVALUATING BASE RUNNER DEFENSE

The DRA evaluations discussed thus far include double-play defense, which is included in the middle-infielder ratings, but nothing about the two other forms of base runner defense: preventing stolen bases and preventing base runner advancement on hits.

At catcher, the best system is probably *Tango(p-wowy)*, which compares how well catchers control the running game and avoid passed balls and wild pitches, taking into account the impact of the pitchers with which they play. Career caught stealing runs for catchers with long careers using the DRA variable *CS.sba* have an over .90 correlation with *Tango(p-wowy)*, though the passed ball and wild pitch calculations under DRA have a lower correlation of about .80. As we shall see when we rate the catchers, there are very good reasons to suspect that all conventional ratings systems are fundamentally wrong.

The last item of defense to discuss is the effect of outfielders on throwing out and holding base runners. The DRA estimates are based, unfortunately, only on assists per nine innings, or runners thrown out. As any fan will tell you, after a few seasons an outfielder with an outstanding arm will have fewer assists because opponent base runners simply won't test their arms.

But an outfielder who essentially intimidates a base runner from taking an extra base, that is, who "holds" a base runner adds value, though not as much as by actually throwing a base runner out. Retrosheet play-by-play data is perfect for measuring this effect, because it records base runner locations before and after a ball is hit into the outfield, and who is playing each outfield position. I believe Clem Comly, who like Tom Ruane, has been one of the leading lights at Retrosheet, first used Retrosheet play-by-play data in 2000 to estimate how many runs outfielders save not just by throwing out base runners, but also by holding them. Comly called his system the Average Run-equivalent Method, or ARM, and estimated that Carl Yastrzemski saved about sixty runs over the course of his career by holding or throwing out base runners. John Walsh developed his own version and published it in *The Hardball Times Baseball Annual 2007*, and Sean Smith followed suit a year or two later. Both Walsh and Smith obtain similar results for Yaz. In general, defensive runs attributable to holding base runners, even by outfielders such as Clemente or Barfield with the most feared arms, rarely exceed a few a year on a consistent basis; however, over the course of a fairly long career, those runs do add up for about five or ten outfielders throughout major league history, and we will definitely address those cases in Part II, thanks to Comly, Walsh, and Smith.

THE ULTIMATE TEST

Some of the highest quality education in the First World is now available to millions of young people in the Third for free on the internet. In addition to the marvelous "Khan Academy," which has ten-minute tutorials for just about every math and science concept covered in grade school, high school, and the first two years of college, a few of our greatest universities, including MIT, Stanford, and Yale, now post videos of complete courses. Yale's Ramamurti Shankar brings a wry sense of humor to his physics lectures, and his students over the years have taken to writing down his stories and sayings. One of my favorites runs as follows:

> You could write a law and think it's correct, and then you'd publish a
> bunch of papers, and eventually you'd realize that your parents are
> the only ones reading them and then you'd know that you were
> wrong. Now, on the other hand, if your friends are reading your

papers, your enemies are reading your papers, and then your enemies are stealing what you've written in your papers, then you'll know that your law is correct.

Translate "enemies" as people I just don't happen to know personally, and "stealing" as "finding useful," and we can proceed with the description of the ultimate test.

This book provides the first public description of the entire DRA system in reproducible detail. However, I first published an article about the basic principles of DRA, which was the first system to use regression analysis on pitching and fielding statistics in a systematic way, back in 2003. That article was reproduced in a follow-up article in 2005, still available on-line at www. hardballtimes.com/main/article/defensive-regression-analysis-complete-series/, which, again, did not reveal the formulas, but compared then-current Davenport defensive runs estimates with DRA and $MGL(S(t,s,d,v,bh))$.

Finally, in 2007, feeling somewhat guilty about not having gotten the formulas out in book form, I disclosed just the outfield formulas of a basic DRA model (without the Retrosheet data of ground outs and fly outs by opponent batter handedness). Clay Davenport subsequently mentioned DRA in one of his on-line chats at baseballprospectus.com, and alluded to the fact that the version of DRA outfielder formulas published included an adjustment for the park effect of Coors Field.

Shortly thereafter, the Davenport outfielder ratings changed, as shown in the table below.

Change in Outfielder Davenport Defensive Runs Estimates After Disclosure of DRA Outfield Formulas

First	Last	Pos	Yr	D'port before Aug-07	DRA as published August 2007 at Hardball Times	D'port after DRA article
Bobby	Abreu	R	2003	-1	4	0
Bobby	Abreu	R	2004	1	-5	-7
Bobby	Abreu	R	2005	-4	-10	-16
Moises	Alou	L	2003	-4	-7	-9
Moises	Alou	L	2004	-6	-9	-1
Carlos	Beltran	C	2003	6	5	6
Carlos	Beltran	C	2005	3	14	9
Pat	Burrell	L	2003	3	-6	-8
Pat	Burrell	L	2005	-4	-19	-14
Mike	Cameron	C	2003	18	44	34
Mike	Cameron	C	2004	0	13	9
Carl	Crawford	L	2003	14	18	13
Carl	Crawford	L	2005	-1	11	8
Jose	Cruz	R	2003	18	12	18

(continued)

Change in Outfielder Davenport Defensive Runs Estimates after Disclosure of DRA Outfield Formulas *(continued)*

First	Last	Pos	Yr	D'port before Aug-07	DRA as published August 2007 at Hardball Times	D'port after DRA article
Jose	Cruz	R	2004	-14	-10	-15
Johnny	Damon	C	2003	7	2	-2
Johnny	Damon	C	2004	10	14	1
Johnny	Damon	C	2005	-3	9	4
Adam	Dunn	L	2004	-15	-17	-23
Adam	Dunn	L	2005	-8	-29	-12
Jermaine	Dye	R	2004	-2	-6	-6
Jermaine	Dye	R	2005	-2	-4	-8
Jim	Edmonds	C	2004	11	5	-2
Jim	Edmonds	C	2005	19	21	22
J.	Encarnacion	R	2003	3	-4	8
J.	Encarnacion	R	2005	-12	-16	-9
Brian	Giles	R	2004	-10	-1	-8
Brian	Giles	R	2005	-3	6	3
Luis	Gonzalez	L	2003	12	-2	2
Luis	Gonzalez	L	2005	2	-4	0
Shawn	Green	R	2003	7	-2	-2
Shawn	Green	R	2005	3	0	6
Marquis	Grissom	C	2003	-15	2	-6
Marquis	Grissom	C	2004	-5	-1	0
Andruw	Jones	C	2003	18	28	19
Andruw	Jones	C	2004	-1	7	15
Andruw	Jones	C	2005	-5	-10	7
Mark	Kotsay	C	2004	13	9	13
Mark	Kotsay	C	2005	2	-6	-8
Carlos	Lee	L	2003	-2	9	6
Carlos	Lee	L	2004	13	2	14
Carlos	Lee	L	2005	-5	10	-1
Juan	Pierre	C	2003	-9	-4	-2
Juan	Pierre	C	2004	-7	-14	-16
Juan	Pierre	C	2005	-6	-18	-20
Manny	Ramirez	L	2004	-9	-14	-18
Manny	Ramirez	L	2005	-10	-30	-19
Gary	Sheffield	R	2003	3	4	-2
Gary	Sheffield	R	2004	-4	-7	-5
Gary	Sheffield	R	2005	-4	-4	-4
Ichiro	Suzuki	R	2003	13	9	11
Ichiro	Suzuki	R	2004	5	6	4
Ichiro	Suzuki	R	2005	9	18	20
Vernon	Wells	C	2003	-2	-16	-13
Vernon	Wells	C	2004	3	0	4
Vernon	Wells	C	2005	2	-16	-9
				D'port Pre-article	DRA Disclosed in article	D'port After article
	Corr w/DRA			0.70	1.00	0.87
	Std			9	13	12

The Davenport ratings have since changed again—more on that shortly below—but this is where they stood a few months after the DRA article came out, as I began work on this book. It is quite remarkable that the post-disclosure correlation rose from .70 to .87 *per season* (not even just over a two- or three-year average) notwithstanding that the Davenport rating includes a little noise from arm ratings included in the total rating. (In addition, some slight difference will always occur using a DRA method if different samples of major league seasons are used.)

Note also the much smaller standard deviation in the Davenport ratings in the outfield before the 2007 article, which were consistent with the Davenport ratings reported in my 2005 article, still on-line.

I do not know for a fact that implementers of the Davenport system began applying the ideas of DRA disclosed in the 2007 article, but it seems to me that they did. This is why the first test in this chapter uses the Davenport numbers as of August 2007, so that we could compare the Davenport system before it ostensibly incorporated DRA outfield methods. I took care not to publish the DRA formulas for infielders, nor the more advanced DRA system. Correlations between Davenport and DRA also rose in the infield, but only very slightly, and had nowhere near the match between the published version of DRA and the latest Davenport outfielder ratings.

Clay Davenport, in addition to being one of the founders of Baseball Prospectus, is a meteorologist by training. Not a TV weatherman, but an accomplished scientist who has developed computer models to predict rainfall from satellite imagery. If Clay Davenport used the portion of DRA that was disclosed, I would consider that good evidence that the basic DRA approach is in some sense of the word correct.

I also hasten to add that there was nothing wrong with Davenport or his colleagues at Baseball Prospectus using my ideas, and I would be in good company if they were. Davenport's Fielding Runs Above Average, when first proposed in general terms in 1998 (it has never been fully disclosed), stated that it applied the key principle of trying to make sure that pitching and fielding runs added up to team runs allowed by *starting* with team runs allowed and attempting to allocate credit and blame around the field, based on traditional statistics. I believe this elegant 'top down' idea was first proposed and published on the nascent internet by Charles Saeger, in the early 1990s.

The 2009 edition of the Baseball Prospectus annual guide includes a description, starting on page 616, of certain elements of the newest version of Davenport's system, which for seasons since the late 1980s is apparently based on Retrosheet play-by-play data with complete trajectory data, and would, under our system for naming systems, be denoted as $D'port(R(t),f,bh,ph,bo)$. Looks familiar? Yes, it appears to be a combination of the *Fox(R(t),f,bh,bo)* and *Smith(R(t),f,bh,ph)* systems described above, which were published in 2008.

But possibly with a new twist. You may recall that the Fox and Smith systems in form apply the well-known "linear weights" values for a single prevented (approximately .48 runs) and the out created (approximately .27 runs) when a shortstop fields a ground ball, though we discovered in this chapter that the arithmetic of their systems backs out a portion of that value. In the 2009 guide, Davenport specifically notes that he does not use "linear weights," which have been around since about 1980, but "something akin to" linear weights to derive the run values for net plays. I would bet that regression analysis, along the lines of our second-stage regression under DRA, is the tool being used to estimate the run values for net plays, which are calculated with a methodology apparently similar to what Smith and Fox developed. In other words, I believe that *D'port(R(t),f,bh,ph,bo)* may be using the Smith and Fox methods for completing step one in our four-step procedure, and the DRA method for completing step three (the second-stage regression), the idea for which I disclosed in my very first DRA article back in 2003.

Yet you need not fear that the results in Part II will already be reflected in the on-line "DT" profiles for historic players available at baseballprospectus. com. Though we will see, after Part II, that many Davenport outfielder ratings have converged to the DRA values, they are still quite different for the Dead Ball Era, because the DRA method for that time period has never been disclosed. And Davenport infielder methods for seasons before the late 1980s still apparently differ from DRA. There are many surprises still in store.

Putting Great Players from Different Eras on an 'Equal' Footing

In chapter one we briefly discussed the concept that the seeming decline over the course of major league history in the performance of the very greatest players is due to the improvement in the quality of bench and everyday players, which has resulted in a compression in the standard deviation in observed performance. As the late Harvard paleontologist Stephen J. Gould first argued, we should celebrate the compression in the standard deviation of baseball performance as evidence that the quality of play in baseball is getting better.

Princeton University Press has published two baseball books by biostatistician Michael J. Schell in which the author carefully applies the idea of adjusting estimates of career offensive runs for the decline in the standard deviation in measured performance over major league history. Schell's second book, *Baseball's All-Time Best Sluggers*, has the most complete discussion of his methodology.

Schell first identifies the pool of major league batters (excluding pitchers) each season who together account for seventy-five percent of the non-pitcher plate appearances that year ("Regulars"). To qualify for the list, a batter might have to have approximately three hundred plate appearances, which is less than a full-time player but more than a bench player.

Schell then determines the "distribution," in other words, the relative frequency, of each offensive event (walks, singles, double/triples, home runs, etc.) among the Regulars for a season (or perhaps a smoothed five-year average). When the distribution of an event is highly skewed, that is, when most of the values are clumped together while one or a very small number of values are very different, such as in 1920 when Ruth hit fifty-four home runs and no one else hit twenty, Schell mathematically transforms the distribution to make it closer to a so-called "normal" or bell-shaped distribution.

Whatever a player's percentile rank among his peer Regulars during his best 9000 plate appearances is for that (possibly "transformed") distribution for an event (for example, hitting homeruns) might be, it is translated to the same percentile rank for that event in 1977–1992, a historical period of relatively stable distributions of outcomes and neither an extremely low nor high scoring environment. All historical players' batting stats are thus translated into the 1977–92 context so that all can be compared in a consistent context.

Finally, Schell applies a well-developed formula for each player's total batting outs, walks, singles, double, triples, and home runs (translated to the 1977–92 scale) into offensive runs for a standard-sized season. Players are rated on the basis of this per-season rate, with a discount to the extent their careers were short of the 9000-plate-appearance standard for a full career.

Schell's book is a treasure trove of valuable insight, unavailable anywhere else, about many contextual factors in baseball history, such as the effects of parks on various offensive events, as well as an outstanding primer geared to baseball fans on many important ideas and techniques in probability and statistics. However, Schell identified two potential issues with ranking players by adjusting for the standard deviation in performance.

First, the approach only works for evaluating the better players of each era; it cannot be used to rank-order every baseball player who ever lived. As Schell explained, variability in outcomes was greater in earlier eras of baseball. Under the Gould hypothesis, that implies that the talent pool was weaker then. The standard deviation adjustment therefore properly pulls down the ratings of the above-average players in prior eras. But is *also* pulls *up* the ratings of the *below*-average players from prior eras, which contradicts the idea that recent players are getting better. Schell concludes that the solution is to "consider the adjustment method as only working for some fraction of the best players, say the top thirty percent." I agree that the adjustments work better for some fraction of the best players, but, as I will suggest later in this chapter, one that focuses our attention on a more select subset than the top thirty percent of Regulars.

Second, Schell acknowledges that estimating the effect of changing talent pools by putting the standard deviation of outcomes into a common scale only "imperfectly measures the talent pool."[1] He later concludes:

> Perhaps the next major statistical advance will be the incorporation
> of a model that estimates how the talent pool may have improved or

---

1. Michael J. Schell, *Baseball's All-Time Best Sluggers* 4 (Princeton University Press, 2005).

declined on a year-by-year basis. The standard deviation [i.e., percentile] adjustment is really just an initial attempt to deal with talent pool issues. The primary assumption [of my book] that a 90th percentile [Regular] in say, 1901, would be a 90th percentile [Regular] today is not likely to be true for each offensive event that we have considered.[2]

The talent pool adjustment introduced in this chapter attempts to "estimate how the talent pool may have improved or declined" over major league history on a year-to-year basis. Dan Fox has come up with an ingenious method for doing this indirectly for batting performance, by showing the relative decline in hitting by pitchers, but his approach cannot be applied to fielding ratings. This, then, is possibly the first attempt at measuring talent pools that could eventually be applied to adjusting all-time ratings for players at all positions, taking into account defensive contributions.

In some sense the talent pool adjustment we'll be introducing merely extends Schell's insight. Whereas his system is designed to put, say, a batter who was among the top ten percent of all major league Regulars in 1901 on the same scale as a batter who was among the top ten percent of all major league Regulars in 2001, the system introduced here does essentially two things.

First, it puts an outstanding 1901 player who was among the top x percent of the *demographic pool from which major league players were drawn in 1901* (young adult white North American males) on the same scale as an outstanding 2001 player who was among the same top x percent of the *same* demographic pool in 2001.

Second, it treats each 2001 player who is *not* a white North American *exactly* the *same* as his 2001 white North American peer.

By operation of steps one and two, an outstanding 1901 player, an outstanding 2001 white North American player, and an outstanding 2001 player who is not white or North American are put on a similar scale that takes into account the growth in the population of young adult white North American males and the introduction of new demographic groups into baseball.

Before describing *how* to do this, let's see *why* we need to do this.

THE OVERFLOWING MAJOR LEAGUE TALENT POOL

What is the only demographic talent pool from which players have consistently been drawn throughout major league history? White U.S. (and

---

2. Id., p. 214.

occasionally Canadian) adult males between twenty and forty years of age. Guess how much this demographic group has grown between 1900 and 2000? Over three times, as shown in the graph below.

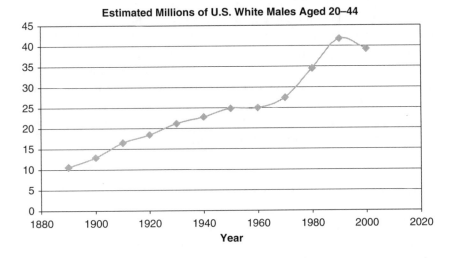

Estimated Millions of U.S. White Males Aged 20–44

These numbers are estimated on the basis of the total resident U.S. population, the percentage of that total consisting of males aged twenty to forty-four, and the overall percentage of the *total* U.S. population that was white, so the numbers are not exact.[3] However, the trend is unmistakable—including the consequences of the Depression baby bust and post-Second World War baby boom.

But the talent pool for baseball players has not merely tripled over the past century—it has grown a great deal more thanks to the inclusion of African-American, Latin American, and Asian players. We'll sometimes call players drawn from any of these talent pools "delta" players, because delta ("Δ") is a Greek letter often used in mathematics to symbolize change. In contrast, we'll sometimes call players from the consistently available (though obviously growing) talent pool of white U.S. males "epsilon" players, because epsilon is a Greek letter often used in mathematics to symbolize very small changes.

About *half* of non-pitchers playing major league baseball today are drawn from the delta pools. Therefore, assuming that players from the epsilon pool are still competing as hard as they always have to become major league baseball stars—and certainly the incentives are vastly greater now

3. Source: www.infoplease.com/ipa/A0110380.html; www.census.gov.

than before—the fact that they can only win about *half* of the roster spots for non-pitchers indicates that, as a practical matter, **the talent pool for major league fielders is arguably *six* times greater than it was a century ago.** That's because the delta pool is generating as much talent as the epsilon pool, which itself has tripled.

That the talent pool for major league fielders could for practical purposes be six times bigger than it was at the beginning of major league history may be difficult to imagine. And indeed there are good arguments against the assumptions that go into this estimate. But there are even better arguments why the estimate is far too low. To understand why, it is important to travel back though the five eras of major league history that we'll be surveying in Part II, with a particular focus on the factors that might impact the talent pool for baseball players, and particularly fielders.

Contemporary Era (1993–Present)

The game as we know it today: stratospheric signing bonuses and salaries attract talent from around the world. In 2009, the Minnesota Twins signed a sixteen-year-old German boy for $800,000, because of his genetic pedigree, extraordinary skills, and training ethic. This "Baryshnikov in baseball cleats," wrote *The Wall Street Journal*, is the son of two ballet stars—his mother would tell him as he was growing up, "Three days away, out of the ballet." I wonder what Babe Ruth would have thought of that.

Since the ideal body size for a non-pitcher is *not* someone unusually tall or big, but rather someone about or a little over six feet tall and about two hundred pounds, there is little reason to believe that the relative increase in popularity of basketball and football has robbed baseball of top fielders. Indeed, as reported a few years ago by *The Wall Street Journal*, virtually *every* athlete given a choice between baseball and another sports career (such as football) chooses baseball.[4] An influx of Latin American players, many of whom have spent most of their young lives training in baseball camps, greatly increases the competitiveness at many key defensive positions, particularly shortstop and catcher.

Players are in the best physical condition ever, by far, and, perhaps more importantly, the *variance* in physical condition is the lowest ever. Probably not a single everyday player smokes cigarettes (though about one-third still chew tobacco, which at least doesn't damage their lungs). Drugs of choice tend to enhance performance, though probably have little impact on fielding.

---

4. *See* Sam Walker, "Football Strikes Out," *Wall Street Journal*, April 16, 2004, p. W4.

Therefore, fewer potentially great players are lost to the talent pool due to poor health or conditioning.

The introduction of batted ball data enables teams to identify low-range fielders who, in prior eras, might have looked good enough to play. So poor fielders are more ruthlessly weeded out now, unless they are very good hitters. Batted ball data also makes it possible for *all* fielders to know where batters tend to hit the ball, so fielders who might not have been bright enough or coached well enough to shift optimally no longer lose their places to those who got by on their wits or those of their managers.

Modern Era (1969–1992)

Baseball is more-or-less fully integrated for the first time around 1970 and the game's demographics are fairly constant for close to a quarter century. Demographic groups not present throughout major league history contribute slightly more than half of outfielders, one-third of all position players, and about one-eighth of pitchers. Free agency begins around 1975 and increases the incentives for potential players at the outset of their careers to choose baseball over football (Dave Winfield), and for good players who are already playing to stretch out their careers.

As Bill James observed, higher salaries also make it economically feasible, for the first time, for players not to work (that is, take another job to make ends meet) in the off-season. This permits more time in the off-season to work *out*. The higher pay also increases the returns to better conditioning. Competition subsequently makes it economically *necessary* for more players to work out during the off season, so player conditioning, though more variable than it will be in the 1990s and 2000s, improves. However, drugs of choice tend not to be performance enhancing (cocaine, nicotine, alcohol), though some probably are (amphetamines). Thus, any given game in the 1970s and 1980s might feature a player who kept himself in superb condition (Brian Downing), another who conspicuously didn't (John Kruk), plus others hallucinating (literally, in the infamous case of Doc Ellis's LSD no-hitter), high on cocaine (too many to mention), or wired on chewing tobacco nicotine (Lenny Dykstra).

Artificial turf greatly increases the demands on outfielders, because it allows batted balls to scoot quickly into the corners and through the gaps, making foot speed more important than ever to cut off doubles, triples, and inside-the-park homeruns. Infielders also have a tougher time; though turf gives truer bounces, ground balls move much more quickly through the infield.

Base stealing becomes more common than at any time since the arrival of the long ball, giving catchers more challenges and opportunities.

The Designated Hitter rule in the American League probably increases average fielding performance in left and at first, as the worst fielders are taken off the field to be designated hitters. Some American League teams with a good designated hitter might also be more willing to carry a defensive star with a weak bat.

Transitional Era (1947–1968)

Jackie Robinson plays his first major league game in 1947, and the percentage of non-white players increases steadily over the next twenty years. Probably most African-American players of undeniable star quality are playing major league baseball by the mid-1950s, but many others who would have impacted replacement-level and average performance levels are only slowly granted admittance to The Show. Players experience jet lag and 162-game schedules for the first time; modern medicine offers a partial remedy (amphetamines). The late Billy Martin and Mickey Mantle (and, no doubt, many others) uphold longstanding drinking traditions. Fielding gloves gradually attain modern size and functionality, thus permitting fielders who might not have had the best hands, but who ran and threw well, to compete more effectively.

Live Ball Era (1920–1946)

The first baseball glove with stitching connecting the thumb and forefinger (Rawlings' "Bill Doak" model) is sold in 1920, making it easier for fielders at almost all positions to 'stab' at batted balls they might otherwise never reach. Errors fall. Double plays soar, as the number of runners reaching first via a walk or a hit increases, stolen bases and sacrifice hits trend down, and strikeouts remain comparatively low. The decreasing importance of fielding bunts and the increasing importance of turning double plays results in second base becoming, for the first time, a more demanding fielding position than third. The overall increase in offense probably permits fewer top fielders to hang on to their jobs if their hitting is weak, unless they are catchers or middle infielders. Probably not that many players play under the influence, but many are unabashedly high-living and not well conditioned. Even Lou Gehrig and Joe DiMaggio smoke cigarettes. The minor league farm system reaches maturity sometime during this period, thereby ensuring that fewer players of major league quality remain stuck in the minor leagues.

Dead Ball Era (1893–1919)

Fielding gloves of some sort are fairly common by 1893, though they look more like leather gardening gloves than what we would identify today as a "baseball glove." Errors are extremely common. The pitcher's mound is moved back to its modern distance in 1893, and the sheer number of batted balls in play is well beyond modern levels until about 1901, when the modern rule counting the first two foul balls as strikes is introduced in the National League (1903 in the American), thus increasing strikeouts and decreasing, slightly, the relative impact of fielding. A probably non-trivial number of players play drunk. The talent pool is probably concentrated somewhat by the collapse of the American Association in 1891, reducing the number of major league teams from seventeen to twelve (and then to eight in 1900), but is then diluted when the number of major league teams increases to sixteen upon the formation of the American League in 1901. Talent procurement is so haphazard that, at the turn of the century, amateur players sometimes just showed up and played in a major league game, if the need arose.

Reversing Direction

Having worked backwards through time, let's quickly march forward, to see again how one talent filter after another has been lifted, to allow much more potential baseball talent from the total population to emerge: The rise of newspapers and wire services around 1900, which increased awareness of major league baseball, especially for kids not living in the Northeast and industrial Midwest. The end, with one exception, of independent minor leagues around 1925, resulting in more talent being concentrated in the major leagues. Penicillin (which saved high-schooler Mickey Mantle from having one of his legs amputated). The development of organized farm systems by Branch Rickey, beginning in the 1930s. Vitamins. Little League. Jackie Robinson and Larry Doby. Expansion West, which finished off the best remaining independent minor league, the Pacific Coast League. Amphetamines. The gradual integration of the major leagues. Contact lenses. Roberto Clemente and the Latin American players he inspired. Free agency and a 250-fold increase in top salaries. Tommy John surgery. Weight training. Batted ball data. Steroids and human growth hormone. Searchable video databases of at-bats, pitch-by-pitch. The most sought-after free agent pitcher of the 2006–07 off-season coming from Japan. . . .

Fewer and fewer potentially great players from the total pool of young men are lost to racism, nativism, the long-term effects of childhood malnutrition or infectious diseases, nearsightedness, child labor, contractual obligations to independent minor league teams, management's inability to project major league ability from minor league statistics, alcoholism, or limited economic motivation. The chances are better now than ever that a boy living in North America, Central America, the Caribbean, Venezuela, Japan, Korea, Taiwan, even now Europe and Australia, with any knack for hitting or throwing a baseball, will discover this talent, play in organized leagues and high school (or full-time instructional baseball 'schools'), attain his optimal height and weight, be motivated to sign a six- or seven-figure minor league signing bonus or get a college baseball scholarship, persist through the day-in-day-out, year-by-year tournament that is minor and major league (and non-U.S.) baseball in order to grasp the American free-agent bonanza, consult major league video and computer data to continue improving his performance, and optimize his diet and exercise regime to stay in phenomenal shape into his forties. Modern technology, broadly defined, has presented solution after solution to problems that would otherwise eliminate talent from the available talent pool, and has thereby effectively expanded the talent pool very far beyond what simple demographic data can show.

For all of the above reasons, we need to make sure that whatever our list of top fielders ultimately turns out to be, it needs to reflect the almost unimaginable growth in baseball's talent pool.

TALENT POOL ADJUSTED RUNS ("TPAR")

Our goal is to put all top fielders throughout major league history on approximately the same scale of career defensive runs as a top fielder whose mid-career season was in 2000, while taking into account the growth of the epsilon talent pool and the increased competition resulting from delta talent pools. We will call this re-calibrated number of career defensive runs a player's talent pool adjusted runs, or "TPAR." Yes, another acronym. Maybe it also makes sense to think of TPAR as promoting Time-independent PARity. Here is how it is calculated.

First, pick the best *epsilon* fielders with at least 3000 innings at that position from each decade of major league history, yielding a total of approximately a hundred. We will rank epsilon fielders with mid-career seasons falling within each decade by career defensive runs at that position ("career runs"). A player's mid-career season is the weighted average calendar year in which he played that position, weighted by innings played at that position ("mid-career season" or "MCS"). The total number of top epsilons drafted from each decade will be based on the relative size of the *epsilon* talent pool in that decade according to the table on the next page.

We will draft our top epsilon shortstops from the following decades based on the relative sizes of the epsilon population (U.S. white males aged twenty through forty-four) at the mid-point of each decade. If we take one player for each percentage point, with rounding, we end up with 101.

Decade-by-Decade Allotment of Top 101
Epsilon Fielders

Decade	Mid-Decade Year	Approx. Epsilon Population (millions)	Percent of Total
1996–2005	2000	39	14
1986–1995	1990	42	15
1976–1985	1980	35	12
1966–1975	1970	27	10
1956–1965	1960	25	9
1946–1955	1950	25	9
1936–1945	1940	23	8
1926–1935	1930	21	7
1916–1925	1920	18	6
1906–1915	1910	17	6
1896–1905	1900	13	5

Therefore, we will draft the top fourteen epsilon fielders by career runs whose mid-career season is between 1996 and 2005, the top fifteen epsilon fielders by career runs whose mid-career season is between 1986 and 1995, the top twelve from 1976 through 1985, and so forth, down to the top five from 1896 through 1905.

Second, plot the career runs of the top epsilon fielders selected in step one by their mid-career season. Examine the plot. Given what we know about major league history, try to explain any trends or patterns.

Third, fit a line or curve that best fits the data. Such line or curve essentially finds the trend in career runs of the very best epsilon fielders over time. Values right on that line are what you would 'project' for a top-flight epsilon fielder with that mid-career season, that is, the "projected career runs" for a top epsilon shortstop with a given mid-career season. Ideally, after backing out the trend indicated by the curve, the points will not only be centered at zero, with no drift, but also have an approximately constant standard deviation over time. We will never achieve that goal, but we will do our best.

Fourth, calibrate the de-trended career runs after step three by adding the projected career runs for a player whose mid-career season is 2000 on the basis of the trend formula determined in step three. This puts the career defensive runs of the top epsilon fielders since the 1890s on approximately the same scale as epsilon fielders whose mid-career season is 2000—in other words, the most recent set of epsilon fielders whose top years as fielders are almost certainly entirely in the past.

Fifth, and most importantly, apply the *same* de-trending and calibration-to-2000 for the career runs of *delta* players, to calculate their TPARs. This assumes nothing at all—in fact, the entire approach taken here for ranking the all-time greats is specifically designed to avoid making *any* assumptions about delta players or the communities from which they are recruited. **We simply treat delta players who performed as well as their epsilon peers exactly the same as their epsilon peers.**

As always, an example will clarify what we're doing in steps one through five and the effects and implications of our key assumptions.

Our First Example

Let's start with a draft of the top epsilon shortstops throughout major league history. Although DRA ratings in this book are calculated for each season from 1893 through 2009, we'll generally only be rating players whose mid-career season was between 1896 and 2005, as we'd rather not rate players who may have had many important fielding seasons before 1893 or whose careers are not yet substantially complete. We draft the fourteen epsilon shortstops with the highest career runs whose mid-career season occurred in 1996–2005, the fifteen with the highest career runs whose mid-career season occurred in 1986–1995, and so forth.

When we conduct the draft at shortstop, we obtain the following graph of career runs for the top 101 epsilon shortstops, ordered by mid-career season.

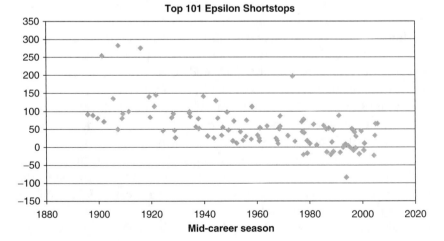

The three highest totals or career runs were recorded in the Dead Ball Era. Things flattened out immediately with the onset of the Live Ball Era. Excluding one outlier, there was a sharp compression after 1960, when integration finally took hold. And sometime in the 1980s the career runs of even some of the *best* epsilon shortstops were below the league-average rate, reflecting the extraordinary competition coming from Latin America.

Though the graph above may tell the story of the relentless increase in competitiveness in fielding at shortstop about as clearly and dramatically as one could wish, there is no simple formula for putting all the top epsilon shortstops on a common scale with constant variance. Though I see a slight bend in the data, when I tried to fit a quadratic curve the coefficients were not statistically significant, so we will be satisfied with the trend line shown immediately below, based on a simple linear regression. The graph thereafter shows the points after the trend is taken out.

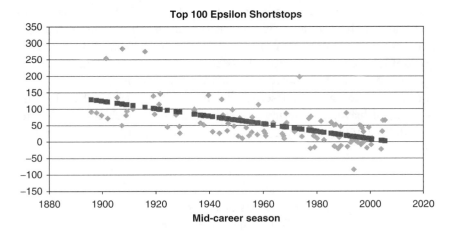

Top 100 Epsilon Shortstops

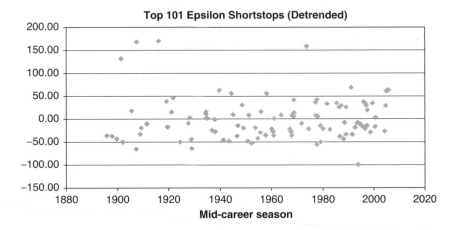

Top 101 Epsilon Shortstops (Detrended)

When you add the number of projected career runs based on the above trend line for a top epsilon shortstop with a mid-career season of 2000, that yields the TPAR for each epsilon shortstop. Therefore, TPAR is equal to career runs ("CR"), minus projected career runs ("PCR"), plus PCR for a player with a MCS of 2000. At shortstop, PCR equals 2306 minus 1.15 multiplied by the player's MCS, so

$$TPAR\text{-}6 = CR - (2306 - 1.15{*}MCS) + (2306 - 1.15{*}2000),$$

which can be more concisely expressed as:

$$TPAR\text{-}6 = CR + 1.15{*}(MCS - 2000).$$

In English, this means that you start with a shortstop's career runs and subtract 1.15 career runs for every year the shortstop's mid-career season falls before 2000, and add 1.15 career runs for each year the shortstop's mid-career season falls after 2000. This puts all top epsilon shortstops on approximately the same scale as a top epsilon shortstop circa 2000, after taking into account the trend showing the effects of increased competition.

Then we apply the same formula to *delta* shortstops. If we sort all delta and epsilon shortstops in descending order by TPAR, we get the following provisional list of top twenty-five shortstop fielding careers of all time, with the symbol for delta ("Δ") indicating a shortstop from the delta talent pool.

Top Twenty-Five Shortstops (Identified Solely by Mid-Career Season) According to Talent Pool Adjusted Runs

MCS	Δ	TPAR
1916		179
1907		177
1974		167
1901		141
1998	Δ	138
1986	Δ	135
1995	Δ	106
1999	Δ	95
1983	Δ	84
2001	Δ	80
1991		78
1978	Δ	73
2006		72
1940		72

(*continued*)

Top Twenty-Five Shortstops (Identified
Solely by Mid-Career Season) According
to Talent Pool Adjusted Runs (*continued*)

MCS	Δ	TPAR
2005		70
1991	Δ	69
1944		65
1958		65
1988	Δ	58
1972	Δ	56
2005	Δ	56
1922		56
1978		51
1969		51
1919		47

I've intentionally omitted the names from this table so that we may focus on the overall patterns without being distracted just yet by individual cases. The three Dead Ball outliers still claim three of the top four spots, which doesn't seem right to me. In any event, we will significantly readjust the list in the shortstop chapter to take into account the many subjective and alternative quantitative factors discussed in the introduction to Part II.

The table below shows what the top twenty-five of all time would look like *without* our demographic adjustment.

Top Twenty-Five Shortstops by
Career Defensive Runs

MCS	Career Runs	Δ
1907	283	
1916	275	
1901	254	
1974	197	
1986	151	Δ
1922	145	
1940	141	
1998	141	Δ
1919	140	
1906	135	
1944	129	
1921	114	
1958	113	
1995	112	Δ
1983	104	Δ
1911	100	
1935	99	
1978	99	Δ
1949	98	

(*continued*)

Top Twenty-Five Shortstops by
Career Defensive Runs (*continued*)

MCS	Career Runs	Δ
1999	97	Δ
1934	96	
1928	94	
1909	94	
1896	92	
1898	89	

Based solely on career runs, there would be only two delta shortstops in the top ten and only six in the top twenty-five; based on TPAR, there are six delta shortstops in the top ten and eleven in the top twenty-five. Based solely on career runs, eight out of the twenty-five greatest shortstops of all time would have played the bulk of their careers in the Dead Ball Era, and six of the top ten would have mid-career seasons of 1922 or earlier. With TPAR, there are still some slightly odd patterns, which we'll address in the final rankings of shortstops, but by *starting* with the TPAR rankings, I believe we'll end up with a much more sensible top forty and top ten.

Our Big Assumptions

Our procedure for obtaining an all-time list of the top fielders at a position based on TPAR relies on two assumptions. The first assumption is that the (miniscule) proportion of the epsilon talent pool capable of fielding at the very highest level has been approximately constant over time. The second assumption is that the very greatest fielding epsilon shortstops across history should be honored equally, and any apparent trend or trends of declining career runs indicate only how much tougher it has become to stand out, due in large part to increasing competition from the new delta talent pools.

Regarding the first assumption, statisticians would rightly object that outcomes at the extreme ends of population distributions are not remotely as regular as elsewhere. And here we're picking the literal "one in a million."

The draft allocation effectively chooses a number of players from each decade proportional to the number of white U.S. males aged twenty to forty-four, or men with twenty-five different birth years at the midpoint year in each decade There were approximately twenty-five million white U.S. males aged twenty to forty-four in 1960, or approximately one million white U.S. males for each birth year in that group. Our chart allocates ten slots for that ten-year period, or one per year. One slot per year, with about a million epsilon males per birth year, yields, on average to one pick from each birth year. The same ratios apply throughout chart by design, so we're effectively picking on average about one white male out of a million per birth year from 1895 through 2005 to create as our cohort of top 101 epsilon shortstops of all time.

In a so-called normal distribution, the top one in a million is about five standard deviations from the average. If you were to randomly generate even ten million numbers from a normal distribution with a mean of zero and standard deviation of one, it is quite likely that you would not generate ten numbers equal to or greater than five. It is quite likely that the number would be surprisingly high and could even be zero. Outcomes at the extremes of a distribution are much less predictable.

Bill James offers the amusing example in *Whatever Happened to the Hall of Fame?* that just because Topeka, Kansas has a larger population than Elizabethan England, one can't use that fact to argue that the best playwrights in Topeka are better than Shakespeare and Marlowe. By the same token, we cannot say that if we allocate two slots among the top English playwrights to Elizabethan England, we must allocate two slots to Jacobin England, and then two more to Georgian England, and then maybe three to Regency England, and five to Victorian England, and so forth. Singularities exist.

But so do trends. Here we're in effect doing our 'random number' test *eleven times*. And finding that our five-standard-deviation outliers are *consistently* getting 'worse' over time in a manner that is consistent with our understanding of baseball history. That cannot be ascribed to the inherent noisiness of sampling from population extremes. By backing out these systematic trends—none of which depends on any particular 'Shakespearian' outlier or 'Shakespearian-Marlovian' pair of outliers—we avoid reaching even more absurd results, such as the conclusion that most of the greatest fielding shortstops of all time peaked before the middle 1920s.

James also argued that once you have a total population (men, women, and children) of at least a million for each major league team (we now have over ten million per team), the actual ratio "no longer means much of anything," because very small populations can generate large numbers of high quality baseball players, while very large ones don't. It is true, as James observed, that a small town in the Dominican Republic, San Pedro de Macoris (population 30,000 when James wrote), has contributed scores of players and more than half a dozen all-stars to major league baseball, whereas China has contributed only one player, who had four plate appearances. But young boys in Macoris are obsessed about baseball, participate in intense development programs, and have few other options for making millions of dollars, whereas there has not been, until very recently, any interest in baseball whatsoever in China. The two are not comparable.

Our 101 top epsilon shortstops were drawn from a large population and large geographic area that has had a fairly strong interest in baseball—not nearly as strong as in the town of Macoris, but consistently stronger than in the world's largest country, China. Given the approximately similar level of interest and participation in baseball across the United States over the past century, the question is whether the population of young adult white males living in the United States between 1896 and 1905 should reasonably be expected to have produced the same (or even close to the same) number of top-flight shortstops as the approximately three times bigger population of young adult white U.S. males did between 1996 and 2005. To the extent one actually tries to take into account the type of non-demographic factors that would account for the different levels of 'Macorian' and 'Chinese' yields of baseball talent, the evidence suggests very strongly that a higher percentage of the best potential baseball talent (in other words, the most relevant subset of this talent pool) is reaching the major leagues from the stable epsilon demographic group than ever before.

Think of some of the factors we identified above, having nothing to do with race or ethnicity, that took talent out of the 1896–1905 epsilon talent pool: childhood malnutrition or infectious diseases, nearsightedness, child labor, contractual obligations to independent minor league teams, management's inability to project major league ability from minor league statistics, alcoholism, limited economic motivation. As we shall see in Part II, some players in those early years chose to stay in so-called minor leagues because they got paid better!

Bill James has pointed out, and I agree with him, that more kids played more baseball (and had more fun doing it) before Little League came along than afterwards, and that is certainly one factor that would mitigate the trend. But I believe that most kids, even today when video games have a hypnotic hold on them, do get to play some baseball, and among the set of kids with any real talent, the obstacles to realizing it are far fewer now than before.

So, to return to the second assumption, we're probably doing a favor to the old-time greats in merely putting them on equal terms with recent epsilon players. And with regard to the players from the delta talent pools, we simply treat them the same as their epsilon peers.

Therefore, I believe the time line adjustments we'll be making still understate the relative value of more recent players. If you are still inclined to disagree, again, in each chapter we will provide five lists—one for each of our five historical eras—of career runs (not converted to TPAR) of all fielders with at least 3000 innings (or estimated innings) at, so you can make your own all-time rankings. But here is how we'll make the time line adjustments at the other positions.

Let's Try That Again

At second base, the top 101 are as shown in the next graph.

Again, not a perfect fit, but not bad, except for two outliers in the 1930s to 1940s that we will explain in chapter twelve. The net effect of the formula for TPAR at second base ("TPAR-4") subtracts (adds) only .51 career runs for each year a second baseman's mid-career season falls before (after) 2000, suggesting that second base has not grown more competitive at the rate that shortstop has.

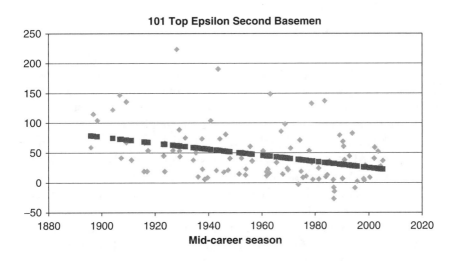

The Near Disappearance of Epsilon Center Fielders

Delta players have so totally dominated center field that we can't find enough epsilon players with 3000 innings played after integration to generate a proportionate sample of approximately a hundred epsilon players throughout major league history. There were only six epsilon centerfielders with at least 3000 innings in center whose mid-career season fell between 1986 and 1995. If we limit that decade's cohort to six, we need to shrink the other decades to keep things in proportion, thus yielding a sample of only forty-two top epsilon centerfielders.

Decade-by-Decade Allotment for Top Forty-Two Epsilon Center

Decade	Mid-Decade Year	Approx. Epsilon Population (millions)	Percent of Total	CF Allocation
1996-2005	2000	39	14	6
1986-1995	1990	42	15	6
1976-1985	1980	35	12	5
1966-1975	1970	27	10	4
1956-1965	1960	25	9	4
1946-1955	1950	25	9	4
1936-1945	1940	23	8	3
1926-1935	1930	21	7	3
1916-1925	1920	18	6	3
1906-1915	1910	17	6	2
1896-1905	1900	13	5	2

Not only is the sample small, the trend line is extremely non-linear. Though it is generally inappropriate to go beyond a quadratic or cubic fit when using simple regression analysis, a quartic curve looked best (see first graph below), as evidenced by the residuals (see graph on the next page).

The trend line of the first graph reflects the steady increase in competition coming from African-American players in center field until about 1990, and the decrease of African-American participation thereafter.

The second graph is by far the closest thing to a constant drift, constant variance model I could obtain. The formula for TPAR in center field is, unfortunately, more complicated, as it involves MCS, MCS-squared, MCS-cubed, and MCS to the fourth power and coefficients with long strings of significant digits. We'll relegate it to appendix A.

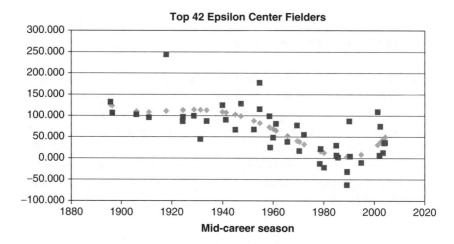

Top 42 Epsilon Center Fielders

Mid-career season

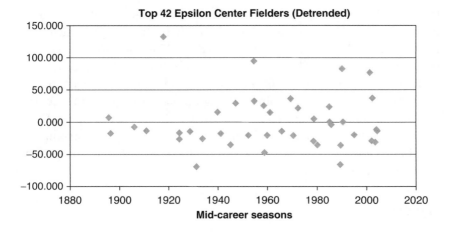

The (First) Exception to the Rule

As we will discuss in evaluating second and third basemen, third base was originally more of a defensive position than second base, until the 1930s, when turning double plays became more important than fielding bunts. The better fielders moved away from the position to second, and the truly outstanding numbers disappeared.

A funny thing happened when integration arrived: the standard deviation exploded.

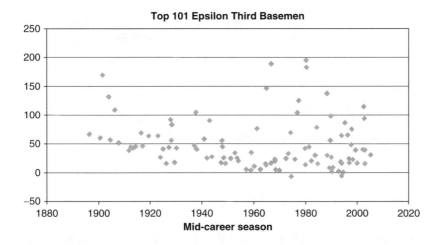

I believe there were two forces at work. Slow non-delta outfielders who could not compete with delta outfielders, but who could hit, were tried at third, where they *under*performed, thus creating *negative* variance. Someone like Killebrew might have played more in the outfield in the 1950s. And slow middle infielders who could not compete with delta middle infielders were tried at third, where they *out*-performed, thus creating *positive* variance. Brooks Robinson might have played short if he had played when Lou Boudreaux did. And Lou Boudreaux, who admitted that he wasn't the quickest on his feet, would probably have played third if he had played in the 1970s.

There is no curve we can fit that won't introduce even more confusion than already exists. In fact, doing nothing results in ratings that reflect the fact that far more fielding talent was located at third base during the Dead Ball Era and after integration was well established. I also see a clear compression in variation in recent years, which I think reflects the weeding out of Killebrew-type third basemen.

Right Field

In right field (see below), we subtract (add) .78 career runs for each year a right fielder's mid-career seasons falls before (after) 2000. Note also that

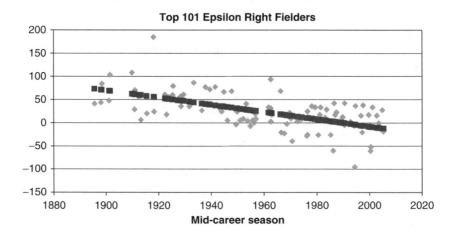

current epsilon right fielders are just about exactly average, which is consistent with the findings in chapter three that ratings in right field have become extremely compressed.

Left Field: Center Field Redux

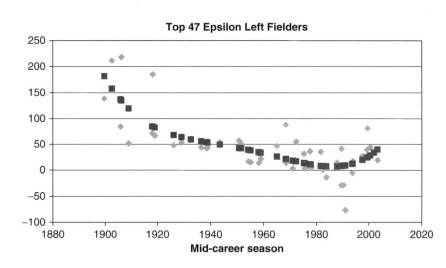

During the Dead Ball Era, left field was a far more important position than right field, in fact, nearly as important as center. So some of the very best fielders were positioned there, and had a huge impact. Three generations later, when integration was more or less complete and artificial turf quite common, speed came into the game. If an outfielder is very fast but can't throw, he plays left, because he can't play center. African-Americans have dominated left field to such an extent that, once again, we have to shrink our draft of epsilon fielder far below a hundred—in fact, to only forty-seven. And once again, as in center, the recent sharp decline in major league participation by African-American players seems to have reduced competitiveness in the field, as epsilon ratings have drifted up since 1990.

Once again, we have a quartic formula too long and ugly to print here but appropriate for appendix A.

First Base: Third Base Redux

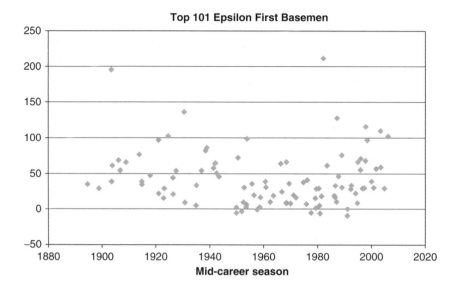

At third, variance exploded around 1960 as integration took hold. For reasons I can't explain, variance also exploded at first base around 1980 (even ignoring the biggest outlier, whom I think many of you can guess). Neither third base nor first base has experienced nearly as much delta competition as was found for outfielders and middle infielders. So, as we did at third, I'm inclined to leave the career runs ratings as they are, without a TPAR calculation.

Our Last Graph

Catcher is similar to third and first insofar as there has been much less competition from delta talent pools than up the middle and in the outfield. All three positions were probably more important in the Dead Ball Era, because of all the bunting and, in the case of catcher, all the base stealing.

However, the increase in variance at catcher since 1960 clearly reflects a change in the demands on the position, rather than demographic factors that I think applied at third. When there were very few stolen bases, it was difficult for Yogi, Campy, or any of their peers to stand out. You can only

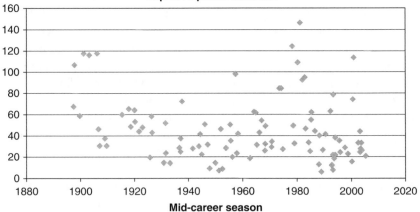

save so many runs by getting the lead runner on an attempted sacrifice bunt, or by preventing wild pitches and passed balls. When base-stealing came back circa 1960, the better catchers could have a fairly large impact.

I don't see a trend in the graph above that can or should be taken out.

A CLOSING PERSPECTIVE

Before beginning the detailed explanation and demonstration of the calculation of TPAR, I said that Michael Schell's book, *Baseball's All-Time Best Sluggers*, effectively puts a batter who was among the top ten percent of all major league Regulars in 1901 on the same scale as a batter who was among the top ten percent of all major league Regulars in 2001, and that the system introduced in this chapter attempts to put a 1901 player who was among the top "x" percent of the demographic talent pool from which major league players were drawn in 1901 on the same scale as a 2001 player who is among *or as good as* the same top "x" percent of players drawn from the *same* demographic talent pool in 2001.

Now that we've shown some of our calculations it is possible to summarize what we're trying to do at each position in just three steps.

First, put the best one-in-a-million fielders drawn from baseball's only consistently available talent pool, young adult white U.S. males, on an approximately equal scale throughout major league history. In other words, take out the trend in top epsilon career runs over time.

Second, add back the number of career defensive runs projected, based on the trend line determined in step one, for a mid-career season of 2000.

Third, apply the exact same de-trending in step one and '2000 mid-career season' add-back in step two to all players who came from demographic groups that have not always been able to participate in major league baseball throughout history.

Though I can easily understand that some might have felt a bit uncomfortable with the concept of "delta" and "epsilon" players, I hope that in the end baseball fans will appreciate that the process yields much fairer assessments of the all-time greats and, if anything, brings greater honor to groups of people who have traditionally been marginalized. And though I am certain that some can and will find disagreement with the particulars of this three-step process just summarized, I do believe that eventually more baseball rankings will incorporate the ideas in this chapter.

In closing, I think it is worth pointing out that TPAR (including TPAR at third, first, and catcher, which simply equals unadjusted career runs) is approximately consistent across positions. The table below shows the the number one, number five, number ten, and number twenty fielder at each position based on TPAR.

Talent Pool Adjusted Runs

POS	#1	#5	#10	#20
SS	179	138	80	56
2B	187	122	90	64
CF	204	134	113	68
3B	195	146	115	79
RF	228	90	46	34
LF	188	128	80	52
IB	212	128	102	75
C	209	117	98	67
Average	**178**	**111**	**80**	**55**

Batted ball data systems have confirmed that a few contemporary fielders at a few positions have probably saved 175 or more runs in their careers, and at other positions certain contemporary fielders could have saved that many if they had remained healthy or had hit well enough to get more playing time. So it appears that TPAR is scaling the top fielders of all time at approximately the current scale of fielder impact. I should also add, however, that (i) the top right fielder is truly off the chart in the sense that no Contemporary Era right fielder has demonstrated an ability to save that many runs on a career basis, (ii) batted ball data systems do not detect quite the same spread of outcomes at first base, and (iii) the very top catcher TPAR is probably about twenty-five runs too high.

The Greatest Fielders
of All Time

Introduction to Part II

We'll rate fielders separately at each position, and each position in approximate order of increasing difficulty, what Bill James termed the "defensive spectrum": first base, left field, right field, third base, center field, second base, and shortstop, with catcher sort of 'off the chart'. We'll address catchers first. This chapter is designed to provide all the background needed to understand the position chapters, whether or not you have gotten through all of Part I.

BASIC FORMAT OF EACH CHAPTER

Each chapter (except the catcher and first base chapters, for reasons discussed therein) marches backward in time, discussing surprising results from the following historical eras: Contemporary (1993 to present), Modern (1969–1992), Transitional (1947–1968), Live Ball (1920–1946), and Dead Ball (1893–1919). The discussion of each historical era will begin with a summary chart of all players who played at least 3000 innings (or estimated innings) and whose "mid-career season" ("MCS," the average calendar year in which he played, weighted by innings played at that position) occurred within that era. Each summary chart will provide the DRA estimate of his career fielding runs above or below the league-average fielding at his position, that is, his "defensive runs" at that position ("Runs"). If he was a "delta" player, that is, a player who would not have been allowed or likely to be recruited to play before 1947, we indicate that with the Greek letter for "delta," or "Δ". Appendix B, available on-line at www:oup.com/us/Wizardry, provides the five historical summary charts at catcher and first base.

Appendix C, available on line, provides all single-season ratings for all fielders (other than pitchers) from 1893 through 2009.

There will be far too many players listed in the summary charts in each chapter for us to say something about each one. Ninety to ninety-five percent of the ratings, however, are hardly worth mentioning, as they are either more or less what one would expect, or so close to average that the fielders in question had little practical impact through their fielding. So we will focus primarily on the surprising or otherwise intriguing results.

In most cases, we'll present the entire fielding record of any fielder discussed. It is important to get fans looking at defensive runs estimates per player and per year. Numbers matter, both to develop appreciation of the reality and significance of fielding contributions, but also to start a conversation to enrich the context around those numbers. This will take time, and I'd like to get as many conversations started as quickly as possible.

The record shown for each player covers just the position being rated (though sometimes we'll separately post results at his other positions), and varies over time based on the amount of data available. For seasons going back to 1952 we will report the following items per season: Year, L (league), Tm (Team), IP (innings played), Runs (and in the case of outfielders, putout runs and assists runs separately), and something denoted as "v-Tm." Innings played are innings or estimated innings played at *that* position. "Runs" are DRA estimates of defensive runs at that position.

The "v-Tm" numbers are the defensive runs by the player *versus* (that is, above or below) the *team* rate, given his total plays made and innings played. That is, if his total plays made, given his innings played, were above the team rate, he will have a positive v-Tm, and vice versa. If a player plays every inning for his team, v-Tm will be zero, because the player's defensive runs at that position will equal the team rating. The more time he misses and the more he over- or under-performs compared to the other players on his team playing that position, the more positive or negative v-Tm will be. A light-hitting defensive specialist should have high v-Tm defensive runs, because he will miss a lot of playing time and should be a significantly better fielder than his better-hitting teammates at that position. Single season v-Tm defensive runs mean little, because they depend on the quality of just one or two other players with any significant impact on the team rating, who may be much better or worse than average. But if there is a clear career trend in v-Tm defensive runs, that will figure into our final assessments.

For seasons before 1952 we lack innings played data, without which it is impossible to calculate v-Tm defensive runs. Following Bill James's advice in *Win Shares*, I have estimated innings played in the infield from 1893 through 1951, and for outfielders from 1920 through 1939, simply by allocating the team defensive runs to each player pro rata based on his share of total plays by his team at that position. This treats all of the fielders on a team at each position as if they were exactly equal in performance, so individual ratings are pulled toward the team rate, generally resulting in more conservative estimates of the impact of individual fielders. For outfielders from 1893 to 1919 and during the 1940s, it is necessary to estimate defensive innings at each respective outfield position in order to derive any defensive runs estimates at all. The methodology is described generally in chapter two and in more detail in appendix A.

After we've finished with the surprises from each historical era, we'll print out a chart of the top forty fielders of all time at that position based on their Talent Pool Adjusted Runs, or TPAR. TPAR translates each player's career defensive runs to a level for a Contemporary Era fielder whose career was centered around the year 2000, as shown in chapter four. The TPAR calculations incorporate a 'talent pool' adjustment going back in time that takes into account the threefold increase in major league baseball's consistently available talent pool, that is, the general population of young adult, white North American males (the "epsilon" talent pool), as well as the sharp growth in talent drawn from the general population of young adult African-American, Latin-American, and Asian males (the "delta" talent pool) since 1947.

At positions such as shortstop, where many players have had long, high-impact careers, more of the top forty merit some commentary, but for other positions, just a few fielders beyond the top ten require any discussion. Each chapter ends with essays about each of the top ten fielders of all time at that position.

BALANCING CAREER AND PEAK VALUE MEASUREMENTS

As Bill James may have been the first to emphasize, there are players with short careers but high peaks in performance, and those with long careers of high value but more modest peaks. Some players miss a lot of playing time within each season, but play at a high level of performance while in the lineup. Others have high-impact seasons because they play virtually every game but then miss entire seasons or otherwise have short careers. How, then, to combine a player's single-season accomplishments into a career rating?

In *The Historical Abstract*, James initially rates players on the basis of an average of their (i) career Win Shares per 162 games played, (ii) average Win Shares for their five best consecutive seasons (regardless of the number of games played in each of those seasons), (iii) average Win Shares for their three best seasonal ratings (regardless of games played in each of those seasons), whether or not consecutive, and (iv) career Win Shares, 'sized' to a typical single-season number using a simple mathematical transformation (the harmonic mean between career Win Shares and twenty-five). James also adds a time-line adjustment (the year of the player's birth, minus 1800, divided by ten).

I tried a few Jamesian approaches to balance overall career, average rate, and peak multi-year performance. One that worked pretty well goes as follows. Calculate for each fielder

1. his defensive runs per 1450 innings (or estimated innings) played at that position ("Rate"),
2. his defensive runs in his *second-best* (to filter out flukey ratings), third-best, and fourth-best seasons in which he was the starting fielder at that position for his team (each a "starting season"), averaged ("Peak"), and
3. his total career defensive runs, *divided by five* ("Career").

If a player has at least four starting seasons, and his Peak exceeds his Rate, take the simple average of Rate, Peak, and Career, which we will call his "Index." If a player does not have at least four starting seasons, or in the extremely rare case in which he does, but his Peak is less than his Rate, calculate his Index by weighting his Rate twice and his Career once.

Here's why it works. In almost every case, the typical fielder at each position good enough to be noteworthy will have a Rate of ten defensive runs per 1450 innings played, a Peak of ten defensive runs in his second, third, and fourth-best starting seasons, and a Career rating of ten as well (that is, fifty career defensive runs, divided by five). Furthermore, the mean and standard deviations of all three measures are remarkably similar to each other across all positions and historical eras, though there is a bit more spread in Career ratings; this causes the Index to be weighted slightly in favor of Career performance, which I believe is appropriate.

In general, an Index of +10 is good, one of +15 very good, and +20 exceptional. The Index also happens to correspond pretty much exactly to the typical number of defensive runs per season by a good full-time fielder (that is, +10 defensive runs), a genuine Gold Glove candidate (about +15 defensive runs), and a clear Gold Glove-quality fielder (about +20 defensive runs). Super-subs who couldn't hit enough to stay in the lineup might have sensational Rate numbers but more modest Career and Peak numbers. Players (and there are many) who had nice Peaks early in their careers but lived off their fielding reputations for too long will have modest Career and Rate numbers but great Peaks.

After laboring on various charts organizing the Career, Rate, Peak, and Index data in all sorts of ways, I made a curious discovery. Each element of the Index, including Career, had at least a .96 correlation with Index, at every position and in each one of the five historical eras we'll survey. Since career defensive runs is one simple number, and it happens to capture the career/ rate/peak components of value indirectly almost all of the time, I decided to do myself, my editors, and my readers a favor, and just rely on career defensive runs as the single number to sum up each fielder career. TPAR is just the talent pool-adjusted version of career defensive runs.

FACTORS TO CONSIDER OTHER THAN TPAR

Of course, no single number can truly sum up a player's fielding career. We will consider all sorts of other evidence before settling upon the final rankings of the very best fielders. Some factors we will consider are as follows:

Late Career Declines

Most fielders have below-average, that is, negative defensive runs in the latter half or third of their careers. In the case of a few historically important fielders, after establishing a clear record of consistent excellence over the course of a handful of seasons, they played too long and pulled their career defensive runs numbers down. We'll highlight those fielders who did establish greatness and not let the decline phase of their careers detract too much from that greatness.

Time Lost for Reasons Beyond the Player's Control

We will give credit for periods of time when a fielder was prevented from playing for reasons beyond his control. The usual legitimate reasons involve war service, segregation, being blocked from playing in the major leagues even when your minor league record shows you're ready to be brought up, and so forth. Players are not credited for time lost to injuries, because being able to avoid or play through injuries is an important skill for which the player is more responsible than anyone else. Bill James explained why this is the right thing to do a quarter century ago.

Evidence from the Best Alternative Systems, When Available

The player essays will primarily address DRA results, but will be informed by other sources of evidence, including good fielding evaluation systems available for different parts of the latter half of baseball history: *Tango* (*p-wowy*) (1993–2007, mainly at catcher and shortstop), *MGL*(*B*(*t,s,d,v,bh*)) (2002–present), *Fox*(*R*(*t*),*f,bh,ph*) (1989–99, 2003–2007), *Smith*(*pgor,bod*) (1952–88, 2000–02), *Smith*(*R*(*t,s,d*)) (1989–99), and *Smith*(*R*(*t*),*f,bh,ph*) (2003–present).

The names given to each system begin with the name of the developer, for example, *Smith* for Sean Smith, or *MGL* for Mitchel G. Lichtman, who often blogs under his initials. If any of the variables 'inside' are subjectively coded by or for an organization, we provide the first initial of the organization, for example, "*R*" for Retrosheet, "*S*" for STATS, and "*B*" for BIS. Retrosheet is a not-for-profit with open source data; STATS and BIS sell proprietary data. For example, a system based on the trajectory ("*t*"), direction or 'slice' of the field ("*s*"), and distance ("*d*") of each batted ball, as estimated by observers at the game (sometimes known as "stringers") and coded by or provided to Retrosheet, or *R*(*t,s,d*), and then converted into defensive runs by computer programs written by Sean Smith, is denoted as *Smith*(*R*(*t,s,d*)).

Here's a brief summary of the strengths and limitations of each system; the detailed analyses that led to these conclusions are provided in chapter three.

Smith(*pgor,bod*) is available on-line at baseball-reference.com under the name "TotalZone." It—is potentially a better system than the current version of DRA for seasons for which we have so-called "play-by-play" data, but not batted ball data, that is, for most seasons since the early 1950s. Play-by-play data does not include subjective estimates of the trajectory, direction and distance of every batted ball, but it does include enormous amounts of objective information about each plate appearance, including the identity of the batter and each player at each position (including the pitcher), whether the batter got a hit, and if the batter grounded or flied out, which fielder converted the batted ball into an out. Using this data, Smith was able to calculate, for each and every batted ball in play, the pitcher's career tendency, relative to the league, to generate ground outs versus fly outs (the "pitcher ground out ratio," or "*pgor*") and the batter's career tendency to generated batted ball outs at each fielding position (the "batter out distribution," or "*bod*").

Though (*pgor,bod*) information is much more limited than batted ball data, it is not subject to coding errors or bias, which is why, even though the data is provided by Retrosheet, we don't 'wrap' the variables around an *R*(·) 'function.' What is really neat about (*pgor,bod*) data is that it can potentially provide an estimate of the likely distribution of batted ball out opportunities throughout the field for a team in any particular season that is much less distorted by the fielding skill of the team's fielders in that particular year. As I've emphasized throughout Part I, DRA may overrate (underrate) an infielder by a few runs in a particular season if his team's outfielders that year, on an overall net basis, are above (below) average. Likewise, DRA may overrate (underrate) an outfielder by a few runs in a particular season if his team's infielders that year, on an overall net basis, are above (below) average. And we will certainly keep that in mind when evaluating players here in Part II.

Using (*pgor,bod*) data, it is possible to develop expected out distribution estimates for a team that are virtually free of distortions created by the fielding skill of the *team's fielders that year*, because (*pgor,bod*) is based on the *career* out distribution tendencies of the team's *pitchers* and opponent *batters*. The tendency of pitchers to generate ground outs or fly outs is very stable from year to year, and the tendency of batters to generate ground outs or fly outs, or pull the ball or go the opposite way, is also very stable. Batters 'face' almost a perfectly average set of fielders over the course of their careers, so the *bod* variable is virtually free of fielding quality bias. And even though certain pitchers might have good or bad outfielders or good or bad infielders behind them in particular seasons, over the course of a typical pitching career those sources of distortion to a pitcher's 'true' ground out or fly out rate should generally average out. Applying the right kind of statistical methods to career (*pgor,bod*) data for each and every batted ball should provide, over the course of a season in which there are typically well over 4000 batted balls hit into the field of play, extremely good estimates of where the outs 'should' have been recorded throughout the field if each and every fielder on the team were exactly average. Then all one needs to do is subtract this estimate per position from the actual number of plays made by the team that year in order to provide an excellent estimate of net skill plays

Unfortunately, as explained in detail in chapter three, certain calculations Smith applies to this raw data reintroduce teammate fielding bias and other biases to an even greater extent than DRA. In addition, the calculations under *Smith*(*pgor,bod*) cause errors to be treated as about half a run worse than simply not making a play, which is incorrect. If you have two fielders at a position who should have, say, +10 defensive runs based on how many successful plays they made, the sure-handed fielder who made his extra plays be avoiding errors might receive +15 defensive runs under *Smith*(*pgor,bod*), and the more error-prone fielder who made more plays by reaching more batted balls that would otherwise be 'clean' hits might receive only +5 defensive runs. This has a massive impact over the course of a few important careers, as we shall see. Fortunately, this error distortion can easily be backed out, so that *Smith*(*pgor,bod*) is very much worth consulting, particularly for infielders.

Smith(*R*(*t,s,d*)) is available on-line at baseball-reference.com, *also* under the name TotalZone. It covers the 1989–99 seasons. This system is based on free Retrosheet batted ball data, the only publicly available, open-source batted ball data in existence. Certain calculations under *Smith*(*R*(*t,s,d*)) cause errors to be over-weighted to an extent that is difficult to calculate exactly, but probably between a quarter and half a run. In addition, the calculation method for locations of the field that are shared by two fielders, such as the hole between third and short and between first and second, as well as the large areas of the outfield labeled left-center and right-center, sharply discounts the value of plays made in those locations—which is precisely where the toughest plays are made. Furthermore, it tends to blend or mix together the fielding performance of neighboring fielders. This will result in good fielders boosting the ratings of lesser fielders playing next to them, and the lesser fielders pulling down the ratings of the good fielders playing next to them. In the infield I've seen evidence that such an approach can shift ten defensive runs per season between players in the shared location. In the outfield, recent studies suggest that the trajectory and location codes in the outfield were subject to significant scorer bias. In theory, $Smith(R(t,s,d))$ should be the best system for 1989–99 because it is based on batted ball data. It is just difficult to estimate how much the calculation and coding issues may impact it.

$Smith(R(t),f,bh,ph)$ is available on-line at baseball-reference.com, *again also* under the name TotalZone. This version of TotalZone utilizes Retrosheet's codes for the trajectory of every batted ball "$R(t)$," which are subject to some subjective coding error—particularly in distinguishing between line drives ("L") and fly balls ("F"). The system also uses purely objective information, such as the position of the fielder ("f") who first touched every batted ball, for example, recording that the left fielder picked up a ground ball hit. This objective but limited data provides a rough proxy for the slice and depth of the field where not only *outs* were recorded, which the ($pgor,bod$) data provides, but where the clean *hits* occurred, which the ($pgor,bod$) data does not. $Smith(R(t),f,bh,ph)$ also tracks whether the batter was right- or left-handed (batter handedness, or "bh"), and whether the pitcher was right- or left-handed (pitcher handedness, or "ph"). Though the outfielder ratings are subject to significant limitations, the infielder ratings are generally very good, except that errors are probably over-weighted by about a quarter of a run and infielders get credit for half of the runs saved by their neighbors, so if a shortstop plays with a very good third baseman and very good second baseman, his ratings can be overstated by quite a bit. We'll just have to keep an eye on those cases. $Fox(R(t),f,bh,bo)$ is a very similar system with similar benefits and limitations. These ratings were posted on Dan Fox's website under the name "Simple Fielding Runs."

$MGL(B(t,s,d,v,bh))$ is available on-line at fangraphs.com, under the name Ultimate Zone Rating, or UZR. It is based on BIS ("B") batted ball data that tracks the trajectory ("t"), slice ("s"), and depth ("d") of each batted ball, like $Smith(R(t,s,d))$, but also the velocity ("v") of each batted ball (useful for ground ball fielding evaluation), batter handedness ("*bh*") and several more variables. The BIS batted ball data, which has been collected since 2002, is also much more refined than the Retrosheet batted ball data, because BIS 'chops up' the field to assign more precise locations for each batted ball. While $MGL(B(t,s,d,v,bh))$ is an excellent system and considered the state of the art, it uses calculations similar to those under $Smith(R(t,s,d))$, which result in significant over-weighting of errors and excessive inter-dependency of ratings of fielders who play next to each other. Still, a terrific gift to baseball fans everywhere.

$Tango(p\text{-}wowy)$ results for shortstops and catchers were reported in *The Hardball Times Baseball Annual 2008*. The system calculates a pitcher's ("*p-*") rate of out conversion at each fielding position "with or without you" ("*wowy*"), that is, with or without the particular fielder being rated. Summing up over all pitchers the fielder played behind, you get an excellent estimate of the number of career plays the fielder *would* have made if he made plays at the same rate as all the *other* fielders at that position who played with the same pitchers. Then all you need to do is subtract that estimate from the actual total number of career plays made by the fielder to get his estimated career net plays made.

With certain refinements $Tango(p\text{-}wowy)$ might very well provide the best estimates of career fielding value. Unfortunately, the current version incorrectly includes fly outs and pop outs for infielders. These plays are over-whelmingly discretionary plays that could be made by two or more fielders, so 'ball hogs' on infield and shallow outfield pop ups could be significantly overrated to a degree that is difficult to estimate. Still, in spite of the 'noise' created by the fly out and pop out data, and the fact that it only includes data since 1993, $Tango(p\text{-}wowy)$ is a very valuable career estimate for shortstops (and certain other isolated ratings Tango has calculated at other positions) of the Contemporary Era.

Data Deterioration

The quality of publicly available data deteriorates almost steadily as we go back in time. Officially, we have complete Retrosheet play-by-play data going back, as of this writing, to 1952. However, several seasons before the 1970s are missing quite a number of games, and the games missed are not distributed randomly but concentrated on a few teams. (It cannot be said emphatically enough that this is not the fault of the volunteers at Retrosheet, who have done an extraordinary job obtaining, checking, and inputting data from original scoresheets.) The number of games missing play-by-play data increases almost steadily as one goes back through the 1950s. For seasons before the 1950s, we not only lack play-by-play data—we even lack reliable counts of the number of innings each fielder played at each position. For seasons before 1920 we lack separate putout totals in left, center, and right field. And for seasons before 1915 or so, the reported number of opponent batters facing each team's pitchers is demonstrably incorrect or just plain missing. Accordingly, the further back in time a player played the more skeptically we will view his ratings, particularly if there appear to be any obvious quirks or outliers, such as an extremely good or bad season, which may be due simply to bad data.

Park Effects

For most seasons since the 1960s or so, parks have had a relatively modest effect on fielding performance except at left field in Fenway and at every outfield position at Coors. However, older ballparks had quirky and often-changing dimensions, which distort some outfielder ratings to a meaningful degree. In general, we lack sufficient outfield data for estimating park effects precisely for the seasons we most need it. However, one general principle is clear: if an outfield position has more (less) territory *relative to* the *other* outfield positions in that park, the outfielder will be overrated (underrated) to some degree. Here's why.

The first adjustment in DRA for estimating net plays is the number of plays made relative to the league average, taking into account the total number of batted balls that land in play *anywhere* in the field. If an outfield is small in *every* direction equally, there will be fewer total batted ball chances for the outfielders (because they'll be hit over the fences), so outfielders should generally not be 'docked' for making fewer plays, all else being equal. (In fact, if the outfield is very small, they will be slightly overrated; in a true 'bandbox' almost every ball not hit over the fence, other than a line drive, would be caught, as happens in the infield.)

However, if the total area of the outfield is close to normal but some areas are small but others large, the *total* number of batted balls landing *somewhere* in the field might be normal, but the number of fly ball chances an outfielder with the relatively large area to patrol will be greater (right field in Crosley Field), and vice versa if the area is relatively smaller (left field in Fenway; right field in the Baker Bowl). So the Crosley right fielder will naturally catch a high proportion of total batted balls, and be overrated, while a Baker Bowl right fielder will catch a low proportion of total batted balls, and be underrated.

In the Dead Ball Era, since there were so few home runs, this factor comes into play only for parks with unusually short fences (such as right field and right-center at the Baker Bowl), because if nobody is hitting home runs, it doesn't matter if you put fences farther back than normal. In the Modern and Contemporary Eras, the dimensions of ball parks have become much more similar, so that really only Coors Field (which is *so* large that all the outfielders are underrated) and left field in Fenway (which is tiny relative to the center and right) require park adjustments.

Player Consistency across Teams

A career assessment is almost certainly essentially correct if a player plays two or three seasons for one team at a given level of performance, is traded, and then has ratings of essentially the same level for two or three years with his second team. This provides the best evidence that we haven't missed a contextual factor in calculating defensive runs. Conversely, if a fielder's outstanding performance for one team suddenly disappears when he joins another team, there is reason to be more skeptical of both sets of ratings.

Player Performance at Other Positions

Whenever a player shows that he can perform well at a more difficult position, he provides good evidence of the quality of his play at his primary position. For example, a left fielder with a couple of good seasons in center, or a third baseman who fills in well at short.

Injuries

Sometimes these can simply be inferred from drops in playing time; the *ESPN Baseball Encyclopedia* also reports, for more recent players, days on the disabled list. If a bad DRA rating in a particular year coincides with a known injury, we can be more confident that good ratings in healthy years were not due to luck.

Evidence from Offensive Statistics of Foot Speed and Changes in Foot Speed

Levels and changes in the level of stolen base attempts and success rate both provide good evidence of how fast a player is and when he loses his speed. Though speed is but one factor in fielding performance, in general, the faster the player, the more credible a record of fielding excellence. Also, *given* a particular level of overall fielding skill, a sudden drop in foot speed usually translates into a sharp decline in fielding performance that would otherwise appear anomalous. The rate at which a player hits triples may also help provide evidence of speed, but park dimensions, particularly in the Dead Ball and Live Ball eras, can distort these numbers substantially.

Specific and Contemporaneous Anecdotes

Testimony (including from the player himself) regarding the degree to which the player focused on fielding, developed new fielding strategies or techniques, or had specific fielding skills or weaknesses, can be illuminating. As we proceed through Part II, I hope you will think of additional specific information that can improve these ratings further. They are, after all, only better approximations to the truth than we've had before.

ONE FACTOR TO IGNORE

Gold Gloves. We will see time and time again that mediocre or even subpar fielders receive Gold Gloves. But before we begin the position chapters, I think it's worth providing the most extreme and illuminating example of how wrong Gold Glove voters can be, and why they are so often wrong.

Derek Jeter

Year	L	Tm	IP	Runs	v-Tm
1995	A	NY	120	-2	-2
1996	A	NY	1371	-10	-1
1997	A	NY	1417	-14	0
1998	A	NY	1305	-12	0
1999	A	NY	1396	-21	1
2000	A	NY	1279	-28	1
2001	A	NY	1312	-29	-3
2002	A	NY	1383	-42	-2
2003	A	NY	1034	-32	0
2004	A	NY	1342	-18	-3
2005	A	NY	1353	-3	0
2006	A	NY	1292	-10	0
2007	A	NY	1318	-13	-2
2008	A	NY	1259	-23	-2
2009	A	NY	1261	-13	-2
Total			18440	-270	-14

Even if Derek Jeter's performance as a fielder is approximately as negative as is estimated by DRA, he has still been a very good all-around player for a very long time, due to his outstanding hitting and base running, with one or two seasons of MVP quality (1999, perhaps 1998) and about four or five all-star quality seasons (2005–07, 2009, maybe 2000). That is a perfect example of a legitimate Hall of Fame candidate. Of course he'll get in on the first ballot, because he'll have over 3000 hits.

The 2002 estimate is certainly too extreme, but Jeter has been consistently far below average under every system. DRA rates him more negatively than $Smith(R(t),f,bh,bh)$, $Fox(R(t),f,bh,bo)$, and $MGL(B(t,s,d,v,bh))$, but those systems incorrectly underweight plays missed in the gaps between third and short and between short and second, and overrate shortstops with high fielding averages. So a low-range, low-errors fielder such as Jeter is overrated. $Tango(p\text{-}wowy)$ would yield an estimate of −267 career defensive runs for Jeter, not even including 2008 and 2009, which for all intents and purposes is the same estimate as DRA. And one of Bill James's characteristically trenchant essays, the "Jeter v. Everett" chapter for *The Fielding Bible* (2006), explained how three different statistical measurements, including some based on BIS batted ball data, along with careful viewings of videotapes of some of Derek's best and worst plays, showed that Derek has been probably "the most ineffective defensive player in the major leagues, at any position."

Derek Jeter has been awarded five Gold Gloves.

Because there has never been a widely known and reliable method of measuring fielding value, people have been left to rely upon their intuitions in Gold Glove voting, and we will see those intuitions have many times led voters far astray. Though Branch Rickey told everybody in 1954 that fielding average is a "worthless," even "deceptive," measure of fielding effectiveness, it is the one fielding number that people are familiar with. Jeter has generally had above-average fielding percentages, and actually led the league once. Since speed is a helpful factor in fielding, a player such as Jeter who has good stolen base numbers will also tend to be rated higher as a fielder. Being flashy or graceful helps. Though I'm not sure that Jeter's patented leap and throw play from the hole is effective (some say it is better to learn to plant your feet quickly to get off a more powerful throw), it looks dramatic. Woody Allen famously said that eighty percent of success in life is showing up. Well, Derek Jeter has shown up game after game for a long time, which has made him more present in the mind of voters. And, to use some marketing jargon, Jeter has probably further increased his 'share of mind' by his highlight reel plays, including his famous 'flip' at home plate in the 2001 playoffs and his leap into the stands to catch a foul ball—possibly the deepest leap into the stands in all of baseball history—that left him literally bloodied but unbowed.

Gold Gloves are honors, and people enjoy honoring people they respect and admire. There's a lot to respect and admire about Derek Jeter as a ballplayer, and his five Gold Gloves are best understood as awards for being one very good ballplayer for a very long time.

It's vital to keep in mind that most of what makes a fielder effective is "invisible," as Bill James explained over thirty years ago: Positioning per opponent hitter. Positioning per pitch. Positioning for base runner defense (for example, playing close to second to defend stolen base attempts, or 'in' to get a double play or a runner at the plate). First step. Acceleration. For outfielders, the path they take to the ball. These components of fielding performance are rarely if ever seen, because they all occur well before the ball and fielder converge into view.

Jeter is only the most spectacular case of why Gold Gloves should be given almost zero weight in evaluating fielders throughout major league history. Time and again we will discover that Gold Gloves are rarely awarded to the most deserving fielders and often awarded to mediocre or even genuinely bad fielders. Now, to be fair, there really haven't been good, widely known, open-source measures of fielding until very recently, such as Sean Smith's various systems. So I'm not blaming anybody. What I *am* saying is that we shouldn't, and therefore won't, trust Gold Glove voters. But, to drive the point home, we'll directly address cases in which the implied fielding value of players who have received multiple Gold Glove awards differs most from our current best quantitative estimates of their actual defensive contribution.

Catcher

We'll begin with our briefest position chapter. Brevity is called for. On the basis of what is 'known', catchers should have had a modest impact on defense throughout most of major league history, and I don't have that much to add to what is already 'known'. Most importantly, what is already 'known' may be largely beside the point.

Catcher evaluation in some sense has nothing to do with "fielding," if by fielding we mean catching a batted ball and turning it into an out. Yes, catchers very occasionally field squibblers that might otherwise result in infield hits, and catch pop ups directly behind the plate that other infielders would not be able to reach. But ninety-five to ninety-nine percent of catcher defense, conventionally defined, is really about preventing the advancement of opponents who have *already* reached base safely, by (i) preventing them from advancing on passed balls and wild pitches, (ii) preventing them from stealing bases, either by throwing them out stealing, picking them off, or scaring them into staying put, (iii) getting the lead runner out on sacrifice bunt attempts, and (iv) blocking the plate.

As has been determined any number of ways by analysts going back at least forty years, preventing base runner advancement is inherently much less important than preventing batters from reaching base safely in the first place. The difference a pitcher makes by striking out (+.27 runs 'saved' on the out created) rather than walking (−.33 runs 'allowed') a batter is worth about .60 runs. The difference a shortstop makes by turning a ground ball into an out (+.27 runs 'saved' on the out created) rather than allowing it go through for a single (−.48 runs 'allowed') is worth about .75 runs. The difference an outfielder makes by catching a deep drive (+.27 runs 'saved' on the

151

out created) rather than allowing a double (–.78 runs 'allowed' on a double) is about 1.05 runs.

The difference a catcher makes by preventing a base runner from advancing one base on a passed ball, wild pitch, or sacrifice bunt is about .20 runs 'saved'—only one-third to one-fifth of the impact of each batter defense outcome. It is true that the difference between throwing out the runner on a stolen base attempt (about +.40 runs 'saved') and allowing that runner to steal the base (about –.20 runs allowed) sums to about +.60 runs saved (as reflected in the DRA formulas after 1952). But once a catcher shows that he is difficult to run on, his opportunities to make that high impact play go down, as was most dramatically seen in the case of Johnny Bench. Of course, if blocking the plate literally prevents a run being scored, that is a high impact play. But how often, over a course of a season, is a run saved *mainly* because the catcher blocked the plate well? Credit for that play must go, in almost every case, to the assisting fielders who made the quick and accurate throws that made the play possible.

This chain of reasoning reaches a similar conclusion to that reached by many studies of team *offense*, which have shown that teams do *not* 'create' a lot of runs for themselves by bunting or stealing bases or advancing on passed balls and wild pitches. So, when you think it through on the basis of the traditional factors for evaluating catcher defense, there would appear to be significant limits to how many runs they can save their teams.

In terms of measuring that impact, we have complete data since the early 1950s on at least the two biggest components of catcher defense: catching or at least blocking pitches, and preventing stolen bases, either by throwing runners out or deterring stolen base attempts. During our tests and descriptions of various recent defensive systems, we mentioned that the system for catchers that probably provides the best career assessments for measuring the impact of catchers on base runner advancement is *Tango(p-wowy)*. By comparing rates of passed balls, wild pitches, stolen bases, and runners caught stealing when *pitchers* are pitching *with* the catcher being rated and when the *same* pitchers are pitching *without* the catcher being rated (that is, to different catchers), the 'pitcher with or without you' *Tango(p-wowy)* approach controls for the known fact that pitchers impact these outcomes. Pitchers who give up a lot of walks, or throw the knuckleball, will 'cause' both a lot of wild pitches and passed balls. Pitchers without a good pickoff move, or who don't have a quick enough motion from the stretch, are easier to steal on.

When we conducted our tests of various defensive systems, DRA appeared to reach similar career results as *Tango(p-wowy)*. However, DRA also provides catcher ratings season by season, as do the various on-line and hard-copy baseball encyclopedias. To the extent DRA ratings diverge on a career basis from *Tango*(*p-wowy*), they tend to do so because they also give catchers credit for the ground ball fielding plays.

For seasons before the early 1950s, we lack the kind of Retrosheet play-by-play data that makes it simple to track, plate appearance by plate appearance, each pitcher–catcher pairing necessary for a *Tango*(*p-wowy*) calculation. We don't have separate individual catcher totals of wild pitches or stolen bases allowed. We don't even have team seasonal totals of stolen bases allowed for most seasons before the early 1950s. This drastically limits the precision of any catcher ratings for the first half of major league history.

Pete Palmer's baseball encyclopedias include his estimates of stolen bases allowed per season per team, but when I tried to incorporate them into the overall DRA model they threw off other aspects of that model. So I went back to estimating catcher value in controlling stolen bases on the basis of simple assists rates. It is well known that assists rates are poor evaluators of exceptional recent catchers such as Bench, because runners just stopped running on them. For most of the Live Ball and Transitional Eras this doesn't matter all that much, because there were so few stolen bases at all. And, during the Dead Ball Era, base runners were far more aggressive— average success rates that have been recorded for team offenses during that period are much lower than for the past fifty years. So perhaps Dead Ball Era base runners were not intimidated by Bench-like arms. Which would mean that assists rates are still meaningful. But, to be clear, we can't really demonstrate this.

Despite the above data limitations, the DRA estimates for catchers who played during the first half of major league history are largely consistent with their reputations. And at catcher, I do believe that subjective evaluations are quite valid, with one vast caveat we'll address shortly. You *can* see how good a catcher's arm is. You *can* see how well he blocks pitches. You *can* see how quickly he can run back to retrieve a pitch that has gotten by him. You *can* see how quickly he pounces on bunts. You *can* see how well he fields squibblers and pop ups far from the plate. You do *not* need to know anything about his 'invisible' range, because he's forced to squat in more or less the same position before each pitch.

Furthermore, because catcher defense is *not* 'invisible', we can reasonably infer a lot about the quality of some catchers' defense from their *offense*. A few of the forgotten catchers of the Dead Ball Era had the worst offensive statistics in history. Their statistics were so obviously bad, even without using modern analytic interpretations, that the only reason they could have been allowed to play is because their teams could *see* how well they handled their catching responsibilities. More was at stake then at catcher. Passed balls and wild pitches were much more common. Opponents were constantly— automatically—bunting and base stealing. Bill James noticed a few years ago that unassisted putouts by catchers were higher years ago, indicating that perhaps catchers fielded more pop ups. And even fielding pop ups was tougher in those days, because catcher mitts were not well designed to 'trap' a ball.

Now perhaps those teams made an incorrect decision to let those catchers play. It is possible that, with perfect information of the *Tango(p-wowy)* variety, the runs they saved on defense did *not* in fact make up for the runs they lost on offense. But the fact that they were allowed to play in spite of their offense is very good evidence that they were very good defensively, even if not by enough to make them objectively good overall players.

Though there are some discoveries of long-forgotten catchers in store, I'm offering up the catcher ratings in some sense both cautiously and cavalierly, because we may be missing the *most* important part of catching: calling pitches and, in general, managing the pitching staff. Now many studies have been done over the years suggesting that catchers actually don't have much impact in this area, or any impact that can be shown to be statistically significant. But Craig Wright, one of the pioneers of baseball statistical analysis, along with Bill James, Pete Palmer, and Dick Cramer, has recently written an article that throws this supposedly well-supported idea into doubt.

In *The Hardball Times Annual 2009*, Wright contributed a long article about the career development of Mike Piazza, which culminated in a 'with or without you' type of analysis estimating the number of walks and hits Mike Piazza saved his teams, based on the rates of unintentional walks, hits, etc., allowed by the pitchers with Piazza catching and without Piazza catching. Wright doesn't provide a defensive runs estimate in the article, but whatever such estimate might be, it would easily exceed Piazza's negative base running defensive runs as measured by *Tango(p-wowy)*, DRA, or any other system.

I believe this is one of the most important studies ever done in defensive evaluations, but I have yet to see a single baseball blog or website that has led any detailed critique about its methods or speculation about its implications for rating large sets of contemporary or historically important catchers. Here are my thoughts.

First, someone should redo the study while taking into some account the fact that Piazza played almost his entire catching career in the two parks, Dodger Stadium and Shea Stadium, which Michael Schell in *Baseball's All-Time Best Sluggers* has shown boosted strikeouts and generally suppressed offense perhaps more than any other stadiums during Piazza's career. I have the feeling that a lot of what Wright found could be attributed to park effects, though probably not all.

Second, assuming Wright's findings are basically correct, we have to find another methodology in order to rate other catchers, because the sample sizes for ninety-nine percent of catchers are simply too small to detect reliably the subtle, but in the very long term, possibly large impact of catchers like Piazza on walks and hits allowed. One approach might be to narrow the analysis solely to strikeouts and unintentional walks per plate appearance, with park effects taken into account, and omit home runs, which are subject to very powerful park effects, as well as non-home runs hits, which are largely controlled by the team's fielders. 'With or without you' differences in the relatively 'pure' binomial outcomes such as unintentional walks per plate appearance (excluding intentional walks), or strikeouts per plate appearance (excluding intentional walks), would generally attain statistical significance in shorter time frames.

Third, again assuming that Wright's ultimate finding is sound, and in fact Piazza was a pretty good catcher even though he was possibly the worst-ever catcher with a long career at controlling the running game, we must substantially—almost entirely—discount almost every quantitative catcher rating ever given, until, at the very least, we can find some reliable methodologies for measuring catcher impact on pitcher strikeout and walk rates.

With that in mind, we'll focus just on our top forty list. Since (anyone's) numbers for catcher must be suspect, we'll be less concerned with validating conventional wisdom than in pointing out interesting cases most worthy of additional exploration.

As we discovered in developing the TPAR models at each position, the three positions that have so far attracted the least delta talent (third base, first base, and catcher) have not shown any historical trends in defensive runs that could or should be 'backed out'. Therefore, catchers are simply ranked on the basis of their estimated career defensive runs, without a separate TPAR calculation.

The five separate charts of players in each historical era with 3000 or more innings are shown in appendix B on-line. It's stunning how many more catchers have been able to rack up at least 3000 innings than players at any other single position could. The damage that playing the position does to each individual player opens up spots to more successors. If you are a mediocre hitter and slow, but willing to take the punishment of playing catcher, it has to be your best shot at making it to The Show and collecting a pension. Something tells me delta talent pools will identify this opportunity and exploit it. This has already happened to a limited extent, as more Latin American players have begun catching.

Let's first deal with the one 'fluke' appearance and the two most noticeable absences from our top forty.

The fluke result is Einar Diaz, who saved about six runs in his career under *Tango(p-wowy)*, which just measures base runner defense, and thirteen runs under Smith's systems. DRA gives Einar full credit for a lot of

Top Forty Catchers of All Time (TPAR equals Runs)

MCS	First	Last	IP	Runs	Δ
2000	Ivan	Rodriguez	19156	209	Δ
1981	Bob	Boone	18456	146	
1978	Steve	Yeager	9421	124	
1906	Bill	Bergen	7950	118	
1901	Jack	Warner	8594	117	
1903	Lou	Criger	8602	116	
2001	Brad	Ausmus	15669	114	
1980	Jim	Sundberg	15896	109	
1898	Duke	Farrell	6362	107	
1957	Del	Crandall	12274	98	
1983	Gary	Carter	17366	95	
1982	Rick	Dempsey	12319	93	
1974	Thurman	Munson	11106	85	
1974	Johnny	Bench	14486	85	
1988	Tony	Pena	15969	79	Δ
1993	Charlie	O'Brien	5970	79	
2001	Einar	Diaz	5181	75	Δ
2001	Mike	Matheny	10049	74	
1938	Al	Lopez	15675	72	
1898	Chief	Zimmer	6355	67	
1918	Ivey	Wingo	9754	65	
1920	Frank	Snyder	9918	64	
1992	Ron	Karkovice	6970	63	
1964	Clay	Dalrymple	7831	62	
1985	Lance	Parrish	15199	62	
1965	Buck	Rodgers	7380	62	
1915	Sam	Agnew	4162	60	
2004	Bengie	Molina	9846	59	Δ
1900	Joe	Sugden	6002	59	
1926	Zack	Taylor	6516	58	
1985	Mike	Heath	8372	55	
1967	Johnny	Edwards	11347	54	
1920	Walter	Schmidt	6053	53	
1999	Charles	Johnson	9717	53	Δ
1931	Gabby	Hartnett	15020	52	
1946	Clyde	Kluttz	4308	51	
1955	Sherm	Lollar	12582	50	
1979	John	Stearns	5867	49	
1968	Mike	Ryan	5000	49	
1919	Hank	Gowdy	6704	49	

ground balls fielded, which may reflect just picking up a lot of bunts that were discretionary chances: 'bunt' hogging analogous to ball hogging on infield and short outfield fly balls. I'm sure he was a fine catcher, but he doesn't belong among the top forty of all time. Though not quite a flukey result, I believe Munson is too high on the list, also because too many of his defensive runs under DRA are attributable to fielding ground balls, many or most of which were probably discretionary plays as well.

The two catchers most fans care about who do not appear on the top forty list are Campy and Yogi. On a rate basis, Roy Campanella was sensational at throwing out base runners in the seasons for which we have stolen base data, even taking into account that the average success rate on stolen base attempts was lower in those days. He also led the league in double plays twice. Though not quite as good as Campy, Yogi Berra was well above average in throwing out baserunners in the years for which we have the data, and probably better than Campy at preventing passed balls and wild pitches. So I would agree with anyone who would say that Berra and Campanella were A or A+ catchers—it's just that they didn't have as many opportunities to make a measurably significant impact, because stolen bases didn't become more frequent until just as their careers were ending.

Honorable Mention: Gabby Hartnett

Year	L	Tm	IP	A2 runs	PB runs	Runs
1922	N	CHI	190	4	1	5
1923	N	CHI	342	-5	3	-2
1924	N	CHI	878	1	-7	-5
1925	N	CHI	981	11	3	13
1926	N	CHI	685	10	-7	3
1927	N	CHI	1075	2	-1	2
1928	N	CHI	962	11	-3	8
1929	N	CHI	8	0	0	0
1930	N	CHI	1229	-5	3	-2
1931	N	CHI	887	3	3	5
1932	N	CHI	974	4	2	6
1933	N	CHI	1189	0	1	1
1934	N	CHI	1092	8	3	10
1935	N	CHI	941	7	7	13
1936	N	CHI	961	2	5	7
1937	N	CHI	843	-2	-1	-3
1938	N	CHI	698	-2	-1	-3
1939	N	CHI	677	2	-3	-1
1940	N	CHI	145	-1	0	-1
1941	N	NY	261	-2	-3	-4
Total			15020	47	5	52

"A2 runs" takes into account both bunts fielded and runners caught stealing. "PB runs" estimates how well the catcher prevented passed balls and wild pitches relative to his backups. The idea is to charge the team's pitchers for all passed balls and wild pitches, since they control both outcomes much more than their catchers (ask Jim Sundberg, who had to catch Charlie Hough). But then you credit or charge each catcher relative to his backups on the basis of his passed ball rate relative to his backups. In a single season this means little, but catchers miss so much playing time and have such short careers, the typical catcher's replacements over the course of his career are generally more diverse and get a lot of playing time, thereby establishing a somewhat reasonable 'control' group against which the catcher you're rating can be compared. In any event, I don't believe any other analyst has shown that any catcher had a major impact (say, anywhere near fifty career defensive runs) by preventing passed balls or wild pitches. I'll soon propose a few from eras in which passed balls were much more common.

Gabby Hartnett could rank much higher. When I tried using Pete Palmer's estimates of stolen bases allowed, Hartnett rocketed up the all-time rankings. When Hartnett started playing close to full time in the mid-1920s, there tended to be about 600 stolen bases per year in the National League; by the mid-1930s, this was down to about 400, where it stayed, more or less, until the early 1960s. So Hartnett was getting many more opportunities to throw out runners than Yogi or Campy.

Honorable Mention: Charlie O'Brien

Year	L	Tm	IP	A2 runs	PB runs	GO2 runs	CS runs	Runs
1985	A	OAK	39	-1	1	-1	0	0
1987	A	MIL	91	3	0	0	3	3
1988	A	MIL	322	3	2	2	1	5
1989	A	MIL	529	6	5	4	1	11
1990	A	MIL	381	3	0	2	1	3
1990	N	NY	211	4	3	1	3	7
1991	N	NY	488	1	3	1	-1	4
1992	N	NY	427	8	3	3	5	11
1993	N	NY	494	3	2	2	1	6
1994	N	ATL	383	3	5	3	0	9
1995	N	ATL	510	-8	5	-6	-3	-3
1996	A	TOR	801	2	6	0	2	9
1997	A	TOR	592	8	1	1	8	9
1998	A	CHI	455	-4	3	-4	0	-1
1998	A	LA	31	0	1	0	0	1
1999	A	LA	171	1	4	0	1	5
2000	N	MON	44	-1	1	1	-1	0
Total			5970	32	47	8	23	79

For catcher seasons since the early 1950s, we still report A2 runs and PB runs, but also report A2 runs disaggregated as GO2 runs (from fielding ground balls) and SB runs based on runners caught stealing and stolen bases allowed.

Charlie O'Brien is sixteenth on our list, despite playing only one season in which he led his team's catchers in innings played. On a rate basis, he is the best catcher since the 1950s under *Tango(p-wowy)*, which credits him with +76 career defensive runs, nearly identical to the DRA estimate. Clay

Dalrymple, number twenty-four, finished second behind Charlie O'Brien on a rate basis under *Tango(p-wowy)*.

Honorable Mention: Rick Dempsey

Year	L	Tm	IP	A2 runs	PB runs	GO2 runs	SB runs	Runs
1969	A	MIN	10	0	0	0	0	0
1970	A	MIN	16	-1	0	0	0	-1
1971	A	MIN	37	0	1	1	0	1
1972	A	MIN	113	-1	-2	-1	0	-3
1973	A	NY	31	-1	0	0	-1	-1
1974	A	NY	237	6	0	1	5	6
1975	A	NY	116	0	1	1	-1	1
1976	A	NY	67	1	1	0	1	2
1976	A	BAL	469	6	-1	0	6	4
1977	A	BAL	745	7	3	-1	8	9
1978	A	BAL	1145	8	-2	2	7	6
1979	A	BAL	1015	19	3	12	7	23
1980	A	BAL	878	4	3	-3	6	6
1981	A	BAL	665	3	6	0	3	9
1982	A	BAL	944	4	-1	4	0	3
1983	A	BAL	989	12	4	10	2	16
1984	A	BAL	907	-2	3	3	-4	1
1985	A	BAL	1008	-2	1	2	-4	-1
1986	A	BAL	922	2	4	3	-1	6
1987	A	CLE	422	-3	3	-4	1	0
1988	N	LA	450	0	0	1	0	1
1989	N	LA	379	6	-1	1	5	5
1990	N	LA	314	4	-3	2	1	0
1991	A	MIL	408	0	-1	2	-1	-1
1992	A	BAL	30	0	-1	0	-1	-2
Total			12319	70	22	33	37	93

Tango(p-wowy) doesn't detect Rick Dempsey's value, but if you drop the flukey outcome for 1979, which probably reflects just a lot of bunt defense of marginal value, DRA matches the career total reported by Sean Smith almost exactly. Dempsey is a great example of a good-field-no-hit player that Earl Weaver rightly rewarded with significant playing time. I can't think of anyone else who contrived to get on a major league roster for twenty-four consecutive seasons while having a below average on-base percentage, far below average slugging percentage, no speed, and not even any particular bunting ability. Nor was he reputed to have a strong arm. Just the kind of guy this book is meant to honor.

Many will say it's crazy to keep Johnny Bench (see next page) off the top ten list, and Smith rates Bench slightly higher overall, based on stronger numbers in the latter half of his career, but a good round hundred runs seems to be a fair

Honorable Mention: Johnny Bench

Year	L	Tm	IP	A2 runs	PB runs	GO2 runs	SB runs	Runs
1967	N	CIN	233	3	0	2	0	3
1968	N	CIN	1301	14	-2	10	4	12
1969	N	CIN	1249	8	1	1	7	9
1970	N	CIN	1158	17	-2	11	6	15
1971	N	CIN	1169	6	5	3	2	10
1972	N	CIN	1139	4	3	-2	6	8
1973	N	CIN	1115	9	3	5	4	12
1974	N	CIN	1133	8	3	2	7	11
1975	N	CIN	1002	4	3	-1	5	7
1976	N	CIN	1071	1	-1	-4	5	0
1977	N	CIN	1065	1	4	-2	3	5
1978	N	CIN	836	2	-4	-3	5	-2
1979	N	CIN	1083	3	3	0	3	6
1980	N	CIN	847	-11	2	-8	-3	-9
1981	N	CIN	60	0	-1	0	0	-1
1982	N	CIN	1	0	0	0	0	0
1983	N	CIN	23	0	0	0	0	0
Total			14486	68	17	12	56	85

upper bound, which would just barely get him there—and we have more interesting cases to promote. Bench may have limited his practical effectiveness by being too obviously good. Nobody ran on him; nobody would bunt the ball anywhere near where he could field it. Since very few teams create net runs on offense by bunting or stealing bases, completely terrifying them from even trying has little or no net impact. Though no current method estimates that Bench was the greatest fielding catcher of all time, he could be

Honorable Mention: Duke Farrell

Year	L	Tm	IP	A2 runs	PB runs	Runs
1893	N	WAS	676	18	10	27
1894	N	NY	943	17	5	22
1895	N	NY	542	0	1	1
1896	N	NY	257	2	1	3
1896	N	WAS	139	2	0	2
1897	N	WAS	494	12	1	13
1898	N	WAS	435	9	1	9
1899	N	WAS	23	1	1	2
1899	N	BRO	656	8	12	21
1900	N	BRO	648	-6	4	-2
1901	N	BRO	489	9	-3	7
1902	N	BRO	448	7	0	7
1903	A	BOS	126	4	-4	-1
1904	A	BOS	425	5	-6	-1
1905	A	BOS	63	0	-3	-3
Total			6362	87	20	107

the greatest catcher of all time, based on all-around value. Our first certifiable smartie, Bench was valedictorian of his high school class.

My first case of a Dead Ball Era catcher whose career deserves more attention and analysis, Duke Farrell (see table on prior page) set a record on May 11, 1897, that stood for a century, by throwing out eight of nine would-be base stealers in one game. We're also missing his first five major league seasons—he began his career in 1888.

Number Ten: Gary Carter

Year	L	Tm	IP	A2 runs	PB runs	GO2 runs	SB runs	Runs
1974	N	MON	48	1	1	1	0	2
1975	N	MON	521	6	2	2	4	8
1976	N	MON	493	4	1	-2	6	5
1977	N	MON	1271	6	2	8	-2	8
1978	N	MON	1304	6	3	-2	8	9
1979	N	MON	1214	9	1	-2	11	9
1980	N	MON	1304	18	5	9	9	23
1981	N	MON	861	6	1	-2	8	7
1982	N	MON	1353	11	2	2	9	14
1983	N	MON	1261	15	1	1	14	16
1984	N	MON	1200	-3	0	-4	1	-4
1985	N	NY	1251	0	4	-4	3	4
1986	N	NY	1078	-6	1	-3	-3	-5
1987	N	NY	1142	-2	3	-1	-2	1
1988	N	NY	998	-8	2	2	-11	-6
1989	N	NY	369	2	0	2	0	1
1990	N	SF	534	-3	0	-1	-2	-3
1991	N	LA	497	5	-2	5	0	2
1992	N	MON	665	-3	5	0	-3	2
Total			17366	62	33	11	51	95

I imagine that Expos fans were angry when Gary Carter got traded for Hubie Brooks, Mike Fitzgerald, Herm Winningham, and Floyd Youmans before the 1985 season. At the time, as a Mets fan, I was ecstatic. However, Carter had already lost his arm the year before the trade, and had only one more noticeably great season at the plate, the year after the trade. But he kept the final inning alive in the sixth game of the 1986 World Series, for which I will always be grateful.

I don't think any catcher in major league history, including Yogi Berra, ever put together a string of nine consecutive full-time catching seasons remotely of the overall (offensive and defensive) quality and consistency of Carter's 1977 through 1985 seasons.

From the 1930s through the 1950s, there were on average only .30 to .40 stolen bases a game in the National League. That jumped up in the early 1960s, just as the career of Del Crandall (see next page) was winding down. One way to put his

Number Nine: Del Crandall

Year	L	Tm	IP	A2 runs	PB runs	GO2 runs	CS runs	Runs
1949	N	BOS	553	3	2			5
1950	N	BOS	581	3	1			4
1953	N	MIL	927	5	1	3	2	6
1954	N	MIL	1167	10	4	10	0	14
1955	N	MIL	1123	3	2	1	2	5
1956	N	MIL	823	3	0	2	2	3
1957	N	MIL	845	6	-1	6	0	5
1958	N	MIL	1076	7	3	4	3	9
1959	N	MIL	1271	8	4	2	5	12
1960	N	MIL	1247	5	6	4	1	11
1961	N	MIL	43	0	1	0	0	1
1962	N	MIL	778	5	3	2	3	9
1963	N	MIL	609	-3	4	-2	0	1
1964	N	SF	510	0	5	1	-1	5
1965	N	PIT	391	2	0	-1	3	2
1966	A	CLE	328	-1	6	-1	-1	5
Total			12274	57	41	31	20	98

career into perspective is that he was about as good as Campanella at stolen base defense, when base-stealing was rare, seemed to prevent passed balls and wild pitches better, and was probably considerably more mobile in fielding bunts.

Jim Sundberg is on anybody's list of the greatest fielding catchers of all time. *Tango(p-wowy)* rates him slightly higher, but Smith shows almost the

Number Eight: Jim Sundberg

Year	L	Tm	IP	A2 runs	PB runs	GO2 runs	SB runs	Runs
1974	A	TEX	1094	6	0	5	1	6
1975	A	TEX	1316	13	1	6	7	14
1976	A	TEX	1204	12	5	4	8	17
1977	A	TEX	1214	26	-1	16	10	25
1978	A	TEX	1294	7	4	-2	9	12
1979	A	TEX	1271	5	-2	1	4	4
1980	A	TEX	1301	1	3	2	-1	4
1981	A	TEX	863	5	2	0	5	7
1982	A	TEX	1136	4	-2	2	3	3
1983	A	TEX	1056	-1	0	-6	5	-1
1984	A	MIL	900	5	5	-2	7	10
1985	A	KC	960	-1	1	0	-2	0
1986	A	KC	1100	-5	-1	-9	3	-7
1987	N	CHI	354	5	4	5	0	9
1988	A	TEX	232	-2	5	0	-1	3
1989	A	TEX	457	1	6	-1	2	6
1988	N	CHI	142	-1	-1	-2	0	-2
			15896	79	30	20	60	109

identical career trends and total. The DRA ratings in the table control for the impact of knuckle-baller Charlie Hough from 1981 through 1983 on wild pitches and passed balls; Sundberg had already lost something before Hough arrived on the scene.

Brad Ausmus was basically a Rick Dempsey with decent speed and an Ivy League degree.

Number Seven: Brad Ausmus

Year	L	Tm	IP	A2 runs	PB runs	GO2 runs	SB runs	Runs
1993	N	SD	402	5	6	3	2	11
1994	N	SD	833	4	3	5	-1	7
1995	N	SD	821	9	4	2	7	13
1996	N	SD	372	0	-3	-1	1	-3
1996	A	DET	621	1	2	-1	2	3
1997	N	HOU	1032	11	-3	1	10	8
1998	N	HOU	1054	3	4	1	2	7
1999	A	DET	1080	1	4	-2	2	4
2000	A	DET	1231	11	5	3	8	16
2001	N	HOU	1056	4	3	-3	7	7
2002	N	HOU	1079	1	3	1	0	4
2003	N	HOU	1158	8	0	5	3	8
2004	N	HOU	1018	2	1	3	-1	3
2005	N	HOU	1065	10	-1	9	1	9
2006	N	HOU	1124	5	7	7	-3	12
2007	N	HOU	907	1	3	1	1	4
2008	N	HOU	570	4	-1	5	-1	3
2009	N	LA	245	-2	-2	-2	0	-4
Total			15669	78	35	37	41	114

Lou Criger (see next page) is our first example of a catcher with truly embarrassing offensive numbers who was obviously allowed to keep playing only because everyone could see how good he was behind the plate. Steve Krah of the Society for American Baseball Research ("SABR") found the following quote from 1910 by Boston writer and former player Tim Murnane:

> Criger is the man who can turn back the fleetest base runner, a man who can nip the boys at first and third unless they are ever on the alert. Criger is the backstop that never drops a ball that he can reach, and who can throw harder and quicker to second than any catcher in the profession … I would like to see some one pick out the equal of Criger.

Criger's batting average—always far below league norms during the high run scoring 1890s—fell below .200 the first year the American League adopted the foul-strike rule, recovered to .211 the following year, and

Number Six: Lou Criger

Year	L	Tm	IP	A2 runs	PB runs	Runs
1896	N	CLE	12	0	1	1
1897	N	CLE	323	-1	3	3
1898	N	CLE	729	6	2	8
1899	N	STL	609	1	1	2
1900	N	STL	664	-1	12	11
1901	A	BOS	634	11	5	16
1902	A	BOS	702	11	5	15
1903	A	BOS	868	19	13	31
1904	A	BOS	911	2	10	12
1905	A	BOS	913	7	8	16
1906	A	BOS	91	-3	4	1
1907	A	BOS	599	11	-2	9
1908	A	BOS	672	7	-6	1
1909	A	STL	661	-6	2	-4
1910	A	NY	205	-4	0	-4
1912	A	STL	10	0	0	0
Total			8602	59	57	116

remained below .200 for the next *seven* years he wore a major league uniform. And yet he played between half and a third of his team's innings.

Perhaps the greatest testament to his defensive value was Cy Young's insistence on keeping Criger as his catcher for almost all of his games between 1897 and 1908. After their run together ended, Young told the *St. Louis Post-Dispatch*, or, rather, that paper reported him as saying:

> in Criger, St. Louis will get one of the greatest catchers that ever donned a glove. I've pitched to him so long that he seems a part of me, and I am positive no one will suffer from the departure more than I. Lou is a great student of the game and knows the weaknesses of every batter in the league. So confident am I of his judgment that I never shake my head. It means that I have to learn a great deal about the batters, features to which I had heretofore paid no attention.

It would be an interesting project to conduct a study similar to Craig Wright's study of Mike Piazza by comparing Cy Young's performances with and without Criger, particularly when it comes to avoiding walks, which was Young's greatest strength. Perhaps Criger framed the pitches well and contributed to Young's extraordinary record of control.

Jack Warner (see next page) had higher batting averages than Criger but he walked less. One surprisingly good and simple rate statistic on offense is a player's "On-base percentage Plus Slugging average, adjusted for park effects, and scaled so that it relative to the league norm, with 100 being average ("OPS+"). Warner's career OPS+ (73) was essentially the same as Criger's (72).

Number Five: Jack Warner

Year	L	Tm	IP	A2 runs	PB runs	Runs
1895	N	BOS	14	1	1	2
1895	N	LOU	510	-9	2	-6
1896	N	LOU	315	-1	11	10
1896	N	NY	159	-2	-5	-7
1897	N	NY	936	8	11	19
1898	N	NY	944	6	20	26
1899	N	NY	708	5	0	5
1900	N	NY	263	1	9	11
1901	N	NY	613	4	20	23
1902	A	BOS	536	4	-5	0
1903	N	NY	700	2	8	10
1904	N	NY	693	2	4	6
1905	N	STL	363	1	3	4
1905	A	DET	333	-4	-4	-8
1906	A	DET	411	5	4	9
1906	A	WAS	294	4	3	7
1907	A	WAS	496	-8	15	7
1908	A	WAS	307	-4	4	0
Total			8594	17	100	117

Both figures are extremely low. Warner and Criger had careers of almost exactly the same (i) length (in terms of estimated innings played), (ii) estimated defensive impact, and (iii) offensive value. Criger attracted a lot of press; I've found nothing on Warner.

Number Four: Bill Bergen

Year	L	Tm	IP	A6 runs	PB runs	Runs
1901	N	CIN	716	2	6	8
1902	N	CIN	804	8	8	16
1903	N	CIN	481	3	4	7
1904	N	BRO	818	10	0	10
1905	N	BRO	651	7	-3	4
1906	N	BRO	938	4	2	6
1907	N	BRO	351	6	1	6
1908	N	BRO	844	6	2	8
1909	N	BRO	952	22	0	22
1910	N	BRO	708	14	8	22
1911	N	BRO	687	7	0	7
Total			7950	90	27	118

The most extreme good field, no hit player in major league history, Bill Bergen had a lifetime batting average of .171, *forty* points lower than the next lowest batting average among all major league players with at least 2500 at bats. No power. No walks. An OPS+ of ... 21. And yet they kept putting him out there. As *The Sporting News* said in 1908: Bergen "ranks with the best receivers in modern baseball. He is an intelligent student of the points of a batsman, a true and fast thrower and is without a peer in judging and capturing foul flies."

Number Three: Steve Yeager

Year	L	Tm	IP	A2 runs	PB runs	GO2 runs	SB runs	Runs
1972	N	LA	306	1	1	2	-1	2
1973	N	LA	361	4	1	5	-1	5
1974	N	LA	808	9	1	8	2	10
1975	N	LA	1179	6	4	8	-1	11
1976	N	LA	948	15	5	11	4	20
1977	N	LA	1014	19	5	17	2	24
1978	N	LA	627	10	4	4	6	14
1979	N	LA	803	4	4	0	4	9
1980	N	LA	613	-1	2	3	-4	1
1981	N	LA	230	0	2	0	1	2
1982	N	LA	523	6	8	1	4	13
1983	N	LA	867	4	10	-4	8	14
1984	N	LA	470	1	-2	2	-1	-1
1985	N	LA	302	5	-1	0	5	4
1986	A	SEA	369	2	-4	1	1	-3
Total			9421	85	39	57	28	124

Steve Yeager had a better arm than Bench, at least according to Lou Brock, who might have been qualified to make such an assessment. Apparently the rest of the league agreed, because they didn't run on him much. Bill James described him as "agile," so perhaps the GO2 runs represent real value by preventing infield hits, rather than fielding sacrifice bunts, which are more or less outs given away by the other team.

Our third certifiably bright guy, Bob Boone (see next page) attended Stanford University. He was the only catcher I'm aware of who was a better fielder in his thirties than in his twenties. *The Historical Abstract* reports that he "was a very smart receiver, who worked as hard to stay in shape as anyone who ever played baseball." *The Historical Abstract* also says that Boone's teammate Steve Carlton "was the hardest working, best-conditioned base-ball player of his generation ... [who] used to exercise by jogging twenty minutes in dry ice[;] every step was a marathon." Well, *there's* a coincidence. Both Carlton and Boone somehow made themselves into better players circa 1980–81 via intense exercise regimes. Carlton went on to have some of his

Number Two: Bob Boone

Year	L	Tm	IP	A2 runs	PB runs	GO2 runs	SB runs	Runs
1972	N	PHI	118	0	-1	0	0	-1
1973	N	PHI	1258	11	-4	4	7	7
1974	N	PHI	1235	-3	0	-3	0	-2
1975	N	PHI	711	4	0	0	4	4
1976	N	PHI	892	-6	-2	-3	-3	-8
1977	N	PHI	1047	6	0	6	0	6
1978	N	PHI	1053	-1	-1	-3	2	-2
1979	N	PHI	963	7	2	1	6	10
1980	N	PHI	1173	3	2	0	2	5
1981	N	PHI	580	-7	0	0	-7	-7
1982	A	LA	1250	19	2	4	15	22
1983	A	LA	1212	16	0	8	8	16
1984	A	LA	1181	10	-1	6	4	9
1985	A	LA	1215	11	1	4	7	12
1986	A	LA	1186	23	3	13	9	26
1987	A	LA	1035	10	1	2	8	12
1988	A	LA	928	11	12	6	5	23
1989	A	KC	1082	6	10	0	6	16
1990	A	KC	335	0	-2	2	-2	-1
Total			18456	123	23	49	74	146

Number One: Ivan Rodriguez

Year	L	Tm	IP	A2 runs	PB runs	GO2 runs	SB runs	Runs
1991	A	TEX	684	15	-2	9	6	13
1992	A	TEX	982	20	5	7	12	24
1993	A	TEX	1117	9	0	3	6	9
1994	A	TEX	837	5	1	2	3	6
1995	A	TEX	1065	14	0	6	8	14
1996	A	TEX	1223	19	-3	7	12	16
1997	A	TEX	1201	17	3	4	13	21
1998	A	TEX	1197	15	-3	1	14	12
1999	A	TEX	1208	19	1	9	11	20
2000	A	TEX	736	4	4	0	5	8
2001	A	TEX	855	12	-1	-1	13	11
2002	A	TEX	836	8	1	8	1	9
2003	N	FLA	1132	-1	-2	-2	0	-4
2004	A	DET	1051	7	6	6	1	13
2005	A	DET	1032	10	-2	1	10	9
2006	A	DET	1054	10	1	3	7	11
2007	A	DET	1053	2	0	0	2	2
2008	A	DET	706	8	6	5	3	14
2008	A	NY	224	1	0	1	0	0
2009	N	HOU	748	-1	1	-1	1	1
2009	A	TEX	214	1	-1	0	2	0
Total			19156	194	15	65	129	209

best years in his mid-thirties, and the weak hitting Boone was able to extend his career far beyond what anyone would have expected at the time. It's stories like these we need to hear to remind ourselves just how hard ballplayers work to keep their dreams alive.

Tango(*p-wowy*) estimates about fifty fewer defensive runs for I-Rod (see prior page) because, as far as I know, *Tango*(*p-wowy*) does not give *any* credit for batted ball defense, whereas DRA's GO2 runs may over-credit 'bunt-hogging'. I would therefore pencil in approximately +175 defensive runs for Rodriguez, pending an analysis of catcher impact on walks and strikeouts.

First Base

This chapter will also be somewhat shorter than subsequent chapters, for three very good reasons. First, there are generally better systems than the current form of DRA for evaluating first basemen since the early 1950s. Second, the best systems for evaluating first basemen since that time suggest that first basemen generally have less impact on team defense than fielders at other positions, which means they can't be as historically important as those fielders. I'm not entirely convinced that this is true, because so many first basemen have been such bad fielders, particularly in leagues without designated hitters, that it should have been possible for exceptional first basemen to exceed the average almost as much as top fielders have at other positions. Nevertheless, that is what the other systems are saying. Third, the findings under DRA for first basemen who played before the mid-1950s, though probably more reliable than those under currently available alternatives, are significantly less reliable than DRA defensive runs estimates at other positions during the same time frame.

Given these caveats, I thought it best to focus, as we did in the catcher chapter, only on our top forty. (The five historical era charts are available on-line at www.oup.com/us/Wizardry.) As we explained in building our talent pool model, there really hasn't been any historical trend in defensive runs estimates for top first basemen that we should back out, probably because first base has attracted relatively little new delta pool talent. Therefore, TPAR is simply equal to career defensive runs. Moreover, as we'll see in the third base chapter, the position was probably more important during the Dead Ball Era, presumably due to the greater importance of bunt defense, so it is appropriate that a fair number of Dead Ball Era first basemen appear on our top forty list.

Despite these caveats, DRA does identify the same top first basemen since the 1950s that are identified under the best systems, and the top DRA ratings before the 1950s appear reasonable.

Before getting to the ratings, we need to clarify the main challenge in evaluating first baseman, which I believe was first identified by Charles Saeger in the early 1990s: the necessity of crediting first basemen for *unassisted* putouts.

THESIS: GENERAL RULE ON INFIELDER PUTOUTS

As we've been saying all along, putouts are essentially meaningless for infielders, because they almost always result from a skill play made by *another* fielder, or from catching an infield or shallow outfield fly that is essentially an automatic out best credited to the *pitcher*. For example, it is wrong to give a second baseman credit for recording a putout by (i) catching a throw from the shortstop who has fielded the ground ball and (ii) merely touching second base for a force out. On that play, the shortstop fielding the ground ball and tossing it to second deserves all of the credit for the hit prevented. It is also wrong to give a middle infielder credit for applying the tag on a stolen base attempt at second. On that play, the catcher (and to a relatively minor extent, the pitcher) deserves the credit for getting the runner out. It is wrong to give a third baseman credit for catching a high fly in short left field that could be caught (i) by any competent third baseman and (ii) by the left fielder and shortstop as well. That outcome should be credited to the pitcher, who has 'won' his contest with the batter by generating an out that is almost as automatic as a strikeout.

Clearly it would *not* be wrong to credit an infielder for catching a scorching line drive by jumping unusually high and at precisely the right moment, or for diving to prevent a true Texas Leaguer from dropping in for a hit. The problem is, you cannot detect the latter two plays from anything other than batted ball data. Furthermore, batted ball data so far hasn't demonstrated that any infielder has the true, repeatable skill of saving anything more than a couple of runs a year by making these kind of do-or-die plays. Unless you have *perfect* batted ball data, crediting infielders on the basis of their putout totals does nothing but add noise and reward ball hogs who take easy chances away from their teammates. Even if you have perfect batted ball data, properly crediting true skill infielder putouts would have virtually no practical impact in a single season, and could have only a marginal impact in a couple of long careers.

ANTITHESIS: THE SAEGER EXCEPTION

As I believe Charles Saeger first noticed, and as Bill James later and independently concluded, you *do* have to credit first basemen for putouts, but only for their *unassisted* putouts, that is, their putouts other than those they record merely by catching throws from other infielders. James illustrated the problem vividly with a real-life example: the careers and career fielding assessments of Steve Garvey and Bill Buckner. Garvey had a very unreliable arm, and knew it, so he avoiding making a throw whenever possible, and would rush to first after fielding a ground ball to record the putout himself. Therefore, his assists totals were very low, and systems based only on assists grossly underrated his ability to prevent hits on balls in play. Bill Buckner, on the other hand, believed it was very important to keep pitchers in the habit of covering the bag, and in later years couldn't run because of bad knees, so he preferred making the throw whenever possible, thus increasing his assists totals above the league norms, which resulted in unjustifiably high ratings.

That is the extreme case. In most cases, first basemen make broadly consistent choices—they make the putout if they are already near the bag, and make the throw if they are not. But even in the non-extreme cases, a first baseman might make up to twenty extra or fewer assists in a single season, either randomly in close cases or because of slight 'Buckner' or 'Garvey' tendency. Since the standard deviation in net skill plays at first is probably also only about twenty per year, any system that relies solely on assists will have a tremendous amount of noise from year to year and, in the rare but real cases such as Garvey and Buckner, will make fundamentally incorrect career assessments.

So we need to credit first basemen for unassisted putouts. It is possible, using just traditional statistics and our old tool, regression analysis, to estimate how many net unassisted putouts a *team* records at first base, taking into account total balls in play allowed by a team's pitchers, as we discussed in explaining the DRA system. You basically 'back out' the net assists, given batted balls in play, at the *other* infield positions, to 'isolate' the remaining unassisted putouts at first. The resulting estimates of team unassisted putouts at first are probably pretty good. But there is one more problem, and I'm not sure Saeger or James explicitly focused on it.

SYNTHESIS

We should neither ignore first base putouts nor credit all unassisted first base putouts; rather, we should only be crediting a *subset* of unassisted first base putouts: unassisted *ground ball* putouts. All the putouts recorded by first basemen on high flies and pop ups should be ignored for the same reason we ignore putouts by second basemen, shortstops, and third basemen.

As of this writing, for seasons since 1952, Retrosheet has gone through original score sheets of major league games and tallied up the precise number of *unassisted ground ball* putouts at first base, so we don't have to estimate unassisted putouts and then estimate the portion of unassisted putouts that are on ground balls. My data provider provided me with team totals of unassisted ground outs at first base, which are used to calculate the team ratings at first for seasons since 1952. However, he was unable to provide the same totals for each individual first baseman on each team. Rather than just allocate the team rating pro-rata based on innings played, I attempted to 'individuate' the ratings on the basis of marginal plays made compared to the rest of the team. Unfortunately, the only individual first base statistic I had that was *predominantly* a skill statistic was assists, so I credited each first baseman for net plays above or below the team rate based on his net assists above or below the team rate. Therefore, a 'Buckner' first baseman will be somewhat overrated compared to a 'Garvey' first baseman under the DRA estimate, unless he plays almost the entire season, in which case the team rating equals his rating and there shouldn't be any distortion.

What about the pre-1952 team and individual ratings? Well, our old tool regression analysis showed that for *post*-1952 seasons the best way to *estimate* total net ground ball outs by first basemen, given total batted balls in play, is to take their net assists and add one-third of their net unassisted putouts given total balls in play, as estimated above,. The resulting estimate best predicted the actual tallies provided by Retrosheet for post-1952 team first base totals.

Therefore, we apply what we learned from looking at the post-1952 data to seasons before 1952: we essentially calculate net unassisted putouts at first base per team by backing out the correct proportion of team assists from the other infield positions, based on regression analysis, and treat one-third of what's left as net unassisted ground ball putouts, which are added to net assists to arrive at net plays for the team at first base.

We lack reliable innings played data for seasons before 1952. Following a slightly simplified version of an approach suggested by James in *Win Shares*, we just assign the total team rating to each first baseman in proportion to his *total* first base putouts as a percentage of *total* team first base putouts. This is fair, because between eighty and ninety percent of first base putouts are *assisted*, and merely reflect playing time. And as to the skill or ball-hogging component of unassisted putouts, that only changes (very slightly) the proportion of the pro-rata team rating assigned to the player—it does *not* cause one player to be rated better or worse on a rate basis than his teammates at that position.

Now we're ready to look at our top forty.

Aside from one clearly incorrect rating, the results raise essentially two major issues: whether the Polo Grounds had a uniquely strong impact on

Top Forty First Basemen of All-Time (TPAR Equals Runs)

MCS	First	Last	POS	IP	Runs	Δ
1982	Keith	Hernandez	1B	17276	212	
1904	Fred	Tenney	1B	15906	195	
2006	Albert	Pujols	1B	8657	138	Δ
1930	Bill	Terry	1B	13915	136	
1987	Pete	O'Brien	1B	11441	128	
1998	John	Olerud	1B	17227	116	
2003	Todd	Helton	1B	15154	110	
1973	George	Scott	1B	15187	102	Δ
2006	Lyle	Overbay	1B	7844	102	
1924	George	Kelly	1B	12004	102	
1954	Gil	Hodges	1B	15761	99	
1921	Wally	Pipp	1B	16060	97	
1998	Tino	Martinez	1B	15648	97	
1939	Buddy	Hassett	1B	6386	86	
1938	Hank	Greenberg	1B	9996	82	
1960	Vic	Power	1B	10362	81	Δ
1914	Ed	Konetchy	1B	17090	77	
1989	Sid	Bream	1B	7316	76	
1951	Ferris	Fain	1B	9567	72	
1996	Rafael	Palmeiro	1B	18500	71	
1968	Tommy	McCraw	1B	6086	70	Δ
1906	Frank	Chance	1B	8655	69	
1998	Jeff	Bagwell	1B	18517	68	
1995	Mark	Grace	1B	18583	66	
1968	Wes	Parker	1B	10325	66	
1909	George	Stovall	1B	8538	66	
1942	Frank	McCormick	1B	12763	64	
1942	Dick	Siebert	1B	8211	64	
1966	Norm	Cash	1B	16214	64	
1985	Willie	Upshaw	1B	9175	63	Δ
1984	Darrell	Evans	1B	6740	62	
1904	Frank	Isbell	1B	5483	61	
2003	Richie	Sexson	1B	10220	59	
1941	Elbie	Fletcher	1B	12403	58	
2002	Travis	Lee	1B	8288	57	
1996	Jeff	King	1B	4010	56	
1907	Tom	Jones	1B	9112	54	
1937	Zeke	Bonura	1B	7873	54	
1928	Phil	Todt	1B	7777	54	
1985	Eddie	Murray	1B	21148	51	Δ

the number of plays made by first basemen, and whether the DRA scale of impact of the best first baseman is overstated.

The one absolutely wrong defensive runs estimate in this book is the career defensive runs estimate for Richie Sexson (see next page). But at least there is a simple explanation for much of the error.

Sexson, six feet six inches tall, and fourteen for twenty-seven lifetime in stealing bases, was a huge, lumbering player who had his last good season

Richie Sexson

Year	L	Tm	IP	Runs	v-Tm
1997	A	CLE	17	-1	-1
1998	A	CLE	363	-3	-1
1999	A	CLE	492	11	7
2000	A	CLE	210	5	3
2000	N	MIL	497	12	10
2001	N	MIL	1372	-2	2
2002	N	MIL	1324	12	1
2003	N	MIL	1452	1	0
2004	N	ARI	204	5	5
2005	A	SEA	1302	4	-1
2006	A	SEA	1310	13	-2
2007	A	SEA	992	-3	1
2008	A	SEA	604	3	2
2008	A	NY	80	2	2
Total			10220	59	29

(and last triple) at age thirty. It would make perfect sense that he would make the 'Buckner' decision to toss to the pitcher covering the bag whenever possible, rather than race to the bag à la Garvey. It would therefore be reasonable to assume that his +29 v-Tm runs, which reflect net assists compared to his teammates, just represent his preference, compared to his teammates, to throw to the pitcher, rather than a real skill at getting to extra ground balls. Subtracting those +29 v-Tm runs, he is still +30 defensive runs in his career, or about +4 defensive runs per 1450 innings played. Sexson's career spans periods in which each of Smith's three systems is applied, and their collective rating for him, backing out the incorrect treatment of errors, is about –4 defensive runs per 1450 innings played. So DRA rates him slightly above average and Smith slightly below.

Zeke Bonura

Year	L	Tm	IP	Runs
1934	A	CHI	1132	10
1935	A	CHI	1208	16
1936	A	CHI	1298	17
1937	A	CHI	1000	1
1938	A	WAS	1149	3
1939	N	NY	1037	8
1940	A	WAS	688	-8
1940	N	CHI	361	7
Total			7873	54

When Branch Rickey wrote that fielding percentage was "utterly useless," "not only misleading, but deceiving," here is the example he gave:

Take Zeke Bonura, the old White Sox first baseman, generally regarded as a poor fielder. The fielding averages showed that he led

American League in fielding for three years. Why? Zeke had "good hands"! Anything he reached, he held. Result: an absence of errors. But he was also slow moving and did not cover much territory. Balls that a quicker man may have fielded went for base hits, but the fielding averages do not reflect this.

Now, DRA completely ignores errors, so the Bonura rating above has nothing to do with fielding average. As we will see, particularly in the outfield, players easily get tagged with the 'bad fielder' label because they are awkward, or strike out a lot, or don't move that quickly, or have a funny sounding name, or for any number of reasons having nothing to do with their ability actually to convert batted balls into outs.

I'm not saying that Bonura was a good fielder. Because the pre-1952 version of DRA only estimates unassisted ground ball putouts but gives full credit for assists, I can imagine that a sluggish guy who made the 'Buckner' choice to throw to the pitcher whenever possible might be overrated somewhat. And Bonura presumably had, unlike Garvey, some confidence in his arm. At age sixteen, he won the javelin competition to become the youngest male ever to win an event at the U.S. national amateur track and field championship. But to claim that Bonura was "slow moving" and "did not cover much territory" says nothing about his 'invisible' range—his ability to position himself well for the hitters, or his reflexes. As we will see at the other corner position, third base, where the 'slice' of the field is narrow, foot speed is not important. Brooks Robinson was one of the slowest players of his time.

In *Win Shares*, Bill James mentions that Zeke Bonura had high assists totals when playing in the Polo Grounds, and takes that as a strong indication that the Polo Grounds had a strong park factor favoring first base assists. We'll address that momentarily. But Bonura played just one season at the Polo Grounds, and his defensive runs estimates were higher his first three seasons with the White Sox, positive in each of his four seasons with the White Sox, one season with the Cubs, and one out of two seasons with the Senators.

I believe that Zeke Bonura, in addition to being a very good hitter, was a solid first baseman, despite his stocky build and lack of foot speed. Perhaps more data and more analysis will confirm this surprising assessment.

POLO GROUNDS PARK FACTOR

James pointed out in *Win Shares* that the unique 'horseshoe' shape of the Polo Grounds resulted in the stands curving sharply inward as they approached the foul lines. Fair balls hit down the first base line would some-times carom against the curving stands at a nearly ninety degree angle back into short right field. When there were no runners on first base, Polo Grounds first basemen would position themselves in short right field, deeper and closer to the hole, to be prepared to field any such 'ricocheting' ball and record an 'extra' assist that would never be recorded in a normal ballpark.

James is on to something, as he almost always is, because three of our top dozen first basemen played mostly in the Polo Grounds: George "Highpockets" Kelly, who started for the Giants from 1920 through 1926, Wally Pipp, who started at first base for the Yankees from 1915 through 1922 while they played at the Polo Grounds, and Bill Terry, who was the Giants' first baseman after Kelly.

Indeed, the Polo Grounds might have inflated first baseman ratings in another way, indirectly. By being positioned closer to second and deeper, Giant first basemen probably made more *non*-ricochet ground ball plays in the hole between first and second, which required the pitcher to cover the bag because the first baseman was too far away.

Now, presumably that would come at the cost of fewer ground ball plays right down the line, which would be handled unassisted, because the Polo Grounds first basemen would be too far from the bag to get those balls right down the line. But some of those balls ricocheted back, and by playing so deep, first basemen might have been in a better position to catch Texas Leaguers hit to right, perhaps permitting them to make enough unassisted *fly out* putouts to make up for the 'lost' unassisted ground ball putouts.

It's too bad we have hardly any truly unique ballparks like the Polo Grounds anymore. Until more research can clarify the issue, we'll relegate Terry, Kelly, and Pipp to Honorable Mention status.

RELATIVE IMPACT OF FIRST BASE DEFENSE

Sean Smith's estimates of career defensive runs for the twenty-two first base-men on our top forty list covered under his three batted ball or play-by-play systems are about one-third smaller than the DRA estimates. A little more technically, regression analysis indicates that the best way to 'predict' Smith's estimate from DRA is to take .65 of the DRA estimate. Such prediction explains eighty-four percent of the variation in the Smith estimates, a pretty nice fit, and the typical difference between the Smith and DRA estimate is twenty-two runs, which is within the twenty-five-run margin of error we're seeking for career defensive runs assessments.

So directionally the DRA estimates of career value, which do not benefit from exact counts of unassisted ground ball putouts for individual first basemen, appear to be consistent with a good system that benefits from having the exact counts. Still, I cannot understand why in some cases the scale is so different; two of those cases are Lyle Overbay and Tino Martinez, both of whom Smith estimates saved about sixty runs, which is why I'll leave them out of the top ten for now. The largest discrepancy between DRA and the Smith systems may, however, be explicable, as we shall see.

MOST NOTABLE NON-TOP TEN GREATS

Ed Konetchy

Year	L	Tm	IP	Runs
1907	N	STL	799	8
1908	N	STL	1367	18
1909	N	STL	1357	4
1910	N	STL	1245	16
1911	N	STL	1402	8
1912	N	STL	1259	3
1913	N	STL	1223	12
1914	N	PIT	1358	13
1916	N	BOS	1406	13
1917	N	BOS	1177	2
1918	N	BOS	1015	-17
1919	N	BRO	1172	-3
1920	N	BRO	1202	-4
1921	N	BRO	486	-3
1921	N	PHI	621	7
Total			17090	77

Notice the nearly identical ratings with St. Louis in 1913, Pittsburgh in 1914, and Boston in 1915. Ed Konetchy may have been even better than we've given him credit for, because DRA does not measure the ability to prevent throwing errors by the other infielders by fielding throws well, and it appears that Konetchy was exceptional in that regard. Brothers Paul and Eric Sallee, writing for SABR, found a contemporaneous report that "Koney has had to handle more weird throws in two years than any two National League guardians of the initial corner. But he dug up and pulled down so many of them that patrons who marveled at these extraordinary performances have come to take them as a matter of course." Mitchel G. Lichtman recently did some research indicating that among contemporary first basemen, any ability to prevent throwing errors is small—perhaps plus or minus two or three runs a season. But the gloves first basemen have been using for the last 50 years bear only a faint resemblance to those used by Konetchy and his peers. 'Scooping' may have mattered a great deal back then.

Gil Hodges

Year	L	Tm	IP	Runs	v-Tm
1948	N	BRO	886	-7	
1949	N	BRO	1403	-2	
1950	N	BRO	1368	-8	
1951	N	BRO	1423	7	
1952	N	BRO	1361	13	1
1953	N	BRO	1035	18	2
1954	N	BRO	1392	26	0
1955	N	BRO	1211	33	1
1956	N	BRO	1120	14	-2
1957	N	BRO	1350	9	0
1958	N	LA	940	4	1
1959	N	LA	952	-6	-7
1960	N	LA	447	-4	-6
1961	N	LA	527	-5	-6
1962	N	NY	288	5	4
1963	N	NY	56	2	1
Total			15761	99	-11

Hodges had a tremendous reputation for fielding, and moved from catcher to first base only because the Dodgers acquired Roy Campanella. It appears it took him a little while to learn the position. The 1954–55 estimates are almost certainly too high: Retrosheet play-by-play data, which provides counts of unassigned ground outs at first, is much sketchier in the early to mid-1950s; the *Smith(pgor,bod)* estimates are considerably lower. Until I'm more confident of the 1952–56 numbers, I think it best to leave Hodges out of the top ten discussion.

OUR POLO GROUNDS HONORABLE MENTIONS

Many fans know that Gehrig replaced Wally Pipp (see next page) as the Yankees' first baseman one fateful afternoon early in the 1925 season. Not many know that Ruth replaced Pipp as the leading home run hitter in the American League in 1918; Pipp had led the league the prior two seasons. Tris Speaker, famous for playing perhaps the shallowest center field in history, said at the time, "I usually play a short field, but of course in the case of such a batter as Pipp it would be foolish to play in." Pipp carried on into the new Live Ball Era, but never topped his home run total in 1916 (twelve), though he did lead the league in triples in 1924. Widely regarded as a top fielder in his day, Pipp continued to field well when he left the Yankees for the Reds in 1926. Oddly, his National League Polo Grounds contemporary, George Kelly (see next page), also had a rebirth as a Crosley Field first baseman. Perhaps there is yet another first base park factor to worry about …

Wally Pipp

Year	L	Tm	IP	Runs
1913	A	DET	63	0
1915	A	NY	1189	10
1916	A	NY	1311	17
1917	A	NY	1411	5
1918	A	NY	829	-9
1919	A	NY	1253	0
1920	A	NY	1350	13
1921	A	NY	1352	13
1922	A	NY	1373	9
1923	A	NY	1297	2
1924	A	NY	1351	1
1925	A	NY	357	13
1926	N	CIN	1359	17
1927	N	CIN	977	3
1928	N	CIN	589	4
Total			16060	97

George "Highpockets" Kelly

Year	L	Tm	IP	Runs
1915	N	NY	48	0
1916	N	NY	86	-1
1917	N	NY	2	0
1917	N	PIT	62	-1
1919	N	NY	272	-5
1920	N	NY	1409	11
1921	N	NY	1329	13
1922	N	NY	1352	23
1923	N	NY	1303	4
1924	N	NY	1104	-4
1925	N	NY	225	3
1926	N	NY	1011	21
1927	N	CIN	389	5
1928	N	CIN	783	16
1929	N	CIN	1283	16
1930	N	CHI	384	5
1930	N	CIN	441	5
1932	N	BRO	521	-6
Year	L		12004	102

The Reds seemed to have a great first baseman in 1926 (Pipp), forced him to compete for the position with another great first baseman in 1927 (Kelly), and then had Kelly for two more apparently great years thereafter.

In *Whatever Happened to the Hall of Fame?* Bill James praised Kelly as a "superb" fielder and alerted me to the fact he had played second base in 1925 when teammate Frankie Frisch shifted from second to short and third. Kelly's DRA rating that year at second is +11 defensive runs. Kelly's Hall of

Fame webpage provides the following quotation by a certain Tom Clark: "George Kelly showed me the first baseman's glove he used in his last season in the big leagues—1932. A mere scrap of leather, it barely covered his large hand, had a sizeable hole in its meager pocket and could not have weighed more than two-to-three ounces."

Bill Terry

Year	L	Tm	IP	Runs
1923	N	NY	18	0
1924	N	NY	274	-2
1925	N	NY	1087	14
1926	N	NY	331	10
1927	N	NY	1325	18
1928	N	NY	1345	-5
1929	N	NY	1336	11
1930	N	NY	1362	26
1931	N	NY	1345	15
1932	N	NY	1369	22
1933	N	NY	1049	1
1934	N	NY	1352	9
1935	N	NY	1268	13
1936	N	NY	455	3
Total			13915	136

Bill Terry began his career as a pitcher, and even had a no-hitter in the minors, so he obviously had a good arm for a first baseman. Fred Stein of SABR reports that Terry was "good-sized for his era, but graceful and extremely fast for his size. (He held his own in foot races with speedy teammates.)" Terry was also a savvy operator who eventually replaced his manager, John McGraw, and successful enough in business at one point to attempt to buy the Giants. So here we have a first baseman who was fast, smart, graceful, threw well, and who put up terrific fielding numbers over a twenty-year period. Were it not for the Polo Grounds question, he'd be in the top five, not just the top ten.

Number Ten: Hank Greenberg

Year	L	Tm	IP	Runs
1933	A	DET	1011	11
1934	A	DET	1352	7
1935	A	DET	1364	13
1936	A	DET	112	1
1937	A	DET	1357	11
1938	A	DET	1345	15
1939	A	DET	1195	2
1946	A	DET	1237	23
1947	N	PIT	1023	0
Total			9996	82

Greenberg worked assiduously, both as a young man and as a seasoned veteran, to improve his batting and fielding game. In the latter case, it seems he sought every possible advantage. In 1939, people started complaining that Greenberg used a glove that was too big. As reported by Ralph Berger of the SABR, one journalist at the time declared, "The glove has three lengths of barbed wire, four corners, two side pockets, a fish net, rod and trowel, a small sled, a library of classics, a compact anti-aircraft gun, a change of clothes and a pocket comb." The Commissioner's office established a rule, more or less designed to get Greenberg, that a glove couldn't be more than eight inches wide or twelve inches high.

Number Nine: Buddy Hassett

Year	L	Tm	IP	Runs
1936	N	BRO	1403	21
1937	N	BRO	1113	15
1938	N	BRO	57	5
1939	N	BOS	1047	12
1940	N	BOS	836	8
1941	N	BOS	821	8
1942	A	NY	1109	17
Total			6386	86

You have to be impressed by Buddy Hassett's consistent performance for three different teams. If and when we obtain more reliable innings played data for his era we may find he was even better, as we're only giving him his pro-rata portion of the team rating based on playing time, without extra credit for exceeding the team rate of plays made per inning. On the basis of the current Retrosheet estimates of innings, which Retrosheet clearly denotes as incomplete, Hassett played fewer innings than the 'pro rata' estimate above, which suggests he did 'out-field' his replacements, and his defensive runs total should be higher. Hassett made about thirty more errors over the course of his career than he would have if his fielding percentage were league-average. Assuming those extra errors did not come from dropping more throws from his infielders, but from his own attempts to field ground balls, they mean nothing, absolutely nothing. Something tells me that if he had a real problem simply catching throws, (i) he would not have played as much as he did, since he was not a good hitter for a first baseman, and (ii) they would not have nicknamed him The Bronx Thrush, which I take to imply that he had the grace of a bird.

The *Smith*(*pgor,bod*) estimate, based on exact individual counts of unassisted ground ball putouts, is better for Vic Power (see next page) than for Hodges, and Power showed consistent excellence for multiple teams over a longer period

Number Eight: Vic Power

1954	A	PHI	155	-1	-1
1955	A	KC	1248	10	1
1956	A	KC	631	11	8
1957	A	KC	935	5	4
1958	A	KC	441	3	7
1958	A	CLE	284	1	3
1959	A	CLE	1063	16	4
1960	A	CLE	1293	17	-1
1961	A	CLE	1246	-1	7
1962	A	MIN	1240	10	3
1963	A	MIN	923	3	7
1964	A	MIN	78	4	4
1964	A	LA	285	-1	1
1964	N	PHI	116	4	3
1965	A	LA	423	0	0
Total			10362	81	50

of time. Like Hodges, Power was someone with a very strong defensive reputation; unlike Hodges, he was not someone who could have been overrated defensively due to slugging, team success, or proximity to New York sportswriters.

Number Seven: Pete O'Brien

Year	L	Tm	IP	Runs	v-Tm
1982	A	TEX	25	-1	-1
1983	A	TEX	1073	24	7
1984	A	TEX	1229	14	4
1985	A	TEX	1346	5	1
1986	A	TEX	1288	14	-1
1987	A	TEX	1301	23	-2
1988	A	TEX	1307	22	3
1989	A	CLE	1331	3	-2
1990	A	SEA	800	16	11
1991	A	SEA	1063	2	-3
1992	A	SEA	625	0	1
1993	A	SEA	52	7	7
Total			11441	128	25

Smith(pgor,bod) evaluates O'Brien more conservatively, which is why I've dropped him a few places. Though O'Brien never made an all-star team, his 1986 season was of all-star quality, and he garnered a few MVP votes.

George Scott's first manager, Dick Williams, thought he was the greatest fielding first basemen ever, and acted on that belief by allowing Scott (see next page) to continue his major league career after the worst hitting season for a first baseman in history. In 1968, "Boomer" batted .171 with only three home runs in 350 at-bats, while playing in the best hitter's park in his league. Like many top-fielding

Number Six: George Scott

Year	L	Tm	IP	Runs	v-Tm
1966	A	BOS	1399	18	0
1967	A	BOS	1329	8	0
1968	A	BOS	820	2	0
1969	A	BOS	411	-2	-4
1970	A	BOS	515	2	0
1971	A	BOS	1270	15	3
1972	A	MIL	1138	6	3
1973	A	MIL	1357	22	3
1974	A	MIL	1306	24	7
1975	A	MIL	1212	-4	0
1976	A	MIL	1366	12	1
1977	A	BOS	1372	3	-2
1978	A	BOS	990	2	-3
1979	A	BOS	370	-3	-6
1979	A	KC	330	-3	-3
1979	A	NY	1	0	0
Total			15187	102	-1

first basemen, Scott started at third. Interestingly, both DRA and *Smith(pgor,bod)* agree that Scott had his best fielding seasons with Milwaukee.

Even taking into consideration how much Coors Field has inflated Todd Helton's offensive statistics, he's given the Rockies, when defense is taken into account, three or four MVP-caliber seasons.

Number Five: Todd Helton

Year	L	Tm	IP	Runs	v-Tm
1997	N	COL	57	3	4
1998	N	COL	1208	11	-3
1999	N	COL	1310	-8	0
2000	N	COL	1349	25	2
2001	N	COL	1370	4	-2
2002	N	COL	1342	12	2
2003	N	COL	1369	29	0
2004	N	COL	1320	20	2
2005	N	COL	1229	10	3
2006	N	COL	1272	-5	2
2007	N	COL	1337	5	2
2008	N	COL	715	5	6
2009	N	COL	1275	-1	2
Total			15154	110	22

I pulled John Olerud (see next page) up a few places because *Smith(R(t,s,d))*, which is based on free Retrosheet data and covers the first ten years of Olerud's career, rates that period +62 defensive runs, just slightly below the DRA estimate, and Smith's other systems have very similar estimates for the

Number Four: John Olerud

Year	L	Tm	IP	Runs	v-Tm
1989	A	TOR	16	1	1
1990	A	TOR	144	-2	-3
1991	A	TOR	1126	9	-4
1992	A	TOR	1096	8	-2
1993	A	TOR	1205	6	3
1994	A	TOR	900	13	2
1995	A	TOR	1173	-4	4
1996	A	TOR	823	4	6
1997	N	NY	1236	10	1
1998	N	NY	1336	20	2
1999	N	NY	1385	13	-1
2000	A	SEA	1358	20	2
2001	A	SEA	1347	5	5
2002	A	SEA	1317	-2	-3
2003	A	SEA	1287	13	0
2004	A	SEA	645	5	0
2004	A	NY	400	-6	-3
2005	A	BOS	431	2	-3
Total			17227	116	7

remainder of his career. In other words, there is simply more evidence for Olerud's excellence than for O'Brien's or Helton's.

Olerud finished third in the MVP vote in 1993 and twelfth in 1998. He was more valuable than 1993's winner, Frank Thomas, because of a vast difference in defensive value, and more valuable than 1998's winner, Sammy Sosa, or Mark McGwire, or Craig Biggio. It's difficult to sell doubles power and fielding contributions at first base, and aside from his ability to draw lots of walks, that's all Olerud had to sell. He was a very valuable player, clearly better than many Hall of Famers.

The 2009 estimate for Pujols is too high because I did not have 2009 team counts of unassisted ground ball putouts at first base, and had to rely on an

Number Three: Albert Pujols

Year	L	Tm	IP	Runs	v-Tm
2001	N	STL	287	2	2
2002	N	STL	144	2	1
2003	N	STL	369	3	-1
2004	N	STL	1338	15	0
2005	N	STL	1358	16	-2
2006	N	STL	1244	19	6
2007	N	STL	1325	28	3
2008	N	STL	1215	14	2
2009	N	STL	1377	39	2
Total			8657	138	12

indirect calculation. Pujols recorded fifty more assists in 2009 than in any prior year, which distorted that calculation. Perhaps he has now decided to take the Buckner rather than Garvey approach, and have his pitchers cover the bag whenever possible.

Leaving that one data hiccup aside, the prior year estimates are completely consistent with $Smith(R(t),f,bh,ph)$. On the basis of his offensive and defensive exploits over this past decade, accomplished during our intensely competitive Contemporary Era, Albert Pujols has already established himself as the greatest all-around first baseman ever.

In the Dead Ball Era and as late as the mid-1980s, when Bill James wrote the first edition of *The Historical Abstract*, the universal consensus was that Hal Chase was the greatest fielding first baseman of all time. Bill James's Fielding Win Shares (developed circa 2000) cannot detect anything exceptional about Chase's fielding, and DRA cannot either. Of course, Chase may have thrown games for gamblers in the field as well as at the plate.

The greatest fielding first baseman of the Dead Ball Era, and arguably the greatest ever, was Fred Tenney, who seems to have invented the modern way of playing the position, including playing far off the bag to be better positioned to prevent hits, starting 3-6-3 double plays, and stretching to catch throws. During his seemingly flukey 1905 season he recorded thirty-eight more assists than any other first baseman.

Number Two: Fred Tenney

Year	L	Tm	IP	Runs
1894	N	BOS	0	0
1897	N	BOS	1133	8
1898	N	BOS	1024	0
1899	N	BOS	1324	21
1900	N	BOS	951	16
1901	N	BOS	1003	17
1902	N	BOS	1197	7
1903	N	BOS	1060	12
1904	N	BOS	1254	11
1905	N	BOS	1316	45
1906	N	BOS	1241	14
1907	N	BOS	1311	15
1908	N	NY	1361	17
1909	N	NY	902	12
1911	N	BOS	831	-1
Year			15906	195

Keith Hernandez (see next page) dropped off the Hall of Fame ballot in his ninth year of eligibility, but will soon be up for consideration by the

Number One: Keith Hernandez

Year	L	Tm	IP	Runs	v-Tm
1974	N	STL	76	-3	-4
1975	N	STL	440	8	5
1976	N	STL	884	18	5
1977	N	STL	1345	19	2
1978	N	STL	1327	6	0
1979	N	STL	1413	23	1
1980	N	STL	1368	20	3
1981	N	STL	873	8	-1
1982	N	STL	1370	16	0
1983	N	STL	491	12	9
1983	N	NY	785	15	13
1984	N	NY	1338	20	1
1985	N	NY	1387	24	-2
1986	N	NY	1302	8	-1
1987	N	NY	1315	12	1
1988	N	NY	767	6	10
1989	N	NY	473	-2	-3
1990	A	CLE	320	2	3
Total			17276	212	42

Veterans Committee. More work needs to be done to estimate his fielding value, because the difference between the DRA estimate of his career defensive runs and the *Smith(pgor,bod)* estimate (just over ninety runs, by far the biggest discrepancy) just about bridges the difference between Hernandez being a marginal and a clearly worthy Hall of Famer.

But for his recent issues with performance-enhancing drugs, Mark McGwire would have been a first ballot Hall of Famer. According to multiple offensive models, Big Mac generated about 550 runs above what the league-average hitter (at all positions) would have produced, or about 55 wins; Hernandez, about 330 runs or 33 wins. The figure of 22 wins that separate McGwire and Hernandez on offense is almost exactly the midpoint number between the DRA and Smith estimates of what separates them on defense. DRA estimates McGwire cost his teams about −80 defensive runs, so the DRA difference between him and Hernandez is about 290 runs, or 29 wins. The various Smith systems that span McGwire's career dock him only about −30 defensive runs, thus creating a spread between him and Hernandez of only 150 runs, or 15 wins. Twenty-two wins of offense is midway between 29 and 15 wins on defense.

If there is any first baseman since the Dead Ball Era who might have saved a couple hundred runs, it would have to be Hernandez. He was the Brooks Robinson of first base—in fact, he charged bunts so aggressively that he occasionally fielded some on the *third* base side. And he threw better than most non-first base infielders, so he frequently took responsibility for relay throws from the outfield—even on throws from *left* field. DRA gives full credit for those relay assists; I'm not sure what *Smith(pgor,bod)* does, but that might account for much of the discrepancy, the largest of any at first base. And, as we saw above, modern batted ball systems show Albert Pujols saving runs at about the same rate as the Hernandez estimates; Pujols just hasn't done it as long. Each one of the single-season numbers is credible.

There is one first base fielding variable not included by DRA that, if included, would boost Hernandez's rating even higher. That factor was, I believe, invented by Bill James, and it is essentially an estimate of the relative number of times a first baseman throws to second or third to get the lead runner, rather than make the easy play at first. James calculated this number for Hernandez, and it indicated he may have thrown out about twenty more lead runners per season than the typical first baseman. The value of getting the lead runner instead of the easy out at first is about .20 runs, which would add about four runs of value, year after year. Hernandez played over 17,000 innings at first, which is about twelve 162-game seasons of 1450 innings per season. So it is possible to add up to another fifty runs to Hernandez's total above.

I'm not prepared to go that far, but for all the reasons above I'm sticking to my estimate that Keef saved about two hundred runs as a fielder, and therefore should be in the Hall of Fame.

Left Field

Precisely because left field is a place were some of the worst fielders are consigned, fast outfielders who don't have the arm to play right or center can often stand out in left. We'll definitely see more high impact fielders in left than in right. In addition, during the Dead Ball Era and probably during the first years of the Live Ball Era, left field was far more important than right field because there were many more plays in left than in right—in fact, nearly as many as in center, particularly in the 1890s and very early 1900s. There may be more undiscovered fielding greats in this chapter than in any other.

Contemporary Era

MCS	First	Last	IP	Runs	Δ
1996	Barry	Bonds	22909	133	Δ
1999	Luis	Gonzalez	20643	81	
2005	Jay	Payton	3777	55	Δ
2001	Brian	Giles	5188	45	
1999	Bobby	Higginson	5435	40	
1995	Bernard	Gilkey	8127	39	Δ
1993	Shane	Mack	3031	36	Δ
2002	Geoff	Jenkins	7624	32	
1995	Tony	Phillips	4273	31	Δ
2004	Randy	Winn	3274	31	Δ
2002	Rondell	White	6066	30	Δ
2002	Jacque	Jones	3952	29	Δ
1998	Marty	Cordova	5742	28	
1995	Greg	Vaughn	10573	25	Δ
2003	Johnny	Damon	4683	19	
1999	B.J.	Surhoff	7500	18	
1994	Phil	Plantier	3080	17	
2002	Garret	Anderson	11600	15	Δ

(continued)

Contemporary Era *(continued)*

MCS	First	Last	IP	Runs	Δ
2001	Ray	Lankford	3436	10	Δ
2000	T.	Hollandsworth	4284	8	
1995	Albert	Belle	8822	8	Δ
2004	Brad	Wilkerson	3249	8	
1994	Derrick	May	4012	7	Δ
1996	Ron	Gant	9683	6	Δ
2004	David	Dellucci	3070	0	
1994	Brady	Anderson	5359	-5	
2000	Dmitri	Young	3100	-6	Δ
2005	Craig	Monroe	3393	-7	Δ
2002	Matt	Lawton	3155	-13	Δ
1999	Troy	O'Leary	5736	-13	Δ
1997	Henry	Rodriguez	5223	-13	Δ
2002	Cliff	Floyd	8759	-14	Δ
1997	Gregg	Jefferies	3017	-19	
2005	Hideki	Matsui	4808	-19	Δ
2002	Lance	Berkman	4059	-21	
2002	Shannon	Stewart	9790	-22	Δ
2002	Chipper	Jones	3065	-23	
1997	Jeff	Conine	6655	-24	
1999	Wil	Cordero	3325	-31	Δ
1998	Rusty	Greer	6908	-33	
2004	F.	Catalanotto	3797	-36	
2001	Gary	Sheffield	4032	-46	Δ
1997	Dante	Bichette	5249	-48	
2000	Moises	Alou	10204	-57	Δ
2005	Adam	Dunn	8376	-61	
2004	Carlos	Lee	13133	-66	Δ
1997	Al	Martin	7307	-69	Δ
2004	Pat	Burrell	9803	-70	
1999	Ryan	Klesko	6398	-74	
2005	Manny	Ramirez	8209	-131	Δ

Of the left fielders of the Contemporary Era whose careers are over or mostly over, only Bonds and Gonzalez have had a significant positive impact as fielders. However, there are some interesting cases to touch upon.

Albert Belle was considered a poor fielder and not a nice guy. *The Historical Abstract* put together a very funny top ten list of "nice" things to say about Belle, one of which implied that he at least took the game seriously ("he played every game"), and another of which claimed that he was an underrated base runner. Might he have been an underrated fielder as well? DRA rates him essentially average, but $Smith(R(t,s,d))$ reports particularly poor performances in 1994 (–10 defensive runs in a strike-shortened season) and 1996 (–15 defensive runs), which would pull Belle down towards a meaningfully negative left field career. (Bell played fewer than 3000 innings in right; DRA estimates he cost his teams –9 defensive runs there; Smith estimates about −18 defensive runs.). I'll defer to conventional wisdom and the batted ball data backing up $Smith(R(t,s,d))$.

Troy O'Leary is only the most recent Red Sox left fielder whose DRA ratings must be adjusted upward by about ten runs per 1450 innings played in left due to the fact that a lot of fly balls bounce off or clear the Green Monster that most left fielders would be able to run down and catch. With that adjustment, O'Leary is slightly above average in left, in agreement with Smith's estimates. With a Fenway park adjustment, Jim Rice (in our upcoming Modern Era chart) would come in slightly below average, and average overall once you add Walsh or Smith credit for holding base runners. But even with a full Fenway adjustment adding back +48 PO7 runs (10*(BOS IP)/1450) to what is reported below, Manny Ramirez was a poor fielder:

Manny Ramirez

Year	L	Tm	IP7	PO7 runs	A7 runs	v-Tm	Runs
2001	A	BOS	482	-5	-1	-1	-6
2002	A	BOS	529	-6	0	-2	-6
2003	A	BOS	1073	-19	2	-4	-17
2004	A	BOS	1088	-19	-2	-1	-21
2005	A	BOS	1225	-28	5	5	-23
2006	A	BOS	1031	-29	-1	-11	-30
2007	A	BOS	995	-21	1	-8	-20
2008	A	BOS	538	-7	1	-5	-5
2008	N	LA	436	7	-1	3	6
2009	N	LA	812	-8	-1	-5	-9
Total			8209	-135	4	-29	-131

Manny Ramirez in Right Field

Year	L	Tm	IP9	PO9 runs	A9 runs	v-Tm	Runs
1993	A	CLE	8	0	0	0	0
1994	A	CLE	676	-1	1	2	1
1995	A	CLE	1131	1	-3	0	-2
1996	A	CLE	1303	0	5	-2	6
1997	A	CLE	1254	-4	0	0	-4
1998	A	CLE	1319	1	0	4	1
1999	A	CLE	1225	8	-2	-3	6
2000	**A**	**CLE**	**799**	**-19**	**0**	**-11**	**-19**
2002	A	BOS	52	1	1	0	2
Total			7767	-12	3	-10	-9

Manny Ramirez began his career in right field and performed adequately there until a leg injury landed him on the disabled list in 2000 for the first time in his career (see the bold line in right field table). The pre-sabermetric

Red Sox signed the injured Manny to what amounted to a $200 million contract in December of that year. Manny largely avoided outfielder duties in 2001 and 2002, when he served as designated hitter. In 2002 he pulled a hamstring and went on the disabled list again. It seems more than plausible that some serious physical ailments limited Manny's fielding after 1999. And since he knew how valuable his hitting was, it would not surprise me in the least if he decided to take things a little easy in the field so that he could establish himself as one of the handful of greatest right-handed hitters of all time.

Even backing out the ten-runs-per-1450 innings effect of the Green Monster, Manny averaged −18 PO7 runs per 1450 innings with the Red Sox, and the batted ball systems largely agree with that estimate. Taking fielding into account, as well as the general explosion in offense that exactly coincided with his career, Manny Ramirez has had only one season of true MVP quality (1999) and about a handful of all-star quality seasons, which should make him a borderline Hall of Fame candidate, even leaving aside the controversy over his suspension for violating major league baseball's current rules regarding performance-enhancing drugs.

Gary Sheffield presents a similar case. Even granting Sheffield the relatively favorable (that is, neutral) DRA estimate of his defensive value at third base, which we will discuss in the third base chapter, Sheffield conservatively cost his teams about a hundred runs in the outfield. While he amassed a lot of career value, when fielding is factored in, Sheffield only had one clear MVP quality season (2003), though he did produce close to ten all-star quality seasons.

Gary Sheffield

Year	L	Tm	IP7	PO7 runs	A7 runs	v-Tm	Runs
1995	N	FLA	20	-1	0	-1	-1
1999	N	LA	1222	-13	-1	-3	-14
2000	N	LA	1133	-9	-1	-6	-11
2001	N	LA	1195	-26	5	-5	-21
2007	A	DET	56	0	0	0	0
2008	A	DET	47	1	0	1	1
2009	N	NY	358	-1	1	-6	-1
Total			4032	-50	3	-20	-46

Sheffield seemed to improve slightly in the outfield (see his right field numbers on the next page for 2002-05), which is possible, as he began his career in the infield and had to learn his new position.

Gary Sheffield in Right Field

Year	L	Tm	IP9	PO9 runs	A9 runs	v-Tm	Runs
1994	N	FLA	744	-14	0	-1	-14
1995	N	FLA	510	-2	0	-1	-2
1996	N	FLA	1342	-16	-2	-4	-19
1997	N	FLA	1115	-4	3	3	-2
1998	N	FLA	323	-6	0	-3	-6
1998	N	LA	776	-4	0	-4	-4
2001	N	LA	7	0	0	0	0
2002	N	ATL	1104	-2	-1	-8	-3
2003	N	ATL	1288	3	-1	0	2
2004	A	NY	1179	-2	1	-3	-1
2005	A	NY	1099	-2	-1	0	-3
2006	A	NY	165	0	0	-1	0
2007	A	DET	50	1	0	1	1
2009	N	NY	144	-7	0	-5	-7
Total			9846	-55	-2	-27	-58

The Modern Era provides some of the best examples demonstrating that errors are irrelevant and foot speed often so.

Modern Era

MCS	First	Last	IP	Runs	Δ
1972	Roy	White	13311	179	Δ
1990	Rickey	Henderson	19932	144	Δ
1983	Jose	Cruz	12379	128	Δ
1982	Willie	Wilson	5187	110	Δ
1978	Warren	Cromartie	4227	74	Δ
1985	Gary	Ward	6831	56	Δ
1972	Pete	Rose	5841	55	
1971	Cleon	Jones	6469	45	Δ
1990	Dan	Gladden	6521	41	
1980	George	Foster	12904	40	Δ
1982	Billy	Sample	4103	37	Δ
1978	Jim	Wohlford	4317	36	
1982	Dave	Collins	5583	35	
1975	Bill	Buckner	4038	32	
1976	Larry	Hisle	3713	32	Δ
1986	Carmelo	Martinez	4671	32	Δ
1983	Larry	Herndon	6774	31	Δ
1972	John	Briggs	5397	30	Δ
1992	Luis	Polonia	7490	29	Δ
1980	Ben	Oglivie	9092	25	Δ
1975	Jose	Cardenal	3290	23	Δ
1989	Bo	Jackson	3423	18	Δ
1980	Gene	Richards	5056	17	Δ
1990	Ivan	Calderon	3120	16	Δ
1988	Kirk	Gibson	3985	15	
1986	Lonnie	Smith	9678	14	Δ
1969	Rick	Reichardt	5859	14	

(continued)

Modern Era (*continued*)

MCS	First	Last	IP	Runs	Δ
1989	Billy	Hatcher	4220	12	Δ
1980	Steve	Henderson	7050	10	Δ
1976	John	Milner	3348	8	Δ
1976	Richie	Zisk	3495	4	
1971	Ken	Henderson	3250	3	
1978	Dave	Kingman	4143	3	
1969	Jesus	Alou	3181	2	Δ
1974	Lou	Piniella	9305	2	
1970	Don	Buford	4379	1	Δ
1985	Gary	Redus	4443	1	Δ
1982	Gary	Roenicke	4420	1	
1979	Al	Woods	4288	-6	Δ
1970	Alex	Johnson	7657	-6	Δ
1970	Manny	Mota	4731	-7	Δ
1989	Tim	Raines	16791	-7	Δ
1974	Joe	Rudi	9692	-7	
1969	Tommy	Harper	5092	-8	Δ
1982	Mike	Easler	3750	-10	Δ
1986	Ken	Griffey	3790	-12	Δ
1984	Brian	Downing	6030	-13	
1976	Don	Baylor	5189	-13	Δ
1980	John	Lowenstein	4503	-14	
1978	Al	Oliver	3954	-15	Δ
1991	Candy	Maldonado	3426	-16	Δ
1988	Mel	Hall	5580	-18	Δ
1976	Steve	Braun	3495	-18	
1991	Kevin	Mitchell	6034	-21	Δ
1991	Joe	Carter	5929	-25	Δ
1989	Kal	Daniels	5127	-26	Δ
1990	Pete	Incaviglia	6509	-28	
1990	Kevin	McReynolds	8537	-29	
1980	Dave	Winfield	3810	-30	Δ
1975	Ralph	Garr	6782	-31	Δ
1989	Vince	Coleman	9861	-31	Δ
1979	Tom	Paciorek	3177	-33	
1980	Steve	Kemp	7920	-34	
1978	Jeff	Burroughs	3522	-34	
1980	Dusty	Baker	9136	-34	Δ
1969	Willie	Stargell	10381	-37	Δ
1972	Carlos	May	5581	-49	Δ
1986	Jeffrey	Leonard	7485	-51	Δ
1971	Lou	Brock	18484	-52	Δ
1972	Bob	Watson	4664	-56	Δ
1987	George	Bell	9593	-57	Δ
1987	Phil	Bradley	7037	-61	Δ
1969	Willie	Horton	9030	-62	Δ
1991	Mike	Greenwell	9514	-77	
1980	Gary	Matthews	12434	-106	Δ
1982	Jim	Rice	13159	-109	Δ
1976	Greg	Luzinski	10091	-152	

Lonnie "Skates" Smith led all National League outfielders in errors in 1983 and 1984, and led all National League left fielders in errors in 1990. Sometime during or just after Smith's 1983-84 accomplishments were in the record book, Bill James wrote a hilarious essay about Lonnie's skill at coping well with his own errors, suggesting that Skates should even become a coach of "defensive recovery and cost containment." Apparently Smith had small feet, which caused him to lose his footing a lot, hence the nickname "Skates." DRA and Sean Smith's methods both show that Lonnie Smith was actually essentially average. His speed (close to four hundred stolen bases lifetime, with a pretty good seventy-three percent success rate) probably helped in the defensive recovery and cost containment.

Speed always helps in the outfield, but it's possible to be a respectably solid corner outfielder and be slow, and to be a disappointingly mediocre left fielder while being fast. Lou Piniella stole only thirty-two bases in his career, and, what's worse, got caught forty-one times. And yet he was a better out-fielder than Tim Raines, Ralph Garr, and Vince Coleman. There's little point in showing all their respective single-season numbers, as they don't form any patterns, except that Coleman did slightly better then tailed off, and Piniella had only one bad year, 1973 (–18 defensive runs). Coincidentally, that was also his worst full-time season as a hitter. Lou added another 2169 innings in right, where he was about average as well.

Piniella's Yankee teammate Sparky Lyle called him the best slow outfielder in baseball, and tells two stories in The Bronx Zoo to back it up. The team had charts prepared showing the batted ball distributions of opponent batters. An assistant with the charts would walkie-talkie bench coach Yogi Berra, who would wave the outfielders to the position indicated in the charts. In one extra inning game, Berra waved Piniella from the position he had taken to one much closer to center, based on what the charts showed. On the next pitch, the batter hit the ball precisely where Piniella had originally posi-tioned himself, for a triple. Afterwards Lou told Yogi, "The next time you move me over, I quit."

Sweet Lou knew more than the sweet spots to play in the outfield. In the famous 1978 Eastern Division sudden death playoff game between the Yankees and Red Sox—the one Bucky Dent won with his three-run homer—Lou performed some "defensive cost containment" that saved the game. The Red Sox came up in the bottom of the ninth behind by one run. Rick Burleson walked, and Jerry Remy hit a fly ball to right (where Lou was playing), that Lou lost in the sun. But Lou pumped his glove like he had it, which fooled Burleson into hugging first. When the ball came down, Burleson was only able to reach second. Rice came up next and flied out—a fly out that would have brought Burleson home from third to tie the game. That set up the final at-bat in which Yaz popped out to Craig Nettles. Bucky Dent may owe his baseball immortality to Lou Piniella's clever fielding.

Transitional Era

MCS	First	Last	IP	Runs	Δ
1951	Gil	Coan	4576	57	
1954	Monte	Irvin	3110	54	Δ
1952	Whitey	Lockman	4204	50	
1965	Tom	Tresh	3951	47	
1967	Tony	Gonzalez	3359	41	Δ
1957	Minnie	Minoso	12614	37	Δ
1962	Hector	Lopez	3619	37	Δ
1958	Charlie	Maxwell	6434	33	
1967	Billy	Williams	14861	28	Δ
1967	Gates	Brown	3158	26	Δ
1961	Frank	Robinson	6730	25	Δ
1959	Norm	Siebern	3282	22	
1954	Stan	Musial	5520	17	
1955	Gene	Woodling	8062	16	
1965	Lee	Maye	4014	16	Δ
1957	Al	Smith	3089	15	Δ
1958	Bob	Cerv	3889	15	
1950	Sid	Gordon	5541	9	
1963	Rocky	Colavito	4418	7	
1964	Chuck	Hinton	3690	7	Δ
1966	Tommy	Davis	8652	5	Δ
1947	Dick	Wakefield	3418	1	
1960	Frank	Thomas	5656	-1	
1960	Jim	Lemon	3594	-2	
1967	Bob	Allison	3980	-2	
1963	Boog	Powell	3429	-5	
1968	Rico	Carty	6365	-6	Δ
1956	Bob	Nieman	5466	-8	
1952	Hank	Sauer	8524	-11	
1968	Carl	Yastrzemski	16476	-12	
1959	Wally	Moon	4720	-17	
1962	Tito	Francona	4454	-20	
1950	Dale	Mitchell	6716	-29	
1953	Gus	Zernial	8482	-30	
1956	Roy	Sievers	5185	-31	
1960	Bob	Skinner	7529	-32	
1956	Rip	Repulski	4068	-39	
1963	Harmon	Killebrew	3937	-53	
1960	Jerry	Lynch	3698	-59	
1952	Del	Ennis	10726	-64	
1951	Ralph	Kiner	10602	-78	
1967	Frank	Howard	7268	-80	
1961	Wes	Covington	5685	-89	Δ
1964	Leon	Wagner	8454	-90	Δ
1951	Ted	Williams	15328	-130	

Give The Kid about 100 runs back to offset what the Green Monster took away. We'll deal with Yaz later in this chapter.

Gil Coan

Year	L	Tm	IP	PO7 runs	A7 runs	v-Tm	Runs
1948	A	WAS	1112	27	1		27
1950	A	WAS	724	7	-2		6
1951	A	WAS	1120	27	4		31
1952	A	WAS	712	-12	0	-10	-12
1953	A	WAS	350	9	-1	8	9
1954	A	BAL	286	1	-1	4	1
1955	A	BAL	258	-6	2	-6	-4
1955	N	NY	9	0	0	0	0
1955	A	CHI	5	-1	0	-1	-1
Total			4576	54	3	-5	57

The Sporting News named Gil Coan Minor League Player of the Year 1945, but with all the boys coming back from the War the next year, he didn't get in a full major season until 1948, when he finished second in league in stolen bases and fielded well. He began hitting in 1950–51 and finished 23rd in MVP voting in 1951. His sharp decline in fielding as well as hitting the following year suggests to me that he sustained a serious injury. The deep left field corner of Griffith Stadium probably gave him extra chances (much the same as the deep right field corner in Crosley boosted right fielder ratings), so I am not prepared to say he was a great fielder, even just on a peak basis.

Seeing Monte Irvin and Whitey Lockman second and third on the list set off alarm bells. Both played for the Giants, one right after the other. Was there a park effect helping them out? On the face of it, one would think not—true, left center was very deep, but the left field line at the Polo Grounds was almost as short as the right field one, so the total area to be covered by the corner outfielders at the Polo Grounds was probably not too unusual. Right field in the Polo Grounds had approximately the same shape (reversed), and Giant right fielders did not dominate. The Giants had a normal team rating with Babe Barna (1942), Sid Gordon (1946–47), Bobby Thomson (1948), as well as in 1952–53, when several players split the position, which would suggest no major park effect. I have not been able to find any accounts of Lockman's fielding, but he had some speed, as evidenced by his possession of one of the lowest rates of grounding into double plays in major league history.

Though he didn't play much in left after 1950, Whitey Lockman continued to save runs there at a very good clip: about +17 defensive runs per 1450 innings played. And he consistently outperformed his teammates there, as

Whitey Lockman

Year	L	Tm	IP	PO7 runs	A7 runs	v-Tm	Runs
1949	N	NY	1298	14	-2		12
1950	N	NY	1036	24	1		25
1951	N	NY	318	-1	0		-1
1953	N	NY	236	3	0	2	3
1954	N	NY	8	0	0	0	0
1955	N	NY	665	6	-2	2	4
1956	N	NY	293	2	-1	4	1
1957	N	NY	104	5	0	6	6
1956	N	STL	190	3	0	3	3
1958	N	SF	57	-1	0	-1	-1
			4204	54	-4	15	50

indicated by his v-Tm runs, starting in 1955. Why, then, was he moved from left to first base between 1950 and 1955? Because his team had an even better left fielder during that interval, Monte Irvin, who will make our top ten list.

The remaining noteworthy Transitional Era cases are sluggish sluggers Gus Zernial and Ralph Kiner.

Gus Zernial

Year	L	Tm	IP	PO7 runs	A7 runs	v-Tm	Runs
1949	A	CHI	368	-13	1		-12
1950	A	CHI	1178	4	-1		3
1951	A	PHI	1171	5	4		9
1951	A	CHI	32	3	0		3
1952	A	PHI	1252	-8	-1	-3	-9
1953	A	PHI	1239	-6	4	-4	-2
1954	A	PHI	753	-15	-1	-8	-15
1955	A	KC	860	5	0	1	5
1956	A	KC	525	-2	3	-5	1
1957	A	KC	941	-7	-1	2	-8
1958	A	DET	163	-3	0	-2	-3
Total			8482	-37	7	-20	-30

The 1949 estimate could be considerably wrong because of the small sample size and the lack of separate putout and innings played data in left, center, and right. Focusing on just his four full-time seasons in left, 1950–53, Gus Zernial would appear to have been a perfectly competent fielder in his time, both for the White Sox and the Athletics. There is some uncertainty about how effective he was at throwing out and holding base runners. He led all American League outfielders in assists in 1951, and generally had high assists totals, as reflected in his good A7 runs above, though Smith estimates he allowed about −15 runs from 1954 onward by failing to hold base runners.

Even if his arm was mediocre, Zernial was hardly a disaster in the field. Then why was he considered *such* a poor fielder, a "comic figure" with "Dave Kingman-like" skills, in Bill James's estimation? Images. Big slugger. Let the league in strikeouts twice, left field errors twice, and all outfielders in errors once. Zernial also got stuck with a funny nickname, Ozark Ike, that he had the good grace to take pride in. The word "eventful" doesn't begin to suggest the life he has led outside of baseball: the short form is that he basically set Joe DiMaggio up with Marilyn Monroe; had careers (presumably some of which were fairly successful) in auto leasing, broadcasting, advertising, marketing, and investment management; recently helped develop a new minor league franchise in his home town, Fresno, California; and has been beating cancer for the past two decades. Sounds like a bright and resourceful character to me.

Ralph Kiner was a bad outfielder, by reputation and by the numbers. But curiously, not always so.

Ralph Kiner in Left Field

Year	L	Tm	IP	PO7 runs	A7 runs	v-Tm	Runs
1947	N	PIT	1307	12	-2		10
1948	N	PIT	1324	21	-3		18
1949	N	PIT	1290	-13	0		-13
1950	N	PIT	1273	-31	1		-29
1951	N	PIT	798	0	-1		-1
1952	N	PIT	1296	-17	-1	1	-18
1953	N	CHI	986	-16	-2	-1	-19
1953	N	PIT	352	-5	1	-8	-4
1954	N	CHI	1274	0	-2	-2	-2
1955	A	CLE	702	-18	-3	-8	-20
Total			10602	-66	-12	-17	-78

People forget that Kiner played more games in *center* than in left in his first season, 1946, and his overall defensive runs that year, in left and center combined, was a mediocre −8 defensive runs, but hardly disastrous. The next two years in left were actually excellent. Perhaps his (subsequently) well-known ankle, leg, and back injuries took their toll on his fielding.

Live Ball Era

MCS	First	Last	IP	Runs	Δ
1933	Al	Simmons	11824	60	
1944	Danny	Litwhiler	4165	54	
1938	Morrie	Arnovich	4006	54	
1929	Goose	Goslin	16690	53	
1926	Ken	Williams	9513	48	
1925	Ray	Blades	4092	45	
1937	Jo-Jo	Moore	10625	44	
1939	Bob	Johnson	12681	44	
1944	Charlie	Keller	6920	39	
1920	Austin	McHenry	3096	38	
1934	Hal	Lee	5921	38	
1937	Moose	Solters	5876	38	
1925	Charlie	Jamieson	11255	34	
1943	Eric	Tipton	3261	33	
1928	Rube	Bressler	6004	30	
1938	Gee	Walker	5889	19	
1940	Augie	Galan	6508	17	
1922	Carson	Bigbee	5676	17	
1931	Adam	Comorosky	4848	14	
1920	Mike	Menosky	4030	12	
1935	Joe	Vosmik	11225	11	
1933	John	Stone	5096	10	
1920	Les	Mann	3354	10	
1930	Riggs	Stephenson	7445	4	
1929	Freddy	Leach	4601	3	
1925	Bill	Lamar	3441	-5	
1921	Tillie	Walker	3748	-6	
1922	Pat	Duncan	5895	-6	
1938	Joe	Medwick	15330	-7	
1924	Bing	Miller	3064	-10	
1927	Bob	Fothergill	4917	-11	
1935	Woody	Jensen	4772	-15	
1943	Jeff	Heath	7105	-16	
1935	Roy	Johnson	4642	-20	
1923	Irish	Meusel	7471	-24	
1930	Chick	Hafey	6629	-25	
1925	Babe	Ruth	8129	-26	
1931	Lefty	O'Doul	6272	-29	
1926	Bob	Meusel	5634	-31	
1925	Bibb	Falk	9489	-63	
1931	Heinie	Manush	11857	-87	
1937	Rip	Radcliff	5106	-97	

Simmons and Goslin were good, not great, in the field and are still remem-bered because of their hitting. Let's discuss the lesser-knowns Litwhiler and Arnovich, who appear to have saved a bunch of runs in very short careers.

Because Danny Litwhiler (see next page) split a lot of time between left and right, the table below gives his estimated innings at all three outfield positions and his combined putout runs anywhere in the outfield (PO789 runs) and assists runs anywhere in the outfield (A789 runs). Though the right field numbers

Danny Litwhiler

Year	L	Tm	IP7	IP8	IP9	PO789 runs	A789 runs	Runs
1940	N	PHI	16	22	236	3	1	4
1941	N	PHI	1264	0	17	20	1	21
1942	N	PHI	1061	0	196	-1	0	-1
1943	N	PHI	276	0	0	9	1	10
1943	N	STL	550	0	0	7	1	8
1944	N	STL	1054	0	0	19	-2	17
1946	N	BOS	484	0	0	3	-2	1
1947	N	BOS	471	0	10	-5	-1	-6
1948	N	BOS	65	0	0	4	0	4
1948	N	CIN	20	5	617	13	-2	11
1949	N	CIN	84	8	516	-4	0	-4
1950	N	CIN	66	0	165	-3	-1	-4
1951	N	CIN	0	0	64	0	0	0
Total			5411	35	1821	65	-5	60

in Crosley may not mean much, because of the park effect we discussed in chapter four, he had good seasons with two different teams, the Phillies and the Cardinals, and great rate stats with both.

In 1941, Litwhiler led all National League outfielders in errors. His new manager the next year, Hans Lobert, somehow found out that all of those errors had been on ground balls. (Did they go though his legs for extra bases? Nobody knows.) Lobert, who as we shall see might have been a historically *bad* third baseman, ordered Litwhiler to start taking infield practice, and Litwhiler came through to become the first major league player to play every game without being charged a single error. But Litwhiler also recorded *eighty-five* fewer putouts, perhaps out of an excessive fear of committing errors.

In addition to the infield practice, two other factors were essential to Litwhiler's errorless season. He later recalled, "I think that my glove [in 1942] was the first one that had the fingers tied together by rawhide. I thought if I tied them together, if I catch a ball, maybe it would stay. Sure enough, during the time of the record, I fielded the ball two times right on the end of the fingers. No way in the world I would have caught [them] if it weren't tied together." The second factor was Johnny Mize, then playing for the Giants. Late in the seasons, Mize hit a line drive to left field in the Polo Grounds, which was extremely muddy after several days of rain. Litwhiler caught the ball on the run, but slipped when setting up to throw, and dropped it. The official scorer charged an error. After the game, Mize, still in his uniform, went up to the press box to argue the call, because he was hitting .299 and wanted to finish the season over .300. Mize won the argument, and thereby enabled Litwhiler to finish the season with a 1.000 fielding average. Mize hit .305 for the year.

Morrie Arnovich

Year	L	Tm	IP	PO7 runs	A7 runs	Runs
1936	N	PHI	155	-1	0	-1
1937	N	PHI	819	8	2	10
1938	N	PHI	1154	11	5	15
1939	N	PHI	1148	16	1	17
1940	N	PHI	298	8	0	8
1940	N	CIN	437	11	1	12
1941	N	NY	426	-8	1	-7
1946	N	NY	7	0	0	0
Total			4443	44	10	54

By all accounts a likable, diligent, hustling player, Morrie Arnovich was probably also very bright—his parents wanted him to become a rabbi. In his best season, 1939, the Phillies team president, Gerry Nugent, is rumored to have said he wouldn't trade Arnovich for Ducky Medwick. Well, the following season Arnovich was hitting .199 as of June 15th, and the Phillies somehow found it in their hearts to trade Arnovich to the Reds for somebody named Johnny Rizzo. Arnovich struggled the next two seasons, and volunteered after Pearl Harbor. Arnovich was thirty-five when he came back from the War, and called it quits after a brief spell with the Giants.

Dead Ball Era

MCS	First	Last	IP	Runs	Δ
1906	Jimmy	Sheckard	14853	218	
1903	Fred	Clarke	18587	212	
1918	Bobby	Veach	14177	185	
1900	Kip	Selbach	9303	138	
1906	Matty	McIntyre	6688	84	
1918	Zack	Wheat	19858	71	
1919	George	Burns	7705	66	
1897	Elmer	Smith	6901	61	
1909	Sherry	Magee	9361	52	
1907	George	Stone	6415	47	
1914	Max	Carey	3734	38	
1898	Ed	Delahanty	6839	33	
1900	Ducky	Holmes	4241	31	
1899	Jesse	Burkett	15040	29	
1910	Rube	Ellis	3675	20	
1917	Possum	Whitted	3052	20	
1915	Jack	Graney	8537	15	
1906	Spike	Shannon	3875	13	
1905	Sam	Mertes	3577	12	
1915	Duffy	Lewis	10801	8	
1899	Joe	Kelley	8026	-2	
1917	Burt	Shotton	3175	-6	
1912	Bob	Bescher	8571	-25	

(continued)

Dead Ball Era (*continued*)

MCS	First	Last	IP	Runs	Δ
1900	Dick	Harley	4568	-26	
1901	Jack	McCarthy	5247	-32	
1903	George	Barclay	3234	-48	
1906	Patsy	Dougherty	10127	-66	
1906	Topsy	Hartsel	6492	-92	

Because we don't have separate putout totals in left, center, and right before 1920, it is necessary to estimate defensive runs for outfielders for all three positions combined. If a player played more than ninety-five percent of his games in a season at one outfield position, we assign the total rating for that season to just that position. If a player split more than five percent of his games, we don't include that season in the separate center field, right field, and left field Dead Ball Era charts. The greatest fielders only rarely split their time in any given season; we'll show seasons with time split among the outfield positions for just one or two important cases.

Kip Selbach

Year	L	Tm	IP	PO7 runs	A7 runs	Runs
1895	N	WAS	993	22	3	26
1896	N	WAS	1052	21	-2	19
1897	N	WAS	1052	38	-1	36
1898	N	WAS	1078	26	4	30
1900	N	NY	1197	9	3	12
1901	N	NY	1061	-7	-2	-10
1902	A	BAL	1078	8	1	9
1904	A	WAS	420	4	0	4
1904	A	BOS	858	13	-2	11
1906	A	BOS	514	1	0	0
Total			9303	134	4	138

Selbach split time between left and center in 1899, saving about thirty runs. I think he got hurt in 1901, because he stole only eight bases, when he had stolen between twenty-five and fifty bases every full-time sea-son before then. His stolen base totals never returned to their prior level. Selbach's best fielding years were played when there was only one major league, so the quality of his competitors in left might well have been relatively high.

Selbach more or less disappeared from baseball history, for several reasons. He peaked before 1901, the year many fans traditionally (and incorrectly) have long viewed as the first year of major league baseball. He played for terrible teams, though he was able to help the Boston Red Sox win the pennant in 1904, thanks in part to a great fielding play he made in the last game of the season. Although a very good offensive player, much of his value came from drawing walks, which weren't even officially tallied for batters in his time. Good fielding, of course, is rarely appreciated, still less good fielding at a position such as left field.

Matty McIntyre

Year	L	Tm	IP	PO7 runs	A7 runs	Runs
1901	A	PHI	714	-3	0	-3
1904	A	DET	1282	36	0	36
1905	A	DET	1112	20	4	24
1906	A	DET	1120	-13	7	-6
1907	A	DET	169	3	1	4
1908	A	DET	1282	22	2	24
1909	A	DET	1010	6	1	7
Total			6688	70	14	84

McIntyre split time between left, center, and right for Tigers in 1910, saving about five runs, and center and right for the White Sox in 1911, saving another sixteen. Though not as consistent as Selbach, McIntyre was clearly outstanding the four seasons in which he was healthy and in the right frame of mind. Shortly after Ty Cobb joined the Tigers in August 1905, Cobb tried fielding a fly ball in McIntyre's territory, causing McIntyre to drop the ball and almost lose the game. Infuriated, McIntyre eventually led the Tigers' notorious hazing campaign against Cobb. The next year, 1906, McIntyre started strong, and his manager Bill Armour praised a number of great catches he made, but in late June Armour accused him of not hustling for a ball that had been hit to the fence, and McIntyre was eventually suspended for "indifferent work." The following year Matty broke his ankle and missed almost all of the season. He came back in 1908 quite strong, but had appendicitis in 1909. The Tigers sold him to the White Sox, where he had his last good season in 1911 (+16 defensive runs, split between center and right).

McIntyre was a leadoff hitter, and good but not exceptional in that role; his almost exact contemporary Topsy Hartsel (see next page) was one of the outstanding leadoff men of all time, thanks to his extraordinary ability to draw walks. His fielding, however, left something to be desired. Here are his numbers when playing in left field. He split time in center in 1904–05, and gave up another dozen runs.

Topsy Hartsel

Year	L	Tm	IP	PO7 runs	A7 runs	Runs
1900	N	CIN	160	-12	-2	-14
1902	A	PHI	1199	-14	1	-13
1903	A	PHI	798	-13	-2	-16
1906	A	PHI	1261	-7	0	-7
1907	A	PHI	1214	-8	-3	-11
1908	A	PHI	1095	-17	-3	-20
1910	A	PHI	682	-8	-2	-10
1911	A	PHI	84	-3	1	-2
Total			6492	-82	-11	-92

If it seems as though the list below says that the very best left fielders of all time played either when the grass was plastic (circa 1980) or when the ball was dead (circa 1900), you're reading it correctly.

Top Forty Left Fielders of All Time

MCS	First	Last	IP	Runs	Δ	TPAR
1972	Roy	White	13311	179	Δ	188
1990	Rickey	Henderson	19932	144	Δ	162
1996	Barry	Bonds	22909	133	Δ	143
1982	Jose	Cruz	11989	119	Δ	138
1982	Willie	Wilson	5187	110	Δ	128
1918	Bobby	Veach	14177	185		127
1906	Jimmy	Sheckard	14853	218		111
1978	Warren	Cromartie	4227	74	Δ	89
1999	Luis	Gonzalez	20643	81		82
1903	Fred	Clarke	18587	212		80
1985	Gary	Ward	6831	56	Δ	76
1972	Pete	Rose	5841	55		65
1990	Dan	Gladden	6521	41		60
1980	George	Foster	12904	40	Δ	57
1982	Billy	Sample	4103	37	Δ	56
1982	Dave	Collins	5583	35		54
1971	Cleon	Jones	6469	45	Δ	53
1995	Bernard	Gilkey	8127	39	Δ	52
1993	Shane	Mack	3031	36	Δ	52
1978	Jim	Wohlford	4317	36		52
1986	Carmelo	Martinez	4671	32	Δ	51
1983	Larry	Herndon	6774	31	Δ	50
1965	Tom	Tresh	3951	47		47
1992	Luis	Polonia	7490	29	Δ	46
1976	Larry	Hisle	3713	32	Δ	45
1975	Bill	Buckner	4038	32		45
1995	Tony	Phillips	4273	31	Δ	44
1967	Tony	Gonzalez	3359	41	Δ	44
1980	Ben	Oglivie	9092	25	Δ	43
2001	Brian	Giles	5188	45		43
1999	Bobby	Higginson	5435	40		42

(continued)

Top Forty Left Fielders of All Time *(continued)*

MCS	First	Last	IP	Runs	Δ	TPAR
1954	Monte	Irvin	3110	54	Δ	41
1951	Gil	Coan	4576	57		41
1972	John	Briggs	5397	30	Δ	39
1995	Greg	Vaughn	10573	25	Δ	37
1989	Bo	Jackson	3423	18	Δ	37
1975	Jose	Cardenal	3290	23	Δ	35
1952	Whitey	Lockman	4204	50		35
1990	Ivan	Calderon	3120	16	Δ	35
2005	Jay	Payton	3777	55	Δ	34

According to the TPAR model, left field became much more competitive as integration advanced, and was most competitive when participation by African-American players reached its peak around 1980. There was an enormous variance in speed among left fielders around that time. This was the era of Greg Luzinski, who played left field from 1972 through 1980, and of Rickey Henderson, who began his career in 1979. And speed mattered more then than it ever has in the outfield, because of Astroturf.

Left field was nearly as important as center field during the Dead Ball Era, particularly before 1900, as nearly as many putouts were recorded in left as in center. This can be confirmed directly for 1911, because Retrosheet has done the research to tabulate separate putout totals in left, center, and right for that season. The Dead Ball DRA model, as shown in appendix A, estimates similar proportions for the other seasons. Although I'm not aware of much, if any, research on this point, it must have been the case that when the pitcher's mound was moved back to its current distance in 1893, it took significantly longer for pitches to reach the plate, so a lot more hitters—almost all of whom were right-handed in those days—were able to pull the ball frequently. It also would seem likely that the hardest hit balls in the outfield would generally be the pulled line drives to left. The situation might have been similar to what it is for slow-pitch softball teams today—you had better have one of your best fielders in left, or you will certainly lose.

Input from $Smith(R(t,s,d))$ suggests we leave Luis Gonzalez (see next page) out of the top ten.

Gonzalez had two careers. Through 1997, his age-twenty-nine season, he maintained a just slightly above average on base percentage (.341) and slugging percentage (.432), and saved in the field somewhere between 130 runs as measured by DRA, and 90 runs as measured by $Smith(R(t,s,d))$. Ninety runs is probably closer to the truth, particularly because Smith's estimate is based on batted ball data and takes into account park factors—the Astrodome was one of the rare post-expansion ballparks with a practically significant park effect. Gonzalez's first negative DRA rating, in 1998, coincided with his first twenty-homer season. He never had another meaningfully above-average fielding season again, as his home runs increased from twenty-three to twenty-six to thirty-one to fifty-seven. $MGL(B(t,s,d,v,bh))$ reports -26 defensive runs in left field over the course of his last two seasons, 2007 and 2008.

Luis Gonzalez

Year	L	Tm	IP	PO7 runs	A7 runs	v-Tm	Runs
1991	N	HOU	1085	14	-1	1	13
1992	N	HOU	859	27	0	7	27
1993	N	HOU	1248	39	0	1	38
1994	N	HOU	928	20	-1	4	19
1995	N	HOU	464	2	-1	-3	1
1995	N	CHI	602	19	0	14	19
1996	N	CHI	1124	3	-1	-5	3
1997	N	HOU	1258	12	1	1	13
1998	A	DET	1143	-11	0	-2	-11
1999	N	ARI	1322	-3	0	3	-2
2000	N	ARI	1431	2	-3	-2	-1
2001	N	ARI	1417	3	-1	0	1
2002	N	ARI	1246	1	-3	-3	-2
2003	N	ARI	1359	0	0	3	0
2004	N	ARI	900	-6	-2	-4	-8
2005	N	ARI	1318	-2	-1	2	-4
2006	N	ARI	1315	-10	-3	-4	-13
2007	N	LA	996	-5	-2	-3	-7
2008	N	FLA	504	-3	-2	2	-5
Total			20518	100	-19	14	81

Honorable Mention: Fred Clarke

Year	L	Tm	IP	PO7 runs	A7 runs	Runs
1894	N	LOU	651	3	2	5
1895	N	LOU	1155	23	1	24
1896	N	LOU	1112	10	1	11
1897	N	LOU	1053	26	1	27
1898	N	LOU	1248	22	-1	21
1899	N	LOU	1222	12	-1	10
1900	N	PIT	883	26	-4	22
1901	N	PIT	1078	22	-1	20
1902	N	PIT	919	5	0	4
1903	N	PIT	857	-4	-3	-8
1904	N	PIT	605	7	-2	5
1905	N	PIT	1163	14	1	15
1906	N	PIT	934	9	2	11
1907	N	PIT	1222	9	-1	8
1908	N	PIT	1273	17	-1	16
1909	N	PIT	1290	21	-2	19
1910	N	PIT	1002	11	-3	8
1911	N	PIT	891	0	-4	-4
1913	N	PIT	22	-3	0	-3
1915	N	PIT	8	-1	0	-1
Total			18587	229	-17	212

Fred Clarke (see preceding page) maintained very consistent defensive runs levels when he was playing full time. Like many (though not all) great fielders, he was a bit cleverer than his fellow players, and was chosen to be his team's manager in 1897 when he was only twenty-four years old. Realizing that he was not good at going back on fly balls, he played deep and developed a special way of diving for balls hit in front of him. Clarke's preference for playing deep might also have motivated him, in his role as manager, to move Honus Wagner from right field to shortstop. As we will discuss in the shortstop chapter, Wagner had an unusually high level of putouts at short, suggesting that he may have 'hogged' a lot of pop ups and short flies. Perhaps Clarke wanted Wagner to serve as a shallow left fielder while Clarke played deep. Since there were almost as many fly balls to left during the Dead Ball Era as there were to center, and perhaps more hard hit balls to left than center, that might have been a very smart thing to do.

From 1900 through 1916, Clarke compiled a .595 winning percentage as a manager, and was brought back to lead a flagging Pirates team to a World Championship in 1925. Clarke later obtained several baseball-related patents, including flip-down sunglasses, and bought a ranch that, luckily for him, just so happened to be sitting on a lot of oil. Within a couple years of his retirement, Clarke was worth (in current dollar terms) well north of $50 million.

Number Ten: Monte Irvin

Year	L	Tm	IP	PO7 runs	A7 runs	v-Tm	Runs
1952	N	NY	234	-3	1	-3	-3
1953	N	NY	725	7	1	4	8
1954	N	NY	1060	23	-1	10	22
1955	N	NY	315	5	0	3	4
1956	N	CHI	775	21	1	1	22
Total			3110	52	2	16	54

The first edition of *The Historical Abstract* reported that everybody in the Negro Leagues believed Monte Irvin would be the one to break the color line, as he was a "consummate gentleman" and an outstanding player. Irvin spent the bulk of his major league career waiting for the call, but did get into the Hall of Fame, mainly on the basis of his Negro and Mexican League record.

What I don't think has been appreciated up to now is that Irvin may have been the greatest fielding left fielder before the Modern Era (1969–92), when integration was largely complete. The table above is missing about twenty-two additional defensive runs of value that Irvin contributed as a corner outfielder, mainly in left and mainly in 1950–51. Irvin split time in 1950–51 about sixty-forty between left and right; on a combined basis he had +19 defensive runs in about 1424 estimated innings. He also picks up about three runs in right in 382 innings post-1951, when we have exact data for putouts and innings played per outfield position. That brings Irvin up to +76 defensive runs in about 4916 innings as a corner outfielder, which come to +22 defensive runs per 1450 innings played, all after the age of thirty, an absolutely amazing rate.

With the possible exception of two other gentlemen we'll be discussing immediately below, I'm not aware of any left fielders in major league history who fielded so well compared with their contemporaries while playing in their mid-thirties. It is easy to imagine that if Irvin had played his entire career in the major leagues, including his prime, he would have saved a couple hundred runs, which, even with a time line adjustment, would place him high up the top ten list. I decided to play it a little conservative in placing him here.

Fenway reduces left fielder defensive runs from fielding batted balls by about ten runs per 162 games, or 1450 innings played. Adding back that

Number Nine: Carl Yastrzmeski

Year	L	Tm	IP	PO7 runs	A7 runs	v-Tm	Green Monster	Runs
1961	A	BOS	1269	-17	0	1	9	-8
1962	A	BOS	1428	13	4	0	10	27
1963	A	BOS	1351	-2	4	4	9	11
1964	A	BOS	136	0	0	1	1	1
1965	A	BOS	1041	-17	2	2	7	-7
1966	A	BOS	1366	18	4	1	9	31
1967	A	BOS	1355	3	2	3	9	14
1968	A	BOS	1320	16	2	2	9	27
1969	A	BOS	1181	-7	4	4	8	5
1970	A	BOS	579	-1	0	0	4	3
1971	A	BOS	1257	0	5	1	9	14
1972	A	BOS	708	-5	2	0	5	3
1973	A	BOS	134	4	-1	3	1	4
1974	A	BOS	537	-16	-1	-4	4	-14
1975	A	BOS	69	-1	0	-1	0	0
1976	A	BOS	429	-8	-1	-3	3	-6
1977	A	BOS	1183	0	4	-6	8	12
1978	A	BOS	552	-7	2	-4	4	-2
1979	A	BOS	290	-7	-1	-3	2	-6
1980	A	BOS	284	-6	0	-3	2	-4
1983	A	BOS	7	-1	0	-1	0	-1
Total			16476	-43	32	-1	114	102

"Green Monster" adjustment for Yaz completely changes his career assessment. His TPAR without the Green Monster adjustment is –7; all you need to do is add +114 to that and his TPAR rises to +107. Also, the missing innings throughout Yaz's left field career were played mainly in center when he was young, and at first when he was not.

There is a good reason to rank Yaz even higher, but also a good reason for placing him lower. In 2007, John Walsh estimated that Yaz saved another thirty-five runs by holding base runners, but alerted people to the fact that the Green Monster *helps* left fielders defend the running game: you have to play shallow, and doubles off the wall can be fielded quickly, making it easier to hold runners. Sean Smith includes a Green Monster factor for base runner defense, and estimates that Yaz saved more like twenty runs holding base runners. I think Smith is probably closer to the mark there, which would legitimately boost Yaz's TPAR to +127. However, all of Yaz's great fielding seasons occurred before 1969, when the American League was still noticeably less integrated than the National. Since the talent pool adjustment behind TPAR is not calculated separately per league, it will slightly overrate American League outfielders over National League outfielders of the Transitional Era (1947–68).

Number Eight: Jimmy Sheckard

Year	L	Tm	IP	PO7 runs	A7 runs	Runs
1898	N	BRO	857	1	-2	-1
1901	N	BRO	1019	23	0	23
1902	N	BRO	1035	26	-2	24
1903	N	BRO	1180	26	10	35
1904	N	BRO	1197	12	1	14
1905	N	BRO	1095	16	6	22
1906	N	CHI	1256	23	-3	20
1907	N	CHI	1205	0	-2	-2
1908	N	CHI	976	0	0	0
1909	N	CHI	1256	8	-1	7
1910	N	CHI	1214	18	2	20
1911	N	CHI	1324	29	7	35
1912	N	CHI	1239	18	3	21
Total			14853	198	20	218

I can't explain the strange gap from 1907 through 1909. But for Jimmy Sheckard to be inexplicably inconsistent on defense would be perfectly consistent with his being inexplicably inconsistent on offense. As pointed out in both editions of *The Historical Abstract*, almost every component of Sheckard's offense waxed and waned unpredictably. He led the league in stolen bases in 1899, with 77, and in 1903, with 67, but never stole more than

35 in any other season. He led the league in slugging (.534) in 1902, but slugged above .400 only once in the remainder of his career. He walked a respectable amount throughout his career, gradually increasing his seasonal totals to a career high of 83 in 1910. In 1911 he upped that by 64 walks, yes, sixty-four, to lead the league with 147, and led the league in walks the following year, his last full-time season, with 122. From 1903, when run scoring really began to fall and sacrifice hits became even more common, through 1912, his sacrifice hits ranged from 46 (in 1909) to 10 (in 1912).

In the end, one way or another, Sheckard put together three seasons of MVP quality (1901, 1903, perhaps 1911) and about a handful of all-star quality seasons. I'd rank him overall, among pre-integration corner outfielders, about as high as (legitimate) Hall of Famers Al Simmons and Goose Goslin.

Number Seven: Bobby Veach

Year	L	Tm	IP	PO7 runs	A7 runs	Runs
1912	A	DET	172	5	2	7
1913	A	DET	1144	3	-1	2
1914	A	DET	1231	22	1	23
1915	A	DET	1290	16	1	17
1916	A	DET	1273	22	-3	19
1917	A	DET	1348	25	-3	22
1918	A	DET	1052	3	-2	1
1919	A	DET	1171	36	0	36
1920	N	DET	1345	23	4	27
1921	N	DET	1300	21	2	23
1922	N	DET	1353	15	-2	13
1923	N	DET	275	-1	0	-2
1924	A	BOS	1141	-2	-2	-4
1925	A	BOS	13	0	0	0
1925	A	NY	70	-1	1	0
			14177	186	-1	185

Another hidden Hall of Famer, Bobby Veach, fielded consistently well in both the Dead Ball Era and the first two or three years of the Live Ball Era, which drastically changed demands on outfielders, as we shall see in the centerfielder chapter. If we use current tools for evaluating offense, Veach created about 140 more runs on offense than the average player at his position. Adding in defense, that puts Veach above the de facto Hall of Fame standard of +300 runs, offense and defense combined.

Bob O'Leary, author of the Veach essay for SABR's Baseball Biography Project, relates a story that illustrates perfectly why I rank Tristram Speaker above Tyrus Cobb in overall value despite the slight edge Cobb has going strictly by the numbers. Cobb took over as player-manager of the Tigers in 1920. One of his first managerial moves was to order Harry Heilmann to yell insults at the easy-going Veach, to get him into a Cobb-like state of intensity. Veach's batting numbers seemed to improve, but most of that was just the change in offensive context brought about by the so-called live ball. Veach's offensive *value* in 1921 was right in line with what it had been the prior half dozen years. But Cobb's machinations were worse than useless; they were deceptive and destructive. Cobb had apparently promised Heilmann before the season that he, Cobb, would tell Veach after the season was over that Heilmann was just following orders. Cobb broke that promise. When Heilmann tried to explain to Veach what had happened, Veach didn't believe him, so now Veach and Heilmann were on the outs. Cobb tried to rid himself of Veach via a trade to the Yankees, which didn't come off, and eventually had him sold to the Red Sox for an undisclosed amount of cash. It doesn't seem as though manager Cobb was deriving the maximum value out of the human resources at his disposal.

Number Six: Warren Cromartie

Year	L	Tm	IP7	PO7 runs	A7 runs	v-Tm	Runs
1974	N	MON	45	-1	0	0	-1
1976	N	MON	26	-2	0	-2	-3
1977	N	MON	1341	19	0	1	18
1978	N	MON	1350	30	5	-2	36
1979	N	MON	1422	22	2	3	24
1980	N	MON	18	-1	0	-1	-1
1982	N	MON	10	0	0	0	0
1991	A	KC	15	0	0	0	0
Total			4227	67	6	-2	74

Warren Cromartie in Right Field

Year	L	Tm	IP9	PO9 runs	A9 runs	v-Tm	Runs
1976	N	MON	119	2	0	2	2
1977	N	MON	28	0	0	0	1
1981	N	MON	325	5	-1	5	3
1982	N	MON	1157	11	0	6	11
1983	N	MON	792	15	3	3	19
1991	A	KC	1	1	0	1	1
Total			2422	34	2	18	37

Adding his +37 defensive runs in right field would bring Warren "Cro" Cromartie's TPAR to +126, right behind Willie Wilson's. Notice Cro's sensational rate of defensive runs compared to his teammates' (the v-Tm runs) in right field; the v-Tm runs in left are not meaningful because Cro either played too much or too little in each of those seasons to outperform the team rate by a significant number of runs. On a rate basis, and taking any reasonable timeline into account, Cromartie may have been the second greatest fielding corner outfielder in history. Since he played mainly in left, he's included in this chapter. In 1980 and part of 1981 he played first base, presumably because of an injury. The gap between 1983 and 1991 was due to Cro's decision to play in Japan, which worked out well: he won the Central League's MVP award in 1989.

Cromartie asked to have a candy bar named after him; echoing his nickname, the bars were named "Cro-bars," and were sold in Montreal's Olympic Stadium, though not, as far as I know, anywhere else. Jonah Keri has written an imaginary—though quite believable—'interview' with Cro for Rich Lederer's website, baseballanalysts.com: "If I Met Warren Cromartie in Front of the Reptile House at the Zoo, This is What I'd Say to Him." Worth checking out.

Number Five: Jose Cruz

Year	L	Tm	IP	PO7 runs	A7 runs	v-Tm	Runs
1971	N	STL	1	0	0	0	0
1972	N	STL	53	-2	0	-1	-2
1973	N	STL	3	0	0	0	0
1974	N	STL	76	-1	0	0	-1
1975	N	HOU	195	-2	1	-1	-1
1976	N	HOU	692	12	0	7	12
1979	N	HOU	1356	18	-2	-3	16
1980	N	HOU	1405	8	3	3	11
1981	N	HOU	929	20	-3	-2	17
1982	N	HOU	1357	24	-3	2	21
1983	N	HOU	1417	20	-2	0	18
1984	N	HOU	1398	11	0	0	11
1985	N	HOU	1193	8	1	1	9
1986	N	HOU	1107	7	-3	2	5
1987	N	HOU	784	6	0	0	5
1988	A	NY	23	-1	0	-1	-1
Total			11989	127	-8	6	119

Cruz saved another twenty-six runs in close to three seasons' worth of play in right field in the early years of his career, though fifteen of those runs occurred in a short season and might not represent a reliable estimate. Sean Smith estimates that Cruz allowed an extra handful of runs in left by being below average in holding base runners. It's possible that the Astrodome, which suppressed Cruz's offensive runs, may have boosted his defensive runs. Luis Gonzalez, as we saw above, had one literally incredible year during his time in Houston. Sean Smith appears to discount both Cruz's and Gonzalez's numbers. More open source research on park effects is needed.

Number Four: Roy White

Year	L	Tm	IP	PO7 runs	A7 runs	v-Tm	Runs
1966	A	NY	602	10	-1	1	9
1967	A	NY	39	-2	0	-2	-2
1968	A	NY	1060	15	3	9	18
1969	A	NY	1106	25	-1	1	24
1970	A	NY	1451	19	-2	2	17
1971	A	NY	1284	29	-1	0	28
1972	A	NY	1370	22	-3	0	20
1973	A	NY	1420	29	-4	0	25
1974	A	NY	570	10	-2	3	8
1975	A	NY	1185	14	1	5	14
1976	A	NY	1224	18	-3	2	15
1977	A	NY	1167	15	-2	9	13
1978	A	NY	611	-5	-2	-8	-7
1979	A	NY	222	-3	1	-4	-3
Total			13311	194	-16	19	179

I dropped Roy White down from number one because of a probable park effect and because his arm was slightly worse than is indicated by his A7 runs. Any outfielder since the Live Ball era who played in a park where the part of the outfield he covered was large *relative to* the other areas of the outfield, like left field in the original Yankee Stadium, will be overrated somewhat. That's because he'll be able to get under more long high flies in his larger area of the field, while the *total* number of outs per batted ball in play will be 'normal', so he'll have an above-average number of putouts for his position, given total balls in play allowed by his team's pitchers. In contrast, a place like Coors, where *all* the outfield positions have to cover an above-average area, *reduces* ratings for *all* the outfielders, because there is more room for hits to *drop in* per batted ball in play.

That said, I think the park effect for White is relatively modest. The Yankees played in Shea Stadium in 1974–75 while Yankee Stadium was being renovated. White had +19 PO8 runs per 1450 innings in those two seasons, even though he was apparently nursing some injury (he was a designated hitter much of 1974). The next two years, White played left in the renovated Yankee Stadium, which had a large, but much less large, left field area than the old Yankee Stadium. And White had +20 PO8 runs per 1450 innings played. White was in his thirties during those four years in Shea and the renovated Yankee Stadium. I therefore do not believe that White's performance in the original Yankee Stadium (+25 PO8 runs per 1450 innings), when he was in his twenties, needs to be discounted much—probably about five runs per season, or no more than thirty runs over what amounts to six full-time seasons patrolling the original Yankee Stadium's left field, which would still leave him above Jose Cruz under TPAR.

There's an old saying, "Take two and hit to right," meaning take two strikes and go the other way (if you're right handed). Because Roy had a weak arm, people said "Take two and hit to White," though I think what they meant to say was "Hit to White and take two [bases]." Walsh and Smith would dock White another dozen runs for not holding base runners well. So when you consider parks and holding base runners, White should have at least +140 career defensive runs.

As Bill James showed in the *Historical Abstract*, when you take into account the major contextual factors impacting offense, which were in fact quite extreme in White's case, White actually contributed more on offense to his teams than recent Hall of Famer Jim Rice. Sean Smith estimates that White was about +140 offensive runs better than the league-average rate for left fielders of his time (about where Jose Cruz is); when you add +140 defensive runs, Roy is very close to the edge for Hall of Fame consideration. Roy also had two seasons of MVP-level performance (1970–71) and several more of all-star quality. Without even considering talent pool adjustments for playing in an integrated league, based on a quick glance at Sean Smith's estimates of career wins above replacement, available at his website, I'd say White was more valuable to his teams than outfield Hall of Famers Enos Slaughter, Kiki Cuyler, Edd Roush, Orlando Cepeda, Ralph Kiner, Earl Averill, Kirby Puckett, Earle Combs, Heinie Manush, Jim Rice, Chuck Klein, Lou Brock, Hack Wilson, and Chick Hafey. Now most of those players don't really belong either, and there are more urgent and worthy cases for Hall of Fame induction, but Roy White was not just, as James argued, a "tremendously underrated" player; he was genuinely great.

Walsh and Smith would credit Barry Bonds (see next page) with about thirty defensive runs for holding base runners, which is why Bonds ranks ahead of Cruz and White. Due to his defense, Barry Bonds was in fact more valuable to his team in the first ten years of his career than Ken Griffey, Jr., was in his.

On the basis of Sean Smith's estimates of offensive runs attributable to base running (base stealing and advancing on hits and sacrifice flies), avoiding double plays, and reaching base on errors, Willie Wilson (also on next page) created about 150 runs on offense from his speed alone. Per full-time season, nobody with a reasonably long career is even close to Wilson's rate, which lends firm support to Bill James's contention that Wilson may have been the fastest man ever to play major league baseball.

Wilson also saved more runs in left field per 1450 innings than any other left fielder in history; the only reason Wilson isn't the greatest left fielder in history on a career basis is because his team moved him to center. He saved

Number Three: Barry Bonds

Year	L	Tm	IP	PO7 runs	A7 runs	v-Tm	Runs
1987	N	PIT	774	26	2	14	28
1988	N	PIT	1134	12	-2	2	10
1989	N	PIT	1338	15	3	3	18
1990	N	PIT	1274	25	2	0	27
1991	N	PIT	1296	9	3	3	12
1992	N	PIT	1241	16	-2	3	14
1993	N	SF	1371	7	-3	2	4
1994	N	SF	959	1	2	-2	3
1995	N	SF	1257	8	2	-1	10
1996	N	SF	1275	3	2	5	5
1997	N	SF	1372	3	-1	3	2
1998	N	SF	1336	23	-5	2	18
1999	N	SF	795	1	-1	0	1
2000	N	SF	1153	10	0	7	10
2001	N	SF	1232	-9	-1	2	-10
2002	N	SF	1115	-5	-2	-1	-7
2003	N	SF	1044	10	-1	-6	8
2004	N	SF	1131	-8	2	-4	-5
2005	N	SF	95	-2	0	-2	-2
2006	N	SF	875	-4	1	-5	-3
2007	N	SF	842	-7	-2	-11	-9
Total			22909	134	-1	14	133

Number Two: Willie Wilson

Year	L	Tm	IP	PO7 runs	A7 runs	v-Tm	Runs
1978	A	KC	365	2	1	0	3
1979	A	KC	1037	27	1	12	28
1980	A	KC	877	30	0	17	29
1981	A	KC	736	21	3	5	24
1982	A	KC	1003	27	-3	7	24
1983	A	KC	551	-6	-1	-5	-8
1990	A	KC	359	3	-1	3	2
1991	A	OAK	258	8	0	5	8
Total			5187	110	0	44	110

more runs in center than any other top left fielder in history. And the estimate on the next page, about +50 defensive runs, is probably too low. Whenever there were runners on base, Wilson, who knew he had a weak arm, intentionally allowed his right fielders to take every fly ball chance they could reach, contra the normal 'rule' under which center fielders take every chance they can. Smith would credit Wilson with another dozen or so runs for holding base runners, which makes sense, because Wilson could cut off batted balls that dropped in for hits and get them back into the infield so quickly.

Willie Wilson in Center Field

Year	L	Tm	IP8	PO8 runs	A8 runs	v-Tm	Runs
1976	A	KC	18	0	1	0	1
1977	A	KC	73	1	0	2	1
1978	A	KC	177	7	-1	7	6
1979	A	KC	180	5	0	6	5
1980	A	KC	524	7	-2	5	6
1981	A	KC	148	1	1	2	2
1982	A	KC	159	8	0	9	8
1983	A	KC	599	0	-3	2	-2
1984	A	KC	1129	8	-1	7	6
1985	A	KC	1245	3	-3	5	0
1986	A	KC	1306	12	-2	2	11
1987	A	KC	1221	3	-2	6	2
1988	A	KC	1194	-4	-2	6	-6
1989	A	KC	832	5	-2	2	3
1990	A	KC	350	-7	-1	-4	-8
1991	A	OAK	212	0	-1	0	-1
1992	A	OAK	903	24	-2	14	22
1993	N	CHI	412	-4	-1	-1	-5
1994	N	CHI	40	-1	0	-1	-1
Year			10721	70	-21	69	49

The same methods used by Sean Smith to estimate Willie Wilson's 'speed' runs on offense indicate that Rickey Henderson created about 180 'speed' runs on offense, in a career about sixty percent longer than Wilson's. Henderson saved essentially the same number of runs on *defense* that he created with his speed on *offense*. The combined value of Henderson's

Rickey Henderson in Center Field

Year	L	Tm	IP8	PO8 runs	A8 runs	v-Tm	Runs
1979	A	OAK	253	0	-1	2	-1
1982	A	OAK	71	3	0	3	3
1983	A	OAK	51	0	0	0	0
1984	A	OAK	22	3	0	3	3
1985	A	NY	1194	16	-1	4	15
1986	A	NY	1185	15	-2	4	13
1987	A	NY	317	6	-1	2	5
1988	A	NY	22	-1	0	-1	-1
1994	A	OAK	68	0	0	-1	0
1996	N	SD	65	-2	0	-3	-3
1997	A	LA	10	2	0	2	2
1997	N	SD	129	2	0	1	2
1998	A	OAK	135	-2	0	-2	-2
2002	A	BOS	27	-1	0	-1	-1
Total			3549	40	-5	12	35

Number One: Rickey Henderson in Left Field

Year	L	Tm	IP7	PO7 runs	A7 runs	v-Tm	Runs
1979	A	OAK	510	-7	0	-1	-7
1980	A	OAK	1401	22	2	-3	24
1981	A	OAK	952	30	-1	0	30
1982	A	OAK	1204	11	-4	2	8
1983	A	OAK	1133	13	-1	-1	13
1984	A	OAK	1108	10	-1	5	9
1985	A	NY	24	1	0	1	1
1986	A	NY	70	-1	0	-1	-1
1987	A	NY	273	11	0	7	10
1988	A	NY	1170	11	0	4	11
1989	A	NY	558	6	-1	3	6
1989	A	OAK	713	9	-1	-3	8
1990	A	OAK	994	25	-2	9	23
1991	A	OAK	982	-1	2	-12	2
1992	A	OAK	884	-4	1	-3	-3
1993	A	OAK	630	7	0	0	7
1993	A	TOR	377	-9	-1	-4	-10
1994	A	OAK	518	13	0	3	13
1995	A	OAK	741	-10	-1	-2	-10
1996	N	SD	932	12	-2	-2	11
1997	N	SD	434	7	0	9	7
1997	A	LA	92	-1	0	-1	-1
1998	A	OAK	1104	13	-4	0	9
1999	N	NY	889	-3	-4	-1	-7
2000	N	NY	214	-4	-1	-4	-5
2000	A	SEA	692	11	-3	7	8
2001	N	SD	813	-10	-1	-3	-11
2002	A	BOS	379	0	1	3	1
2003	N	LA	140	-2	0	-1	-2
Total			19932	162	-18	10	144

defensive runs (including in center, where he averaged about +14 defensive runs per 1450 innings played) and 'speed' offensive runs on offense was so great that even if he had been a league-average hitter for his position he would merit inclusion in the Hall of Fame, based on the de facto standard of 300 runs of value above league-average performance. But his ability to get on base and occasional power also generated about 450 runs of career offensive runs above the rate of average left fielders of his day. Bill James was asked once whether Henderson was a Hall of Famer. James replied, "If you could split him in two, you'd have two Hall of Famers."

Right Field

Right fielders can't be too fast, because if they were, they'd be centerfielders. But they can't be too slow, either, because if they're too slow getting to balls hit down the right field line or in the gap, a great arm will be of no use in preventing runners from advancing to third. With the speed of all right fielders clustered in the middle, there is generally not nearly as big a difference in the spread of defensive runs as we saw in left or will see in center.

Contemporary Era

MCS	First	Last	IP	Runs	Δ
1998	Sammy	Sosa	17111	91	Δ
1998	Brian	Jordan	7804	79	Δ
2005	Ichiro	Suzuki	9901	76	Δ
1999	Reggie	Sanders	9536	49	Δ
1994	David	Justice	7202	48	Δ
1999	Raul	Mondesi	11513	47	Δ
1998	Tim	Salmon	10937	38	
2003	Richard	Hidalgo	4289	37	Δ
1995	Paul	O'Neill	15388	36	
2001	Shawn	Green	13792	34	
1993	Mark	Whiten	5794	31	Δ
2005	J.D.	Drew	8562	28	
2000	Matt	Lawton	6502	27	Δ
2005	Jacque	Jones	4097	25	Δ
2004	Jose	Cruz, Jr.	3601	24	Δ
1996	Orlando	Merced	4696	20	Δ
2003	Jermaine	Dye	14276	20	Δ
2000	Mark	Kotsay	3149	17	
2003	Trot	Nixon	7795	16	

(*Continued*)

Contemporary Era *(continued)*

MCS	First	Last	IP	Runs	Δ
1997	Dave	Martinez	4757	15	
2000	Michael	Tucker	5513	10	Δ
1995	Stan	Javier	3175	8	Δ
1993	Jim	Eisenreich	4102	2	
2002	V.	Guerrero	13650	2	Δ
1998	Jeffrey	Hammonds	3305	2	Δ
2004	Jay	Gibbons	3540	-1	
2003	Jose	Guillen	9396	-1	Δ
2000	Danny	Bautista	3928	-3	Δ
2000	Bobby	Higginson	5319	-5	
1994	Dante	Bichette	7264	-6	
1997	Troy	O'Leary	3009	-9	Δ
1997	Manny	Ramirez	7767	-9	Δ
1999	Alex	Ochoa	3441	-14	Δ
2005	Brian	Giles	7583	-19	
1997	Larry	Walker	14235	-21	
2004	Juan	Encarnacion	6640	-26	Δ
1994	Willie	McGee	3753	-26	Δ
1999	Moises	Alou	4760	-29	Δ
2003	Bobby	Abreu	16024	-30	Δ
2001	Matt	Stairs	4124	-52	
2003	Magglio	Ordonez	13300	-53	Δ
2000	Gary	Sheffield	9846	-58	Δ
1995	Glenallen	Hill	3650	-60	Δ
2000	Jeromy	Burnitz	11267	-61	
2000	Ben	Grieve	3686	-61	
1999	Juan	Gonzalez	6341	-72	Δ
1998	Derek	Bell	6923	-77	Δ
1994	Jay	Buhner	11421	-95	

The Contemporary Era ratings generally conform to expectations. Ichiro Suzuki, Brian Jordan, Sammy Sosa, Raul Mondesi, Jermaine Dye, and Paul O'Neill generally demonstrate good numbers under the better fielding evaluation systems, at least for their better seasons (for example, Dye's seasons before he broke his leg in 2001). Our main surprise introduces an important general lesson about fielding evaluation.

The career of Larry Walker (see next page) shows the impact parks can have on fielding outcomes. In Montreal, Walker's DRA estimates he saved 44 runs catching fly balls (PO9 runs); *Smith(R(t,s,d))*, which uses batted ball data, estimates 37 runs. Once Walker moved to Coors, his DRA ratings drop substantially, whereas Smith's systems, which have park adjustments, suggest that Walker was essentially average over the course of his right field Coors career. On the basis of the fact that DRA appears to rate Walker at about a dozen runs below average per 1450 innings played in right, I would consider that to be the 'rule of thumb' estimate for corner outfielders at Coors, with perhaps an

Larry Walker

Year	L	Tm	IP	PO9 runs	A9 runs	v-Tm	Runs
1989	N	MON	106	-2	1	-2	-1
1990	N	MON	1004	10	2	7	12
1991	N	MON	790	19	-1	5	19
1992	N	MON	1217	9	4	-2	13
1993	N	MON	1145	10	1	3	11
1994	N	MON	607	-2	0	-5	-2
1995	N	COL	1097	-7	2	1	-5
1996	N	COL	169	0	0	2	0
1997	N	COL	1235	-20	1	-1	-19
1998	N	COL	1011	2	0	3	2
1999	N	COL	943	-13	3	-2	-9
2000	N	COL	422	-2	3	3	2
2001	N	COL	1097	-6	0	-1	-6
2002	N	COL	1037	-10	4	-8	-7
2003	N	COL	1103	-17	0	-2	-17
2004	N	COL	267	1	1	4	2
2004	N	STL	337	-4	-1	-2	-5
2005	N	STL	649	-10	0	-6	-10
Total			14235	-42	21	-3	-21

even larger adjustment needed in center field. Smith has gone on record that for purposes of his systems going back to the 1950s, park adjustments are only really needed for Coors outfielders and left fielders in Fenway.

Modern Era

MCS	First	Last	IP	Runs	Δ
1987	Jesse	Barfield	10877	178	Δ
1974	Bobby	Bonds	12475	63	Δ
1981	Tony	Armas	5135	48	Δ
1991	Joe	Orsulak	4617	43	
1986	Glenn	Wilson	7779	42	
1979	Bake	McBride	4639	38	Δ
1978	Leon	Roberts	4236	36	
1981	Dwight	Evans	17737	33	
1979	Sixto	Lezcano	8845	33	
1984	George	Vukovich	3311	29	
1975	Reggie	Jackson	16124	28	Δ
1980	Hosken	Powell	3642	27	Δ
1976	Reggie	Smith	7303	25	Δ
1973	Willie	Crawford	5147	25	Δ
1976	Jay	Johnstone	4195	25	
1987	Tom	Brunansky	13080	23	
1970	Jim	Northrup	5721	22	
1984	Lee	Lacy	4558	19	Δ
1981	Joel	Youngblood	3093	17	

(continued)

Modern Era *(continued)*

MCS	First	Last	IP	Runs	Δ
1987	Von	Hayes	4196	17	
1976	Jose	Cruz	4076	16	Δ
1985	Mike	Davis	5536	16	Δ
1990	Rob	Deer	7336	13	
1977	Oscar	Gamble	3550	12	Δ
1977	Greg	Gross	3536	12	
1983	Terry	Puhl	6242	11	
1981	George	Hendrick	7124	9	Δ
1970	Pete	Rose	5125	9	
1974	Bernie	Carbo	3211	8	
1984	Harold	Baines	8718	7	Δ
1989	Cory	Snyder	6359	6	
1974	Leroy	Stanton	4319	6	Δ
1972	Jim	Wynn	3096	6	Δ
1988	Ivan	Calderon	3176	6	Δ
1973	Merv	Rettenmund	3088	3	
1986	Pat	Sheridan	3316	2	
1970	Ollie	Brown	7130	2	Δ
1970	Vada	Pinson	4377	2	Δ
1989	Dale	Murphy	6445	2	
1992	Felix	Jose	5142	1	Δ
1969	Ron	Swoboda	3955	-2	
1986	Chili	Davis	3883	-3	Δ
1987	Chet	Lemon	3810	-4	Δ
1981	Dave	Parker	15610	-5	Δ
1990	Jose	Canseco	5653	-5	
1988	Candy	Maldonado	4853	-6	Δ
1988	Kevin	Bass	7391	-7	Δ
1992	Joe	Carter	4978	-7	Δ
1973	Jose	Cardenal	4406	-8	Δ
1979	Ellis	Valentine	6453	-12	Δ
1975	Charlie	Spikes	3155	-13	Δ
1979	Gary	Matthews	3714	-14	Δ
1979	Dan	Ford	6346	-14	Δ
1989	Hubie	Brooks	4678	-19	Δ
1988	Andre	Dawson	10807	-20	Δ
1980	Al	Cowens	10660	-23	Δ
1992	Bobby	Bonilla	5651	-24	Δ
1972	Pat	Kelly	5681	-24	Δ
1976	Richie	Zisk	4191	-25	
1985	Kirk	Gibson	3798	-26	
1980	Jack	Clark	8641	-26	
1988	D.	Strawberry	11044	-28	Δ
1976	Jerry	Morales	4501	-28	
1974	Bobby	Darwin	3526	-30	Δ
1971	Rusty	Staub	13966	-40	
1992	Eric	Anthony	3179	-44	Δ
1991	Tony	Gwynn	18375	-47	Δ

(continued)

Modern Era *(continued)*

MCS	First	Last	IP	Runs	Δ
1991	Ruben	Sierra	11999	-47	Δ
1976	Ken	Singleton	10891	-53	Δ
1984	Keith	Moreland	4618	-54	
1986	Mike	Marshall	5413	-60	
1976	Bobby	Murcer	7106	-62	
1983	Larry	Parrish	3462	-62	
1983	Ken	Griffey	10186	-70	Δ
1983	Dave	Winfield	15957	-74	Δ
1982	C.	Washington	9075	-75	Δ
1990	Danny	Tartabull	7636	-119	Δ
1976	Jeff	Burroughs	7287	-125	

Aside from Barfield, there were no consistently dominant right fielders in the Modern Era, which dramatically illustrates the point about right fielders being neither very quick nor very slow. It is nothing but an amusing coincidence that Reggie Smith, so often (and often unjustly) overshadowed by his almost exact contemporary Reggie Jackson, ranks just two spots below Jackson. Both were very good right fielders when young. Walsh would credit

Tony Gwynn

Year	L	Tm	IP	PO9 runs	A9 runs	v-Tm	Runs
1982	N	SD	99	-2	-1	-3	-2
1983	N	SD	468	-4	1	-2	-3
1984	N	SD	1337	9	1	4	9
1985	N	SD	1334	7	1	4	8
1986	N	SD	1396	9	4	0	13
1987	N	SD	1329	14	1	4	16
1988	N	SD	893	-1	1	0	0
1989	N	SD	633	-2	2	0	0
1990	N	SD	1266	6	0	0	6
1991	N	SD	1176	8	-2	3	6
1992	N	SD	1128	-2	0	1	-1
1993	N	SD	1012	-2	-1	1	-3
1994	N	SD	900	-3	-2	0	-5
1995	N	SD	1127	2	-1	0	1
1996	N	SD	960	-7	-3	3	-10
1997	N	SD	1203	-29	-1	-4	-30
1998	N	SD	902	-21	-1	-10	-23
1999	N	SD	806	-18	-1	-10	-19
2000	N	SD	202	-7	0	-7	-8
2001	N	SD	103	-4	1	-4	-3
Total			18375	-45	-1	-20	-47

Dwight Evans with another thirty runs for holding base runners, and Smith close to another twenty on top of that, which would bring Dewie up to where Bobby Bonds is—good, but not a notable all-time great. The biggest surprises are Gwynn and Winfield.

Tony Gwynn (see prior page) had two careers as a right fielder. Gwynn was good enough in the mid-1980s to be promoted to center in 1988–89 (hence the drop in innings played in right). He gradually put on weight; by the late 1990s, he must have been one of the heaviest singles hitters in baseball history, and a liability in the field as measured under any system, though the estimates above for the 1997–99 are probably a bit extreme.

Dave Winfield

Year	L	Tm	IP	PO9 runs	A9 runs	v-Tm	Runs
1974	N	SD	297	-3	0	0	-4
1975	N	SD	1237	10	0	2	10
1976	N	SD	1090	4	3	5	7
1977	N	SD	1379	10	2	5	12
1978	N	SD	713	5	-2	2	3
1979	N	SD	1385	15	0	-2	16
1980	N	SD	1194	-13	3	1	-10
1983	A	NY	49	1	0	1	1
1984	A	NY	1088	-5	-4	1	-9
1985	A	NY	1352	-8	1	-3	-7
1986	A	NY	1266	-5	-1	1	-6
1987	A	NY	1263	-23	-3	1	-26
1988	A	NY	1261	-24	-4	-4	-28
1990	A	LA	920	-26	0	-6	-26
1991	A	LA	984	-6	-1	1	-6
1992	A	TOR	217	1	-1	1	0
1993	A	MIN	253	0	1	6	0
1994	A	MIN	9	0	0	0	0
Total			15957	-68	-6	11	-74

As a Padre, Dave Winfield was probably a 'plus' outfielder, both in terms of catching batted balls and also in eliminating and holding base runners. This is consistent with his having 'plus' speed, as indicated by an above-average rate of total stolen base attempts and successful stolen base attempts, and his obviously strong arm. Nineteen eighty-one was his first year with the Yankees and the last year of anything other than ordinary base stealing or fielding accomplishment. Though some of the seasonal totals differ, the aggregate career assessment above is broadly consistent with *Smith(pgor, bod)* (through 1988) and *Smith(R(t,s,d))* (1989–94). Winfield gave up another thirty runs in 3800 innings in left field, mainly in 1981–83 for the Yankees. When a fielder is consistently below average in multiple settings, I see no alternative but to conclude that he was below average, no matter how many Gold Gloves he was awarded (seven in Dave's case).

We'll address the eye-popping number for Clemente at the close of the chapter; other than that one number, the results below seem pretty reasonable.

Transitional Era

MCS	First	Last	IP	Runs	Δ
1964	Roberto	Clemente	19920	256	Δ
1963	Hank	Aaron	18869	134	Δ
1963	Al	Kaline	16879	93	
1966	Johnny	Callison	13423	69	
1948	Tommy	Holmes	5179	68	
1967	Tony	Oliva	9950	61	Δ
1953	Carl	Furillo	11636	41	
1962	Bob	Allison	5335	34	
1963	Jim	King	5344	32	
1950	Willard	Marshall	6686	24	
1961	Willie	Kirkland	6558	21	Δ
1957	Wally	Post	7037	20	
1963	Lou	Clinton	4963	17	
1968	Jesus	Alou	5160	10	Δ
1964	Floyd	Robinson	5758	10	Δ
1957	Walt	Moryn	3052	9	
1952	Johnny	Wyrostek	3194	9	
1951	Vic	Wertz	6002	6	
1964	Felipe	Alou	5689	6	Δ
1956	Hank	Bauer	8493	5	
1966	Frank	Robinson	10835	4	Δ
1954	Andy	Pafko	3456	4	
1963	Roger	Maris	9534	3	
1956	Jackie	Jensen	10539	1	
1949	Elmer	Valo	5130	-3	
1962	George	Altman	3371	-3	Δ
1965	Mike	Hershberger	5539	-5	
1959	Al	Smith	5448	-6	Δ
1962	Rocky	Colavito	11117	-6	
1955	Gus	Bell	5681	-7	
1956	Jim	Rivera	4253	-8	
1966	Billy	Williams	3219	-12	Δ
1953	Dave	Philley	5042	-17	
1961	Gino	Cimoli	3256	-18	
1959	Joe	Cunningham	3128	-18	
1967	Ron	Fairly	5094	-21	
1968	Tony	Conigliaro	6361	-23	
1964	Lee	Thomas	3254	-23	
1957	Jim	Lemon	3929	-27	
1962	Frank	Howard	4348	-39	
1959	Wally	Moon	3187	-53	
1954	Don	Mueller	8779	-61	

Carl Furillo

Year	L	Tm	IP	PO9 runs	A9 runs	v-Tm	Runs
1949	N	BRO	1157	18	0		18
1950	N	BRO	1307	-15	4		-11
1951	N	BRO	1367	23	5		29
1952	N	BRO	1000	10	1	2	10
1953	N	BRO	1093	4	-1	1	3
1954	N	BRO	1268	19	-2	3	17
1955	N	BRO	1221	-1	-1	4	-2
1956	N	BRO	1238	-1	-1	1	-2
1957	N	BRO	903	-7	-1	-4	-8
1958	N	LA	927	-6	-3	5	-9
1959	N	LA	146	-2	-1	0	-2
1960	N	LA	10	0	0	0	0
			11636	42	-1	13	41

Furillo played mostly in center his first few years (1946–48), and his esti-mated defensive runs under DRA for those three seasons are quite high. However, the version of DRA applicable for those seasons can overestimate full-time outfielders who play significant portions of the season at more than one outfield position. Playing almost exclusively in right from 1949 through 1954, he appears to have been saving about a dozen runs per 1450 innings, not taking into account his arm. The Reading Rifle must have con-vinced the league by 1952 not to run on him anymore; Smith credits him with another ten runs for holding base runners, which actually seems low. I'd pencil in about +75 total defensive runs, including center, for Skoonj. A very moving essay about Furillo that I recommend can be found at ottobruno.org.

Tony Oliva

Year	L	Tm	IP	PO9 runs	A9 runs	v-Tm	Runs
1962	A	MIN	10	0	0	0	0
1964	A	MIN	1356	5	-4	2	1
1965	A	MIN	1233	17	1	3	17
1966	A	MIN	1230	17	0	3	17
1967	A	MIN	1282	7	-1	7	6
1968	A	MIN	1099	-2	0	-1	-3
1969	A	MIN	1370	12	1	1	12
1970	A	MIN	1345	23	1	3	24
1971	A	MIN	1018	-13	-1	-3	-14
1972	A	MIN	8	0	0	0	0
Total			9950	65	-4		61

On the basis of the above defensive runs estimates and standard offensive runs estimates, Tony Oliva put together at least three MVP-quality seasons

(1965, 1966, and 1970), another 'high' all-star or 'low' MVP year (1964, his Rookie of the Year season), and four other seasons of all-star or close to all-star-level performance (1967, 1969, and 1971)—before his knees completely gave way in 1972, when he was only thirty-three years old. It's a fair question whether a ballplayer who has put together the string of MVP-level and all-star-level seasons expected of a Hall of Famer should be required to hang around adding 'average' ballplayer value to punch his ticket for Cooperstown. I think the answer is no.

Live Ball Era

MCS	First	Last	IP	Runs	Δ
1933	Paul	Waner	18783	86	
1926	Sam	Rice	13739	80	
1942	Wally	Moses	10782	77	
1938	Ival	Goodman	7725	76	
1939	Gene	Moore	6096	72	
1945	Bill	Nicholson	11418	66	
1923	Billy	Southworth	6548	61	
1929	Kiki	Cuyler	6783	61	
1925	Cliff	Heathcote	6231	60	
1929	Bing	Miller	8318	57	
1924	Bob	Meusel	4519	56	
1927	Babe	Ruth	9768	51	
1939	Pete	Fox	8947	40	
1929	Harry	Rice	3511	36	
1932	Roy	Johnson	4258	35	
1944	Roy	Cullenbine	4016	29	
1936	George	Selkirk	3178	27	
1926	Curt	Walker	9393	26	
1944	Buddy	Lewis	3976	25	
1927	Bill	Barrett	3340	19	
1923	Frank	Welch	3274	18	
1929	Lance	Richbourg	5172	17	
1938	Lou	Finney	3904	15	
1941	Taffy	Wright	3602	13	
1932	Carl	Reynolds	5139	13	
1942	Tommy	Henrich	4313	12	
1935	John	Stone	3803	9	
1922	Ross	Youngs	10223	7	
1946	Enos	Slaughter	11152	6	
1932	George	Watkins	3466	0	
1925	George	Harper	4808	-3	
1936	Mel	Ott	18599	-4	
1935	Ben	Chapman	3957	-5	
1930	Earl	Webb	4356	-5	
1920	Max	Flack	7714	-11	
1937	Frank	Demaree	3908	-32	
1944	Dixie	Walker	6514	-47	
1932	Dick	Porter	4981	-49	

(*Continued*)

Live Ball Era (*Continued*)

MCS	First	Last	IP	Runs	Δ
1926	Homer	Summa	6131	-50	
1935	Johnny	Moore	3121	-54	
1923	Jack	Tobin	7342	-65	
1938	Beau	Bell	4740	-71	
1936	Bruce	Campbell	9401	-83	
1945	Ron	Northey	5953	-84	
1933	Chuck	Klein	10668	-84	
1931	Babe	Herman	8467	-90	
1925	Harry	Heilmann	11833	-92	

Many fans today are not aware that there were two baseball Babes of enduring historical interest.

Babe Herman

Year	L	Tm	IP	PO9 runs	A9 runs	Runs
1926	N	BRO	228	0	0	1
1928	N	BRO	1041	-5	-1	-5
1929	N	BRO	1210	-33	-4	-36
1930	N	BRO	1312	-35	-6	-41
1931	N	BRO	1329	-33	4	-29
1932	N	CIN	1254	34	2	37
1933	N	CHI	1163	-5	0	-5
1934	N	CHI	912	-5	-2	-8
1945	N	BRO	17	-2	0	-3
Total			8467	-84	-6	-90

Babe Herman came up with Brooklyn, which in retrospect seems inevitable, began playing first base, and led the league in errors there his second year (1927), despite fielding that position in only 105 games. Then they tried him in right field, which should be some indication that the Dead Ball Era tradition of putting the worst outfielders in right field still retained currency in the late 1920s. The Babe led outfielders at all *three* positions in errors in 1928 and 1929, despite missing significant amounts of playing time (the latest Retrosheet data suggests he must have been frequently replaced late in games). Now I have been repeating throughout this book that errors are meaningless. They are meaningless for a normal major league fielder. Babe Herman was not a normal major league fielder. In any event, those errors are already counted as plays not made, as can be seen in the above defensive runs estimates. Though the Babe didn't lead the league in errors in 1930 or 1931, Brooklyn apparently had had enough, and traded him to the Reds.

I do not believe that Babe Herman enabled the 1932 Reds to allow thirty-seven fewer runs than an ordinary right fielder would have playing for them that year. Crosley Field had a very deep right field corner, and relatively more space than in left and center, so right fielders got comparatively more chances out there. This is why I am not prepared to say that Ival Goodman, who played his entire career in Crosley and who sits high up on our list of Live Ball right fielders, was really that good. Still, it must be said that Babe Herman, for whatever reason, actually caught 392 pop ups, fly balls, and line drives playing right field (his only outfield position) for the 1932 Reds, while missing ten games. I believe it may be the record for putouts in right field in a single season, and if it's not, it's very close. (Such a record could not have been officially tallied in major league history, because the official records never recorded putouts separately for each outfield position.)

Though I do not believe Babe Herman saved thirty-seven (or even twenty) runs for the 1932 Reds, I do believe that Herman was a naturally good athlete (he finished in the top five in stolen bases in 1929–1931), and by some accounts not unintelligent. Possibly shocked by being traded, and realizing he had to transform his game to save his career, the Babe probably hustled to take some pop flies that would ordinarily have been caught by the center fielder or the first or second baseman. He might also have taken a few deep chances from his teammates in center field, who included the formerly great but long since faded Taylor Douthit. The Babe just so happened to lead the league in outfield double plays that year—the signature play of outfield excellence, because you have to catch a ball expected to drop in for a hit, and then throw the runner out. For the brief remainder of his right field career, Babe Herman reverted to something reasonably close to the mean, which, in his case, was pretty good.

Babe Ruth

Year	L	Tm	IP7	IP8	IP9	Runs
1919	A	BOS	942			0
1920	A	NY	252	225	722	7
1921	A	NY	1141	255		2
1922	A	NY	642		405	0
1923	A	NY	720	75	695	14
1924	A	NY	460	14	960	14
1925	A	NY	270		634	1
1926	A	NY	678		619	2
1927	A	NY	542		847	13
1928	A	NY	419		878	-2
1929	A	NY	362		599	2
1930	A	NY	404		772	-4
1931	A	NY	354		720	-18
1932	A	NY	276		715	-9
1933	A	NY	357		658	-14
1934	A	NY	200		545	10
1935	N	BOS	112			-1
Total			8129	569	9768	18

Ruth being Ruth, it was necessary to invent a different format just for him, as he split time more or less evenly between left and right but also played a bit in center. The defensive runs shown are for all positions combined.

Through 1927, Ruth fielded better than indicated by his defensive runs total, probably averaging comfortably more than +10 defensive runs per season, and with a much higher defensive runs total for 1923. Why might I say this? Well, even though Retrosheet now has putout totals in left, center, and right for the seasons Ruth played after 1919, the innings played estimates are much sketchier. Whenever we lack individual innings played data to 'individuate' the player ratings, I follow a simplified version of an approach Bill James took in *Win Shares*, allocating innings based on the percentage of the team's plays the player made—in other words, give all the fielders essentially a pro-rata portion of the team's rating.

When we do that for Ruth, we find his total estimated innings (his percentage of team plays, multiplied by team innings) exceeds the maximum number of innings he could have played through 1927, meaning that, on average, he significantly exceeded the team rate of making putouts in those seasons, particularly 1923.

According to the *The Big Bam*, the most recent Ruth biography, the Bambino reported to spring training in 1923 in the best shape of his life, having spent the whole winter working out to atone for losing almost one-third of his prior season to suspensions for various infractions on and off the field. When I first calculated the above defensive runs estimate, I surmised that Ruth played his left field games that year at home, where the just-opened Yankee Stadium's enormous gap in left-center would have afforded him more batted ball opportunities. According to recently released Retrosheet data, however, Ruth generally played in right field at Yankee Stadium, even during his early years there. So he probably had the park effect working *against* him as a fielder.

If the above estimates are anywhere near to being correct, and I think they are probably a little too conservative, the discovery that Ruth was actually a good fielder when he was young and in decent shape should increase even further the estimates of Ruth's peak or prime overall value relative to his league to a level far above any measured for any other player, including Barry Bonds, whose top seasons with the bat did not coincide with his top fielding seasons. Of course, such assessment does not take into account talent pool adjustments. The method for making such adjustments introduced in this book can readily be adapted to overall estimates of player value, including offense, and I believe that if and when such adjustments are made, Ruth might just fall from his perch.

Though Paul Waner appears at the top of the list for Live Ball Era right fielders, almost thirty of those runs occurred in a fluke season years after his prime. I'd give the nod to Sam Rice, who had several very good seasons in right field and in center.

Sam Rice

Year	L	Tm	IP9	PO9 runs	A9 runs	Runs
1917	A	WAS	1316	12	3	15
1918	A	WAS	55	0	2	2
1919	A	WAS	1197	18	-1	17
1921	A	WAS	17	0	0	0
1923	A	WAS	1301	9	0	9
1924	A	WAS	1108	13	-1	12
1925	A	WAS	1147	10	2	12
1926	A	WAS	1023	3	3	6
1927	A	WAS	1197	3	-2	1
1928	A	WAS	1284	-17	-3	-21
1929	A	WAS	1291	4	2	7
1930	A	WAS	1156	20	-1	20
1931	A	WAS	664	7	-1	5
1932	A	WAS	332	4	2	6
1933	A	WAS	76	1	1	1
1934	A	CLE	574	-9	-2	-12
Total			13739	76	3	80

Sam Rice in Center Field

Year	L	Tm	IP8	PO8 runs	A8 runs	Runs
1920	A	WAS	1339	34	3	37
1921	A	WAS	1215	10	0	10
1922	A	WAS	1348	10	4	14
1924	A	WAS	244	2	-1	1
1925	A	WAS	212	-2	0	-2
1926	A	WAS	326	-4	2	-2
1930	A	WAS	99	1	0	1
1931	A	WAS	102	3	-1	2
1932	A	WAS	77	1	0	2
1933	A	WAS	45	1	1	2
Total			5008	57	8	65

Rice fell into the stands after making a leaping, game-saving catch in the 1925 World Series between the Senators and the Pirates. Because it took him some time to re-emerge from the crowd, some suspected that he had dropped the ball. The umpire called the batter out, but the Pirates' manager protested, and even Commissioner Landis met with Rice after the game to ask him whether he had, in fact, caught and held onto the ball. Rice replied, "The umpire said I did." And Landis agreed to leave it at that, probably because altering the umpire's call wouldn't have made baseball fans any happier: 1600 fans had sent Landis signed and sworn affidavits that were split almost perfectly evenly on the issue. Though the Pirates went on to win that World Series anyway, this particular catch remained a mystery that continued to matter to a lot of people, mainly because Rice refused to say whether he had caught the ball. His motives are themselves somewhat of a mystery, but Rice decided to write out his answer on the condition it be opened only after his death. Here is what he wrote:

> It was a cold and windy day—the right field bleachers were crowded with people in overcoats and wrapped in blankets, the ball was a line drive headed for the bleachers towards right center. I turned slightly to my right and had the ball in view all the way, going at top speed and about fifteen feet from bleachers jumped as high as I could and back handed and the ball hit the center of pocket in glove (I had a death grip on it). I hit the ground about five feet from a barrier about four feet high in front of bleachers with all the brakes on but couldn't stop so I tried to jump it to land in the crowd but my feet hit the barrier about a foot from top and I toppled over on my stomach into first row of bleachers. I hit my [Adam's] apple on something which sort of knocked me out for a few seconds but [Senator outfielder Earl] McNeely around about that time grabbed me by the shirt and picked me out. I remember trotting back towards the infield still carrying the ball for about halfway and then tossed it towards the pitchers mound. (How I have wished many times I had kept it.) At no time did I lose possession of the ball. "Sam" Rice

Dead Ball Era

MCS	First	Last	IP	Runs	Δ
1918	Harry	Hooper	16192	185	
1910	Mike	Mitchell	6466	108	
1902	Elmer	Flick	9241	104	
1898	Patsy	Donovan	12746	85	
1911	Chief	Wilson	3700	71	
1913	Ty	Cobb	5104	55	
1901	Willie	Keeler	17152	48	
1898	Fielder	Jones	4279	44	
1896	Jimmy	Ryan	4032	41	
1897	Dusty	Miller	4014	38	
1905	Socks	Seybold	5751	37	
1911	Steve	Evans	5176	29	
1918	Shano	Collins	3144	24	
1915	Gavvy	Cravath	4766	20	
1904	Danny	Green	3238	16	
1913	Wilbur	Good	3055	6	

(Continued)

Dead Ball Era (*Continued*)

MCS	First	Last	IP	Runs	Δ
1904	Cozy	Dolan	3412	5	
1906	Harry	Lumley	5929	5	
1905	George	Browne	5595	4	
1913	Gus	Williams	3289	-5	
1911	Doc	Miller	3174	-7	
1919	Tommy	Griffith	10716	-10	
1911	Danny	Murphy	4165	-14	
1918	Casey	Stengel	7553	-15	
1917	Elmer	Smith	5107	-16	
1909	John	Titus	8536	-21	
1910	Frank	Schulte	8070	-26	
1909	Doc	Gessler	5006	-35	
1919	Braggo	Roth	3697	-41	
1902	Buck	Freeman	5855	-48	
1915	Eddie	Murphy	4624	-57	
1910	Sam	Crawford	11290	-80	

Mike Mitchell

1907	N	CIN	1214	27	10	37
1908	N	CIN	976	2	0	2
1909	N	CIN	1231	16	-1	15
1911	N	CIN	1177	20	2	23
1912	N	CIN	1222	6	-2	4
1914	N	PIT	646	29	-1	28
Total			6466	100	8	108

The 1914 number is suspect, but the 1907, 1909, and 1911 are solid, and he had a fine season in 1913 (not shown because split between left and right). Mike Mitchell set a major league record for outfield assists in his first season, led the league in triples twice, led National League right fielders in putouts for the one season after 1893 and before 1920 (1911), for which we have separate putout data per outfield position, routinely stole thirty bases a season, and could hit. The reason you've probably never heard of him is that he only played eight major league seasons. He didn't even begin playing professional ball until he was twenty-two, effectively turned down a major league contract with the Cubs when he was twenty-four because they were offering him less money than his minor league team, and spent his age twenty-five and age twenty-six seasons in the Pacific Coast League.

Elmer Flick's numbers (see next page) are weird but not inexplicable. The Phillies played in the notorious Baker Bowl, where the right field corner was only 280 feet from home plate and, even more bizarrely, the right-center

Elmer Flick

Year	L	Tm	IP	PO9 runs	A9 runs	Runs
1898	N	PHI	1129	9	2	11
1899	N	PHI	1061	20	2	22
1900	N	PHI	1171	5	4	9
1901	N	PHI	1163	37	2	38
1902	A	PHI	117	-2	0	-2
1902	A	CLE	934	0	1	1
1903	A	CLE	1137	14	0	14
1904	A	CLE	1180	10	3	12
1905	A	CLE	1112	3	2	5
1908	A	CLE	80	-1	0	-1
1910	A	CLE	158	-3	-2	-5
Total			9241	91	13	104

power alley only 300 feet away. Most right fielders who played there had very low putout totals. But Flick decided to play shallow, so shallow that sometimes he threw batters out at first base on what would otherwise have been clean hits. Twice in 1899 he literally fought with his second baseman, Nap Lajoie, over short fly ball chances in right field. Perhaps Lajoie 'won the war', so to speak, because Flick's putouts went way down in 1900. In 1901, Lajoie jumped to the new American League—and you can see from the table what happened to Flick's putouts. I don't believe Flick is too overrated as a right fielder by DRA, however, both because I think his strategy of playing very shallow at the Baker Bowl was clever, and also because of his strong performance in Cleveland, where his second base teammate was … Nap Lajoie. I guess they had patched things up by then. Flick led the leagues in triples three times, stolen bases two times, was so good in right that Cleveland shifted him to

Sam Crawford

Year	L	Tm	IP	PO9 runs	A9 runs	Runs
1901	N	CIN	1069	0	1	1
1904	A	DET	1265	3	2	5
1905	A	DET	895	2	4	6
1906	A	DET	968	-1	2	1
1911	A	DET	1239	-12	-5	-17
1912	A	DET	1265	-20	-3	-23
1913	A	DET	1188	-6	-4	-11
1914	A	DET	1365	-5	-2	-7
1915	A	DET	1365	-7	-8	-15
1916	A	DET	645	-20	-2	-22
1917	A	DET	26	1	0	1
Total			11290	-65	-15	-80

center for two seasons, and was almost being traded even up for the young Ty Cobb. A mysterious gastrointestinal condition ended his career prematurely.

The first edition of *The Historical Abstract* took note of the extremely low putout rates by Sam Crawford (see prior page), who was not regarded as a poor fielder and who actually holds the career record for triples. James suspected a park effect of some sort. Given that Harry Heilmann, who played in Tiger Stadium right after Crawford, also has abysmal DRA ratings, I thought that might be right.

Well, for what it's worth, Crawford's fielding fell off in 1911, the year before the Tigers moved to Tiger Stadium, Tiger Stadium's dimensions were almost perfectly symmetric, and Heilmann's successor, the drinking man Pete Fox, did just fine in right, with not one negative rating during his full-time seasons there (1934–39). As saw earlier in this chapter, pretty good right fielders (Tony Gwynn and Dave Winfield) can go very bad.

Top Forty Right Fielders of All Time

MCS	First	Last	Pos	IP	Runs	Δ	TPAR
1964	Roberto	Clemente	RF	19920	256	Δ	228
1987	Jesse	Barfield	RF	10877	178	Δ	167
1918	Harry	Hooper	RF	16192	185		121
1963	Hank	Aaron	RF	18869	134	Δ	105
1998	Sammy	Sosa	RF	17111	91	Δ	90
2005	Ichiro	Suzuki	RF	9901	76	Δ	80
1998	Brian	Jordan	RF	7804	79	Δ	78
1963	Al	Kaline	RF	16879	93		64
1999	Reggie	Sanders	RF	9536	49	Δ	48
1999	Raul	Mondesi	RF	11513	47	Δ	46
1994	David	Justice	RF	7202	48	Δ	43
1974	Bobby	Bonds	RF	12475	63	Δ	43
1966	Johnny	Callison	RF	13423	69		42
2003	Richard	Hidalgo	RF	4289	37	Δ	39
1910	Mike	Mitchell	RF	6466	108		38
1998	Tim	Salmon	RF	10937	38		36
1967	Tony	Oliva	RF	9950	61	Δ	36
1991	Joe	Orsulak	RF	4617	43		35
2001	Shawn	Green	RF	13792	34		35
1933	Paul	Waner	RF	18783	86		34
1981	Tony	Armas	RF	5135	48	Δ	34
1995	Paul	O'Neill	RF	15388	36		32
1986	Glenn	Wilson	RF	7779	42		32
1942	Wally	Moses	RF	10782	77		32
2005	J.D.	Drew	RF	8562	28		31
2005	Jacque	Jones	RF	4097	25	Δ	29
1938	Ival	Goodman	RF	7725	76		28
2000	Matt	Lawton	RF	6502	27	Δ	27
1902	Elmer	Flick	RF	9241	104		27
1948	Tommy	Holmes	RF	5179	68		27
2004	Jose	Cruz, Jr.	RF	3601	24	Δ	26

(Continued)

Top Forty Right Fielders of All Time (*Continued*)

MCS	First	Last	Pos	IP	Runs	Δ	TPAR
1993	Mark	Whiten	RF	5794	31	Δ	25
1939	Gene	Moore	RF	6096	72		25
1945	Bill	Nicholson	RF	11418	66		23
1979	Bake	McBride	RF	4639	38	Δ	22
2003	Jermaine	Dye	RF	14276	20	Δ	22
1926	Sam	Rice	RF	13739	80		22
1981	Dwight	Evans	RF	17737	33		19
1978	Leon	Roberts	RF	4236	36		19
2003	Trot	Nixon	RF	7795	16		18

Once you get below number eight on the TPAR list, it's very hard to make any clear distinctions. The Walsh and Smith methods would give Mondesi another forty runs for holding base runners, but Smith's methods would take back even more than that for not catching as many fly balls.

Number Ten: David Justice

Year	L	Tm	IP	PO8 runs	A8 runs	v-Tm	Runs
1989	N	ATL	115	-4	0	-3	-4
1990	N	ATL	509	-6	0	-3	-6
1991	N	ATL	957	1	0	0	1
1992	N	ATL	1198	13	-1	-4	12
1993	N	ATL	1394	14	-2	1	12
1994	N	ATL	879	5	-1	-3	4
1995	N	ATL	1035	9	0	5	9
1996	N	ATL	347	7	0	0	7
1997	A	CLE	27	0	0	0	0
1998	A	CLE	18	1	0	1	0
1999	A	CLE	124	5	-1	4	4
2000	A	CLE	188	1	0	3	1
2000	A	NY	148	5	0	3	5
2001	A	NY	67	-1	0	0	-1
2002	A	OAK	195	5	-1	6	4
Total			7202	55	-7	9	48

David Justice was a very fine player, but he will probably be remembered most for being (briefly) married to Halle Berry.

Reggie Sanders (see next page) gets the nod over Justice because Walsh and Smith credit Sanders with about another fifteen runs for holding base runners.

Al Kaline (also on next page) had a great arm, and the league finally gave up challenging it by about 1959. Walsh would credit another twenty runs for holding base runners. Smith would add another thirty on top of that. Since the difference between the Walsh and Smith estimates for Kaline is larger

Number Nine: Reggie Sanders

Year	L	Tm	IP	PO9 runs	A9 runs	v-Tm	Runs
1993	N	CIN	1161	9	-4	5	5
1994	N	CIN	912	0	2	-1	2
1995	N	CIN	1028	-4	2	-3	-2
1996	N	CIN	692	3	1	6	4
1997	N	CIN	753	6	-2	-5	4
1998	N	CIN	384	4	-1	3	3
1999	N	SD	254	4	-1	7	3
2000	N	ATL	207	1	1	-1	2
2001	N	ARI	1020	5	-2	-1	3
2002	N	SF	1136	12	2	-1	14
2003	N	PIT	666	0	0	3	0
2004	N	STL	652	2	0	5	1
2005	N	STL	6	-1	0	-1	-1
2006	A	KC	601	6	0	3	6
2007	A	KC	63	5	0	4	5
Total			9536	52	-3	24	49

Number Eight: Al Kaline

Year	L	Tm	IP	PO9 runs	A9 runs	v-Tm	Runs
1953	A	DET	6	-1	0	-1	-1
1954	A	DET	1181	9	3	1	13
1955	A	DET	1326	8	1	-2	8
1956	A	DET	1260	7	2	4	9
1957	A	DET	1131	8	0	6	9
1958	A	DET	1209	28	6	6	34
1959	A	DET	130	5	0	6	5
1961	A	DET	1147	16	-1	5	15
1962	A	DET	882	3	1	9	5
1963	A	DET	1215	-9	-2	2	-11
1964	A	DET	1193	15	-2	5	14
1965	A	DET	444	-2	-1	2	-3
1966	A	DET	453	0	-1	-5	0
1967	A	DET	1086	8	3	-3	11
1968	A	DET	584	8	-2	-4	6
1969	A	DET	974	-5	0	0	-4
1970	A	DET	687	0	-2	-2	-2
1971	A	DET	967	-4	-1	3	-5
1972	A	DET	570	-9	0	-3	-9
1973	A	DET	435	1	-1	0	0
Total			16879	88	6		93

than for any other outfielder, I would split it and credit Kaline about thirty-five runs for holding base runners. *Smith*(*pgor, bod*) and DRA agree almost precisely on runs saved from catching fly balls.

I dropped Kaline down a bit because he never demonstrated any sustained fielding excellence outside of the practically non-integrated American League of the 1950s; the timeline adjustment under TPAR does not differentiate between the two leagues, and I believe the American League was significantly weaker in the outfield. Al suffered from numerous foot and leg injuries throughout his career, which may explain some of the ups and downs in his ratings and playing time.

Number Seven: Sammy Sosa

Year	L	Tm	IP	PO9 runs	A9 runs	v-Tm	Runs
1989	A	TEX	2	0	0	0	-1
1989	A	CHI	64	-1	0	-1	-1
1990	A	CHI	1255	11	2	2	13
1991	A	CHI	699	19	-1	12	19
1993	N	CHI	836	7	2	5	10
1994	N	CHI	841	13	-2	3	10
1995	N	CHI	1274	15	1	0	17
1996	N	CHI	1087	10	4	-2	14
1997	N	CHI	1417	3	2	-1	5
1998	N	CHI	1379	1	2	-2	3
1999	N	CHI	1220	5	-3	8	3
2000	N	CHI	1373	-2	-4	-4	-6
2001	N	CHI	1385	13	-2	3	11
2002	N	CHI	1295	4	-2	1	2
2003	N	CHI	1179	-7	-4	-4	-11
2004	N	CHI	1098	7	-2	-2	5
2005	A	BAL	577	-3	0	-4	-4
2007	A	TEX	131	1	0	0	1
Total			17111	98	-6		91

Sosa is the only top right fielder with a mediocre arm, even taking into account the Walsh and Smith methods for estimating runs saved by holding base runners. As good as his fielding was, his on-base percentage was essentially league average, which is poor for a right fielder. Regardless of how the issues surrounding performance-enhancing drugs play out in the next few years, he does not belong in the Hall of Fame.

Brian Jordan (see next page) played defensive back for the Atlanta Falcons in 1989–91, which, when you think about it, is possibly the best training for playing the outfield, other than actually playing the outfield. Jordan's decision to concentrate on baseball proved profitable, as his career earnings topped $50 million.

Jordan could rank higher. $Smith(R(t,s,d))$ credits Jordan with sixty-six more runs from catching fly balls. In principle, the batted ball data used in that version of Smith's systems can provide better answers, as discussed in chapter three, but studies have shown that the 'stringers' at the games make systematic mistakes in coding the trajectories and locations of batted balls,

Number Six: Brian Jordan

Year	L	Tm	IP	PO9 runs	A9 runs	v-Tm	Runs
1992	N	STL	179	-2	0	-3	-3
1993	N	STL	80	4	0	3	3
1994	N	STL	181	4	1	0	4
1995	N	STL	978	10	-3	4	7
1996	N	STL	1045	22	0	10	22
1997	N	STL	210	3	0	5	4
1998	N	STL	947	1	1	-6	2
1999	N	ATL	1281	2	-1	-1	2
2000	N	ATL	1108	15	-1	3	14
2001	N	ATL	1234	17	1	4	18
2002	N	LA	34	0	0	0	0
2003	N	LA	26	0	0	0	0
2004	A	TEX	359	4	-1	2	3
2005	N	ATL	142	3	0	4	3
2006	N	ATL	2	0	0	0	0
Total			7804	82	-4	25	79

especially in the outfield. Though I believe that the DRA estimates during 1997–99 are too low, Jordan was in fact seriously injured in 1997. The $Smith(R(t, s, d))$ estimates, which translate into +26 defensive runs per 1450 innings over that time frame, are probably a little too high. Smith would also give credit for another fifteen runs for holding base runners.

Number Five: Ichiro Suzuki

Year	L	Tm	IP9	PO9 runs	A9 runs	v-Tm	Runs
2001	A	SEA	1314	25	-2	6	23
2002	A	SEA	1285	17	-1	1	16
2003	A	SEA	1367	10	1	3	12
2004	A	SEA	1405	6	0	3	6
2005	A	SEA	1388	18	1	4	19
2006	A	SEA	1062	0	0	6	0
2008	A	SEA	788	-4	1	3	-4
2009	A	SEA	1291	6	-3	1	4
Total			9901	78	-1	26	76

Ichiro Suzuki in Center Field

Year	L	Tm	IP8	PO8 runs	A8 runs	v-Tm	Runs
2002	A	SEA	24	0	0	0	0
2006	A	SEA	338	8	-1	6	7
2007	A	SEA	1339	7	1	0	8
2008	A	SEA	602	7	6	0	13
Total			2303	23	6	7	29

Ichiro! is one of the reasons baseball is still worth watching. At a time when more and more plate appearances end in one of the so-called Three True Outcomes (a strikeout, a walk, or a home run), this man almost always hits the ball into the field of play—and legs out more doubles and infield hits than anyone. He has the best outfield arm; nobody runs on him, and Walsh and Smith would add another twenty runs for holding base runners. Suzuki tried out center, which he handled well (which presents even more evidence of his fielding skill), but has returned to right.

Number Four: Hank Aaron

Year	Lg	Team	IP	PO9 Runs	A9 Runs	Runs
1954	N	MIL	107	-4	0	-4
1955	N	MIL	900	7	-1	6
1956	N	MIL	1341	14	2	16
1957	N	MIL	745	7	0	6
1958	N	MIL	1019	16	0	16
1959	N	MIL	1226	-10	0	-10
1960	N	MIL	1342	16	-1	14
1961	N	MIL	655	20	2	22
1962	N	MIL	622	2	0	2
1963	N	MIL	1446	-3	-1	-4
1964	N	MIL	1171	9	2	11
1965	N	MIL	1309	15	-1	13
1966	N	ATL	1346	9	0	8
1967	N	ATL	1249	14	0	14
1968	N	ATL	1291	23	1	24
1969	N	ATL	1248	5	0	4
1970	N	ATL	1060	5	-1	4
1971	N	ATL	516	-10	-1	-12
1972	N	ATL	118	0	2	2
1973	N	ATL	158	1	0	1
Total			18869	132	2	134

One has to be impressed with Hank Aaron's fielding contributions as he played into his mid-thirties. I'm sure he could have been a very solid career center fielder. Bill Bruton was the Braves' center fielder when Aaron came up, and a good one, but Bruton hung on to the position for too long. Aaron didn't get a real opportunity to play centerfield until his eighth season (1961), and though he did fine, he quickly returned to right (1963).

After serving with distinction as a member of the "Golden Outfield," with Tris Speaker in center and Duffy Lewis in left, Harry Hooper (see next page)

Number Three: Harry Hooper

Year	L	Tm	IP	PO9 runs	A9 runs	Runs
1911	A	BOS	1103	16	4	20
1912	A	BOS	1248	10	1	11
1914	A	BOS	1180	20	3	24
1915	A	BOS	1265	21	3	24
1916	A	BOS	1282	22	1	23
1917	A	BOS	1282	0	-1	-1
1918	A	BOS	1069	13	-1	12
1919	A	BOS	1086	21	1	22
1920	A	BOS	1153	16	2	18
1921	A	CHI	905	1	-1	0
1922	A	CHI	1324	19	1	20
1923	A	CHI	1222	-7	-3	-9
1924	A	CHI	1070	11	3	14
1925	A	CHI	1004	6	2	8
Total			16192	171	14	185

was traded by the Red Sox to the White Sox in exchange for Shano Collins and Nemo Liebold. They sure don't name ballplayers like they used to.

About that Golden Outfield, also known as the Million Dollar Outfield and honored mainly for its fielding excellence: my impression is that fans, sportswriters, and players assessed relative fielding skill *more* accurately a century ago than they have more recently. I am not aware of any pre-Second World War cases, analogous to Jeter and many other examples we will see in center, second, and short, in which a poor fielder was widely and persistently viewed as the best fielder at his position. That's probably because the variance in basic athleticism was so much more obvious then than it is today. Most, nearly all, major league fielders since the dawn of TV at least 'look' reasonably good out in the field. In contrast, I'm sure way back when there were some who clearly looked slow, tentative, or clumsy, and others who looked fast, confident, and in charge.

Though Hooper's election to the Hall has been criticized, if you add the above DRA estimates of his fielding value to any of the widely known estimates of offensive value, he comes well within striking distance, based either on overall runs above the average right fielder of his time or using runs over replacement value. Hooper had a solidly above-average on-base percentage and slugging percentage, decent speed, and all-time great fielding ability. The only reason he didn't play center was because Speaker was on his team. Very bright, too—an engineering graduate of a small Catholic college most recently made famous by upsetting Villanova to reach the Sweet Sixteen in the 2010 NCAA March Madness tournament.

Number Two: Jesse Barfield

Year	L	Tm	IP	PO9 runs	A9 runs	v-Tm	Runs
1981	A	TOR	219	8	0	8	8
1982	A	TOR	973	-2	4	-3	2
1983	A	TOR	873	4	5	-3	10
1984	A	TOR	648	13	3	7	17
1985	A	TOR	1290	25	6	1	31
1986	A	TOR	1297	28	4	4	32
1987	A	TOR	1249	29	3	4	33
1988	A	TOR	1053	25	1	1	26
1989	A	TOR	171	1	1	-1	2
1989	A	NY	997	-6	3	-7	-3
1990	A	NY	1193	8	4	7	12
1991	A	NY	678	8	3	7	10
1992	A	NY	236	-2	1	-1	-1
Total			10877	139	38	26	178

Jesse Barfield really had only four great fielding seasons, all with one team, and dropped off as soon as he was traded to the Yankees, which makes me wonder if there was some park effect or other contextual factor that inflated his numbers. During his 1985–88 peak with Toronto, he played next to Lloyd Moseby in center, whose ratings fell a bit during that time. Perhaps Moseby, secure in his position and recognizing that his arm was weaker than Barfield's, allowed Barfield, whenever runners were on base, to break the unwritten code under which corner outfielders yield to the center fielder on balls they both can field. In 1990–91 Barfield played next to Roberto Kelly, who, while fighting to stay in the line up, might have been reluctant to yield any chances to Barfield.

DRA estimates that Robert Clemente (see next page) saved more runs, compared to the average fielder of his time at his position, than all but two fielders, both of whom played shortstop in the Dead Ball Era. Clemente also has the highest TPAR of any fielder at any position. Walsh would credit Clemente with about twenty more runs for holding runners, and Smith would credit close to twenty more on top of that, which would potentially bring Clemente up to about +300 career defensive runs. Could he really have been that good?

There are reasons to wonder. Clemente's defensive runs estimates have more year-to-year variability than those of any top fielder. At first I thought that could be partly explained by Clemente's numerous injuries. Problem is, there seems to be no relationship between his injuries and his measured fielding performance. For example, Clemente was seriously injured in 1957 and unusually healthy in 1960; the defensive runs estimates would imply he was healthy in '57 and hurt in '60. Another factor I considered is faulty data—there are probably more Pirates games missing in the Retrosheet play-by-play database going back to 1952 than for any other team, except possibly the Braves. But the biggest swings in Clemente's annual performance do not coincide with the biggest gaps in the play-by-play data for the Pirates.

Number One: Roberto Clemente

Year	L	Tm	IP	PO9 runs	A9 runs	v-Tm	Runs
1955	N	PIT	897	11	5	12	16
1956	N	PIT	839	4	4	2	8
1957	N	PIT	843	28	0	14	28
1958	N	PIT	1151	32	7	-2	38
1959	N	PIT	900	13	2	8	15
1960	N	PIT	1256	-2	3	0	1
1961	N	PIT	1236	-9	8	1	-1
1962	N	PIT	1229	12	4	6	16
1963	N	PIT	1243	3	0	5	3
1964	N	PIT	1362	12	0	2	12
1965	N	PIT	1265	19	3	1	23
1966	N	PIT	1374	19	3	1	22
1967	N	PIT	1248	3	4	-4	6
1968	N	PIT	1159	34	-1	1	33
1969	N	PIT	1124	0	2	0	2
1970	N	PIT	901	5	2	-2	8
1971	N	PIT	1081	12	1	-2	13
1972	N	PIT	812	14	-1	4	13
Total			19920	211	46	48	256

Though more research is needed to refine the estimate of Clemente's fielding contribution, I think future methods will confirm that it was indeed vast. And there is a probably a simple explanation for it. Even more than Hooper or Aaron or Jordan, Clemente was meant to play center. If you took an all-time great center fielder and replayed his career in right field, where he would have been compared against a rather middling set of fielders, he'd be right where Clemente is.

When Clemente came up in 1955, the Pirates tried eight different players in center, Clemente among them. Although he had not hit well in his rookie year, as the 1956 season opened Clemente seemed to be winning the battle, though occasionally left fielder Lee Walls started and Bobby Del Greco came in late to substitute for Clemente. Since Del Greco and Clemente were both right-handed hitters, they couldn't have been making the change to get a platoon advantage, so, strange as it may seem, apparently the Pirates were pulling Clemente out late in games because they thought Del Greco was a better fielder. (Del Greco's DRA numbers are pretty good, and he later served as a defensive backup in center for Mickey Mantle.)

On May 17, 1956, the Pirates traded Del Greco and relief pitcher Dick Littlefield to the Cardinals, in exchange for the 1955 National League Rookie of the Year, Bill Virdon, who was the Cardinals' starting centerfielder. I have no idea why Cardinals' general manager Frank Lane unloaded Virdon. St. Louis fans were furious. A certain Mrs. Eleanor Esstman was quoted at the time in a local newspaper to the effect that "all these deals would be fine if the Cards were getting value received. But this deal, like the [Harvey] Haddix trade, seems to be change for the sake of change." Perhaps Virdon's slow start that year (he was hitting under .200) had something to do with it. In any event, Virdon immediately took over in center field for the Pirates, and the Pittsburgh Post-Gazette reported that "[t]his move will mean that Roberto Clemente will be a spare outfielder and come in handy as a pinch-hitter."

Clemente managed to win a full-time job that year, playing some in left, but mostly in right, and hit .311. Problem was, he led all National League outfielders in errors, while Virdon led all National League center fielders in fielding average and finished with a .319 batting average, in spite of his slow start. The one man in baseball able and willing to inform the public how "meaningless," indeed "deceptive," fielding average could be, Branch Rickey, had retired as the Pirates' general manager the prior year, for health reasons. Something tells me that if Rickey's ticker had been working better, Clemente would have been moved back to center. But then he wouldn't have been remembered as the greatest fielding right fielder of all time.

Third Base

Gold Glove voters haven't made any major, or at least repeated, mistakes at third base—not a single third baseman has won more than one Gold Glove who was not at least a decent or good fielder. I think that's because, with one exception we'll get to, third base defense *can* be reasonably well evaluated by sight. The most important skills for a third baseman are fearlessness, quick reflexes, a strong arm, and the ability to field bunts. Those are all readily observable skills. In addition, because the slice of the field covered by third basemen is so much narrower than at second, short, or in the outfield, sheer range, including invisible range in the form of positioning, is relatively less important, though still important.

Contemporary Era

MCS	First	Last	IP	Runs	Δ
2003	Scott	Rolen	15139	115	
2003	David	Bell	7952	94	
1995	Matt	Williams	14763	87	
1998	Scott	Brosius	7873	76	
2004	Adrian	Beltre	14332	72	Δ
1996	Robin	Ventura	15929	66	
1994	Ken	Caminiti	14253	65	
1998	Shane	Andrews	3814	48	
2002	Aaron	Boone	7957	40	
1999	Jeff	Cirillo	11255	39	
2003	Eric	Chavez	10659	39	
2005	Joe	Crede	7479	30	
1997	Travis	Fryman	11699	24	
1998	John	Valentin	3147	23	
1993	Scott	Leius	3395	19	

(continued)

Contemporary Era *(continued)*

MCS	First	Last	IP	Runs	Δ
1997	Cal	Ripken	5727	17	
2000	Phil	Nevin	4001	17	
1994	Scott	Cooper	3812	16	
2003	Troy	Glaus	11394	16	
2004	Geoff	Blum	4781	16	
2000	Vinny	Castilla	14305	11	
2002	Tony	Batista	6925	11	Δ
1997	Willie	Greene	3139	10	Δ
2004	Mike	Lowell	12611	9	
2005	Morgan	Ensberg	5055	9	
2001	Bill	Mueller	9240	6	
1993	Jeff	King	4706	2	
2002	Corey	Koskie	7745	1	
1994	Jim	Thome	4109	1	
2004	Sean	Burroughs	3257	-5	
1994	Dave	Magadan	4845	-6	
2001	Edgardo	Alfonzo	7345	-7	Δ
1993	Leo	Gomez	4665	-11	
2001	Joe	Randa	11396	-14	
2003	Eric	Hinske	3798	-15	
2003	Shea	Hillenbrand	3839	-17	
2003	Mike	Lamb	3579	-17	
1999	Ron	Coomer	3009	-17	
1997	Craig	Paquette	3639	-18	
1994	Charlie	Hayes	10987	-21	Δ
1995	Sean	Berry	4735	-23	
1996	Ed	Sprague	8719	-23	
2005	Wes	Helms	3313	-27	
2000	Fernando	Tatis	5634	-32	Δ
2005	Ty	Wigginton	4557	-33	
2005	Hank	Blalock	5976	-40	
1998	Russ	Davis	4533	-40	
1995	Mike	Blowers	4822	-43	
1995	Dave	Hollins	6516	-44	
1996	Todd	Zeile	12855	-47	
2004	Aramis	Ramirez	11804	-47	Δ
2002	Chipper	Jones	14507	-108	
1996	Dean	Palmer	9852	-113	

The above list matches well with the latest batted ball data estimates, with one major exception: Chipper Jones (see next page).

From 2000 onward, DRA is broadly consistent with all other systems, except that they rate Chipper slightly above average, while DRA rates him slightly below average. The discrepancy is nowhere very large except for 2001, when I believe he might have been injured. His own team, one of the best-managed baseball organizations of our time, sent him to left field after that 2001 season, just so that they exploit the golden opportunity to play

Chipper Jones

Year	L	Tm	IP	Runs	v-Tm
1995	N	ATL	1055	-2	4
1996	N	ATL	1037	-25	-7
1997	N	ATL	1301	-13	2
1998	N	ATL	1400	-10	2
1999	N	ATL	1381	-26	-1
2000	N	ATL	1311	-7	-1
2001	N	ATL	1297	-18	-1
2004	N	ATL	802	-3	-2
2005	N	ATL	830	-5	-1
2006	N	ATL	888	-3	3
2007	N	ATL	1081	5	4
2008	N	ATL	987	7	-2
2009	N	ATL	1137	-9	-9
Total			14507	-108	-9

thirty-four-year-old Vinnie Castilla, a good but unspectacular fielder and ordinary hitter, at third. In general, you don't move a competent third baseman who hits like Chipper into left field—it's relatively easier and cheaper to find a competent left fielder who can hit better than Vinny Castilla. My sense is there must have been a real problem in 2001. Whatever it was, it was resolved by 2004. Since then, Chipper has played part-to-full-time at third at a more or less average level.

The real discrepancy among the systems concerns Chipper's first four full-time seasons at third: 1996–99. DRA estimates –21 defensive runs per 1450 innings over that period; $Smith(R(t,s,d))$, which is based on free Retrosheet batted ball data from 1989 through 1999, estimates –5 defensive runs per 1450 innings over that period; the $Fox(R(t),f,bh,bo)$ play-by-play system estimates –3 defensive runs per 1450. So the batted ball and play-by-play systems suggest that Chipper was probably slightly below average in 1996–99, whereas DRA sees Chipper, during those four years, as a very poor fielder essentially playing out of position. What is even more peculiar is that Chipper came up as a shortstop; you would think that he'd be, if anything, *above* average after moving to an easier position. And in general you'd be right. But there are exceptions. Batted ball systems currently show that A-Rod has not been an above-average third baseman, even though he was a competent shortstop. And we'll soon see another example from recent history of a shortstop who struggled at third.

Though I could believe it possible that Chipper was well below average in his first years at his new position, the weight of evidence from the batted ball and play-by-play systems was leading me to concede that, at least in this case, DRA had made a significant valuation error. Then noted analyst Tom Tango published a $Tango(p\text{-}wowy)$ estimate that Chipper made 261 plays below expectation over the course of his career through 2008, which could translate into close to *minus 200 defensive runs*.

Tango(p-wowy) compares how many batted ball outs were recorded by third basemen per batted ball in play throughout *pitchers'* careers when they were pitching *with* Chipper as their third baseman compared to when they were pitching *without* Chipper, that is, with another third baseman ("with or without you," or "wowy"). *Tango(p-wowy)* would seem perfectly designed to control for any unusual batted ball distributions generated by the remarkably stable pitching staff that Braves had in place for most of Chipper's tenure at third, particularly during 1996–99, when Maddux, Smoltz, and Glavine were each pitching about 200 innings or more, year in and year out. Most importantly for purposes of applying *Tango(p-wowy)*, Maddux, Smoltz, and Glavine have each pitched much if not most of their careers *without* Chipper as their third baseman, so there should be large enough samples with and without Chipper to make a good comparison. And *Tango(p-wowy)* can account not only for batted ball distributions generated by pitchers, but also for the extent to which *pitcher fielding* might interfere with third base opportunities. Maddux and Glavine were among the best fielding pitchers of our time. It is reasonable to think they might have taken more than a few bunts that would normally be handled by their third basemen. *Tango(p-wowy)* automatically takes into account this factor as well. However, one problem with Tango(p-wowy) is that *Tango(p-wowy)* includes pop outs and fly outs caught by infielders, which should be ignored as discretionary plays usually playable by more than one fielder. Perhaps Chipper's shortstop and left field teammates 'hogged' a lot of those discretionary chances from him.

Given this mixed evidence, I'm currently inclined to think that Chipper was indeed well below average as a fielder, though perhaps somewhat better than the DRA estimate. And even if the DRA estimate of approximately −100 defensive runs is correct, Chipper generated so many runs in offense he's a worthy first ballot Hall of Famer.

Modern Era

MCS	First	Last	IP	Runs	Δ
1980	Mike	Schmidt	18946	195	
1980	Buddy	Bell	18966	183	
1988	Tim	Wallach	17766	137	
1977	Graig	Nettles	20625	125	
1990	Terry	Pendleton	15395	119	Δ
1977	Darrell	Evans	12223	104	
1990	Gary	Gaetti	19227	98	
1984	Tom	Brookens	7925	79	
1974	A.	Rodriguez	15961	70	
1989	Kelly	Gruber	6776	56	

(*continued*)

Modern Era (*continued*)

MCS	First	Last	IP	Runs	Δ
1981	Doug	DeCinces	13121	45	
1980	George	Brett	14582	42	
1985	Luis	Salazar	6554	38	Δ
1973	Wayne	Garrett	6379	33	
1984	Garth	Iorg	3153	30	
1988	Tim	Hulett	3514	30	
1990	Steve	Buechele	10203	27	
1972	Doug	Rader	11848	25	
1976	Eric	Soderholm	6267	23	
1982	Phil	Garner	6515	20	
1969	Tony	Perez	6655	20	Δ
1985	Ken	Oberkfell	8166	16	
1980	Jerry	Royster	4007	14	
1980	John	Castino	3364	11	
1983	Hubie	Brooks	4460	10	Δ
1979	Ron	Cey	17140	9	
1990	Kevin	Seitzer	8746	9	
1978	Mike	Cubbage	3428	8	
1989	Jack	Howell	5120	8	
1978	Lenny	Randle	4198	5	Δ
1970	Denis	Menke	3048	4	
1985	Paul	Molitor	6898	3	
1976	Dave	Chalk	3830	3	
1990	C.	Worthington	3134	2	
1991	Tony	Phillips	3053	2	Δ
1992	Gary	Sheffield	3994	0	Δ
1992	Bobby	Bonilla	8017	-1	Δ
1977	Steve	Ontiveros	4833	-1	Δ
1984	Pedro	Guerrero	3115	-5	Δ
1974	Don	Money	8718	-7	
1970	Ed	Spiezio	3337	-7	
1986	Chris	Brown	3562	-7	Δ
1985	Rance	Mulliniks	4931	-10	
1972	Al	Gallagher	3005	-12	
1990	Wade	Boggs	18921	-13	
1984	Jim	Morrison	4801	-13	
1974	Dave	Roberts	3135	-17	
1991	Chris	Sabo	7056	-17	
1978	Roy	Howell	7092	-17	
1991	Edgar	Martinez	4605	-25	
1978	Bill	Stein	4119	-25	
1973	Rico	Petrocelli	6233	-27	
1972	Bill	Melton	7686	-31	
1978	Enos	Cabell	7403	-32	Δ
1983	Ray	Knight	8047	-32	
1969	Paul	Schaal	8709	-34	
1978	Larry	Parrish	8769	-36	
1980	Wayne	Gross	6898	-36	
1989	Mike	Pagliarulo	9286	-37	

(*continued*)

Modern Era (*continued*)

MCS	First	Last	IP	Runs	Δ
1987	Jim	Presley	7803	-39	
1981	Bob	Horner	5703	-39	
1987	Rick	Schu	3181	-40	
1986	Vance	Law	5294	-43	
1973	Sal	Bando	16392	-47	
1977	Ken	Reitz	11216	-50	
1987	Brook	Jacoby	9740	-54	
1976	Pete	Rose	5249	-54	
1974	Richie	Hebner	10522	-56	
1978	Butch	Hobson	5601	-58	
1988	Howard	Johnson	8097	-59	
1972	Joe	Torre	4309	-67	
1980	Toby	Harrah	9210	-106	
1984	Carney	Lansford	14640	-122	
1980	Bill	Madlock	12144	-123	Δ

The Modern Era provides us with an example of someone for whom playing third might have been tougher than playing short.

Toby Harrah

Year	L	Tm	IP	Runs	v-Tm
1971	A	WAS	46	1	2
1973	A	TEX	409	-7	1
1974	A	TEX	27	1	1
1975	A	TEX	160	5	5
1976	A	TEX	45	-1	-1
1977	A	TEX	1404	-16	0
1978	A	TEX	772	-9	0
1979	A	CLE	1021	-37	-8
1980	A	CLE	1332	-10	2
1981	A	CLE	871	-12	-1
1982	A	CLE	1355	-13	-2
1983	A	CLE	1199	-3	-1
1984	A	NY	569	-5	0
Total			9210	-106	-3

Toby Harrah had +8 career defensive runs at shortstop, which was his primary position through 1976. He consistently underperformed at his new position with two different teams (actually, with three, though the sample size of innings played with the Yankees is too small to be reliable). He tended to position himself nearer the third base line, out of a concern of giving up too many doubles; it seems that resulted in too many singles going through the gap between third and short. Nevertheless, he was a genuine all-star quality player for more than a few years, thanks to his excellent on-base percentage, speed, and decent power.

Though you can see a lot by looking at third basemen, the one visible phenomenon that has distorted evaluations of third basemen is errors.

Bobby Bonilla

Year	L	Tm	IP	Runs	v-Tm
1986	N	PIT	30	1	1
1987	N	PIT	690	-2	-4
1988	N	PIT	1404	7	0
1989	N	PIT	1383	12	0
1990	N	PIT	80	3	3
1991	N	PIT	520	-2	2
1993	N	NY	426	0	0
1994	N	NY	918	11	1
1995	N	NY	366	-5	-6
1995	A	BAL	203	4	2
1996	A	BAL	34	-2	-2
1998	N	LA	474	-7	-5
1997	N	FLA	1269	-17	1
1998	N	FLA	216	-5	-4
2000	N	ATL	4	0	0
Total			8017	-1	-10

While praising Bobby Bonilla for his effort, arm, and quickness, *The Historical Abstract* concludes that he was worse at third than the "awful" Carney Lansford. Lansford indeed had absolutely no range; Bonilla had good range, but just made a lot of errors. In every season that he played more than a few innings at third he had a below-average fielding percentage. During his first two full-time seasons at third, 1988–89, he led the league in errors. But he also led the league in 1988 in assists, with 336, and recorded 330 assists the following year. In 1994, he led the league in errors again, even though he played only 918 innings. In all three of those seasons, notwithstanding his errors, Bonilla made more plays than expected, given the many factors taken into account by DRA.

Smith's systems charge Bonilla −49 career defensive runs at third base. Bonilla made close to fifty extra errors because of his lower fielding percentage; that is, if he had had the same number of balls reached (putouts, assists, and errors) but had a league-average fielding percentage, he would have made about fifty fewer errors. If you add back the half run that Smith's systems tend to overpenalize errors as being something worse than a play not made, Bobby is about −25 defensive runs under Smith's systems, which comes to −5 defensive runs per 1450 innings. Not good, but hardly awful.

Bonilla might rate a little too high under DRA due to extra bunt opportunities. If you were an opponent given the sign to bunt, and you thought the third baseman was a lousy fielder because he made a lot of errors, you might *decide* to bunt toward third base. In other words, a third baseman such as Bonilla with a bad fielding reputation might attract extra chances that way, record some more assists, and thereby slightly increase his DRA rating, though I have not yet seen direct evidence that is the case.

Tony Perez

Year	L	Tm	IP	Runs	v-Tm
1967	N	CIN	1237	-13	1
1968	N	CIN	1463	10	1
1969	N	CIN	1422	6	-1
1970	N	CIN	1309	3	-2
1971	N	CIN	1223	15	-4
Total			6655	20	-5

Tony Perez's first full-time position was third base. He led the league in double plays in 1968 (thirty-three) and 1969 (thirty-five), and recorded another thirty-four double plays in 1970. He also led the league in assists in 1969 and 1971. But his team thought they had a 'problem', because he led the league in errors in 1968, 1969, and 1970. So in the famous multi-player trade with Houston in 1971 that brought Joe Morgan over to join The Big Red Machine, the Reds made sure they also got Denis Menke, a below-average-fielding shortstop they thought could play third. And he did play third all right. But he couldn't hit like Tony Perez, or even over .200 by his second year. So then they tried Dan Driessen at third. He hit well enough but couldn't field, so they let him take Perez's job at first, gave the third base job to Pete Rose, and traded Tony Perez to Montreal.

Gary Sheffield

Year	L	Tm	IP	Runs	v-Tm
1989	A	MIL	177	2	0
1990	A	MIL	1069	-4	3
1991	A	MIL	369	-6	-3
1992	N	SD	1248	4	3
1993	N	SD	565	-1	2
1993	N	FLA	565	4	2
2004	A	NY	2	0	0
Total			3994	0	6

Throughout his career, Gary Sheffield courted all manner of controversy. We'll focus here on just one controversial finding of DRA: that Sheffield might not have been such a terrible fielding third baseman. I see nothing in his record through 1992 to indicate that he couldn't field the position. Nor am I convinced he was ineffective in 1993; as shown by his v-Tm runs, he was *better* than his replacements that year, for *both* of the teams he played for. However, by leading the league in errors, and compiling an embarrassing .899 fielding percentage, he provided his second team, the Marlins, an excuse to exile him to the outfield. Given that he had once proven the ability to play third competently, and subsequently proved over the course of the next seventeen years that he was below average in the outfield, I wonder whether his career could have been even greater if he'd stayed at third.

Transitional Era

MCS	First	Last	IP	Runs	Δ
1967	Brooks	Robinson	25038	189	
1965	Clete	Boyer	12349	146	
1961	Ken	Boyer	15340	76	
1953	Hank	Thompson	5463	56	Δ
1948	Hank	Majeski	7298	55	
1948	Billy	Johnson	7626	45	
1959	Eddie	Mathews	19011	35	
1953	Al	Rosen	8077	34	
1957	Hector	Lopez	3840	27	Δ
1948	Floyd	Baker	3974	26	
1954	Fred	Hatfield	3211	26	
1951	Billy	Cox	5619	24	
1968	Bob	Bailey	9559	23	
1965	Ed	Charles	8049	21	Δ
1954	Gil	McDougald	3895	20	
1968	Tony	Taylor	3277	20	
1947	Frankie	Gustine	3070	17	
1967	Ron	Santo	18777	17	
1949	Johnny	Pesky	3996	16	
1964	Charley	Smith	5174	15	
1965	Pete	Ward	4729	13	
1960	Eddie	Kasko	3336	11	
1962	Jim	Gilliam	5469	9	Δ
1963	Jim	Davenport	8304	6	
1957	Andy	Carey	6951	6	
1968	Ken	McMullen	11035	5	
1953	Bobby	Adams	5351	5	
1959	Don	Hoak	10350	4	
1954	Randy	Jackson	7340	2	
1968	Joe	Foy	5639	2	Δ
1955	Ray	Boone	4407	-1	
1961	Bubba	Phillips	6402	-7	
1966	Dick	Allen	5723	-9	Δ
1961	Frank	Malzone	11969	-11	
1965	Rich	Rollins	6910	-18	
1966	Jim Ray	Hart	5728	-20	Δ
1968	Mike	Shannon	4228	-23	
1950	Grady	Hatton	8009	-24	

(continued)

Transitional Era *(continued)*

MCS	First	Last	IP	Runs	Δ
1949	Sid	Gordon	3815	-27	
1959	Al	Smith	3020	-27	
1967	Don	Wert	8940	-30	
1958	Frank	Thomas	3231	-32	
1960	Gene	Freese	6414	-41	
1947	Bob	Elliott	11742	-47	
1965	Harmon	Killebrew	6242	-50	
1950	George	Kell	14633	-50	
1955	Ray	Jablonski	4973	-55	
1966	Max	Alvis	8484	-60	
1954	Willie	Jones	14158	-61	
1949	Bob	Dillinger	5760	-68	
1966	Bob	Aspromonte	9323	-71	
1954	Eddie	Yost	17240	-204	

Here's another controversial fellow underrated due to errors:

Dick Allen

Year	L	Tm	IP	Runs	v-Tm
1963	N	PHI	1	0	0
1964	N	PHI	1419	11	0
1965	N	PHI	1431	-2	2
1966	N	PHI	806	-5	-3
1967	N	PHI	1085	-2	1
1968	N	PHI	72	-1	-1
1970	N	STL	331	-5	2
1971	N	LA	562	-3	-8
1972	A	CHI	16	-1	-1
Total			5723	-9	-7

Dick Allen never played third base before coming to the major leagues, and he did lead the league in errors in 1964 and 1967. But over that four-year period he was second only to Ron Santo in assists and starting double plays. And he might have been even better if not for three severe injuries. In the middle of 1965, Allen got into a fight with (ex-third baseman) Frank Thomas over the latter's racist hazing of another black player on the team. During the fight, Thomas hit Allen's shoulder with a baseball bat, apparently with some force. Allen was hitting .341 before the fight; over the rest of the season he hit .271, and his defensive runs performance fell sharply as well. Before the 1966 season opened, Allen dislocated a shoulder (not sure if it was the same one), and the next year he cut his throwing hand in a freak accident while pushing a stalled car in his driveway. The last injury reduced the feeling in two of his fingers, which prevented him from gripping the ball properly and forced his move to first, where he wouldn't have to throw so much. Yet in spite of his lack of experience and three severe injuries, Dick Allen acquitted himself decently well at third.

The top National League third baseman when Allen was playing the position also made a lot of errors, at least in the beginning of his career.

Ron Santo

Year	L	Tm	IP	Runs	v-Tm
1960	N	CHI	836	-20	-3
1961	N	CHI	1352	-14	-1
1962	N	CHI	1373	8	0
1963	N	CHI	1457	5	-1
1964	N	CHI	1422	5	0
1965	N	CHI	1472	-11	0
1966	N	CHI	1351	12	3
1967	N	CHI	1440	22	0
1968	N	CHI	1444	8	1
1969	N	CHI	1413	4	0
1970	N	CHI	1321	13	6
1971	N	CHI	1295	-10	-2
1972	N	CHI	1116	7	1
1973	N	CHI	1275	-9	1
1974	A	CHI	210	-3	-1
Total			18777	17	6

Ron Santo started weakly and finished weakly as a fielder, but in between he was good-to-excellent, and those seasons of strong fielding coincided with his batting prime, thus contributing to at least four consecutive seasons of MVP-level overall value (1964–67). Santo's career offensive runs, along with a slight positional adjustment for playing third base and his net fielding contribution, easily surpass 350 runs of total value above the level of the average third basemen of his era, and thus safely exceed a reasonable threshold for career value necessary to qualify for the Hall. Santo's Hall of Fame candidacy has been undermined by three things beyond his control: his teams were unsuccessful, his outstanding four-year peak occurred right within the modern Dead Ball period, which made his offensive numbers look less impressive, and, perhaps most of all, his peak almost exactly coincided with Willie Mays's best years. It's past time for the Veterans Committee to vote Santo in.[1]

The Veterans Committee admitted George Kell to the Hall in 1983, I believe in part for a good fielding reputation: Kell led the league in fielding percentage

1. Now it is truly too late. Ron Santo died while this book was in production.

George Kell

Year	L	Tm	IP	Runs	v-Tm
1943	A	PHI	15	0	
1944	A	PHI	1274	-3	
1945	A	PHI	1346	8	
1946	A	PHI	235	3	
1946	A	DET	998	-7	
1947	A	DET	1370	8	
1948	A	DET	750	-6	
1949	A	DET	1238	6	
1950	A	DET	1403	-7	
1951	A	DET	1320	2	
1952	A	DET	343	-5	-5
1952	A	BOS	625	-8	-5
1953	A	BOS	1008	-12	-3
1954	A	BOS	208	-4	-3
1954	A	CHI	220	-3	-4
1955	A	CHI	834	-13	-5
1956	A	CHI	143	-3	-3
1956	A	BAL	749	-4	-1
1957	A	BAL	553	-5	0
Total			14633	-50	-28

five times. And he did lead the league in assists four times, which is a much better, if still imperfect, sign of excellence for an infielder. However, the reason he recorded all those assists was because he led the league in innings played at

Ed Yost

Year	L	Tm	IP	Runs	v-Tm
1944	A	WAS	19	0	
1946	A	WAS	76	0	
1947	A	WAS	960	-11	
1948	A	WAS	1282	-19	
1949	A	WAS	994	-1	
1950	A	WAS	1365	-24	
1951	A	WAS	1321	-21	
1952	A	WAS	1424	-23	0
1953	A	WAS	1341	-2	0
1954	A	WAS	1296	-6	-1
1955	A	WAS	899	-15	-4
1956	A	WAS	1187	-9	0
1957	A	WAS	937	-10	4
1958	A	WAS	942	-12	4
1959	A	DET	1267	-11	-3
1960	A	DET	1181	-25	-5
1961	A	LA	523	-11	-10
1962	A	LA	226	-5	-2
Total			17240	-204	-17

third and played behind a ground ball pitching staff. Taking into account those factors, as well as others, Kell was actually a consistently average fielder with two different teams throughout his twenties, and a consistently below-average fielder with three different teams throughout his thirties.

In both *The Historical Abstract* and *Win Shares*, Bill James criticizes Pete Palmer's ratings for Ed Yost (see prior page) for fluctuating up and down excessively, due to failure (since corrected to some extent) to account for changes in the level of left-handed pitching on Yost's teams. DRA makes these kinds of adjustments, and finds Yost to be consistently very poor at the beginning of his career, consistently below average at his peak, and consistently poor at the end of this career with three different teams. Yost compensated for his defensive limitations with an uncanny ability to draw walks (eight seasons of 123 or more walks).

Third base became for the first time a less demanding fielding position than second base sometime during the 1930s. The shift came about mainly

Live Ball Era

MCS	First	Last	IP	Runs	Δ
1938	Billy	Werber	9995	105	
1928	Pie	Traynor	16497	92	
1943	Ken	Keltner	13235	91	
1928	Ossie	Bluege	13209	84	
1923	Babe	Pinelli	6232	64	
1941	Pinky	May	5613	58	
1928	Willie	Kamm	14714	56	
1937	Lew	Riggs	5431	47	
1927	Chuck	Dressen	4780	44	
1930	Wally	Gilbert	5153	42	
1938	Buddy	Lewis	5832	42	
1925	Bernie	Friberg	4161	41	
1938	Red	Rolfe	9764	41	
1944	Steve	Mesner	3699	28	
1924	Frankie	Frisch	4096	27	
1942	Lee	Handley	5908	25	
1939	Harlond	Clift	13521	25	
1939	Cecil	Travis	3995	19	
1925	Rube	Lutzke	4612	18	
1930	Marty	McManus	6373	18	
1936	Odell	Hale	3808	17	
1926	Sammy	Hale	5904	16	
1945	Bob	Kennedy	4491	12	
1928	F.	Lindstrom	6791	8	
1922	Frank	Ellerbe	3023	7	
1933	Woody	English	3514	5	
1944	Mark	Christman	3727	3	
1945	Whitey	Kurowski	7411	2	

(continued)

Live Ball Era *(continued)*

MCS	First	Last	IP	Runs	Δ
1925	Fred	Haney	3803	2	
1921	Bob	Jones	6381	2	
1946	Pete	Suder	3263	1	
1933	Pinky	Whitney	11925	-1	
1934	Pepper	Martin	3613	-2	
1925	Howard	Freigau	3180	-3	
1931	Joe	Sewell	5779	-4	
1934	Joe	Stripp	7773	-5	
1940	Cookie	Lavagetto	5838	-11	
1921	Howie	Shanks	4175	-16	
1938	Tony	Cuccinello	3726	-19	
1931	Sparky	Adams	4664	-27	
1942	Jim	Tabor	8518	-27	
1922	Jimmy	Johnston	3835	-32	
1939	Don	Gutteridge	3398	-32	
1930	Jimmy	Dykes	10999	-36	
1927	Frank	O'Rourke	5162	-38	
1926	Gene	Robertson	4633	-40	
1933	Johnny	Vergez	5400	-43	
1921	Tony	Boeckel	6621	-44	
1936	Marv	Owen	8088	-48	
1926	Andy	High	6567	-48	
1927	Les	Bell	6985	-50	
1940	Stan	Hack	16317	-57	
1924	Joe	Dugan	8914	-77	
1920	Milt	Stock	13303	-80	
1939	Pinky	Higgins	15418	-167	

because double plays opportunities increased with the live ball (as there was less sacrifice hitting and base-stealing), so it became a practical necessity for the second basemen to be good on the double play pivot and less important for the third baseman to handle bunts.

Pie Traynor was for decades almost universally regarded by baseball fans as the greatest ever third baseman, mainly because his career batting average was .320 and he was believed to be a good fielder, which he in fact was. Bill James argued for many years, however, that Stan Hack was actually a much better overall player because he drew more walks and had a much higher on-base percentage, especially relative to his peers. Without going through a season-by-season analysis, it is clear that Traynor's approximately 150-run advantage on defense more than makes up for Hack's advantage on offense. Kell, Traynor, and Hack were all very fine players, but, based on the best measures of overall value, not Hall of Fame impact players of the caliber of Ron Santo.

Ken Keltner has long been recognized as a good fielder, and Billy Werber will be one of our honorable mentions when we settle upon our top ten, so let's highlight the lesser knowns: Bluege, Pinelli, and May.

Ossie Bluege

Year	L	Tm	IP	Runs
1922	A	WAS	119	0
1923	A	WAS	936	-10
1924	A	WAS	962	0
1925	A	WAS	1249	11
1926	A	WAS	1182	-13
1927	A	WAS	1312	29
1928	A	WAS	1265	17
1929	A	WAS	357	1
1930	A	WAS	1205	13
1931	A	WAS	1361	5
1932	A	WAS	1329	17
1933	A	WAS	1184	5
1934	A	WAS	343	3
1935	A	WAS	209	4
1936	A	WAS	154	2
1937	A	WAS	19	0
1938	A	WAS	8	0
1939	A	WAS	15	0
Total			13209	84

Ossie Bluege, who played only a little after Pinelli and could rank right up with him, served the Washington Senators–Minnesota Twins franchise as a (i) third baseman on its first World Championship team, (ii) all-star short-stop for one year, (iii) manager for five years, (iv) farm director for several years, and (v) financial controller for about a dozen years. Truly a five-tool company man.

Babe Pinelli

Year	L	Tm	IP	Runs
1918	A	CHI	152	-2
1920	A	DET	652	6
1922	N	CIN	1655	3
1923	N	CIN	1032	8
1924	N	CIN	1300	17
1925	N	CIN	1010	22
1926	N	CIN	354	8
1927	N	CIN	77	1
Total			6232	64

Babe Pinelli's career passed just before third base became less difficult than second, so I would give him the nod as the best fielding third baseman during the Live Ball Era on a rate basis. Though not a terrible hitter, his bat for some reason died after he turned thirty, which prevented him from amassing significant career fielding value. He went on to become the umpire who called the most famous strike in history: the last pitch of Don Larsen's perfect game.

Merrill Glend "Pinky" May

Year	L	Tm	IP	Runs
1939	N	PHI	1155	15
1940	N	PHI	1175	22
1941	N	PHI	1205	11
1942	N	PHI	903	10
1943	N	PHI	1175	0
Total			5613	58

Pinky May didn't get his shot until he was twenty-eight, and presumably was drafted in 1944 and never made it back, since he hit well enough in 1943 to keep on playing. He probably deserved a longer run; clearly fielded third very well, and maintained an above-average on-base percentage.

Dead Ball Era

MCS	First	Last	IP	Runs	Δ
1902	Jimmy	Collins	15116	169	
1904	Tommy	Leach	8417	132	
1906	Lee	Tannehill	6042	109	
1916	Eddie	Foster	10380	69	
1896	Billy	Clingman	3684	67	
1919	Heinie	Groh	11221	64	
1901	Lave	Cross	14288	60	
1904	Bill	Bradley	11593	57	
1908	Art	Devlin	10607	52	
1917	Ossie	Vitt	7371	46	
1914	Home Run	Baker	13807	46	
1912	Buck	Herzog	4145	44	
1913	Terry	Turner	5221	43	
1912	Mike	Mowrey	9143	39	
1915	Heinie	Zimmerman	8261	34	
1910	George	Moriarty	6937	32	
1901	Bobby	Wallace	3755	30	
1914	Jimmy	Austin	12327	29	
1898	John	McGraw	6446	27	
1917	Larry	Gardner	14536	27	
1906	Dave	Brain	3912	24	
1902	Sammy	Strang	3332	20	
1907	Wid	Conroy	5639	19	
1905	Harry	Steinfeldt	12439	14	
1911	Bobby	Byrne	10269	12	
1899	Barry	McCormick	3636	8	

(*continued*)

Dead Ball Era (*continued*)

MCS	First	Last	IP	Runs	Δ
1915	Red	Smith	9486	7	
1917	Doug	Baird	4747	-1	
1918	Charlie	Deal	6672	-7	
1903	Jimmy	Burke	3766	-7	
1902	Harry	Wolverton	6726	-8	
1918	Buck	Weaver	3938	-8	
1902	Ed	Gremminger	3273	-10	
1906	Ernie	Courtney	3101	-14	
1896	Billy	Shindle	6471	-16	
1910	Eddie	Grant	6691	-18	
1903	Doc	Casey	9530	-22	
1909	Roy	Hartzell	3767	-24	
1899	Charlie	Irwin	7457	-26	
1899	Fred	Hartman	4933	-27	
1896	Bill	Joyce	3700	-28	
1915	Fritz	Maisel	3739	-41	
1900	Billy	Lauder	4219	-50	
1905	Bill	Coughlin	8557	-73	
1910	Harry	Lord	6968	-114	
1911	Hans	Lobert	8458	-153	

Several Dead Ball Era third basemen are included in the top forty chart. I can find but one startling rating in the Dead Ball Era.

Hans Lobert

Year	L	Tm	IP	Runs
1903	N	PIT	15	0
1905	N	CHI	123	1
1906	N	CIN	336	-3
1907	N	CIN	48	0
1908	N	CIN	861	-1
1909	N	CIN	1048	-13
1910	N	CIN	763	0
1911	N	PHI	1324	-36
1912	N	PHI	440	-7
1913	N	PHI	1254	-27
1914	N	PHI	1116	-56
1915	N	NY	908	-12
1916	N	NY	151	0
1917	N	NY	71	1
Total			8458	-153

Hans Lobert was the fastest man in baseball, and maybe the world, as he beat Olympian Jim Thorpe and track star Vince Campbell in publicly held footraces. He also led National League third basemen in fielding percentage twice (1913 and 1914) and sometimes played shortstop. How, then, could he have been the worst fielding third baseman who played 3000 innings in the Dead Ball Era? First, some more facts: the four teams for which Lobert played more than 1000 innings in a season at third base were the 1909 Reds and the 1911, 1913, and 1914 Phillies. These teams were all last in the league in third base assists, in two cases by what have to be record-breaking margins. In 1911, Phillies third basemen had *sixty-two* fewer assists than the team with the second-to-lowest number of assists; in 1914, *forty-nine* fewer. Again, that is not sixty-two or forty-nine below *average*, but below the *second lowest* number.

But all four teams were also first or second in the league in *third base putouts*. Normally, infielder putouts are meaningless. Perhaps Lobert may have elected, whenever possible, to tag or force out runners coming from second on a ground ball to third in order to avoid making a throw, making much the same 'avoid making an error on a throw' Steve Garvy choice we discussed in the first base chapter. Retrosheet has play-by-play data for about two-thirds of the Phillies games in 1911; perhaps a close review will reveal that Lobert did indeed record an abundant number of unassisted putouts after fielding *ground* balls, which should properly offset the missing assists. Or perhaps Lobert used his extraordinary speed to serve as an extra short outfielder—which might have been useful in the Dead Ball Era, when there were more fly out opportunities in left than right field.

Top Forty Third Basemen of All Time (TPAR Equals Runs)

MCS	First	Last	IP	Runs	Δ
1980	Mike	Schmidt	18946	195	
1967	Brooks	Robinson	25038	189	
1980	Buddy	Bell	18966	183	
1902	Jimmy	Collins	15116	169	
1965	Clete	Boyer	12349	146	
1988	Tim	Wallach	17766	137	
1904	Tommy	Leach	8417	132	
1977	Graig	Nettles	20625	125	
1990	Terry	Pendleton	15395	119	Δ
2003	Scott	Rolen	15139	115	
1906	Lee	Tannehill	6042	109	
1938	Billy	Werber	9995	105	
1977	Darrell	Evans	12223	104	
1990	Gary	Gaetti	19227	98	
2003	David	Bell	7952	94	
1928	Pie	Traynor	16497	92	
1943	Ken	Keltner	13235	91	

(continued)

Top Forty Third Basemen of All Time (TPAR Equals Runs) *(continued)*

MCS	First	Last	IP	Runs	Δ
1995	Matt	Williams	14763	87	
1928	Ossie	Bluege	13209	84	
1984	Tom	Brookens	7925	79	
1961	Ken	Boyer	15340	76	
1998	Scott	Brosius	7873	76	
2004	Adrian	Beltre	14332	72	Δ
1974	A.	Rodriguez	15961	70	
1916	Eddie	Foster	10380	69	
1896	Billy	Clingman	3684	67	
1996	Robin	Ventura	15929	66	
1994	Ken	Caminiti	14253	65	
1919	Heinie	Groh	11221	64	
1923	Babe	Pinelli	6232	64	
1901	Lave	Cross	14288	60	
1941	Pinky	May	5613	58	
1904	Bill	Bradley	11593	57	
1989	Kelly	Gruber	6776	56	
1928	Willie	Kamm	14714	56	
1953	Hank	Thompson	5463	56	Δ
1948	Hank	Majeski	7298	55	
1908	Art	Devlin	10607	52	
1998	Shane	Andrews	3814	48	
1937	Lew	Riggs	5431	47	

As we mentioned in explaining the talent pool adjustment model, third base did not follow the normal historical trend of ostensibly declining performance by top fielders over time. Since there was no apparent historical trend to back out, we'll just use the actual defensive runs of third basemen in lieu of a separate calculation of TPAR.

Darrell Evans (see next page) was Bill James's choice for the most underrated player of all time when *The Historical Abstract* was last updated. The DRA estimates of Evans's defensive runs, both at third base and first base, when combined with his offensive runs as estimated by Smith, put him more than 350 runs above the average player at the positions he played. That would suggest that Darrell Evans had about as much career value as Santo. I advocate more for Santo's Hall of Fame candidacy because he's waited longer than Evans, but also because Santo had a sustained peak (1964–67) during which, aside from Willie Mays, he was the best player in the league. Evans had at most two MVP level seasons (1973 and 1974) and only a few all-star level seasons scattered throughout his career, mainly because he missed large blocks of playing time to injuries in at least ten seasons.

Darrell Evans

Year	L	Tm	IP	Runs	v-Tm
1969	N	ATL	45	-1	-1
1970	N	ATL	99	1	1
1971	N	ATL	572	3	2
1972	N	ATL	1093	14	3
1973	N	ATL	1295	16	4
1974	N	ATL	1425	24	1
1975	N	ATL	1359	10	1
1976	N	ATL	37	1	0
1976	N	SF	34	0	1
1977	N	SF	266	2	5
1978	N	SF	1363	6	1
1979	N	SF	1385	6	2
1980	N	SF	1237	10	0
1981	N	SF	758	7	5
1982	N	SF	691	-4	-1
1983	N	SF	199	7	6
1984	A	DET	109	0	-1
1985	A	DET	37	2	1
1986	A	DET	11	-1	-1
1987	A	DET	20	2	1
1989	N	ATL	187	-1	0
Total			12223	104	32

Duke University's first All-American basketball player, Billy Werber sipped from two cups of coffee served by the Yankees (only one game at third in 1930 and one in 1933), but those brief appearances eventually enabled him to qualify as the oldest living ballplayer to have played with Babe Ruth. He

Honorable Mention: Billy Werber

Year	L	Tm	IP	Runs
1930	A	NY	0	0
1933	A	NY	0	0
1933	A	BOS	304	0
1934	A	BOS	1157	25
1935	A	BOS	1101	11
1936	A	BOS	781	-6
1937	A	PHI	1088	2
1938	A	PHI	1143	0
1939	N	CIN	1334	16
1940	N	CIN	1247	25
1941	N	CIN	1009	16
1942	N	NY	832	15
Total			9995	105

died recently at the age of 100. As a third basemen he displayed above-average and at times very good fielding for two teams in the National League and one in the American. He successfully expanded his father's insurance business after retiring from baseball.

Lee Tannehill was an exemplar of the 1906 Chicago White Sox "Hitless Wonders," who somehow won the World Series while collectively generating a batting average of .198, an on-base percentage of .279, and a slugging

Honorable Mention: Lee Tannehill

Year	L	Tm	IP	Runs
1904	A	CHI	1376	37
1905	A	CHI	1310	35
1906	A	CHI	956	28
1907	A	CHI	326	-1
1908	A	CHI	1199	23
1909	A	CHI	737	-9
1910	A	CHI	51	0
1911	A	CHI	77	-2
1912	A	CHI	10	0
Total			6042	109

average of .283. Tannehill started as a shortstop, and led the league in double plays there in 1903 before moving over to third base to make room for the returning George Davis. I do not know why Tannehill's career petered out— it may have been simply that he was a very weak hitter.

Terry Pendleton's odd hiccup in 1987 and decline after 1991 are also detected by *Fox(R(t),f,bh,bo)*, *Smith(pgor,bod)* (1987), and *Smith(R(t,s,d))* (1989 onward). My best guess as to why Pendleton did not maintain his value as a fielder is that he slowed down a bit—he was a fairly active base stealer and triples hitter until 1991, but not so much after.

Number Ten: Terry Pendleton

Year	L	Tm	IP	Runs	v-Tm
1984	N	STL	585	4	-1
1985	N	STL	1274	23	0
1986	N	STL	1376	26	1
1987	N	STL	1385	-1	-1
1988	N	STL	863	7	8
1989	N	STL	1391	29	5
1990	N	STL	1010	10	5
1991	N	ATL	1284	12	3
1992	N	ATL	1389	0	-1
1993	N	ATL	1393	9	1
1994	N	ATL	677	-2	-4
1996	N	ATL	342	0	6
1995	N	FLA	1129	4	1
1996	N	FLA	928	5	3
1997	N	CIN	220	-5	-4
1998	A	KC	150	0	3
Total			15395	119	24

Number Nine: Tommy Leach

Year	L	Tm	IP	Runs
1898	N	LOU	24	0
1899	N	LOU	735	3
1900	N	PIT	247	2
1901	N	PIT	790	18
1902	N	PIT	1178	27
1903	N	PIT	1124	17
1904	N	PIT	1292	41
1905	N	PIT	515	7
1906	N	PIT	601	0
1907	N	PIT	270	2
1908	N	PIT	1343	15
1909	N	PIT	121	1
1911	N	PIT	0	0
1912	N	CHI	32	0
1913	N	CHI	9	0
1914	N	CHI	137	-1
Total			8417	132

Truly unique. Can you think of any other player in history who was an outstanding infielder for several years, then an outstanding centerfielder for several more? Leach saved 130 runs at what was then the second toughest infield position and another 100 or so in center outfield. Leach made the move to center after breaking two ribs in a home plate collision in 1905 and experiencing difficulty throwing. Leach was also a pretty good hitter for his time, with a slightly above-average on-base percentage and slugging percentage, and often hit third in the Pirates lineup in front of Honus Wagner. I'd estimate his overall value to be surprisingly close to a Hall of Fame standard.

Number Eight: Tim Wallach

Year	L	Tm	IP	Runs	v-Tm
1981	N	MON	100	1	3
1982	N	MON	1391	10	2
1983	N	MON	1389	4	2
1984	N	MON	1396	27	-2
1985	N	MON	1348	34	-2
1986	N	MON	1124	20	2
1987	N	MON	1305	4	2
1988	N	MON	1344	15	2
1989	N	MON	1358	-4	0
1990	N	MON	1426	9	0
1991	N	MON	1321	2	1
1992	N	MON	701	16	6
1993	N	LA	1076	10	8
1994	N	LA	947	-4	1
1995	N	LA	792	-3	2
1996	N	LA	385	-6	1
1996	A	LA	363	1	-4
Total			17766	137	22

I dropped Tim Wallach (see prior page) back somewhat because of inconsistency. Though the slight drop in 1987 could easily be due to after-effects of the injury that ended his 1986 season, there is no apparent reason for his fielding decline in 1989–91. Like many good fielding third baseman, he had no foot speed to lose, and nothing in his offensive record suggests a change in foot speed anytime in his career. Wallach was named AAA Pacific Coast League Manager of the Year in 2009 for leading the Albuquerque Isotopes to the title, and shortly thereafter named "Best Manager Prospect" by *Baseball America*. I'm sure we'll be reading more about him.

Number Seven: Graig Nettles

Year	L	Tm	IP	Runs	v-Tm
1968	A	MIN	37	1	1
1969	A	MIN	141	-2	0
1970	A	CLE	1313	18	2
1971	A	CLE	1403	36	3
1972	A	CLE	1351	17	-2
1973	A	NY	1370	27	2
1974	A	NY	1368	14	0
1975	A	NY	1389	14	0
1976	A	NY	1432	21	1
1977	A	NY	1379	3	-2
1978	A	NY	1413	8	-1
1979	A	NY	1243	4	0
1980	A	NY	769	-6	2
1981	A	NY	840	5	-1
1982	A	NY	961	-2	1
1983	A	NY	1060	-14	1
1984	N	SD	946	-3	-3
1985	N	SD	1078	-6	0
1986	N	SD	847	-4	-3
1987	N	ATL	221	-5	-2
1988	N	MON	64	0	-1
Total			20625	125	-3

It is always reassuring when assessing defensive runs estimates to see a player's measured performance remain essentially the same after changing teams (see Nettles's 1970–76 seasons). Nettles's 1977 World Series fielding heroics were in some sense his last hurrah as a great fielder, though he was able to extend his career another decade by hitting about twenty homers a year, which in those somewhat more innocent times was the threshold for being considered something of a power hitter.

All the most sophisticated metrics agree: Scott Rolen (see next page) is an outstanding fielder who has already established his place among the greatest third basemen of all time. Rolen may in fact be the very greatest fielding third baseman of all time, because he has dominated the position when it has been apparently much more competitive. There are two pieces of evidence to suggest that third base has gotten much tougher: first, the variance

Number Six: Scott Rolen

Year	L	Tm	IP	Runs	v-Tm
1996	N	PHI	322	-8	-3
1997	N	PHI	1337	9	2
1998	N	PHI	1419	3	0
1999	N	PHI	962	14	3
2000	N	PHI	1080	8	5
2001	N	PHI	1329	12	1
2002	N	PHI	874	4	-6
2002	N	STL	486	10	6
2003	N	STL	1339	2	4
2004	N	STL	1228	21	4
2005	N	STL	486	12	6
2006	N	STL	1216	18	3
2007	N	STL	935	6	-4
2008	A	TOR	1007	9	-6
2009	A	TOR	779	-5	0
2009	N	CIN	339	0	1
Total			15139	115	16

in performance has dropped substantially during the Contemporary Era, after rising dramatically in the Transitional and Modern Eras. Second, analyst Tom Tango has done several studies of the performance of fielders who play multiple positions; on the basis of these studies, Tango suggests that third base is now about as competitive as second base, meaning that fielders who field both positions field both about equally well, and lose approximately the same value when shifted to short. Rolen's hitting is also first rate. Were he to retire now, I would certainly support his election to the Hall of Fame, though I'm concerned that time lost to injuries has diminished the superficial impressiveness of his offensive statistics.

Clete Boyer (see next page) couldn't hit as well as his brother Ken, and had the bad luck to begin playing full-time precisely when Brooks Robinson had already established himself as the presumptive American League Gold Glover at third. Clete was awarded a Gold Glove in 1969, after he moved to the National League Atlanta Braves. There is little evidence he deserved it then, but, given his prior performance, it was a nice gesture.

Jimmy Collins (see next page) was the first player to be inducted into the Hall of Fame who mainly played third base. It cannot be emphasized enough how primitive the statistical record is before 1920 and particularly before 1901. Nevertheless, the estimates above Collins defensive runs are generally

Number Five: Clete Boyer

Year	L	Tm	IP	Runs	v-Tm
1955	A	KC	61	1	0
1956	A	KC	48	1	1
1957	A	KC	2	0	0
1959	A	NY	90	2	2
1960	A	NY	782	18	5
1961	A	NY	1200	26	2
1962	A	NY	1397	33	2
1963	A	NY	1243	12	4
1964	A	NY	1076	12	-3
1965	A	NY	1275	12	-5
1966	A	NY	741	17	0
1967	N	ATL	1299	1	-1
1968	N	ATL	615	2	-1
1969	N	ATL	1198	7	6
1970	N	ATL	1092	1	0
1971	N	ATL	229	2	1
Total			12349	146	13

Number Four: Jimmy Collins

Year	L	Tm	IP	Runs
1895	N	LOU	693	3
1896	N	BOS	764	16
1897	N	BOS	1183	30
1898	N	BOS	1340	22
1899	N	BOS	1330	41
1900	N	BOS	1233	6
1901	A	BOS	1210	20
1902	A	BOS	980	10
1903	A	BOS	1174	9
1904	A	BOS	1397	22
1905	A	BOS	1165	5
1906	A	BOS	338	-7
1907	A	BOS	320	1
1907	A	PHI	905	-5
1908	A	PHI	1084	-4
Total			15116	169

consistent from year to year, demonstrate a normal aging pattern, and reflect the universal opinion of his contemporaries that he was far and away the greatest fielding third baseman of his time. John McGraw praised Collins as "the real pioneer of the modern style of playing third base." Collins figured out the only way to deal with the rising number of bunts in the game was to play in on the grass, charge the ball, and, if need be, throw in one uninterrupted underhand motion.

Collins also pounced on the new opportunity presented by the formation of the American League as a major league. He negotiated a high salary with the predecessor to the Red Sox, and the right to ten percent of team profits above $25,000. His former "owner" accused him of disloyalty, to which Collins responded: "I would not go back now if they offered me the whole outfit. These National League magnates have a way of frightening a man into believing that he has committed a crime, and unless a player has a good, stiff backbone, he will usually cave."

Number Three: Mike Schmidt

Year	L	Tm	IP	Runs	v-Tm
1972	N	PHI	76	1	1
1973	N	PHI	939	14	15
1974	N	PHI	1433	30	1
1975	N	PHI	1329	21	0
1976	N	PHI	1424	13	1
1977	N	PHI	1299	24	4
1978	N	PHI	1215	5	1
1979	N	PHI	1344	15	-1
1980	N	PHI	1315	24	5
1981	N	PHI	849	15	2
1982	N	PHI	1296	13	0
1983	N	PHI	1337	12	3
1984	N	PHI	1225	8	4
1985	N	PHI	432	2	7
1986	N	PHI	1034	-7	-2
1987	N	PHI	1160	10	4
1988	N	PHI	898	3	9
1989	N	PHI	340	-8	-5
Total			18946	195	49

The best systems for overall player evaluation will tend to agree that the greatest all-around player between the reigns of Willie Mays and Barry Bonds must have been either Joe Morgan or Mike Schmidt. I favor Schmidt. Morgan may have had the greatest five-year peak (1972–76), but was not really close to being an MVP-quality player outside those five years and often not even a borderline all-star. Again, using DRA estimates for defensive runs and any of the many good estimates for offensive runs, Schmidt had three seasons about as great as any of Morgan's (1974, 1977, 1980), a fourth that would have been as great as Morgan's best if it had not been shortened by the strike (1981), five more seasons of clear MVP-level performance (1975–76, 1979, 1982–83), and five more seasons of very strong all-star performance (1978, 1984–87). Schmidt, like Morgan, played in a fully integrated league throughout his career. I believe that as defensive runs estimates gain in credibility and more efforts are made to adjust all-time ratings properly for talent pools,

Number Two: Buddy Bell

Year	L	Tm	IP	Runs	v-Tm
1972	A	CLE	49	1	0
1973	A	CLE	1367	24	-1
1974	A	CLE	1011	14	7
1975	A	CLE	1328	-4	4
1976	A	CLE	1391	12	-1
1977	A	CLE	1017	13	2
1978	A	CLE	1211	15	6
1979	A	TEX	1232	35	4
1980	A	TEX	1046	13	8
1981	A	TEX	836	29	4
1982	A	TEX	1228	23	3
1983	A	TEX	1375	14	-1
1984	A	TEX	1277	22	2
1985	A	TEX	711	12	6
1985	N	CIN	585	-8	-6
1986	N	CIN	1344	-6	-1
1987	N	CIN	1228	-19	-4
1988	N	CIN	108	-1	-2
1988	N	HOU	565	-5	-5
1989	A	TEX	58	0	-1
Total			18966	183	24

Michael Jack Schmidt will eventually be recognized as one of the ten greatest players who ever lived.

For defensive purposes, I rank Bell above Schmidt because Bell excelled with two different teams, Schmidt with only one, so there is more evidence that Bell did not benefit from an unusual and undetected contextual factor. Bell represents the middle generation of the greatest three-generation family of baseball players. Buddy's dad Gus was a poor fielding centerfielder who was eventually moved over to the corner outfield positions, but Buddy's son David is, along with Scott Rolen and Adrian Beltre, among the best fielding third basemen of our Contemporary Era.

It is always important to remember that no fielding evaluation system provides an exact measurement of defensive runs, only an approximation. This is especially true at third base, where even the best systems tend to correlate more weakly with each other than at any other position, other than right field. The version of DRA used for generating ratings since 1952 provides the estimates below for Brooks Robinson. The unusual trends are consistent with those shown by *Smith(pgor,bod)*. Brooksie immediately established himself as a very good fielder, had some sort of injury in 1965, took another year to recover, and then gave us nearly a decade of superlative performance.

The table credits the Vacuum Cleaner with 'only' +189 defensive runs in his career. *Smith(pgor,bod)* credits an additional hundred. That is a

Number One: Brooks Robinson

Year	L	Tm	IP	Runs	v-Tm
1955	A	BAL	44	-1	-1
1956	A	BAL	101	1	1
1957	A	BAL	284	-1	2
1958	A	BAL	1119	8	5
1959	A	BAL	723	5	3
1960	A	BAL	1355	14	0
1961	A	BAL	1460	4	1
1962	A	BAL	1445	14	1
1963	A	BAL	1414	8	0
1964	A	BAL	1457	5	0
1965	A	BAL	1299	-4	0
1966	A	BAL	1431	0	-1
1967	A	BAL	1413	35	1
1968	A	BAL	1435	23	1
1969	A	BAL	1393	19	-2
1970	A	BAL	1390	-1	2
1971	A	BAL	1372	12	1
1972	A	BAL	1323	11	2
1973	A	BAL	1342	17	2
1974	A	BAL	1362	17	-1
1975	A	BAL	1224	9	-4
1976	A	BAL	552	-5	0
1977	A	BAL	100	1	1
Total			25038	189	14

big difference. It represents the cumulative effect of about five extra runs credited per year.

One of the major goals of this book, stated at the outset, is to see if we can, among other things, get the discrepancies in career defensive runs estimates among the best systems down below twenty-five runs. I can eliminate almost the entire amount of this discrepancy, but will introduce a new one. *Smith(pgor,bod)* mistakenly charges half a run for errors above the league-average rate and credits half a run extra for errors below that rate. Brooks Robinson made 176 errors below what he would have made if he had had a league-average fielding percentage. Now, to be clear, DRA still gives Robinson full credit for each of those extra plays made; DRA just avoids adding an extra credit for errors avoided, because they are already credited as extra plays made. Making that adjustment more or less wipes out the difference with DRA.

As we discussed in explaining the DRA model and the testing of the DRA model, I developed two alternative models for years since the 1950s, so that instead of one model covering 1952 through 2009 I had separate models for 1952 through 1977, and for 1978 through 2009. Under the 1952–77 alternative version of DRA, Robinson had approximately 270 defensive runs, again, because of an extra few runs per season adding up over the course of what was the longest fielding career at a single position in major league history. So, taking the average of the two DRA models, and adjusting Smith's numbers for the impact of errors, I arrive at the belief that Robinson probably saved about 225, maybe 250 runs in his career. (Applying the alternative versions of DRA to Mike Schmidt's career increases his defensive runs, but less so.) On the basis of these multiple quantitative evaluations and the impressions Brooksie made almost from the very start of his career until its end, I can only join in the consensus that Brooks Robinson was the greatest fielding third baseman of all time.

Center field

This chapter catches more Gold Glove mistakes than any other. In a few cases in center field, the voters have always been wrong about a player; in other cases, they guessed right early in a player's career, but kept awarding him Gold Gloves well after he'd lost a step or two or three.

Contemporary Era

MCS	First	Last	IP	Runs	Δ
2002	Andruw	Jones	14732	208	Δ
2003	Mike	Cameron	14416	121	Δ
2001	Jim	Edmonds	14263	109	
1994	Devon	White	14538	95	Δ
2004	Carlos	Beltran	13115	79	Δ
2002	Darin	Erstad	4536	74	
1993	Stan	Javier	4989	66	Δ
1995	Darren	Lewis	7713	53	Δ
1994	Chuck	Carr	3618	52	Δ
2004	Torii	Hunter	12100	42	Δ
1994	Lance	Johnson	11057	42	Δ
2000	Ruben	Rivera	3227	42	Δ
1994	Otis	Nixon	8997	39	Δ
2004	Rocco	Baldelli	3332	36	
2004	Mark	Kotsay	8346	35	
1999	Kenny	Lofton	16743	30	Δ
1998	Brian	Hunter	5548	28	Δ
2000	Doug	Glanville	7181	23	Δ
2003	Jay	Payton	4832	23	Δ
1999	Gerald	Williams	3584	21	Δ
2003	Milton	Bradley	3941	16	Δ

(continued)

Contemporary Era (*continued*)

MCS	First	Last	IP	Runs	Δ
1997	Rondell	White	4290	15	Δ
2000	Garret	Anderson	3393	14	Δ
2003	Luis	Matos	3352	13	
2001	Chris	Singleton	4880	12	Δ
1997	Marquis	Grissom	16800	12	Δ
2003	Randy	Winn	5602	8	Δ
2002	Johnny	Damon	10835	7	
1997	Rich	Becker	3751	6	
1998	Steve	Finley	19376	4	
2004	Dave	Roberts	4122	-1	
1994	Ray	Lankford	9658	-4	Δ
1995	Chad	Curtis	5609	-10	
1998	Damon	Buford	3896	-11	Δ
1999	Marvin	Benard	3645	-13	Δ
1994	Deion	Sanders	3361	-15	Δ
2001	Terrence	Long	3463	-16	Δ
2004	Gary	Matthews, Jr.	4105	-16	Δ
1999	Q.	McCracken	3076	-17	Δ
1998	Tom	Goodwin	6828	-20	Δ
2005	Scott	Podsednik	3136	-23	
2005	Corey	Patterson	7585	-23	Δ
2001	Gabe	Kapler	3594	-27	
1999	Carl	Everett	5318	-31	Δ
1996	Brady	Anderson	7707	-44	
1996	Darryl	Hamilton	6763	-45	Δ
2000	Jose	Cruz, Jr.	5039	-50	Δ
1995	Brian	McRae	11242	-58	Δ
2005	Vernon	Wells	10376	-60	Δ
1998	Bernie	Williams	16130	-61	Δ
2004	Juan	Pierre	10176	-66	Δ
2002	Preston	Wilson	7374	-78	Δ
1997	Ken	Griffey, Jr.	18037	-91	Δ

Ken Griffey, Jr., received ten straight Gold Gloves (1990–1999) and was named to the Rawlings all-time Gold Glove team, joining Mays and Clemente in the outfield. But Junior was never clearly better than average when he was winning those Gold Gloves, and in later years may have actually cost his teams more runs in the field than all but a half-dozen or so center fielders in major league history. For some reason, $Smith(R(t,s,d))$ estimates about +40 defensive runs in 1995–96 fielding batted balls; otherwise, Smith's estimates would be virtually the same. Given the difficulties batted ball data systems have had coding outfield data, I'm inclined to discount those two years as a coding aberration by the stringers for those seasons.

Junior genuinely excelled in throwing out and holding base runners. DRA estimates he saved about fifteen runs throwing out base runners, but

Ken Griffey, Jr.

Year	L	Tm	IP	PO8 runs	A8 runs	v-Tm	Runs
1989	A	SEA	1060	-4	3	-7	-1
1990	A	SEA	1333	-9	1	0	-8
1991	A	SEA	1272	-1	4	0	4
1992	A	SEA	1187	-6	0	1	-5
1993	A	SEA	1208	-6	0	0	-6
1994	A	SEA	862	-12	4	1	-8
1995	A	SEA	596	6	1	6	7
1996	A	SEA	1173	4	1	0	5
1997	A	SEA	1331	2	1	0	3
1998	A	SEA	1345	8	1	1	9
1999	A	SEA	1315	-11	0	-2	-11
2000	N	CIN	1227	11	0	1	11
2001	N	CIN	757	-16	-2	-8	-18
2002	N	CIN	424	-13	1	-13	-12
2003	N	CIN	356	-8	0	-6	-8
2004	N	CIN	656	-11	0	-13	-11
2005	N	CIN	1066	-24	0	-9	-24
2006	N	CIN	870	-17	1	-7	-16
Total			18037	-106	15	-55	-91

can't really measure runs saved by holding base runners. Walsh would add another twenty-five runs; Smith would add another twenty more on top of that. (In general, the Smith estimates are higher than the Walsh estimates; I could not say which is better.) Even with credit granted for those runs, Junior was a poor center fielder. In some ways, he's the Jeter of the outfield: admired by fans, fellow players, and management for many good reasons, but clearly a below-average fielder under several well-constructed defensive models.

Junior is also in some ways like a contemporary Joe DiMaggio. He started out as a decent centerfielder, with a truly outstanding arm, just like DiMaggio, as we shall see, though Joe was genuinely good, not just decent, for his first few seasons. Junior played a lot of games before he turned twenty-one, just like DiMaggio, when Joe's three or so seasons in the Pacific Coast League (which had 180-game seasons) are included. Both were high-average, high-power hitters, with good but not great plate discipline. Neither player was known for being particularly conscientious about conditioning. And both players declined sharply in their fielding performance after age thirty.

Steve Finley received five Gold Gloves, but his single-season DRA ratings are nothing but a patternless string of numbers clustered around zero. Bernie Williams received four Gold Gloves, but he presents a rather interesting pattern of performance:

Bernie Williams

Year	L	Tm	IP	PO8 runs	A8 runs	v-Tm	Runs
1991	A	NY	754	-1	-1	6	-2
1992	A	NY	485	6	0	5	6
1993	A	NY	1225	17	-2	3	15
1994	A	NY	939	5	1	2	6
1995	A	NY	1275	18	-4	0	14
1996	A	NY	1231	-7	1	-5	-6
1997	A	NY	1123	-17	-3	0	-19
1998	A	NY	1095	2	-2	-1	0
1999	A	NY	1355	4	-1	0	4
2000	A	NY	1170	-3	-3	1	-6
2001	A	NY	1267	-4	-3	3	-7
2002	A	NY	1317	-22	-4	3	-26
2003	A	NY	1001	-9	-1	1	-10
2004	A	NY	830	-12	-2	-7	-13
2005	A	NY	863	-10	1	-2	-9
2006	A	NY	200	-6	-1	-5	-7
			16130	-38	-23	5	-61

Like Griffey, Williams also overstayed his welcome in center field, as even his most loyal fans were admitting towards the end. In fact, he was only a really good fielder for four seasons, in which his speed (as a teenager, he was a world-class 400-meter runner) enabled him to cover a lot of ground. Bernie didn't start winning his four Gold Gloves (1997–2000) until he had *lost* his 'plus' range. But by then his batting numbers had begun drawing some attention.

Torii Hunter bagged his first Gold Glove in 2001. He deserved to. *Smith(pgor,bod)*, the best alternative system for that season and one you can easily look up on the internet, also rates that season highly, with +20 defensive runs. Hunter has received Gold Gloves every year since then. He hasn't deserved even one. Both $MGL(B(t,s,d,v,bh))$ and $Smith(R(t),f,bh,ph)$ agree with DRA on his post-2001 ordinariness. $Dewan(B(t,s,d,v))$, which tracks

Torii Hunter

Year	L	Tm	IP	PO8 runs	A8 runs	v-Tm	Runs
1998	A	MIN	45	-3	0	-3	-3
1999	A	MIN	770	4	0	-2	4
2000	A	MIN	825	0	5	-3	5
2001	A	MIN	1295	26	3	4	29
2002	A	MIN	1235	-18	0	4	-19
2003	A	MIN	1299	2	-1	2	1
2004	A	MIN	1100	1	-1	-1	1
2005	A	MIN	813	-3	3	4	0
2006	A	MIN	1232	3	1	1	3
2007	A	MIN	1315	0	4	-2	5
2008	A	LA	1193	6	-1	-2	4
2009	A	LA	977	8	4	-2	12
Total			12100	26	16	1	42

Marquis Grissom

Year	L	Tm	IP	PO8 runs	A8 runs	v-Tm	Runs
1989	N	MON	162	-5	0	-4	-5
1990	N	MON	258	5	0	3	5
1991	N	MON	1141	10	4	5	14
1992	N	MON	1402	2	-1	-2	1
1993	N	MON	1357	14	0	0	14
1994	N	MON	980	20	0	1	20
1995	N	ATL	1159	13	1	1	14
1996	N	ATL	1380	-5	1	-4	-4
1997	A	CLE	1251	7	0	1	7
1998	N	MIL	1170	-3	-1	2	-4
1999	N	MIL	1285	-12	-4	-1	-16
2000	N	MIL	1259	-6	-3	-2	-9
2001	N	LA	765	-5	1	0	-5
2002	N	LA	492	-7	-1	-5	-8
2003	N	SF	1237	2	-3	-4	-1
2004	N	SF	1219	-1	-3	-3	-3
2005	N	SF	285	-7	-1	-10	-8
Total			16800	22	-10	-24	12

separately home runs saved—Hunter's highlight reel speciality—would add only about three runs per season of extra value for those home runs saved.

Marquiss Grissom received four Gold Gloves, and had about four seasons in which he would have been a solid choice for a Gold Glove. He stopped having seasons like that after he turned twenty-eight, but garnered major

Kenny Lofton

Year	L	Tm	IP	PO8 runs	A8 runs	v-Tm	Runs
1991	N	HOU	151	-1	0	0	-1
1992	A	CLE	1256	6	4	9	10
1993	A	CLE	1245	-2	2	1	0
1994	A	CLE	975	-5	4	-1	-1
1995	A	CLE	974	-6	3	-5	-3
1996	A	CLE	1334	5	2	4	8
1997	N	ATL	1047	9	0	-8	9
1998	A	CLE	1322	-15	6	-3	-9
1999	A	CLE	991	-3	2	-7	-1
2000	A	CLE	1152	15	-1	1	14
2001	A	CLE	1077	3	-2	3	0
2002	A	CHI	744	3	-1	-5	2
2002	N	SF	372	2	0	-2	3
2003	N	CHI	456	4	0	4	4
2003	N	PIT	714	2	0	-1	2
2004	A	NY	539	3	0	6	3
2005	N	PHI	741	7	2	-2	8
2006	N	LA	961	-11	-1	1	-11
2007	A	CLE	21	-2	-2	0	-4
2007	A	TEX	669	-4	2	1	-2
			16743	11	20	-4	30

league paychecks for another decade on the basis of his prior performance. Major league organizations throughout history have allowed centerfielders past their prime to play in center if they've previously established a reputation for fielding excellence. Now that more and more teams are using batted ball data, slowing center fielders won't be able to hang onto their jobs. Which is one of many reasons why I believe baseball is much more competitive now that it was even thirty years ago, to say nothing of sixty or ninety years ago.

Smith($R(t,s,d)$), which uses Retrosheet's free batted ball data from 1989 through 1999, rates Kenny Lofton (see prior page) much higher than DRA for every season he played in Cleveland while such batted ball data was available (1992–96 and 1998–99), approximately +15 defensive runs per season. However, Smith's two other systems, Smith($pgor,bod$) (2000–02) and Smith($R(t),f,bh,ph$) (2003 onward) rate him basically average, including the first two years in Cleveland after the batted ball data ran out, when he was still stealing bases at the same clip he had been in 1999. Given some of the massive coding problems we're discovering in outfielder batted ball data, I strongly suspect some coding bias in Cleveland for those seasons. For the time being, I would pencil in the average between Smith's estimates and DRA, which would be about +75 defensive runs, a good but not great total.

Modern Era

MCS	First	Last	IP	Runs	Δ
1971	Paul	Blair	13857	152	Δ
1988	Gary	Pettis	8799	119	Δ
1978	Garry	Maddox	13736	112	Δ
1982	Chet	Lemon	12425	109	Δ
1990	Lenny	Dykstra	9831	87	
1969	Ken	Berry	8015	77	
1976	Bill	North	8348	70	Δ
1969	Tommie	Agee	7777	68	Δ
1985	Eddie	Milner	4635	66	Δ
1976	Cesar	Geronimo	7728	57	Δ
1972	Del	Unser	9061	55	
1980	Ruppert	Jones	7734	53	Δ
1986	Willie	Wilson	10721	49	Δ
1985	Mookie	Wilson	8621	45	Δ
1987	Dave	Henderson	9419	39	Δ
1971	Bobby	Tolan	4655	38	Δ
1977	Mickey	Rivers	9697	37	Δ
1986	Rickey	Henderson	3549	35	Δ
1974	Elliott	Maddox	3487	32	Δ
1980	Al	Bumbry	7395	32	Δ
1980	Andre	Dawson	9007	30	Δ
1985	Bob	Dernier	4640	30	
1980	Omar	Moreno	10273	30	Δ
1980	Tony	Scott	5025	29	Δ

(continued)

Modern Era (*continued*)

MCS	First	Last	IP	Runs	Δ
1983	Dwayne	Murphy	10025	27	Δ
1988	Mitch	Webster	3318	27	Δ
1981	Jerry	Mumphrey	7621	23	Δ
1979	Rick	Bosetti	3261	22	
1988	Milt	Thompson	3896	20	Δ
1970	Mickey	Stanley	9082	17	
1970	Cesar	Tovar	3553	15	Δ
1989	Gerald	Young	3913	15	Δ
1983	George	Wright	3670	13	Δ
1978	Juan	Beniquez	5975	12	Δ
1990	Eric	Davis	6863	11	Δ
1969	Jim	Wynn	10108	11	Δ
1970	Reggie	Smith	6877	7	Δ
1985	Kevin	McReynolds	3817	7	
1975	Bake	McBride	3208	6	Δ
1984	Chili	Davis	4466	4	Δ
1990	Andy	Van Slyke	9522	4	
1992	Darrin	Jackson	3871	3	Δ
1987	Willie	McGee	11471	3	Δ
1983	Rudy	Law	3722	3	Δ
1970	Jay	Johnstone	3961	2	
1986	Von	Hayes	3011	2	
1973	Dusty	Baker	4056	-3	Δ
1987	Oddibe	McDowell	5196	-3	Δ
1992	Milt	Cuyler	3164	-4	Δ
1992	Mike	Devereaux	6381	-5	Δ
1978	Larry	Herndon	3041	-6	Δ
1987	John	Shelby	5823	-7	Δ
1988	Daryl	Boston	3470	-9	Δ
1989	Joe	Carter	3610	-9	Δ
1972	Dave	May	4481	-13	Δ
1978	Rick	Miller	6586	-13	
1988	Kirby	Puckett	12245	-14	Δ
1988	Herm	Winningham	3496	-16	Δ
1977	Jerry	Morales	3921	-17	
1991	Dave	Martinez	6276	-18	Δ
1973	Ken	Henderson	4220	-19	
1985	Lloyd	Moseby	11296	-21	Δ
1980	Rick	Manning	11093	-22	
1974	Johnny	Grubb	3376	-22	
1977	Ron	LeFlore	7236	-23	Δ
1976	Cesar	Cedeno	12664	-25	Δ
1983	Tony	Armas	4990	-27	Δ
1974	Al	Oliver	7246	-27	Δ
1986	Marvell	Wynne	5178	-27	Δ
1972	Larry	Hisle	4140	-28	Δ
1989	Brett	Butler	16831	-32	
1979	Jerry	Martin	3076	-32	

(*continued*)

Modern Era *(continued)*

MCS	First	Last	IP	Runs	Δ
1979	Lee	Mazzilli	5441	-35	
1970	Cito	Gaston	3466	-36	Δ
1992	Roberto	Kelly	7328	-38	Δ
1970	Jim	Northrup	3399	-38	
1976	Von	Joshua	3352	-39	Δ
1992	Alex	Cole	3029	-39	Δ
1989	Billy	Hatcher	4462	-41	Δ
1976	George	Hendrick	6307	-46	Δ
1972	Bobby	Murcer	6727	-49	
1977	Rowland	Office	4779	-55	Δ
1980	Gorman	Thomas	8137	-55	
1989	Robin	Yount	9925	-63	
1984	Dale	Murphy	9040	-67	
1991	Ellis	Burks	8792	-78	Δ
1981	Fred	Lynn	13510	-90	
1982	Ken	Landreaux	6895	-91	Δ
1976	Amos	Otis	15715	-95	Δ
1972	Rick	Monday	12386	-121	

The top part of list looks about right, but surprises lurk below.

Once again, we need to address many poor choices made by Gold Glove voters. There have been two recurring patterns to the mistakes made. First, there were the centerfielders who were superb for one or two years and genuinely deserved one, maybe two Gold Gloves, but kept getting Gold Gloves after they declined to roughly average performance: Andre Dawson (eight), Kirby Puckett (six), Willie McGee (three), and Eric Davis (three). Second, there were the guys who were merely decent fielders initially but excellent all-around players, so they received Gold Gloves and then kept getting them even when their fielding fell significantly below average: Dale Murphy (five), Cesar Cedeno (five) (Cesar didn't actually decline until his very last full season), Fred Lynn (four), and Amos Otis (three). In most of these cases the players also had high stolen base totals, so Gold Glove voters not unreasonably assumed they ran well. Speed is helpful, but positioning, jumps, reads on balls, understanding wind and other game conditions—so much more goes into great centerfield performance than just foot speed. Andy Van Slyke also stole a lot of bases, but probably won his first Gold Glove in 1988 because he led the league in triples. They gave him another three in a row when he was basically average.

Andre Dawson (see next page) won a Gold Glove every year from 1980 through 1988. I think he was a worthy candidate in 1981–82 and in 1984 (+17 defensive runs in right field). He was below average in right field in each of his remaining Gold Glove seasons.

Andre Dawson

Year	L	Tm	IP	PO8 runs	A8 runs	v-Tm	Runs
1976	N	MON	119	5	0	6	5
1977	N	MON	1126	11	0	3	11
1978	N	MON	1348	-4	5	-4	1
1979	N	MON	1367	-10	-2	-1	-12
1980	N	MON	1274	2	2	-1	4
1981	N	MON	898	17	2	2	19
1982	N	MON	1310	10	-1	-1	10
1983	N	MON	1401	-7	-1	0	-8
1985	N	MON	165	0	0	-1	0
Total			9007	26	5	4	30

Kirby Puckett was actually very good for two seasons, and arguably deserved perhaps a couple of Gold Gloves, thus establishing his fielding

Kirby Puckett

Year	L	Tm	IP	PO8 runs	A8 runs	v-Tm	Runs
1984	A	MIN	1126	26	5	5	30
1985	A	MIN	1404	5	6	-1	10
1986	A	MIN	1385	-14	-1	-1	-15
1987	A	MIN	1273	-17	2	-1	-15
1988	A	MIN	1350	-6	1	0	-4
1989	A	MIN	1328	-3	3	1	0
1990	A	MIN	1041	-8	0	-7	-8
1991	A	MIN	1217	-6	3	-2	-2
1992	A	MIN	1275	6	0	3	7
1993	A	MIN	807	-17	2	-14	-16
1994	A	MIN	5	0	1	0	0
1995	A	MIN	34	0	0	0	0
Total			12245	-36	22	-16	-14

reputation, but declined sharply. What happened in 1986? He hit thirty-one home runs, after hitting just four in his previous 299 major league games. How did he do that? He bulked up—going from approximately 175 pounds in his first season to approximately 225 in very short order. Bulking up apparently cost him his fielding speed and agility. (It may have also eventually cost him his life, as he had a serious weight problem almost as soon as he retired, and died at the age of forty-seven from cardiovascular disease.) Kirby played very deep. That enabled him to make memorable homer-saving plays like the one in the sixth game of the 1991 World Series, but probably at the cost of allowing a lot more singles to drop in front of him.

Like Kirby Puckett, Willie McGee had a nice season in 1984 (+19 defensive runs) and they gave him a Gold Glove. The rest of his DRA numbers are clustered around zero. Eric Davis was outstanding during his first full season in center, in 1987 (+23 defensive runs), but immediately fell to slightly below average performance, where he remained for the rest of his career. Perhaps he fielded more conservatively to avoid injury (he was extremely injury prone).

Dale Murphy

Year	L	Tm	IP	PO8 runs	A8 runs	v-Tm	Runs
1980	N	ATL	1113	2	2	7	3
1981	N	ATL	897	-6	1	3	-5
1982	N	ATL	946	4	-2	6	3
1983	N	ATL	1150	-10	0	2	-10
1984	N	ATL	1427	-5	1	0	-4
1985	N	ATL	1421	-21	-1	1	-22
1986	N	ATL	1346	-19	-1	-3	-20
1989	N	ATL	730	-11	-2	-8	-12
1990	N	PHI	9	0	0	0	0
Total			9040	-66	-1	7	-67

Dale may be the only player who began his career at the positions requiring the least foot speed (catcher and first base) but was moved by his team to the position requiring the most foot speed (center field). Though never a good fielder in center, he kept receiving Gold Gloves because he made few errors, hustled, and was durable, respected, and the most dominant hitter of his time at a demanding fielding position. When the Braves finally figured out that he wasn't really a center fielder, he put together a couple of nice seasons in right. I wondered whether some park factor had been suppressing his ratings, but Otis Nixon played a great centerfield at Atlanta's Fulton County stadium from 1991 to 1993.

Cesar Cedeno's defensive runs estimates also fall in the category of 'patternless string of numbers clustered around zero'. Fred Lynn's show a strong downward trend.

Fred Lynn

Year	L	Tm	IP	PO8 runs	A8 runs	v-Tm	Runs
1974	A	BOS	30	-1	0	-2	-2
1975	A	BOS	1250	-4	1	-5	-3
1976	A	BOS	1102	-11	2	-12	-9
1977	A	BOS	1093	-9	-1	3	-10
1978	A	BOS	1336	-17	0	3	-17
1979	A	BOS	1218	3	0	3	4
1980	A	BOS	949	3	3	8	6
1981	A	LA	589	-2	0	-1	-2
1982	A	LA	1116	5	-1	3	4
1983	A	LA	1000	-13	1	-1	-12
1984	A	LA	457	-5	0	-8	-4
1985	A	BAL	1046	-13	-1	-5	-14
1986	A	BAL	910	-16	-2	-3	-19
1987	A	BAL	840	-10	-1	-4	-11
1988	A	BAL	508	1	-2	0	-1
1988	A	DET	20	0	0	0	0
1990	N	SD	46	-1	0	0	-1
Total			13510	-90	0	-23	-90

It is difficult to imagine an opening act more likely than Fred Lynn's to cause a player to be overrated. Not only was Lynn the first rookie to win an MVP; he led the Red Sox, the team of baseball's intelligentsia, to a World Series so dramatic that many credited it with preserving major league baseball's status as "a" if no longer quite "the" principal American spectator sport. Not surprisingly, Lynn received a Gold Glove for that magic 1975 season. He didn't deserve it. Nor did he deserve the ones he won in 1978 through 1980. Injuries pulled his performance even further down over the years, and his defensive backups consistently out–performed him during the last half of his career.

Amos Otis

Year	L	Tm	IP	PO8 runs	A8 runs	v-Tm	Runs
1967	N	NY	117	-6	1	-6	-5
1969	N	NY	120	1	0	0	1
1970	A	KC	1414	-10	4	0	-6
1971	A	KC	1241	14	1	-2	14
1972	A	KC	1190	2	-1	0	1
1973	A	KC	1160	-7	0	2	-7
1974	A	KC	1258	10	-1	7	9
1975	A	KC	1098	-8	0	-3	-8
1976	A	KC	1326	-21	-4	0	-26
1977	A	KC	1181	-13	0	-2	-13
1978	A	KC	1152	-6	0	-7	-5
1979	A	KC	1266	-18	1	-6	-17
1980	A	KC	913	-1	0	-5	-1
1981	A	KC	758	-5	-1	-2	-6
1982	A	KC	1056	-19	-1	-11	-20
1983	A	KC	465	-5	0	-4	-5
Total			15715	-93	-2	-38	-95

The Historical Abstract describes Otis as a "magnificent" fielding center fielder, but DRA and *Smith(pgor,bod)* indicate otherwise. Otis was a solid fielder until about 1976 (aged twenty-nine). There is nothing wrong with being an average fielding centerfielder if you also have an above-average on-base percentage, above average power, and above average base-running skill. Otis fell off after age thirty, as seems to happen to many center fielders, and consistently played worse than his backups, though partly that was because his backups included Willie Wilson.

I would imagine that the biggest surprises among the Transitional Era centerfielders shown in the next table are Mantle, Pinson, and Snider.

Transitional Era

MCS	First	Last	IP	Runs	Δ
1962	Willie	Mays	24276	195	Δ
1955	Richie	Ashburn	16378	177	
1968	Willie	Davis	19188	133	Δ
1947	Dom	DiMaggio	10882	128	
1955	Jim	Busby	9580	115	
1964	Curt	Flood	14142	100	Δ
1959	Jim	Piersall	10005	98	
1961	Jim	Landis	9310	81	
1952	Chuck	Diering	3256	67	
1960	Bill	Virdon	12816	48	
1966	Vic	Davalillo	5797	38	
1951	Irv	Noren	3007	38	
1953	Jim	Rivera	3261	34	
1967	Adolfo	Phillips	4141	33	Δ
1958	Bill	Bruton	13055	30	Δ
1959	Bobby	Del Greco	4677	25	
1948	Hoot	Evers	3129	22	
1952	Bobby	Thomson	7565	16	
1962	Jackie	Brandt	5228	14	
1968	Jose	Cardenal	7067	12	Δ
1965	Russ	Snyder	3170	11	
1967	Felipe	Alou	3944	10	Δ
1962	Lenny	Green	5003	-2	Δ
1965	Don	Lock	5327	-5	
1947	Andy	Pafko	5894	-7	
1965	Jimmie	Hall	3572	-7	
1962	Gary	Geiger	4325	-8	
1951	Dave	Philley	3611	-9	
1961	Albie	Pearson	4666	-13	
1961	Al	Kaline	4005	-22	
1962	Don	Demeter	4355	-23	
1968	Matty	Alou	7123	-27	Δ
1960	Willie	Tasby	3732	-27	Δ
1965	Mack	Jones	3779	-31	Δ
1954	Larry	Doby	9853	-37	Δ
1957	Bill	Tuttle	8743	-40	
1958	Mickey	Mantle	14854	-52	
1965	Tony	Gonzalez	7587	-54	Δ
1968	Ted	Uhlaender	5123	-62	
1952	Johnny	Groth	8041	-75	
1964	Vada	Pinson	14579	-94	Δ
1954	Duke	Snider	12981	-118	
1955	Gus	Bell	7187	-131	

I hate to knock the last living member of the 1955 Woild Champeens, but the Duke of Flatbush did not reign with authority over center field.

Duke Snider

Year	L	Tm	IP	PO8 runs	A8 runs	v-Tm	Runs
1949	N	BRO	1200	-17	1		-16
1950	N	BRO	1290	-9	2		-8
1951	N	BRO	1306	-18	-1		-19
1952	N	BRO	1245	-6	-2	-1	-7
1953	N	BRO	1312	-8	1	-2	-8
1954	N	BRO	1329	-15	1	-2	-14
1955	N	BRO	1278	-3	0	0	-4
1956	N	BRO	1287	7	-2	0	6
1957	N	BRO	1194	-12	-2	-1	-14
1958	N	LA	579	-15	-1	-5	-16
1959	N	LA	366	-8	-1	-5	-9
1960	N	LA	344	-5	0	-3	-5
1961	N	LA	169	-3	0	-3	-4
1962	N	LA	10	0	0	0	0
1963	N	NY	72	-2	0	-1	-2
Total			12981	-113	-6	-25	-118

Some of his teammates thought he was good at going back for the ball, but not so good charging in. For what it's worth, Snider was a poor percentage base stealer, and essentially stopped trying after his age-twenty-six season (1953). He was probably better than his numbers indicate, for the simple reason that for much of his career one-*fourth* of the league he is compared against generally consisted of two of the greatest centerfielders of all time, Mays and Ashburn. Even if you give Snider a few runs a season for that (because the average of eight teams is overstated by, say, an extra twenty runs a year by having not just one, but two, outstanding center fielders), Snider is still a below-average fielder.

Vada Pinson's numbers (see next page) are among the most surprising at any position. By reputation and on the basis of the evidence of his non-fielding statistics he was one of the fastest players of his time. He led the league in triples twice, and hit ten or more triples five times. During 1974, when he turned thirty-six, he stole twenty-one bases in only twenty-six attempts. Crosley Field had a slightly shallow center and deep right corner, but Vada's rate of defensive runs per 1450 innings was higher when he played for the Reds (–9 defensive runs) than when he played for the Indians, Angels, and Royals (–13 defensive runs). Nor do I think that is just because Vada was getting older—Vada kept his speed right till the end.

Pinson ran well and threw great, which is something you can generally judge just by sight, whereas *effective* range (positioning and jumps) is largely, as Bill James first put it, and as I keep emphasizing, "invisible." Like many outfielders with great arms, he had high DRA assists runs saved in his first

Vada Pinson

Year	L	Tm	IP	PO8 runs	A8 runs	v-Tm	Runs
1958	N	CIN	37	0	0	1	0
1959	N	CIN	1355	-7	1	-1	-6
1960	N	CIN	1384	-11	0	0	-11
1961	N	CIN	1334	5	5	4	10
1962	N	CIN	1343	-8	3	0	-6
1963	N	CIN	1258	-8	-1	0	-8
1964	N	CIN	1376	-21	1	1	-19
1965	N	CIN	1427	-13	0	0	-13
1966	N	CIN	1186	-2	-2	5	-4
1967	N	CIN	1408	-12	-2	1	-15
1968	N	CIN	1055	-8	0	5	-8
1969	N	STL	3	0	0	0	-1
1970	A	CLE	101	-3	0	-1	-2
1971	A	CLE	822	-2	2	-5	-1
1972	A	LA	105	-3	0	-4	-3
1973	A	LA	243	-2	0	-3	-2
1974	A	KC	43	-3	0	-3	-3
1975	A	KC	100	-1	0	-1	-1
Total			14579	-99	5	1	-94

couple of years (see 1961–62). Once the league caught on, they stopped running on him. Walsh and Smith would add another twenty or twenty-five runs for holding base runners. It does not alter the overall assessment that Pinson was a significantly below-average fielder.

When healthy, Mickey Mantle (see next page) certainly could play center, but never demonstrated sustained, above-average ability. Mantle was a shortstop until he came to the major leagues.

One of the biggest thrills I've experienced as a baseball fan occurred while writing this book, when I had the chance to attend a public viewing of a film made of the television broadcast of Don Larsen's perfect game. When Mantle strode to the plate for his first at-bat, the entire audience spontaneously began applauding—something they did for no one else. Mantle homered, and later preserved the perfect game with a backhanded catch at full speed of a Gil Hodges drive hit deep into Yankee Stadium's Death Valley. An inning or two after Mantle made the play against Hodges, Mel Allen observed that Mickey wasn't known for getting good jumps on batted balls, but was so fast he could make up for it. I find that an incredibly useful subjective observation: an announcer who at that point had seen this particular player field at least a thousand batted balls clearly pointed out a specific strength and a specific weakness in how the player fielded his position. In *My Favorite Summer 1956*, Mantle admitted that his mind (and eyes) wandered sometimes during

Mickey Mantle

Year	L	Tm	IP	PO8 runs	A8 runs	v-Tm	Runs
1952	A	NY	1069	6	8	2	15
1953	A	NY	998	-1	-3	0	-3
1954	A	NY	1239	-14	-4	4	-18
1955	A	NY	1277	2	2	2	4
1956	A	NY	1262	-1	0	0	-2
1957	A	NY	1225	2	-2	1	0
1958	A	NY	1310	-13	-3	1	-16
1959	A	NY	1258	10	-2	2	8
1960	A	NY	1280	-9	0	-2	-9
1961	A	NY	1294	4	-1	1	3
1962	A	NY	764	-13	0	-8	-13
1963	A	NY	382	1	0	3	1
1964	A	NY	819	-9	-3	4	-12
1966	A	NY	677	-8	-2	-6	-9
Total			14854	-41	-10	4	-52

a ballgame. As he put it, "I'd be showing Hank [Bauer] something in the stands and all of sudden I'd hear *crack!* And I'd look to see where everybody's running."

Live Ball Era

MCS	First	Last	IP	Runs	Δ
1940	Mike	Kreevich	8104	124	
1929	Taylor	Douthit	8663	99	
1924	Johnny	Mostil	7426	97	
1941	Vince	DiMaggio	8708	90	
1934	Sam	West	12382	87	
1924	Jigger	Statz	5223	86	
1922	Max	Carey	12166	79	
1945	Thurman	Tucker	4175	67	
1922	Sam	Rice	5008	65	
1938	Johnny	Cooney	4614	64	
1931	Tom	Oliver	4271	44	
1939	Harry	Craft	4618	41	
1934	Wally	Berger	8179	41	
1943	Joe	DiMaggio	14028	39	
1928	Jimmy	Welsh	3392	36	
1930	Johnny	Frederick	4381	34	
1943	Tommy	Holmes	3737	34	
1933	Kiddo	Davis	3526	30	
1926	Ira	Flagstead	6148	23	
1945	Sam	Chapman	7101	17	
1940	Terry	Moore	9947	14	
1925	Eddie	Brown	3685	11	
1923	B.	Jacobson	8301	9	

(continued)

Live Ball Era *(continued)*

MCS	First	Last	IP	Runs	Δ
1941	Roy	Weatherly	3989	7	
1921	Nemo	Leibold	3292	6	
1931	Fred	Schulte	8754	1	
1929	Al	Simmons	6780	-5	
1921	Ray	Powell	5878	-5	
1921	Hi	Myers	4554	-5	
1941	Barney	McCosky	3395	-6	
1933	Lloyd	Waner	13842	-6	
1928	Harry	Rice	4033	-9	
1936	Ben	Chapman	4748	-10	
1929	Earle	Combs	9683	-14	
1941	Wally	Judnich	3435	-15	
1946	Johnny	Hopp	3018	-16	
1931	Ethan	Allen	6237	-20	
1923	Whitey	Witt	3669	-22	
1937	Mel	Almada	3981	-22	
1937	Hank	Leiber	4378	-27	
1931	Mule	Haas	6946	-32	
1920	Cy	Williams	11365	-35	
1944	Stan	Spence	6248	-37	
1937	Jo-Jo	White	4080	-39	
1939	Joe	Marty	3619	-42	
1943	Johnny	Rucker	4730	-49	
1923	Edd	Roush	13531	-50	
1932	Kiki	Cuyler	5617	-52	
1933	Earl	Averill	12746	-93	
1928	Hack	Wilson	7704	-94	
1939	Doc	Cramer	16814	-102	

Pistol Pete Reiser is missing from the table above, even though he probably had more than 3000 innings in center, because of the way I had to estimate innings in the absence of hard data. According to DRA, Reiser had +30 defensive runs in his first (and really only) complete season, which combined with his batting and base running accomplishments, holds up as probably the greatest season in baseball history for a twenty-two year old non-pitcher—except for the season put together that very same year by his exact contemporary, Ted Williams. The following year, Reiser had the first of his many brutal encounters with the outfield walls of Ebbets Field, and fell to −16 defensive runs. Now of course both numbers are just estimates, but I think it is clear that had he just stayed away from the walls, Pete Reiser would have been among the greatest fielding center fielders of all time.

Joe DiMaggio

Year	L	Tm	IP	PO8 Runs	A8 Runs	Runs
1936	A	NY	459	-5	1	-4
1937	A	NY	1307	9	4	13
1938	A	NY	1232	7	4	12
1939	A	NY	998	21	2	23
1940	A	NY	1111	11	-3	9
1941	A	NY	1195	19	3	22
1942	A	NY	1348	6	-1	5
1946	A	NY	1112	-3	3	0
1947	A	NY	1187	-37	-5	-42
1948	A	NY	1290	3	-3	0
1949	A	NY	660	4	-3	1
1950	A	NY	1170	3	-2	1
1951	A	NY	959	0	-1	-1
Total			14028	38	1	39

It's past time to put to rest the notion that Joe DiMaggio was the greatest all-around player after Ruth. This myth has rested on the premise that his statistics couldn't capture his value. Yes, Yankee Stadium hurt his numbers. Retrosheet has recently released home-road batting splits for all seasons since 1920. Hitting in Yankee Stadium, where the wall in left-center and straightaway center was about 460 feet from home plate, did cost the right-handed Joltin' Joe, when all is said and done, the equivalent of about sixty home runs, which translates into something close to ninety offensive runs. But giving DiMaggio back those runs doesn't bring him remotely near the overall value of Ted Williams, even taking into consideration that Ted played an easier position with little enthusiasm.

Fans projected all sorts of things onto DiMaggio, including fielding excellence, because he was the most graceful and hardest slugging star of one of the most dominant teams in major league history, Joe McCarthy's Yankees of 1936–39. Even Jeter never had such an advantage in attracting an undeserved reputation for fielding prowess. But now we can begin to measure DiMaggio's fielding with some confidence, and it is absolutely clear that he was not a great fielder. He was a good fielder, perhaps a very good fielder, when young, averaging +15 defensive runs per 1450 innings through 1942. But he seemed to be fading, both as a hitter and a fielder, even before the War came.

After the War he was clearly a different player, even ignoring 1947. When I wrote my first internet article about DRA in 2003, I expressed my hope that "the *im*perfection of the output will reassure the skeptics among you that the ratings were not just cooked up." DiMaggio's rating for 1947 is obviously imperfect—it is, in fact, obviously wrong, as even the 1947 version of Joe DiMaggio could not possibly have caused the Yankees to give up an extra forty-two runs. A very big part of what this book is about is ending the game of 'hide the ball' when it comes to fielding metrics. The formulas are revealed, the data is public, the output is what it is, and some of it must be wrong.

But to give you some idea of how such a seemingly whacky number could pop up, consider the following. Joe played in 139 games, during some of which he probably left early for a defensive replacement (total games played by other Yankee centerfielders were twenty, thus 159 total player games, when only 154 total games were played, thus yielding five 'shared' games). So let's say Joe played the equivalent of about 135 complete games, or eighty-eight percent. A centerfielder typically catches forty percent of his team's outfield putouts. The Yankee outfielders made 1079 putouts. Eighty-eight percent of forty percent of 1079 is 378 putouts. Joe made 316, *sixty-two* fewer than expected, given this rough, rule-of-thumb calculation.

Before the season began, DiMaggio had surgery to remove a three-inch "bone spur" from his left heel. Perhaps when he came back, his outfield teammates Tommy Heinrich, Charlie Keller, and Johnny Lindell agreed that, in contrast to the standard practice then and now of having the center fielder handle every chance he can, including soft flies that could in theory be taken by corner outfielders, *they* would handle every play for Joe that they possibly could. Given that the 1947 Yankee outfield, as a whole, was actually +5 defensive runs in catching fly balls, it appears that the plan worked. The Yankees' fourth outfielder, Johnny Lindell (+33 PO8 runs), picked up most of the slack for Joe.

The best fielding center fielder during Joe DiMaggio's peak years before the War was Mike "Little Ikey Pikey" Kreevich.

Mike Kreevich

Year	L	Tm	IP	PO8 runs	A8 runs	Runs
1936	A	CHI	450	5	3	9
1937	A	CHI	1204	26	0	26
1938	A	CHI	1131	19	-3	15
1939	A	CHI	1219	18	4	22
1940	A	CHI	1230	27	1	28
1941	A	CHI	929	19	-1	18
1942	A	PHI	915	11	-2	8
1945	A	STL	673	10	-2	8
1945	A	WAS	352	-10	-1	-10
Total			8104	126	-2	124

Kreevich got a late start. He actually played a few games for the Cubs in 1931, but didn't make it back to the major leagues until 1936, by which time he was already twenty-eight. He made the all-star team in 1938, and played well the next year. It is widely documented that he had a drinking problem, which apparently worsened in 1940. Though his hitting declined, his fielding didn't seem to. With some help from Luke Sewell, manager of the Browns, Kreevich pulled it together to help the Browns to the pennant in 1944, turning in a very solid year with the bat. In 1943–44, Kreevich split time in the outfield, which is why those seasons are not shown among his 'pure' centerfield seasons. He was more or less average those years, as he was on a combined basis for his two 1945 teams. I don't know how the rest of his life turned out, but he did live to be eighty-five.

During Bob Feller's Opening Day no-hitter in 1940 Kreevich took a called strike, and must have made a face. The ump asked, "What's wrong with it?" Kreevich replied, "It sounded a little high."

The most overrated center fielder of the 1930s and 1940s was Doc Cramer.

Doc Cramer

Year	L	Tm	IP	PO8 runs	A8 runs	Runs
1930	A	PHI	64	0	0	0
1931	A	PHI	408	-1	0	0
1932	A	PHI	440	8	0	8
1933	A	PHI	1330	-18	0	-17
1934	A	PHI	1332	6	0	6
1935	A	PHI	1304	-1	-3	-4
1936	A	BOS	1350	17	4	21
1937	A	BOS	1165	-2	0	-3
1938	A	BOS	1288	6	0	6
1939	A	BOS	1184	-9	0	-9
1941	A	WAS	1307	-36	-2	-38
1942	A	DET	1303	-13	2	-11
1943	A	DET	1179	13	-2	11
1944	A	DET	1212	-23	-1	-24
1945	A	DET	1183	-10	-3	-13
1946	A	DET	420	-16	-1	-17
1947	A	DET	330	-17	0	-17
1948	A	DET	16	-2	0	-2
Total			16814	-97	-5	-102

Over the course of his career, Cramer had a below-average on-base percentage, a below-average slugging percentage, and was an abysmal base-stealer, with a success rate below fifty percent. Therefore, one would think, he had to have been a outstanding fielder for his teams to keep putting him in the lineup. He appears to have been nothing more than solid during the 1930s, and nobody noticed when he went into massive and persistent decline, even though he was a relatively old player (thirty-four in 1939).

Actually, it appears that Boston did notice, and first tried moving Doc off center and into left and right in 1940 (missing from the chart above for only center field performance), then traded him to Washington. The fences at Griffith Stadium were very far back, which may have left too much ground for Doc to cover. So Washington traded him to Detroit. When the Second World War came, good players were so scarce that even a slow, light-hitting thirty-seven-year-old centerfielder could find full-time employment. Cramer hung on to play part-time for bits of three more seasons after the War.

The most overrated center fielder of the 1920s was Edd Roush, who is in the Hall of Fame, and had a reputation as a good fielder.

Edd Roush

Year	L	Tm	IP	PO8 runs	A8 runs	Runs
1913	A	CHI	18	-1	0	-1
1916	N	CIN	582	11	-1	10
1917	N	CIN	1130	-7	-2	-9
1918	N	CIN	959	2	-1	1
1919	N	CIN	1129	7	3	9
1920	N	CIN	1214	16	-1	15
1921	N	CIN	910	1	-4	-4
1922	N	CIN	340	-1	2	1
1923	N	CIN	1164	-6	-2	-8
1924	N	CIN	959	-3	-1	-4
1925	N	CIN	1151	0	1	2
1926	N	CIN	1210	-31	-1	-32
1927	N	NY	1208	-20	2	-17
1928	N	NY	318	2	2	4
1929	N	NY	906	-20	4	-15
1931	N	CIN	332	-2	0	-2
Total			13531	-52	1	-50

I surmise that Roush's fielding reputation was based on three factors we have repeatedly seen will cause a fielder to be overrated: a nice start, a graceful style, and good hitting. Roush was a solid-to-good fielder through 1920. The *Historical Abstract* quotes the following description of Roush from *The Chicago Tribune*: "[Roush has the] legs of a gazelle." However, Roush was not a good base stealer—his stolen base totals were unexceptional for the Dead Ball Era, and his success rate during the seasons for which we have caught stealing data was poor. But he led the league in batting average twice during the Dead Ball Era, and enjoyed even higher batting averages when the live ball arrived.

One man who did make the transition from the Dead Ball Era to the Live Ball Era fairly well was Max Carey.

Carey should perhaps receive some credit as a centerfielder for his high performance during his first years as a left fielder in Forbes Field (+38 defensive runs), where the left field corner was 365 feet from home plate. After trying out what seems to have been about a dozen centerfielders from 1911 through 1915, the Pirates finally gave the job to Carey. Carey led his league in stolen bases ten times. Retrosheet has compiled caught stealing numbers for selected Dead Ball seasons, and Carey's stolen base percentage was far better than Cobb's. I believe he may have created more offensive runs from his base-stealing than anybody before the Modern Era (1969 onward).

Max Carey

Year	L	Tm	IP	PO8 runs	A8 runs	Runs
1917	N	PIT	1299	13	4	18
1918	N	PIT	1103	20	5	24
1919	N	PIT	550	0	-2	-2
1920	N	PIT	1098	-5	-5	-10
1921	N	PIT	1236	19	-4	15
1922	N	PIT	1329	-2	1	0
1923	N	PIT	1345	7	5	13
1924	N	PIT	1302	17	0	18
1925	N	PIT	1146	-11	4	-6
1926	N	BRO	219	2	-2	0
1926	N	PIT	704	1	0	1
1927	N	BRO	265	6	0	6
1928	N	BRO	561	3	1	4
1929	N	BRO	9	0	0	0
			12166	71	8	79

The first set of centerfielders who played most of their careers after 1920 and who proved themselves even more adept at running down the long line drives of the new era were Johnny Mostil, Jigger Statz, and Taylor Douthit.

Johnny Mostil

Year	L	Tm	IP	PO8 runs	A8 runs	Runs
1921	A	CHI	800	0	0	0
1922	A	CHI	931	12	-2	10
1923	A	CHI	1158	24	1	24
1924	A	CHI	791	5	3	7
1925	A	CHI	1301	16	-3	13
1926	A	CHI	1283	27	-1	27
1927	A	CHI	15	0	1	1
1928	A	CHI	1077	16	-1	15
1929	A	CHI	69	1	-1	0
Total			7426	100	-4	97

I generally have avoided citing the opinions of players who merely say that so-and-so was a great fielder, because such vague, 'global' assessments are so often flat-out wrong. However, Eddie Collins was, by common consent, one of the smartest players of his era, and had played against Tris Speaker for many years. Collins said Mostil was better. Johnny Mostil lost time to some sort of injury in 1924, and attempted suicide in 1927 after his girlfriend dumped him for one of his teammates. The prior year he had just put together an MVP-quality season. He returned in 1928 to play at an all-star quality level.

Jigger Statz

Year	L	Tm	IP	PO8 runs	A8 runs	Runs
1920	N	NY	55	0	0	0
1922	N	CHI	956	11	1	12
1923	N	CHI	1348	21	4	25
1924	N	CHI	1150	14	6	20
1925	N	CHI	321	2	0	2
1927	N	BRO	1054	25	1	25
1928	N	BRO	338	2	0	1
Total			5223	75	11	86

Listed as five feet, seven inches tall and 150 pounds, which probably meant he was even smaller than that, Jigger Statz had trouble hitting but found his way back to the Pacific Coast League, where he had begun his career. Jigger won the PCL MVP award in 1932, and ended up playing more documented games of professional baseball than anybody except Pete Rose and Hank Aaron.

Taylor Douthit

Year	L	Tm	IP	PO8 runs	A8 runs	Runs
1924	N	STL	206	-2	0	-2
1925	N	STL	139	2	0	1
1926	N	STL	1201	33	0	33
1927	N	STL	1128	28	-4	24
1928	N	STL	1348	49	-3	46
1929	N	STL	1300	-3	-5	-8
1930	N	STL	1348	9	-3	6
1931	N	STL	330	2	-2	0
1931	N	CIN	862	-4	-1	-6
1932	N	CIN	692	8	-2	7
1933	N	CHI	111	-1	0	-1
Total			8663	120	-21	99

"Ball Hawk" Douthit put up three of the greatest fielding seasons of all time, beginning in 1926, which exactly coincided with the first glory years in St. Louis Cardinals history. Douthit fell to earth the fourth year, as did the Cardinals. Branch Rickey, then in his first general manager role (though it was not called that back then), traded Douthit two years later to Cincinnati. Rickey is famous now for having repeatedly detected the moment his players began to decline, and for being generally successful in unloading them onto other organizations. Rickey was also infamously cheap, and Douthit's salary had reached $14,000, a large sum at the time. Douthit retired due to arthritis in the hip, which may have been what cut his speed four years before, and entered his family's insurance business.

Dead Ball Era

MCS	First	Last	IP	Runs	Δ
1918	Tris	Speaker	23091	244	
1896	Mike	Griffin	6111	132	
1896	Bill	Lange	5713	106	
1904	Fielder	Jones	9812	106	
1906	Cy	Seymour	9153	102	
1911	Tommy	Leach	6916	95	
1918	Happy	Felsch	5351	79	
1902	Emmet	Heidrick	4727	72	
1904	Jimmy	Slagle	3397	59	
1897	Steve	Brodie	7648	57	
1904	Roy	Thomas	11480	52	
1897	George	Van Haltren	7819	46	
1913	Fred	Snodgrass	3371	44	
1903	Jimmy	Barrett	5045	39	
1897	Dummy	Hoy	8653	23	
1913	Burt	Shotton	3890	23	
1897	Billy	Hamilton	7836	22	
1912	Rebel	Oakes	3568	22	
1914	Clyde	Milan	12862	14	
1916	Dode	Paskert	8120	11	
1910	Joe	Birmingham	4354	9	
1917	Hy	Myers	4261	4	
1918	Amos	Strunk	4657	-8	
1904	Chick	Stahl	6593	-8	
1918	Ping	Bodie	3008	-14	
1918	Ty	Cobb	16280	-18	
1904	Ginger	Beaumont	11495	-18	
1904	Homer	Smoot	4516	-21	
1908	Danny	Hoffman	4027	-26	
1903	John	Dobbs	3479	-27	
1896	Jake	Stenzel	5503	-37	
1908	Sam	Crawford	3539	-38	
1909	Rube	Oldring	3090	-45	
1918	Benny	Kauff	4790	-46	

Ginger Beaumont and Billy Hamilton were both very fast runners, despite their short, highly-muscled frames. But as we've discovered in our historical review thus far, the very speediest players can be mediocre (Mantle) or poor (Pinson) centerfielders. Hamilton was basically average until his last full-time season; Beamont slightly below average:

For many years, Beaumont's fielding was rated very badly in baseball encyclopedias. DRA includes an adjustment for infield fly outs, because in most cases short outfield fly balls or pop ups can be caught by either outfielders or infielders, and outfielders should not be penalized if 'ball hogging' infielders take those chances, or vice versa. Honus Wagner played shortstop during many of Beaumont's years with the Pirates, and seems to have been, based on

Ginger Beaumont

Year	L	Tm	IP	PO8 runs	A8 runs	Runs
1899	N	PIT	853	6	3	9
1900	N	PIT	1171	-8	-6	-14
1901	N	PIT	1129	15	-4	11
1902	N	PIT	1096	9	-1	8
1903	N	PIT	1197	2	-1	1
1904	N	PIT	1299	-2	-3	-4
1905	N	PIT	830	-2	-1	-3
1906	N	PIT	680	-13	-1	-14
1907	N	BOS	1265	-12	7	-5
1908	N	BOS	1034	-7	1	-7
1909	N	BOS	942	-2	0	-1
Total			11495	-13	-5	-18

his putout totals, a ball hog on what amounted to discretionary plays. DRA effectively adds some of them back to Beaumont's total, so Beaumont is not underrated. That adjustment brings Beaumont's DRA results with the Pirates more or less in line with his results with the Braves: average to a little below average.

In the DRA system, we don't care whether a player makes more plays because he avoids errors or because he has more range. *The Historical Abstract* reports that Mike Griffin had the lowest error rate, relative to his peers, of any outfielder in history. When errors were as common as they were back then, being sure-handed was definitely one way to excel.

Mike Griffin

Year	L	Tm	IP	PO8 runs	A8 runs	Runs
1893	N	BRO	789	14	2	16
1894	N	BRO	900	21	-3	18
1895	N	BRO	1112	28	2	30
1896	N	BRO	1035	27	-4	23
1897	N	BRO	1137	26	-4	23
1898	N	BRO	1137	21	2	23
Total			6111	138	-6	132

Griffin played the first half of his career before 1893, the year I have chosen as the first year of truly major league baseball. I chose that cutoff point because that was the first year that pitchers pitched from the modern distance of sixty feet, six inches, and even more importantly, because the American Association had collapsed the prior year, resulting in a stronger concentration of talent in the remaining major league, the National League. Others may not agree, and perhaps will apply their own version of DRA methods to rate fielders from before 1893. We may discover that Mike Griffin was even greater in his younger years, and arguably the greatest defensive outfielder before integration.

The other top nineteenth-century centerfielder was Bill Lange, who was apparently rangier than Griffin. *The Historical Abstract* cites a study by

Bill Lange

Year	L	Tm	IP	PO8 runs	A8 runs	Runs
1894	N	CHI	900	-1	4	3
1895	N	CHI	1044	12	6	17
1896	N	CHI	1027	26	2	28
1897	N	CHI	1002	4	1	4
1898	N	CHI	942	23	3	26
1899	N	CHI	799	22	6	28
Total			5713	86	20	106

William Akin for the *1981 Baseball Research Journal* that concludes, "in the absence of logically compelling statistical evidence, the impression of contemporary observers must be given greater weight.

The evidence points to Bill Lange of Chicago." Had he qualified for the Hall of Fame by playing at least ten seasons (he retired after his seventh in deference to the wishes of his prospective father-in-law), he might very well have earned a plaque in Cooperstown.

Top Forty Center Fielders of All Time

MCS	First	Last	IP	Total Runs	Δ	TPAR
2002	Andruw	Jones	14732	208	Δ	196
1918	Tris	Speaker	23091	244		159
1962	Willie	Mays	24276	195	Δ	157
1988	Gary	Pettis	8799	119	Δ	141
1971	Paul	Blair	13857	152	Δ	141
1982	Chet	Lemon	12425	109	Δ	124
1955	Richie	Ashburn	16378	177		120
1978	Garry	Maddox	13736	112	Δ	120
1994	Devon	White	14538	95	Δ	114
1968	Willie	Davis	19188	133	Δ	114
1990	Lenny	Dykstra	9831	87		109
2003	Mike	Cameron	14416	121	Δ	105
2001	Jim	Edmonds	14263	109		102
1993	Stan	Javier	4989	66	Δ	86

(continued)

Top Forty Center Fielders of All Time *(continued)*

MCS	First	Last	IP	Total Runs	Δ	TPAR
1985	Eddie	Milner	4635	66	Δ	85
1976	Bill	North	8348	70	Δ	73
1986	Willie	Wilson	10721	49	Δ	70
1994	Chuck	Carr	3618	52	Δ	70
1995	Darren	Lewis	7713	53	Δ	69
1964	Curt	Flood	14142	100	Δ	69
1980	Ruppert	Jones	7734	53	Δ	65
1985	Mookie	Wilson	8621	45	Δ	65
2002	Darin	Erstad	4536	74		63
1969	Ken	Berry	8015	77		62
1976	Cesar	Geronimo	7728	57	Δ	61
1987	Dave	Henderson	9419	39	Δ	61
1994	Lance	Johnson	11057	42	Δ	60
1955	Jim	Busby	9580	115		58
2004	Carlos	Beltran	13115	79	Δ	58
1994	Otis	Nixon	8997	39	Δ	57
1986	Rickey	Henderson	3549	35	Δ	56
1947	Dom	DiMaggio	10882	128		55
1959	Jim	Piersall	10005	98		52
1969	Tommie	Agee	7777	68	Δ	51
1985	Bob	Dernier	4640	30		50
1988	Mitch	Webster	3318	27	Δ	48
1972	Del	Unser	9061	55		48
1980	Al	Bumbry	7395	32	Δ	45
1983	Dwayne	Murphy	10025	27	Δ	44
1980	Omar	Moreno	10273	30	Δ	43

Ken (the "Bandit") Berry spent most of his career with the White Sox in the 1960s, when the American League was still not quite fully integrated, though he did have four excellent part-time seasons with the Angels and Brewers from 1971 through 1974, when the American League could fairly be said to have fully integrated and regained parity with the National. Note

Ken Berry

Year	Lg	Team	IP	PO8 Runs	A8 Runs	DRA
1962	A	CHI	8	0	1	1
1963	A	CHI	14	1	0	1
1964	A	CHI	89	-3	0	-3
1965	A	CHI	1245	20	0	20
1966	A	CHI	84	2	0	2
1967	A	CHI	317	-1	0	-1
1968	A	CHI	1248	7	1	8
1969	A	CHI	794	5	1	6
1970	A	CHI	1147	5	0	5
1971	A	LA	706	14	-1	13
1972	A	LA	961	9	4	13
1973	A	LA	892	8	-2	6
1974	A	MIL	510	6	2	7

his consistently high quality of play for the White Sox, Angels, and Brewers, particularly given the relatively low number of innings played.

Mark Liptak of baseball-almanac.com interviewed Berry in August 2005. The Bandit spoke convincingly about just how much thought and grueling physical work go into being a first-rate centerfielder:

> You know I've been wanting to get this off my chest for a long time. One time I was watching ESPN baseball with Jon Miller and Joe Morgan. Miller reminded Morgan that late in his career he played some outfield and asked what it was like. Morgan said, "it wasn't like being at second base, you could relax out there." I was sitting at home and started shaking my head. When I played center field I was responsible for my other two outfielders as far as positioning them. I had to know who was hitting, I had to know what my pitchers were going to throw them, when I was in Comiskey Park I'd have to keep checking the wind because it would often shift or swirl. I had to always be ready. Yet Morgan said you could 'relax,' when you played the outfield.
> I worked on those leaping catches every single day. Every day I practiced stealing home runs. During batting practice I'd clear out the other guys from center field and start working. I'd throw my hat down to give me an idea of where I started from and I'd just start going after fly balls. After I'd make the catch I could see how far I went to get them and that gave me an idea of what I could do in a game.

Lenny ("Nails") Dykstra

Year	L	Tm	IP	PO8 runs	A8 runs	v-Tm	Runs
1985	N	NY	522	8	1	4	9
1986	N	NY	957	8	1	-6	9
1987	N	NY	866	5	-1	-3	4
1988	N	NY	869	9	-1	9	8
1989	N	NY	379	4	1	6	6
1989	N	PHI	738	-6	-1	-5	-7
1990	N	PHI	1289	25	0	6	25
1991	N	PHI	546	4	0	2	4
1992	N	PHI	751	3	1	1	4
1993	N	PHI	1422	11	-5	2	6
1994	N	PHI	725	7	0	7	7
1995	N	PHI	464	6	0	9	6
1996	N	PHI	304	5	1	5	6
Total			9831	90	-3	36	87

Both Lenny Dykstra and Gary Pettis are ranked higher by TPAR than many might expect. That's because their careers were centered around the late 1980s and early 1990s, when, according to the analysis conducted in chapter four, center field (and left field) were most competitive.

With the Mets, Nails averaged +15 defensive runs per 1450 innings. It looks as though it took one season for him to adjust to playing at Philadelphia's Veterans stadium (a turf ballpark; Shea had grass), but overall, his average defensive runs per 1450 innings with the Phillies was almost exactly what it had been for the Mets. That said, he never could keep himself in the lineup consistently.

Jim Edmonds

Year	L	Tm	IP	PO8 runs	A8 runs	v-Tm	Runs
1993	A	LA	9	1	0	1	1
1994	A	LA	27	2	0	2	2
1995	A	LA	1190	14	0	2	14
1996	A	LA	923	3	0	3	3
1997	A	LA	967	8	2	0	10
1998	A	LA	1313	7	0	3	7
1999	A	LA	376	3	1	-2	4
2000	N	STL	1211	4	0	1	4
2001	N	STL	1215	-7	3	-3	-4
2002	N	STL	1160	9	2	-5	11
2003	N	STL	1017	15	3	8	18
2004	N	STL	1242	6	2	2	9
2005	N	STL	1153	23	0	6	22
2006	N	STL	792	6	0	6	6
2007	N	STL	828	-3	2	2	-2
2008	N	CHI	628	0	5	-2	5
2008	N	SD	212	0	-1	0	-1
Total			14263	91	17	25	109

The 2005 rating is too high; I am skeptical that he could have had his best fielding season at age thirty-five. However, Walsh indicates that Edmonds may have saved an additional twenty-five runs holding base runners, and Smith estimates twice that many. And he did have a couple of good seasons for separate teams and leagues (1995 and 1997 for the Angels and 2002–03 for the Cardinals), and consistently outperformed his backups. He generated Hall of Fame value, offense and defense combined, over the course of his career. Like almost all players with a balance of skills rather than one or two notable ones, he will be undervalued by Hall of Fame voters, and may have to wait a while to get in.

Chet Lemon was a player with a very odd mix of strengths and weaknesses. As usually happens in such cases, the weaknesses draw inordinate attention. *The Historical Abstract* cites a certain "Scouting Report: 1987" to the effect that Lemon was an "enigma … whose judgment on throws from the outfield has been called into question and [who is] prone to missing the cutoff man."

Honorable Mention: Chet Lemon

Year	L	Tm	IP	PO8 runs	A8 runs	v-Tm	Runs
1975	A	CHI	8	-1	0	-1	-1
1976	A	CHI	1042	4	2	4	5
1977	A	CHI	1302	30	1	6	31
1978	A	CHI	690	10	0	3	10
1979	A	CHI	1281	2	1	2	3
1980	A	CHI	1185	-3	2	-4	-1
1981	A	CHI	781	2	-2	1	0
1982	A	DET	217	1	0	-1	1
1983	A	DET	1247	21	0	-1	21
1984	A	DET	1208	24	-2	4	22
1985	A	DET	1272	14	-3	2	11
1986	A	DET	1002	8	0	-2	8
1987	A	DET	1171	1	-1	-8	0
1990	A	DET	18	-1	0	-1	-1
Total			12425	110	-2	4	109

He didn't walk that much, but led the league four times in being hit by pitches, and maintained a good on-base percentage. Decent power, particularly for the time. Terrible base runner—would frequently slide into first, which is almost always ineffective and dangerous—and perhaps the only top flight centerfielder whose stolen base success rate was below fifty percent. It isn't clear what brought his fielding performance down in 1979–81; whatever it was, the Tigers thought he'd be better off in right field, where he played most of 1982. Since base running is the least important part of both offense

Honorable Mention: Garry Maddox

Year	L	Tm	IP	PO8 runs	A8 runs	v-Tm	Runs
1972	N	SF	810	-6	0	-5	-6
1973	N	SF	1236	-9	-2	1	-11
1974	N	SF	1124	2	-3	5	-1
1975	N	SF	123	0	1	1	2
1975	N	PHI	840	21	2	6	23
1976	N	PHI	1240	19	0	10	20
1977	N	PHI	1205	20	-1	5	19
1978	N	PHI	1324	20	-1	0	19
1979	N	PHI	1194	21	2	1	23
1980	N	PHI	1247	12	-1	2	11
1981	N	PHI	750	12	1	5	13
1982	N	PHI	903	-1	0	-9	-1
1983	N	PHI	736	2	-1	2	1
1984	N	PHI	497	4	0	4	4
1985	N	PHI	492	-1	0	-2	-1
1986	N	PHI	14	-2	0	-1	-2
Total			13736	115	-3	24	112

and defense, I would have been quite happy to accept Lemon's weaknesses in those areas, given his strengths in everything else.

In the 1970s it was frequently said, "Seventy percent of the earth is covered by water. The other thirty percent is covered by Garry Maddox." (See table on prior page). Why have I kept him off the top ten list? Questions about consistency and context. As shown above, he was at best an average fielder when he came up with the Giants. Traded to the Phillies, he played next to possibly the worst outfielder of all time: Greg "The Bull" Luzinski. On almost all teams, the centerfielder takes all chances in the outfield that he can, including soft flies that could be handled in the gaps by the corner outfielders. But with The Bull, Maddox may have taken what would normally be fly ball chances of the left fielder. Maddox had only one good season when he wasn't playing next to Luzinski, the strike-shortened 1981. Notwithstanding these caveats, Garry Maddox was almost certainly an excellent centerfielder. It's just difficult to be completely convinced that he belongs among the very, very best of all time.

Number Ten: Dom DiMaggio

Year	L	Tm	IP	PO8 runs	A8 runs	v-Tm	Runs
1941	A	BOS	1230	7	3		10
1942	A	BOS	1265	36	5		41
1946	A	BOS	1191	10	-1		9
1947	A	BOS	1137	19	6		25
1948	A	BOS	1356	13	0		12
1949	A	BOS	1230	18	2		20
1950	A	BOS	1188	15	2		17
1951	A	BOS	1239	1	-1		0
1952	A	BOS	1045	-5	-1	1	-7
Total			10882	113	15	1	128

The best fielding center fielder of the 1940s, Dom DiMaggio averaged +17 defensive runs per 1450 innings played throughout his career. If we credit Dom with +54 runs saved in 1943–45, which is conservative, as he was saving runs at a higher rate, on average, in 1941–42 and 1946, that brings his TPAR up to 109. In fact, one could argue that, like Phil Rizzuto, Dom should get credit for his last year in the minor leagues—he was named the most valuable player in the Pacific Coast League, the independent league closest in quality to the major leagues. Add another seventeen runs for that, and Dom would be number seven on the TPAR list.

Dom wasn't known as the Little Professor just because he wore glasses. He studied the hitters, and carefully positioned himself in the field. He would lean one way or the other as a pitch was delivered, and got great jumps.

An acquaintance of mine who saw both Dom and Joe play thought there was no contest—Dom was much the better fielder.

And about as valuable a player overall, after the War. On the basis of Sean Smith's Runs Above Replacement ("RAR"), with DRA estimates replacing Smith's defensive estimates, Dom had +269 RAR from 1946 through 1951; Joe +264 RAR. Now perhaps, as explained earlier, Joe should not be fully charged for his –42 defensive runs in 1947, the year of his bone spur surgery, because his outfield teammates, particularly Lindell, took up the slack. Even leaving fielding out of the analysis, though, Dom hit about as many singles and doubles as Joe, was better at staying in the lineup, drew more walks, and stole more bases (though not enough to matter all that much). So it's really Joe's homers versus Dom's defense. As far as I can tell, the only season after the War Joe clearly out-produced Dom was 1948, when Joe led the league with thirty-nine home runs.

In the seventh game of the 1946 World Series Dom tied things up for the Red Sox in the top of the eighth inning by doubling in two runners, but pulled a hamstring coming into second and had to be taken out. In the bottom half of the inning, with two outs, the Cardinals had Enos Slaughter on first, with the left-hander Harry "The Hat" Walker at the plate, a Tony Gwynn-type hitter who hit a lot of soft singles, often to left field. (Walker led the league in batting average the following year.) Dom's substitute, Leon Culberson, was playing Walker to hit straightaway. From the dugout, DiMaggio waved Culberson over toward left, but Culberson hardly budged. DiMaggio frantically tried again to wave him over. Too late. Slaughter broke to steal second—pulling shortstop Johnny Pesky toward the bag—the pitch came in, and Walker hit what he later called a "dying seagull" in left center, almost exactly where DiMaggio had feared he would. Slaughter later said, "I knew I was going to score before I hit second base, because I knew Culberson was in center, not Dom DiMaggio." Culberson, anxious about bad hops—the Sportsman's Park outfield was in terrible condition, because it was the end of the year and both the Browns and the Cardinals played all their games there—failed to charge the ball quickly enough once it hit the ground, and rather than throw directly home to get Slaughter, tossed the ball weakly to Pesky, who had to spin around to make his throw, which was off target—but probably too late anyway. The Red Sox got a couple of runners on in the top of the ninth, but couldn't get them home.

Dominic DiMaggio is my nominee for the greatest baseball player at the game of life. As recalled by David Halberstam, "Nothing came easily to him." And yet he always prevailed. A very weak hitter when he first came up with the San Francisco Seals in the Pacific Coast League, he listened hard to his first manager, Lefty O'Doul, and completely changed his batting mechanics, eventually finishing second in batting his final year with the Seals. Small and quiet, but proud, Dom found a way to fit in with the tempestuous Red Sox team of the late 1940s. When Red Sox management (Lou Boudreau) foolishly tried to bench him, he retired on his own terms and, with no particular training or preparation, started a hugely successful plastics business, eventually amassing enough wealth that he once considered buying the team he had played for. He died, aged ninety-two, in 2009.

Number Nine: Willie Davis

Year	L	Tm	IP	PO8 runs	A8 runs	v-Tm	Runs
1960	N	LA	193	2	0	4	2
1961	N	LA	787	6	-2	7	4
1962	N	LA	1358	11	1	2	12
1963	N	LA	1248	11	4	5	15
1964	N	LA	1378	23	4	2	27
1965	N	LA	1244	16	-1	1	15
1966	N	LA	1333	16	-1	-2	15
1967	N	LA	1218	-1	0	-4	-1
1968	N	LA	1392	-5	-1	-2	-6
1969	N	LA	1067	4	-1	1	3
1970	N	LA	1214	8	2	-5	10
1971	N	LA	1355	9	-1	-5	7
1972	N	LA	1318	9	1	0	10
1973	N	LA	1297	7	-1	0	6
1974	N	MON	1276	11	-1	-5	10
1975	A	TEX	350	-1	-1	-2	-2
1975	N	STL	114	-3	0	-3	-3
1976	N	SD	1044	9	-1	2	8
Total			19188	132	0	-4	133

The late Willie Davis is largely forgotten, mainly because Dodger Stadium prevented him from being a consistent .300 hitter with 3000 career hits. I can find nothing to suggest that his numbers misrepresent his value as a fielder. I'm also impressed that he maintained value as a 'plus', if not outstanding, centerfielder deep into his thirties.

The most demonstrably consistent fielder in history, Mike Cameron (see next page) has posted good numbers in center field for each of the five teams for which he has played through 2009. Here are his defensive runs in center field per 1450 innings played: White Sox (+8), Reds (+14), Mariners (+19), Mets (+5, but with a small sample of less than 1450 innings), Padres (+11). Consistent, high-level results in multiple contexts provide the best possible evidence of truly outstanding fielding ability, as it then makes it very hard to believe the player is somehow being helped by a contextual factor that hasn't been factored out. Unlike most fielders, Cameron more or less estimates where the ball is going to land almost as soon as it's hit, runs straight to that

Number Eight: Mike Cameron

Year	L	Tm	IP	PO8 runs	A8 runs	v-Tm	Runs
1995	A	CHI	20	0	0	0	0
1996	A	CHI	22	0	0	0	0
1997	A	CHI	837	7	0	2	7
1998	A	CHI	972	5	-1	4	4
1999	N	CIN	1261	13	-1	1	12
2000	A	SEA	1270	8	-1	5	7
2001	A	SEA	1272	20	0	3	20
2002	A	SEA	1318	4	-1	0	3
2003	A	SEA	1284	38	-2	0	36
2004	N	NY	1184	8	-1	2	7
2005	N	NY	79	-3	0	-3	-3
2006	N	SD	1244	9	-1	-4	9
2007	N	SD	1329	3	-1	0	2
2008	N	MIL	1057	3	-1	-2	2
2009	N	MIL	1268	11	4	-3	15
Total			14416	126	-5	4	121

location, and then starts looking for the ball. Cameron credits much of his success to intensive coaching he received from Gary Pettis.

Devon White deserved almost all of his Gold Gloves. Following a classic, nearly universal pattern in center field, Devon declined during his age-thirty-one season, when his stolen base attempts, adjusted for estimated times he reached first base (his singles plus his walks), dropped by a third. Neither his running game nor his fielding performance ever returned to their prior levels.

Number Seven: Devon White

Year	L	Tm	IP	PO8 runs	A8 runs	v-Tm	Runs
1985	A	LA	7	-1	0	-1	-1
1986	A	LA	57	2	0	1	2
1987	A	LA	452	15	1	4	16
1988	A	LA	978	22	1	11	23
1989	A	LA	1366	23	1	2	24
1990	A	LA	1015	3	2	4	6
1991	A	TOR	1384	20	0	2	20
1992	A	TOR	1306	14	0	-1	14
1993	A	TOR	1264	10	-1	4	9
1994	A	TOR	811	10	-1	2	9
1995	A	TOR	862	-4	1	3	-3
1996	N	FLA	1201	-2	-1	0	-3
1997	N	FLA	587	1	0	1	1
1998	N	ARI	1219	7	-4	-5	3
1999	N	LA	1065	-8	-3	-5	-11
2000	N	LA	296	-4	0	-5	-4
2001	N	MIL	668	-10	-1	-5	-11
Total			14538	100	-5	12	95

Number Six: Richie Ashburn

Year	L	Tm	IP	PO8 runs	A8 runs	v-Tm	Runs
1949	N	PHI	1348	31	1		32
1950	N	PHI	1299	14	-3		11
1951	N	PHI	1348	37	1		38
1952	N	PHI	1373	3	-1	3	2
1953	N	PHI	1369	28	0	4	28
1954	N	PHI	1342	24	1	0	24
1955	N	PHI	1217	11	6	0	17
1956	N	PHI	1368	21	1	0	22
1957	N	PHI	1382	17	4	-1	21
1958	N	PHI	1370	18	-2	2	16
1959	N	PHI	1255	-6	-3	-1	-9
1960	N	CHI	805	-5	1	-5	-4
1961	N	CHI	489	-16	-1	-15	-17
1962	N	NY	413	-3	0	-1	-3
Total			16378	174	3	-14	177

Something happened to Ashburn in 1959, his age-thirty-two season. In 1958 he hit thirteen triples, stole thirty bases while being caught twelve times, and saved about sixteen runs in the field. In 1959 he hit only two triples, stole only nine bases and was caught eleven times, and cost his team about nine runs in the field.

A lot has already been written about Ashburn's fielding numbers, which, without any contextual adjustments, were staggering. DRA adjusts for the tendency of Robin Roberts and other Phillies' pitchers of Ashburn's time to give up fly balls rather than ground balls.

The trickier factor, requiring more investigation, is the effect of Shibe Park, where Ashburn played during his prime, which had a vast centerfield area. The field as a whole was shaped like a symmetric diamond, without a 'rounding off' of the upper corner of the 'diamond' in centerfield. I once did a quick-and-dirty home-road analysis for Ashburn using Retrosheet data available for the 1957–58 seasons, and he did save about five runs more per season at home than on the road. So perhaps we could shave another couple of runs per season. On the other hand, I would imagine that most fielders with long careers perform better in their home parks, just because the field is more familiar.

Some have wondered whether Ashburn may have boosted his numbers by covering for an immobile Del Ennis in left field, as Garry Maddox may have been covering for Greg Luzinski. But Ashburn's ratings were not unusually high when Ennis had his worst seasons, in 1953 (–16 defensive runs) and 1956 (–35 defensive runs). Over the course of his career, Ashburn's fellow outfielders were only very slightly below average, so I don't believe Ashburn was a ball hog when it came to his fellow outfielders. And infield fly ball hogging is adjusted out by DRA.

Finally, Ashburn's single season numbers are consistent with the batted ball data estimates of today's best fielders, who face much stiffer competition than Ashburn did, leaving aside Willie Mays, so it's reasonable to believe he could dominate as much as he did. I'm confident that Ashburn was truly outstanding, saved at least 150 runs in the outfield, and accordingly deserved his spot in the Hall of Fame.

Number Five: Gary Pettis

Year	L	Tm	IP	PO8 runs	A8 runs	v-Tm	Runs
1982	A	LA	15	1	0	1	1
1983	A	LA	172	-3	2	-1	-1
1984	A	LA	950	14	3	8	17
1985	A	LA	1055	18	3	6	21
1986	A	LA	1324	36	1	3	36
1987	A	LA	991	21	-2	-3	20
1988	A	DET	1025	15	0	3	15
1989	A	DET	1022	3	-3	-3	0
1990	A	TEX	1031	-4	3	-4	-2
1991	A	TEX	782	6	0	3	5
1992	A	DET	389	5	0	9	5
1992	N	SD	44	1	0	1	1
Total			8799	113	6	25	119

Number Four: Paul Blair

Year	L	Tm	IP	PO8 runs	A8 runs	v-Tm	Runs
1964	A	BAL	9	-1	0	-1	-1
1965	A	BAL	908	3	1	-7	3
1966	A	BAL	787	-2	-1	-1	-3
1967	A	BAL	1269	20	3	0	22
1968	A	BAL	977	11	2	2	13
1969	A	BAL	1339	22	1	1	23
1970	A	BAL	1086	22	2	3	24
1971	A	BAL	1115	-2	-3	-6	-5
1972	A	BAL	1084	14	-1	-2	13
1973	A	BAL	1154	18	2	4	20
1974	A	BAL	1285	19	-2	-2	16
1975	A	BAL	1033	19	0	7	19
1976	A	BAL	957	8	-2	5	7
1977	A	NY	312	-2	-1	-5	-4
1978	A	NY	211	2	0	-1	2
1979	A	NY	4	0	0	0	0
1979	N	CIN	327	1	-1	-1	0
1980	A	NY	1	0	0	0	0
Total			13857	151	0	-3	152

The talent pool model data suggests that fielding competition in center field might have weakened slightly in the past decade or two as African-American participation has declined in baseball, and the timeline adjustment therefore favors players such as Gary Pettis (see prior page), whose weighted average season was 1988, over players such as Cameron, whose weighted average season is 2003. Perhaps more sophisticated talent pool modeling will modify this result, but for the time being, I'll leave Cameron's brilliant fielding coach, Gary Pettis, right where he is.

The drop in 1971 for Paul Blair (see prior page) was probably due to the after-effects of a terrible beaning the prior year and an embarrassing and probably distracting attempt, abandoned by the end of the season, at switch hitting. Walsh and Smith would boost his ratings another thirty runs for holding base runners over the course of his career.

Number Three: Tris Speaker

Year	L	Tm	IP	PO8 runs	A8 runs	Runs
1908	A	BOS	266	-4	3	0
1909	A	BOS	1205	12	10	21
1910	A	BOS	1188	29	0	29
1911	A	BOS	1171	5	2	7
1912	A	BOS	1348	20	7	27
1913	A	BOS	1180	25	5	30
1914	A	BOS	1324	41	6	47
1915	A	BOS	1273	20	0	20
1916	A	CLE	1282	2	2	4
1917	A	CLE	1205	13	2	15
1918	A	CLE	1078	28	-2	26
1919	A	CLE	1137	29	3	32
1920	A	CLE	1289	-4	3	-1
1921	A	CLE	1094	8	-1	7
1922	A	CLE	966	-9	1	-9
1923	A	CLE	1314	-8	6	-2
1924	A	CLE	1092	-9	5	-4
1925	A	CLE	967	-1	3	2
1926	A	CLE	1310	6	2	8
1927	A	WAS	1010	-15	0	-16
1928	A	PHI	390	-1	2	1
Total			23091	186	57	244

I very much wanted Tris Speaker's defensive runs to vault him past Cobb in overall value. Sean Smith estimates Cobb was about 260 runs better than Speaker, over the course of their respective careers, based on runs above replacement level, leaving aside fielding. The difference between DRA's estimates of their respective defensive value (including Cobb's good performance in right field) almost bridges the difference, but not quite; Cobb is probably still between fifty and seventy-five runs ahead. If I were a general manager at the time, I would still have preferred Spoke on my team.

Speaker's contemporary Edd Roush once said that he had to move forty feet back when the live ball arrived circa 1920. Speaker, of course, played shallower than any centerfielder in history, and apparently couldn't make the necessary adjustments to continue to dominate as a fielder in the live ball era, though, as Bill James has pointed out, he did adjust fairly well as a hitter, leading the league in doubles for four straight years (1920–23) and even hitting seventeen homeruns in 1923. It's also possible that Speaker's sharp decline as a fielder after 1919 might have been attributable simply to a normal, age-related decline in foot speed—his stolen bases dropped into the single digits for the first time in 1920 (when he turned thirty-two) and stayed there for the remainder of his career.

Number Two: Willie Mays

Year	L	Tm	IP	PO8 runs	A8 runs	v-Tm	Runs
1951	N	NY	1036	16	1		17
1952	N	NY	311	8	7	1	15
1954	N	NY	1346	29	1	1	30
1955	N	NY	1361	12	-1	6	11
1956	N	NY	1345	18	1	2	19
1957	N	NY	1354	9	2	-1	11
1958	N	SF	1352	15	2	-1	18
1959	N	SF	1281	5	-2	0	3
1960	N	SF	1348	6	0	0	6
1961	N	SF	1335	2	-3	-2	-1
1962	N	SF	1394	15	-2	4	13
1963	N	SF	1387	4	-1	-1	3
1964	N	SF	1346	13	0	0	12
1965	N	SF	1242	6	2	0	8
1966	N	SF	1247	25	0	8	25
1967	N	SF	1075	18	-2	5	16
1968	N	SF	1135	4	-1	-6	3
1969	N	SF	853	-6	-3	-1	-9
1970	N	SF	1040	-4	0	0	-5
1971	N	SF	654	1	-1	-4	1
1972	N	SF	113	-2	0	-2	-1
1972	N	NY	382	-1	0	0	-1
1973	N	NY	339	3	-1	3	3
Total			24276	195	0	14	195

John Walsh estimated that Mays saved about twenty-five more runs by holding base runners; Smith would add another twenty-five on top of that. Again, I have no idea which estimate is better. Mays missed a year and a half in the Service. DRA shows a suspiciously high rating for the partial season (1952), but I see no reason not to give Mays another twenty runs for 1953. So when you add an average of the Walsh and Smith estimates of runs saved by holding runners and grant credit for a full 1952 and 1953, Mays is well above +250 career defensive runs, pulling him past Speaker, without even considering talent pool effects.

I've wondered time and again why Mays seemed to decline as a fielder around 1960, only to recover in 1962. In 1958 and 1959 the San Francisco Giants played in Seals Stadium, which had conventional dimensions and normal weather. Mays' average annual defensive runs during those two years was almost exactly what it had been his last year in the Polo Grounds. Then the Giants moved into Candlestick Park. As Mays later explained, it took him a while to develop a strategy for coping with the crazy Candlestick wind. Eventually he figured out that the best thing to do was literally to stand still after a fly ball was hit and count to five, to see where the wind was taking the ball.

Let's try putting together a new answer to a question that baseball fans have been asking for about half a century: Mantle or Mays? After Mantle's injuries took him down in the mid-1960s and Mays carried on as an excellent-to-effective player at least through his penultimate season (1972), there was no doubt about who had had the most valuable career, so the question changed to: Who was better in his prime, Mantle or Mays?

The first edition of *The Historical Abstract* stated that "Mickey Mantle was, at his peak in 1956–57 and again in 1961–62, clearly a greater player than Willie Mays—and it is not a close or difficult decision." Bill James showed that Mantle was about twenty-five to thirty-five runs per season better on offense in 1956–57 and 1961–62 under a variety of measures than Mays during his peak seasons, and argued that Mays was probably only about five or seven runs per season better on defense. Fifteen years later, the second edition of *The Historical Abstract* reported Mantle as clearly better than Mays in Win Shares (overall value, offense and defense) per 162 games, Win Shares in each player's top three seasons, and Win Shares in each player's five best consecutive seasons. Mays beat Mantle only in career Win Shares.

DRA is more significantly more accurate than Win Shares in assessing fielding value, particularly in the outfield. In addition, there are now slightly better offensive runs estimates now available on-line that take into account how much a batter improved the probability of his team winning, literally plate appearance by plate appearance, based on ideas first proposed by brothers Harlan and Eldon Mills circa 1970 and implemented by several other top analysts since then. (Harlan had more sheet brainpower than any baseball analyst who ever lived; he worked at Princeton University's Institute for

Advanced Study during the 1950s while Albert Einstein and John von Neumann were there, and made lasting contributions to software engineering.) The concept is now referred to as Win Probability Added ("WPA"). Tom Tango contributed the idea of 'weighting' WPA by the leverage of a situation. If a player is good and the game is close, his good hitting will have a huge impact on the probability of his team winning. If the game is a blow-out (either way), good hitting won't have much impact on WPA. Tango developed a Leverage Index ("LI") to back out the leverage of the situation, which obviously is not under the player's control, in order to create WPA/LI, which is posted for seasons where the data is available at baseball-reference.com.

Applying WPA/LI to measure offense (including base running) ("Off"), DRA to measure defense ("Def"), slight positional adjustments provided by Smith (see the penalty for Mantle for playing first base in 1967–68) ("Pos"), and Smith's adjustment for value below average value but above replacement value ("Rep"), here is how Mays and Mantle stack up year by year.

Mays played in a qualitatively more integrated and competitive league, as Mark Armour has shown in his essential article, *The Effects of Integration, 1947–1986*. This may explain why Smith's replacement-level adjustments are

Mays

Year	L	Tm	PA	Off.	Def.	Pos	Rep	RAR
1951	N	NY	523	12	17	-1	17	45
1952	N	NY	144	7	15	0	5	27
1954	N	NY	633	57	30	-1	21	107
1955	N	NY	663	37	11	-1	21	68
1956	N	NY	647	38	19	-1	21	77
1957	N	NY	662	60	11	-1	21	91
1958	N	SF	679	61	18	-1	21	99
1959	N	SF	642	54	3	-1	21	77
1960	N	SF	660	45	6	0	22	73
1961	N	SF	655	53	-1	0	22	74
1962	N	SF	703	67	13	0	23	103
1963	N	SF	664	71	3	0	22	96
1964	N	SF	661	78	12	0	22	112
1965	N	SF	634	72	8	0	22	102
1966	N	SF	624	53	25	0	21	99
1967	N	SF	539	20	16	0	19	55
1968	N	SF	567	44	3	0	20	67
1969	N	SF	455	16	-9	0	16	23
1970	N	SF	560	44	-5	-2	17	54
1971	N	SF	532	46	1	-4	16	59
1972	N	SF	66	1	-1	0	2	2
1972	N	NY	239	15	-1	-1	7	20
1973	N	NY	237	-3	3	-1	7	6

Mantle

Year	L	Tm	PA	Off.	Def.	Pos	Rep	RAR
1951	A	NY	384	7	-12	-4	11	2
1952	A	NY	624	36	13	-2	16	63
1953	A	NY	540	30	-4	-1	15	40
1954	A	NY	645	54	-18	-1	17	52
1955	A	NY	633	73	4	-1	17	93
1956	A	NY	647	93	-2	-1	17	107
1957	A	NY	620	100	0	-1	17	116
1958	A	NY	650	80	-16	-1	17	80
1959	A	NY	636	37	8	-1	17	61
1960	A	NY	639	52	-9	0	18	61
1961	A	NY	640	88	3	0	18	109
1962	A	NY	500	72	-17	-1	14	68
1963	A	NY	212	23	-1	0	6	28
1964	A	NY	564	63	-9	-2	16	68
1965	A	NY	434	19	-13	-5	12	13
1966	A	NY	390	36	-2	0	11	45
1967	A	NY	548	43	-4	-8	16	47
1968	A	NY	542	33	-10	-8	16	31

more generous for Mays than Mantle, even when they had approximately equal playing time. The extra five runs given to Mays for his peak seasons in 1962–66 seem appropriate, given just how much more competitive the more or less fully integrated National League was than the barely integrated American League of Mantle's peak seasons through 1961. If you sort the seasons in descending order of overall value and subtract the cumulative difference between Mays and Mantle (see the "Cum.Diff." column in the table on the next page), it appears that Mantle has a very slight edge, well within measurement error, for the top three or four years.

If one wants to define "peak" as the player's three best seasons, in whatever order, Mantle's ten run advantage might mean something. But if the definition is altered to be the three best *consecutive* seasons, Mays' 1964–66 (313 RAR) is just so close to Mantle's 1955–57 (316) that the only reasonable thing to say is that they're tied. And once you go to four consecutive seasons, Mays starts to pull away.

Mays has been overshadowed since his retirement by Mantle's personal charm and tragic but inspirational end, and perhaps as well by the statistical revolution in baseball, which quantified how much better Mantle was as a hitter, due to his substantially higher on-base percentage. Yet if I could pick one player from history around which to build a franchise, it would be Mays. No one else ever demonstrated his breadth of skills, intensity, durability, and adaptability. He would have been the dominant player of any time and place, as he was of his own, because he would have found a way to be.

Mays v. Mantle in Descending Order of Best
Seasons

Mays		Mantle		Mays - Mantle Cum.Diff.
Year	RAR	Year	RAR	
1964	112	1957	116	-4
1954	107	1961	109	-5
1962	103	1956	107	-10
1965	102	1955	93	-1
1966	99	1958	80	17
1958	99	1964	68	48
1963	96	1962	68	76
1957	91	1952	63	104
1956	77	1959	61	120
1959	77	1960	61	136
1961	74	1954	52	158
1960	73	1967	47	184
1955	68	1966	45	207
1968	67	1953	40	234
1971	59	1968	31	262
1967	55	1963	28	289
1970	54	1965	13	331
1951	45	1951	2	374
1952	27			401
1969	23			424
1972	22			446
1973	6			452

Some combination of the Walsh and Smith defensive runs estimates for runners held would boost Andruw Jones to close to 250 career defensive runs, and a TPAR total comfortably ahead of Mays. Jones was always a power hitter, typically hitting thirty-five homers a year. Prior to the 2005 season he

Number One: Andruw Jones

Year	L	Tm	IP	PO8 runs	A8 runs	v-Tm	Runs
1996	N	ATL	71	3	0	3	3
1997	N	ATL	415	15	3	8	18
1998	N	ATL	1373	28	6	-2	33
1999	N	ATL	1447	46	2	2	48
2000	N	ATL	1430	19	-1	1	19
2001	N	ATL	1435	26	0	0	26
2002	N	ATL	1358	23	-2	2	21
2003	N	ATL	1329	24	-1	5	23
2004	N	ATL	1347	8	1	-1	9
2005	N	ATL	1366	-6	2	-3	-4
2006	N	ATL	1317	-1	-2	-4	-4
2007	N	ATL	1346	11	-1	-3	10
2008	N	LA	496	4	2	-1	6
Total			14732	199	9	7	208

worked out, bulked up, hit fifty-one homeruns—and had his first negative DRA rating. His fielding career in center appears to be over.

With the possible exception of Richie Ashburn, Andruw Jones in his peak seasons (however defined) recorded more putouts relative to his contemporary centerfielders, given the total number of batted allowed by his team's pitchers, than anyone in history. With the possible exceptions of Tris Speaker and Paul Blair, Andruw Jones has also played the most shallow centerfield relative to his contemporary centerfielders than anyone in history.

The two facts are connected: Jones has positioned himself to catch a high number of short high flies that would normally be caught by middle-infielders. He obviously shouldn't be given credit for making plays on what amount to automatic outs that could readily be made by any one of two or three fielders. DRA has an adjustment that takes this into account, and it has a substantial impact on Jones's DRA rating, so I believe that the numbers for Jones reasonably measure his real value to his teams. The $Smith(R(t,s,d))$ estimate for 1997–99, which uses batted ball data and calculation methods that would generally avoid crediting Jones for a lot of runs saved by taking discretionary chances, is nearly identical for that period.

Despite his disappointingly early decline, Andruw Jones deserves to be elected to the Hall of Fame. Based on Sean Smiths' Wins Above Replacement, Jones had four seasons of MVP-candidate value (1998–2000 and 2005), three exceptionally strong all-star quality seasons (2002–03 and 2006), and three more seasons that were well above average (1997, 2001, and 2004). As he would have had at most only four borderline all-star quality seasons without his well-documented defensive value, it will be interesting to see if and when Hall of Fame voters recognize his excellence.

Second Base

As we will see at shortstop, second base became much more competitive during the Contemporary Era due to the influx of talent from Latin America. Ratings generally compressed toward the mean, and Gold Glove voters couldn't identify the great fielders.

Contemporary Era

MCS	First	Last	IP	Runs	Δ
2001	Pokey	Reese	4223	96	Δ
1994	Mark	Lemke	7674	82	
2002	Craig	Counsell	4298	59	
2004	M.	Grudzielanek	9271	52	
1999	Fernando	Vina	8733	51	Δ
1999	Rey	Sanchez	3724	50	Δ
1993	Jody	Reed	8870	45	
2002	Tony	Graffanino	4100	40	
2000	Damion	Easley	9736	38	Δ
2005	Jose	Valentin	1265	37	
1994	Luis	Sojo	3322	34	Δ
2005	Placido	Polanco	8379	29	Δ
1999	Keith	Lockhart	3674	29	
1994	Pat	Kelly	4492	29	
2004	Marcus	Giles	6319	28	
2004	Alex	Cora	3339	26	
2003	Neifi	Perez	1752	26	Δ
1996	Luis	Alicea	8010	25	Δ
2004	Adam	Kennedy	10045	25	
1996	Roberto	Alomar	19871	21	Δ
2002	Jerry	Hairston	4522	21	Δ
2002	Marlon	Anderson	5442	17	Δ

(*continued*)

Contemporary Era *(continued)*

MCS	First	Last	IP	Runs	Δ
1995	Mark	McLemore	9935	12	Δ
2000	Warren	Morris	3323	9	
1998	Randy	Velarde	5214	7	
2001	Miguel	Cairo	5630	6	Δ
1993	Bip	Roberts	3734	6	Δ
2003	Junior	Spivey	3543	5	Δ
1998	David	Bell	3273	4	
1998	Quilvio	Veras	6143	4	Δ
2004	Ronnie	Belliard	9861	3	Δ
1996	Mickey	Morandini	10172	3	
2004	Mark	Loretta	6551	2	
1995	Carlos	Baerga	8947	1	Δ
1999	Eric	Young	10857	0	Δ
1993	Mariano	Duncan	4566	-3	Δ
2000	Tony	Womack	4403	-5	Δ
2001	Ray	Durham	15711	-7	Δ
1995	Brent	Gates	3890	-8	
1999	Edgardo	Alfonzo	4573	-10	Δ
1996	Jeff	Frye	4372	-11	
2001	Jeff	Kent	17056	-11	
1996	Mark	Lewis	3265	-12	
2002	Michael	Young	3566	-14	
2001	Carlos	Febles	4036	-14	Δ
2005	Jose	Castillo	3219	-16	Δ
2004	D'Angelo	Jimenez	3514	-17	Δ
1995	Carlos	Garcia	4358	-18	Δ
2003	Luis	Rivas	4804	-24	
1999	Bret	Boone	15219	-25	
1995	Terry	Shumpert	3264	-31	Δ
2000	Jay	Bell	3435	-33	
1997	Mike	Lansing	7421	-34	
1999	Jose	Offerman	4966	-39	Δ
1995	Delino	DeShields	11736	-42	Δ
2003	Luis	Castillo	13799	-45	Δ
2002	Todd	Walker	8272	-55	
1995	Chuck	Knoblauch	11802	-64	
2003	Alfonso	Soriano	6754	-66	Δ
1995	Joey	Cora	7825	-78	
2002	Jose	Vidro	8707	-79	Δ
1999	Craig	Biggio	17155	-111	

The three most overrated multi-Gold Glove winners of the Contemporary Era have been Alomar (ten), Boone (four), and Biggio (five). Luis Castillo (three) has not been a good fielder on a career basis, but somehow the voters picked out the three seasons (2003–05) in which he fielded as well as a legitimate Gold Glove candidate.

Luis Castillo

Year	L	Tm	IP	Runs	v-Tm
1996	N	FLA	352	-2	0
1997	N	FLA	576	-1	-6
1998	N	FLA	378	-5	-4
1999	N	FLA	1068	-11	-7
2000	N	FLA	1176	-6	0
2001	N	FLA	1157	-1	2
2002	N	FLA	1258	-8	3
2003	N	FLA	1312	13	6
2004	N	FLA	1274	8	-1
2005	N	FLA	1012	11	11
2006	A	MIN	1239	3	3
2007	A	MIN	726	-11	-9
2007	N	NY	432	-15	-12
2008	N	NY	690	-7	-6
2009	N	NY	1147	-14	3
Total			13799	-45	-19

Roberto Alomar also had a nice three-year run of good-to-excellent fielding (1996–99).

Roberto Alomar

Year	L	Tm	IP	Runs	v-Tm
1988	N	SD	1244	12	8
1989	N	SD	1399	8	-2
1990	N	SD	1226	6	0
1991	A	TOR	1419	0	0
1992	A	TOR	1275	-12	-8
1993	A	TOR	1305	-5	0
1994	A	TOR	873	2	1
1995	A	TOR	1125	-6	0
1996	A	BAL	1218	26	6
1997	A	BAL	897	9	6
1998	A	BAL	1236	10	5
1999	A	CLE	1306	8	4
2000	A	CLE	1309	2	4
2001	A	CLE	1324	0	-1
2002	N	NY	1266	-18	-4
2003	N	NY	584	-10	0
2003	A	CHI	557	-2	-3
2004	A	CHI	103	0	-1
2004	N	ARI	203	-8	-4
Total			19871	21	12

The other six Gold Gloves (1991–95 and 2000–01) were not deserved, though it's nice to imagine that, having been given his early Gold Gloves, he was encouraged to improve his performance, rather like students who have been shown to improve when prompted to self-identify as capable and hard working.

Brett Boone won all of his Gold Gloves with his bat. His first Gold Glove coincided with the first season in which he hit more than twenty home runs.

Brett Boone

Year	L	Tm	IP	Runs	v-Tm
1992	A	SEA	278	0	1
1993	A	SEA	622	-10	-8
1994	N	CIN	892	-7	2
1995	N	CIN	1214	-2	3
1996	N	CIN	1206	7	4
1997	N	CIN	1115	8	-1
1998	N	CIN	1358	1	-3
1999	N	ATL	1297	12	0
2000	N	SD	1097	-17	-6
2001	A	SEA	1370	2	2
2002	A	SEA	1317	-13	-5
2003	A	SEA	1375	10	2
2004	A	SEA	1309	-14	-2
2005	A	SEA	647	-8	-8
2005	A	MIN	122	5	5
Total			15219	-25	-16

The remaining three, from 2002 to 2004, can only be attributed to a second, four-year power surge he enjoyed, beginning in 2001, when he turned thirty-two and led the league in runs batted in.

Craig Biggio

Year	L	Tm	IP	Runs	v-Tm
1991	N	HOU	25	0	0
1992	N	HOU	1408	-27	-1
1993	N	HOU	1353	3	4
1994	N	HOU	980	-5	1
1995	N	HOU	1271	-15	-1
1996	N	HOU	1409	-15	2
1997	N	HOU	1384	18	4
1998	N	HOU	1368	-9	2
1999	N	HOU	1351	-18	-10
2000	N	HOU	853	2	8
2001	N	HOU	1345	-16	2
2002	N	HOU	1237	-21	-3
2005	N	HOU	1172	8	5
2006	N	HOU	1062	-1	-4
2007	N	HOU	937	-15	-2
Total			17155	-111	5

Craig Biggio may have been the only middle-infielder in history who began his major league career as a catcher. He caught almost four hundred games—and made the All Star team—before moving to second base. When interviewed in 2003 by Jayson Stark, Biggio said, "Going from catcher to second base was like telling me I'm going to be president of Wal Mart tomorrow." Biggio went down a list of new skills he had to acquire having absolutely nothing to do with being a catcher: fielding batted balls coming toward you rather than going away from you, positioning, cutoffs, relays, and double play pivots. In his own words, it took him "two-and-a-half to three years" to get even "comfortable" in the position.

The Gold Glove voters apparently sensed when he got comfortable, as they awarded him his first Gold Glove in his third full-time season at second, 1994. Actually, I doubt they were that perceptive. Biggio probably got his first Gold Glove that year because he hit over .300 for the first time and led the league in doubles and stolen bases. $Smith(R(t,s,d))$ agrees with DRA that Biggio was still below average in 1994, and also agrees that the only season Biggio deserved the Gold Glove was in 1997. However, over the entire 1992–99 period, $Smith(R(t,s,d))$, which is based on Retrosheet batted ball data, estimates that Biggio was average overall (almost exactly zero defensive runs), whereas DRA estimates –68 defensive runs. Retrosheet does not have batted ball data after 1999. The two Smith systems applicable to the Retrosheet data available in 2000–02 and 2003 onward, $Smith(pgor,bod)$ and $Smith(R(t),f,bh,ph)$ respectively, are much closer to the DRA estimate: those systems charge Biggio –34 defensive runs at second from 2000 to 2007; DRA –43 defensive runs.

So the argument that Biggio was only slightly below average in his career at second base, rather than being a downright poor fielder, comes down to saying that $Smith(R(t,s,d))$, by virtue of being based on batted ball data, must provide a more accurate assessment of Biggio's 1992–99 performance than DRA. Further research is needed, but there is one very good reason to believe that DRA is closer to the mark.

In chapter three, we discussed a couple of technical issues with certain batted ball systems. In particular, we highlighted that some batted ball systems use what I called a "mixed method" calculation for shared locations on the field. For example, under the mixed method, extra plays *made* in the batted ball location 'slice' of the field in the gap between third and short by a *good* third baseman, such as a Scott Brosius or Robin Ventura, are effectively mixed together with the extra plays *not* made by a *poor* shortstop, such as Jeter, in the same slice of the field shared by the third baseman and shortstop. The net effect of the mixed method when a good and a poor fielder share the same location is that the defensive runs estimate for the good fielder is pulled down and the defensive runs estimate for the poor fielder is pulled up.

Back in 2003 I worked with an analyst who had used the mixed method for his own batted ball data system and had been coming up with surprisingly average ratings for Jeter when he was playing next to Brosius and Ventura. When we eliminated the mixed method, Jeter was restored to his normal rate of giving up at least ten runs per season. Yes, Brosius and Ventura were effectively subsidizing Jeter under the mixed method by close to ten runs per season.

I think we have exactly the same issue with Biggio, who played next to one of the very best fielding first basemen of all time, Jeff Bagwell. The Killer Bees shared the mirror image of the gap between third and short: the gap between first and second. And $Smith(R(t,s,d))$ *applies the mixed method to that gap.* Over the same 2002–09 period, $Smith(R(t,s,d))$ rates Bagwell only +42 defensive runs, about +5 defensive runs per season. I believe that if $Smith(R(t,s,d))$ (correctly) abandoned the mixed method, Biggio's defensive runs over that period would approach the –8 defensive runs per season indicated by DRA, and Bagwell would be properly credited with something more like +10 to +15 defensive runs per season in his prime.

Craig Biggio will be a first-ballot Hall-of-Famer, because he eventually collected over 3000 hits. He probably deserves to be in the Hall of Fame because of his exceptional doubles power, his very good 'total' on-base percentage (taking into account reaching first base by being hit by a pitch, reaching base on errors, and avoiding hitting into double plays), his excellent base running, and his exemplary willingness to play wherever his team most needed him. He just wasn't a good fielding second baseman. Simply developing into an adequate—if generally well below average—second baseman was a historic accomplishment.

Modern Era

MCS	First	Last	IP	Runs	Δ
1984	Glenn	Hubbard	11206	137	
1979	Bobby	Grich	15155	133	
1984	Willie	Randolph	18675	118	Δ
1986	Lou	Whitaker	19069	101	Δ
1976	Rennie	Stennett	8922	101	Δ
1969	Dick	Green	9542	98	
1982	Julio	Cruz	9409	85	Δ
1982	Frank	White	17808	83	Δ
1989	Ryne	Sandberg	17233	79	
1980	Manny	Trillo	12798	72	Δ
1974	Ted	Sizemore	10832	71	
1990	Robby	Thompson	10720	69	
1989	Tony	Phillips	5844	66	Δ
1991	Mike	Gallego	4442	61	
1971	Tommy	Helms	9640	58	
1989	Harold	Reynolds	11279	54	Δ
1978	Mike	Tyson	4678	53	
1991	Jose	Lind	8901	47	Δ
1975	Dave	Cash	11349	44	Δ
1991	Scott	Fletcher	5725	38	
1985	Jim	Gantner	12237	35	
1979	Phil	Garner	8220	34	
1990	Jeff	Treadway	4104	32	
1972	Sandy	Alomar	9525	30	Δ
1981	Rob	Wilfong	6232	24	
1970	Tim	Cullen	3223	24	

(*continued*)

Modern Era (*continued*)

MCS	First	Last	IP	Runs	Δ
1970	Davey	Johnson	10289	21	
1990	Jose	Oquendo	4975	21	Δ
1986	Johnny	Ray	10993	21	Δ
1975	Jack	Brohamer	5127	19	
1979	Larry	Milbourne	3252	17	Δ
1984	Ron	Oester	9753	13	
1977	Rob	Andrews	3315	11	
1979	Bump	Wills	6912	10	Δ
1984	Jack	Perconte	3227	10	
1975	Marty	Perez	3490	9	
1990	Billy	Ripken	6169	7	
1973	Tito	Fuentes	10759	7	Δ
1981	Paul	Molitor	3458	6	
1979	Dave	McKay	3032	6	
1987	S.	Lombardozzi	3261	5	
1985	Vance	Law	3026	5	
1981	Jerry	Royster	3057	2	Δ
1984	Tim	Flannery	3978	-1	
1977	Bob	Randall	3372	-1	
1974	Denny	Doyle	7485	-2	
1983	Juan	Bonilla	3244	-3	
1973	Gary	Sutherland	5584	-3	
1969	Dick	McAuliffe	7960	-4	
1987	Bill	Doran	11417	-8	
1975	Lenny	Randle	3569	-14	Δ
1987	Donnie	Hill	3395	-14	
1971	Rod	Carew	9463	-17	Δ
1971	Ken	Boswell	4544	-17	
1979	Rodney	Scott	3611	-18	Δ
1973	Dave	Nelson	3666	-19	Δ
1972	Ted	Kubiak	3295	-19	
1974	Pedro	Garcia	4620	-20	Δ
1976	Derrel	Thomas	4806	-20	Δ
1984	Tony	Bernazard	8394	-23	Δ
1969	Glenn	Beckert	10833	-25	
1978	Davey	Lopes	12032	-25	Δ
1983	Damaso	Garcia	8031	-26	
1987	Tim	Teufel	6170	-27	
1990	Julio	Franco	5696	-29	Δ
1970	Horace	Clarke	9519	-29	Δ
1973	Doug	Griffin	5166	-33	
1980	Doug	Flynn	7404	-33	
1986	Wally	Backman	6129	-40	
1986	Tom	Herr	11890	-40	
1979	Jerry	Remy	9615	-40	
1986	Marty	Barrett	7696	-40	
1981	Rich	Dauer	7727	-50	
1970	Cookie	Rojas	11813	-52	
1978	Duane	Kuiper	7660	-56	

(*continued*)

Modern Era (*continued*)

MCS	First	Last	IP	Runs	Δ
1991	Nelson	Liriano	4437	-63	Δ
1969	Mike	Andrews	6679	-66	
1972	Felix	Millan	12667	-67	Δ
1989	Jerry	Browne	4894	-69	Δ
1988	Juan	Samuel	10117	-92	Δ
1976	Jorge	Orta	5837	-95	Δ
1974	Joe	Morgan	21543	-124	Δ
1987	Steve	Sax	14644	-129	

The ratings at second base for the Modern Era generally conform to expectations. There is just one major surprise and a couple of minor ones.

Joe Morgan

Year	L	Tm	IP	Runs	v-Tm
1963	N	HOU	54	-1	0
1964	N	HOU	95	-5	-4
1965	N	HOU	1409	-7	-1
1966	N	HOU	1038	-10	6
1967	N	HOU	1127	0	4
1968	N	HOU	43	-4	-3
1969	N	HOU	1138	-20	-1
1970	N	HOU	1254	-4	-1
1971	N	HOU	1381	4	0
1972	N	CIN	1338	-2	-1
1973	N	CIN	1341	7	1
1974	N	CIN	1215	5	3
1975	N	CIN	1205	8	-6
1976	N	CIN	1127	-17	5
1977	N	CIN	1245	-10	1
1978	N	CIN	1011	-21	-7
1979	N	CIN	1018	-17	-3
1980	N	HOU	1037	-6	4
1981	N	SF	744	-8	2
1982	N	SF	1034	-8	6
1983	N	PHI	919	3	6
1984	A	OAK	771	-13	-1
Total			21543	-124	10

Joe Morgan received his Gold Gloves from 1973 through 1977 for many of the same reasons Jeter has received his. During his Gold Glove run, Morgan had five of his six highest batting averages, was by far the greatest offensive force among major league middle infielders, twice led the league in fielding percentage, always finished in the top five in stolen bases, was perceived as a leader of the most dominant team in his league, and won back-to-back MVP awards. In all fairness, even if we credit him with almost exactly average fielding performance during his peak years (1972–76), which we do above, those were the greatest five consecutive seasons of any ballplayer after Mays and before Bonds.

Still, he was not in fact a good fielder. Morgan did lead the league once in assists, in 1971 when he was with the Astros, but only because that team had a ground ball staff. Morgan led second basemen in putouts twice. Putouts by infielders should be ignored, because almost all infield putouts are force outs (for which the assisting player deserves credit) or catches of fly balls or pop ups that are more or less automatic outs, for which DRA credits the pitcher. Morgan may have been a 'ball hog' on those pop ups and fly balls. Being a ball hog is not a character flaw, and doesn't hurt your team, but it doesn't help your team either. Seeing Joe catching all those fly balls and pop ups just might have contributed to his reputation as a top fielder.

Smith(pgor,bod) rates Morgan negatively as well, though about eighty runs more favorably than DRA. About twenty-five runs of that difference can be explained by the fact that Morgan made fifty-four fewer errors over the course of his career, given his total chances, than the league average fielder would have, and *Smith(pgor,bod)* generally (and incorrectly) gives an extra half a run credit per error avoided, on top of credit for the play made. That still leaves fifty-five runs to account for.

I think I can get the difference down to about forty runs. For reasons of simplicity, when first developing the DRA model I did not include unassisted *ground ball* putouts at second, third, and short, because they are so rare. I subsequently received more data on unassisted ground ball putouts for infielders other than first basemen as this book was being finalized, and it appears that in the latter half of his career, Morgan's team (the Reds) had about thirty more unassisted ground ball putouts at second than the league-average team. Perhaps when fielding ground balls near the bag, Joe grew to prefer running to record the putout rather than tossing to the shortstop. If we credit Joe with those extra thirty ground out plays, we should credit him with at least fifteen runs.

Taking into consideration Smith's estimates and DRA, I'm reasonably confident Morgan caused his teams to allow about eighty runs more than they otherwise would have, and probably something closer to a hundred. He's still one of the twenty or so greatest players, at any position, who ever played the game.

Morgan was overrated as a fielder partly because people could see that he didn't make errors, that he hustled, and that he was fast. There actually is a particular skill relevant to second baseman that does not depend on "invisible" range that we've been talking so much about: making the double play pivot. And if you're adept at the pivot, it's good for your job security at second; if you're not, it's not.

Tommy Herr

Year	L	Tm	IP	Runs	v-Tm
1979	N	STL	29	0	0
1980	N	STL	388	-1	-1
1981	N	STL	925	5	0
1982	N	STL	1088	6	7
1983	N	STL	693	-7	7
1984	N	STL	1247	-2	-1
1985	N	STL	1404	-16	0
1986	N	STL	1331	-6	0
1987	N	STL	1168	-14	-6
1988	N	STL	131	-5	-5
1988	A	MIN	625	3	3
1989	N	PHI	1213	11	2
1990	N	NY	223	-4	-1
1990	N	PHI	947	-2	-6
1991	N	SF	99	-3	-3
1991	N	NY	378	-7	0
Total			11890	-40	-2

Tommy Herr was terrific at turning two, and accordingly kept his job as a second baseman. Rod Carew was perceived as awkward around the bag, and

Rod Carew

Year	L	Tm	IP	Runs	v-Tm
1967	A	MIN	1151	-5	-1
1968	A	MIN	982	-9	-4
1969	A	MIN	965	-7	-9
1970	A	MIN	377	-9	-9
1971	A	MIN	1209	-8	4
1972	A	MIN	1184	7	3
1973	A	MIN	1241	2	3
1974	A	MIN	1285	1	2
1975	A	MIN	1038	10	4
1976	A	MIN	13	0	0
1977	A	MIN	6	1	1
1978	A	MIN	5	0	0
1983	A	LA	6	-1	-1
Total			9463	-17	-6

got shifted to first. Though turning double plays is important, preventing hits is slightly more so. Carew had better range than Herr, and was overall a more effective fielder. Since it is so much easier to find a good hitting first baseman than a good hitting second baseman, Carew's teams would have derived considerably more value from his services by keeping him at second and, if need be, averting their eyes when he turned double plays, which he somehow managed to do at close to a league-average rate anyway, at least according to *Smith(pgor,bod)*.

Transitional Era

MCS	First	Last	IP	Runs	Δ
1963	Bill	Mazeroski	18335	149	
1967	Bobby	Knoop	9295	86	
1947	S.	Stirnweiss	6656	81	
1956	Gil	McDougald	4678	61	
1950	Jackie	Robinson	6454	57	Δ
1960	Don	Blasingame	11005	53	
1953	W.	Terwilliger	4964	51	
1962	Jerry	Kindall	3933	44	
1952	Red	Schoendienst	15863	41	
1948	Jerry	Priddy	10238	41	
1965	Julian	Javier	12958	39	Δ
1956	Danny	O'Connell	5971	36	
1954	Bobby	Avila	9877	34	Δ
1965	Hal	Lanier	3409	34	
1954	Billy	Goodman	5183	23	
1962	Chuck	Schilling	4286	23	
1947	Eddie	Stanky	9859	21	
1957	Jim	Gilliam	8626	20	Δ
1962	Chuck	Cottier	3752	18	
1955	Gene	Baker	3968	17	Δ
1963	Jerry	Lumpe	9145	16	
1951	Jerry	Coleman	4544	15	
1968	Jim	Lefebvre	5157	15	
1954	Granny	Hamner	4677	13	
1962	Billy	Moran	3790	12	
1958	Billy	Gardner	7034	8	
1960	Frank	Bolling	12984	6	
1956	Ted	Lepcio	3168	5	
1950	Cass	Michaels	6905	4	
1953	Davey	Williams	3903	2	
1949	Bobby	Adams	3097	-5	
1960	Charlie	Neal	5520	-6	Δ
1963	Chuck	Hiller	4295	-7	
1952	Eddie	Miksis	3047	-8	
1948	Pete	Suder	6867	-11	
1965	Jerry	Adair	6746	-17	
1966	Bernie	Allen	7209	-18	
1948	Connie	Ryan	8540	-19	
1962	Joey	Amalfitano	3096	-19	
1958	Pete	Runnels	5314	-20	

(continued)

Transitional Era (*continued*)

1956	Billy	Martin	6119	-26	
1953	Bobby	Young	5647	-26	
1962	Jake	Wood	3518	-33	Δ
1957	Nellie	Fox	20214	-35	
1965	Pete	Rose	5408	-37	
1964	Tony	Taylor	12420	-56	Δ
1968	Ron	Hunt	10509	-57	
1962	Bobby	Richardson	11548	-85	
1958	Johnny	Temple	11132	-93	

James Nelson ("Nellie") Fox presents my toughest case, at any position, and I can't say I can give you a good answer. Fox was a twelve-time all-star, a three-time Gold Glove winner, and the American League Most Valuable Player in 1959. DRA would not find the 1957 Gold Glove objectionable, and would support a Gold Glove in 1955 if the award had existed (the first year was 1957). Other than those two seasons, DRA cannot find a meaningfully above-average season for Nellie, and rates him a poor fielder after 1960. In contrast, *Smith(pgor,bod)* indicates Fox was always an above-average fielder and a top flight fielder from 1954 through 1960.

Nellie Fox

Year	L	Tm	IP	Runs	v-Tm	*Smith (pgor,bod)*
1947	A	PHI	0	0		0
1948	A	PHI	17	0		-1
1949	A	PHI	588	6		4
1950	A	CHI	1085	-7		1
1951	A	CHI	1349	-2		7
1952	A	CHI	1355	3	-4	8
1953	A	CHI	1369	-3	-1	0
1954	A	CHI	1373	-8	0	11
1955	A	CHI	1364	24	-1	12
1956	A	CHI	1380	-8	0	-4
1957	A	CHI	1393	12	0	15
1958	A	CHI	1377	-8	1	7
1959	A	CHI	1406	1	1	21
1960	A	CHI	1324	2	1	16
1961	A	CHI	1382	-11	1	4
1962	A	CHI	1338	-11	-4	6
1963	A	CHI	1148	-12	-3	10
1964	N	HOU	962	-13	-4	-5
1965	N	HOU	6	0	0	0
Total			20214	-35	-12	112

I can explain about forty runs of the difference in career value: Nellie made eighty-two fewer errors, given his total chances, than the average second baseman of this time would have. Again, this causes Nellie to be overrated by about forty runs under *Smith*(*pgor,bod*), but that still leaves a gap of approximately a hundred runs, perhaps the largest inexplicable gap at any position. Fox led league in putouts ten straight times, but his teams were not significantly above average in unassisted *ground ball* putouts by second basemen, so the Joe Morgan adjustment discussed above would not help bridge the difference. It would appear that Nellie may have been a ball hog on infield fly outs, judging by his raw putout totals.

Even if the *Smith*(*pgor,bod*) estimate (+112 defensive runs) reduced for the over-crediting of errors (approximately −40 defensive runs) is correct, and I am not convinced that it is, that would leave Nellie with only +72 defensive runs. With the TPAR adjustment, that would only put him among the top 30 or 35 second basemen of all time. Good, but not great.

Nellie Fox led the league in singles eight times and almost never struck out, but also didn't walk that much and almost never homered. A somewhat similar hitter, though not as good, was Bobby Richardson, who also won multiple Gold Gloves.

Bobby Richardson

Year	L	Tm	IP	Runs	v-Tm
1955	A	NY	54	-4	-5
1956	A	NY	23	-2	-2
1957	A	NY	734	2	0
1958	A	NY	379	-1	-1
1959	A	NY	950	-5	-3
1960	A	NY	1123	-11	-11
1961	A	NY	1405	-15	0
1962	A	NY	1440	-3	1
1963	A	NY	1337	9	6
1964	A	NY	1430	-26	4
1965	A	NY	1404	-19	1
1966	A	NY	1270	-11	3
Total			11548	-85	-8

Richardson presents us with another massive gap between the DRA estimate of career defensive runs and the *Smith*(*pgor,bod*) estimate, which is essentially average. Richardson did not have a significantly better than average fielding percentage, so we can't bridge the gap, even partly, by backing out the different treatment of errors under *Smith*(*pgor,bod*). However, there is another factor, more difficult to reduce to a simple calculation but very real, that probably accounts for the difference. Under *Smith*(*pgor,bod*), a fielder is indirectly given partial credit for every additional fielding out made by his teammates and infield fly out generated by his pitchers. The 1960–64 Yankees converted by far the highest percentage of total balls in play into outs in their league over that time frame. Though the Yankees were a very poor fielding team in 1965–66, I'm fairly confident that overall Yankee team performance during 1960–66 explains most of the difference between DRA and *Smith(pgor,bod)*.

Perhaps the most direct proof that Richardson could not have been a superior fielder is that during five of the six seasons (1955–60) in which Richardson shared second base time with Gil McDougald, Gil outperformed Bobby (see the v-Tm numbers for Bobby (above) and Gil (below)), and Bobby never once outperformed Gil.

Gil McDougald

Year	L	Tm	IP	Runs	v-Tm
1951	A	NY	413	3	
1952	A	NY	317	-4	-6
1953	A	NY	109	-1	-1
1954	A	NY	735	8	0
1955	A	NY	1067	31	11
1956	A	NY	218	5	4
1957	A	NY	156	1	0
1958	A	NY	996	1	1
1959	A	NY	438	4	4
1960	A	NY	228	14	14
Total			4678	61	29

McDougald played wherever in the infield he was most needed. He started primarily at third, gradually spent more time at second, and in the middle of his career was more or less the Yankee shortstop between Rizzuto and Kubek. Though only particularly good at second, he did save another dozen or so runs at third and short. McDougald decided to retire at age thirty-two after being drafted by the newly-created Washington Senators in the expansion draft for the 1961 season.

Jackie Robinson

Year	L	Tm	IP	Runs	v-Tm
1948	N	BRO	1035	8	
1949	N	BRO	1409	14	
1950	N	BRO	1229	7	
1951	N	BRO	1261	27	
1952	N	BRO	1235	4	2
1953	N	BRO	69	2	1
1954	N	BRO	36	-1	-1
1955	N	BRO	10	-1	-1
1956	N	BRO	171	-3	-6
			6454	57	-3

Even more than McDougald, Jackie Robinson was the multi-positional player par excellence. Though he never played much at shortstop, and was only average at first base and in left field, he was outstanding at both second and third. Combined with his broad range of offensive contributions, Jackie's

Jackie Robinson at Third Base

Year	L	Tm	IP	Runs	v-Tm
1948	N	BRO	57	0	
1953	N	BRO	366	6	4
1954	N	BRO	377	5	3
1955	N	BRO	712	9	-5
1956	N	BRO	595	20	4
Total			2107	40	6

fielding enabled him to put together at least two seasons of historic aggregate value, far above standard MVP norms (1949 and 1951), three more seasons of clear MVP quality (1950, 1952, and 1953), and two very strong all-star quality seasons (1948 and 1956). He would have deserved to be a first-ballot Hall of Famer even if he hadn't played a leading role in desegregating not only baseball, but the entire country.

Live Ball Era

MCS	First	Last	IP	Runs	Δ
1928	Frankie	Frisch	15530	224	
1944	Joe	Gordon	13453	191	
1941	Lonny	Frey	8384	104	
1929	Max	Bishop	10491	89	
1931	Ski	Melillo	11447	75	
1938	Billy	Herman	15978	74	
1944	Bobby	Doerr	16405	74	
1924	Aaron	Ward	7044	67	
1927	Sparky	Adams	4697	54	
1929	Hughie	Critz	12862	53	
1935	Rabbit	Warstler	3831	50	
1923	Jimmy	Dykes	6354	45	
1929	Freddie	Maguire	5102	44	
1934	Jackie	Hayes	7735	38	
1933	Tony	Piet	4294	24	
1938	B.	Whitehead	6113	23	
1943	Mickey	Witek	3784	21	
1924	Bucky	Harris	11341	19	
1946	Eddie	Mayo	4635	18	
1928	George	Grantham	7210	18	
1923	Sam	Bohne	3114	15	
1933	C.	Gehringer	19396	14	
1946	Emil	Verban	6825	12	
1925	Rogers	Hornsby	13682	10	
1936	Odell	Hale	4333	10	

(*continued*)

Live Ball Era *(continued)*

MCS	First	Last	IP	Runs	Δ
1940	Jimmy	Brown	3419	9	
1939	Stu	Martin	3849	6	
1931	Johnny	Hodapp	3977	1	
1937	Pep	Young	4112	1	
1943	Jimmy	Bloodworth	7526	-2	
1924	Lew	Fonseca	3021	-2	
1924	Hod	Ford	5041	-2	
1925	Marty	McManus	8247	-6	
1945	Don	Johnson	4262	-6	
1942	Ray	Mack	6947	-6	
1935	Tony	Cuccinello	10380	-7	
1942	Pete	Coscarart	5610	-8	
1945	Don	Kolloway	5349	-9	
1929	R.	Maranville	4441	-14	
1928	Bill	Regan	5303	-19	
1920	Bill	Wambsganss	10442	-21	
1933	Bill	Cissell	4241	-23	
1946	Danny	Murtaugh	5171	-24	
1939	Don	Heffner	4936	-24	
1921	Johnny	Rawlings	6096	-34	
1932	Tony	Lazzeri	12868	-37	
1945	Johnny	Berardino	3847	-39	
1937	Alex	Kampouris	5208	-42	
1942	Frankie	Gustine	5837	-47	
1923	Cotton	Tierney	3916	-49	
1928	Bernie	Friberg	3617	-53	
1944	Don	Gutteridge	5042	-56	
1934	Buddy	Myer	11679	-88	
1929	Fresco	Thompson	5379	-118	

As far as fielding at second base is concerned, the Live Ball Era was the transitional era. Over the course of the Live Ball Era, second base gradually switched places with third base along the defensive spectrum to become the second most difficult fielding position after shortstop (leaving aside the sheer physical demands of catching). We'll discuss and deal with this issue when we get to our top ten list. Though the Frankie Frisch rating is probably about thirty runs too high, for reasons we'll explain later in this chapter, the ratings are more or less what you would expect.

In *Whatever Happened to the Hall of Fame?* Bill James argued that Buddy Myer (see next page), who did not make the Hall, was a more valuable player over the course of his career than his near contemporary over in the National League, Billy Herman (also on next page), who did. However, both players were approximately equal on offense, based on the various offensive runs models available on many websites, and DRA credits Herman with 150 more defensive runs.

Charles Solomon "Buddy" Myer began his career playing a little bit at third, short, second, and outfield, before settling in at second base. Although slightly below average for his first few full seasons there, he didn't have any really bad years until 1934–35, after which his innings played never returned to a full-time level. His stolen base data does suggest a slight slowing down.

Billy Herman

Year	L	Tm	IP	Runs
1931	N	CHI	227	-2
1932	N	CHI	1375	14
1933	N	CHI	1357	17
1934	N	CHI	1028	2
1935	N	CHI	1394	16
1936	N	CHI	1371	12
1937	N	CHI	1213	25
1938	N	CHI	1352	19
1939	N	CHI	1381	-7
1940	N	CHI	1230	2
1941	N	BRO	1133	0
1941	N	CHI	54	1
1942	N	BRO	1332	-6
1943	N	BRO	1038	-16
1946	N	BOS	329	-2
1946	N	BRO	118	0
1947	N	PIT	46	-1
Total			15978	74

Buddy Myer

Year	L	Tm	Runs	v-Tm
1927	A	BOS	11	0
1929	A	WAS	754	-8
1930	A	WAS	1125	-1
1931	A	WAS	1239	-11
1932	A	WAS	1220	-12
1933	A	WAS	1119	6
1934	A	WAS	1204	-24
1935	A	WAS	1347	-29
1936	A	WAS	393	-1
1937	A	WAS	1015	-8
1938	A	WAS	1039	0
1939	A	WAS	559	0
1940	A	WAS	507	-2
1941	A	WAS	150	1
Total			11679	-88

He hit a good many triples throughout his career, but that was probably mainly due to Griffith Stadium, which had a large outfield perfect for hitting triples. Ralph Berger wrote an interesting bio for Myer for the SABR website, where we learn that Myer was a unique combination of scholar, brawler, and banker: he refused to sign a baseball contract until he had finished college, started a couple of epic fist fights in the field, and became a successful mortgage banker after his playing days were over.

Dead Ball Era

MCS	First	Last	IP	Runs	Δ
1907	Nap	Lajoie	18043	147	
1909	Johnny	Evers	15246	136	
1904	Hobe	Ferris	9063	123	
1897	Cupid	Childs	9099	115	
1898	Bobby	Lowe	11565	104	
1909	Miller	Huggins	13429	67	
1916	Morrie	Rath	4495	67	
1896	Bid	McPhee	6958	59	
1917	Del	Pratt	14809	54	
1903	John	Farrell	3988	44	
1907	Whitey	Alperman	3165	41	
1911	Dick	Egan	5984	38	
1904	Billy	Gilbert	6322	35	
1910	Otto	Knabe	8853	34	
1905	Jimmy	Williams	10416	33	
1913	Dots	Miller	5789	30	
1917	Eddie	Collins	23503	19	
1917	George	Cutshaw	13376	19	
1916	Bert	Niehoff	3711	19	
1909	Amby	McConnell	3379	18	
1913	Dave	Shean	4915	13	
1912	Bill	Sweeney	4976	13	
1900	G.	DeMontreville	4241	2	
1903	Claude	Ritchey	12994	1	
1905	Danny	Murphy	7544	-3	
1909	John	Hummel	4750	-3	
1913	Steve	Yerkes	3562	-13	
1901	Kid	Gleason	13653	-13	
1915	Ray	Morgan	6086	-17	
1907	Germany	Schaefer	5128	-20	
1906	Ed	Abbaticchio	3642	-28	
1917	Buck	Herzog	4199	-28	
1910	Frank	LaPorte	4121	-30	
1914	Jim	Viox	3699	-31	
1900	Dick	Padden	6401	-32	
1906	Frank	Isbell	3095	-32	
1918	Ralph	Young	8780	-33	
1918	Joe	Gedeon	4974	-40	
1909	Jim	Delahanty	4290	-44	
1896	Bill	Hallman	7157	-44	
1898	Tom	Daly	9045	-72	
1897	Joe	Quinn	6576	-99	
1914	Larry	Doyle	14921	-187	

The most striking number belongs to Laughin' Larry Doyle.

Doyle appears to have cost his teams more runs in the field than any other second baseman in history. If one also takes into account that second base was the least demanding infield position (other than first base) before

Larry Doyle

Year	L	Tm	IP	Runs
1907	N	NY	543	-11
1908	N	NY	879	-3
1909	N	NY	1209	-22
1910	N	NY	1327	-18
1911	N	NY	1214	-31
1912	N	NY	1185	-10
1913	N	NY	1165	-10
1914	N	NY	1273	-30
1915	N	NY	1318	-28
1916	N	NY	1025	2
1916	N	CHI	99	0
1917	N	CHI	1060	3
1918	N	NY	675	-5
1919	N	NY	828	6
1920	N	NY	1121	-29
Total			14921	-187

the 1930s, and that competition was clearly much, much weaker than now, it is probably fair to say that Doyle was the worst fielding infielder (excluding first basemen) in history. *The Historical Abstract* reports that Doyle had spells in which he lost confidence in his ability to make the throw to first, as Chuck Knoblach did in the 1990s. Somewhere else I read that Doyle played too close to the bag at second, thereby letting more hits through the hole in right. Second basemen in general only gradually moved to their current standard position in the early part of the 20th century. Perhaps Doyle made this adjustment later in his career, because he seemed to solve his fielding problems during the last four years of the Dead Ball Era.

There is certainly one undiscovered great second baseman: Cupid Childs.

Cupid Childs

Year	L	Tm	IP	Runs
1893	N	CLE	1082	8
1894	N	CLE	1016	7
1895	N	CLE	1043	20
1896	N	CLE	1169	45
1897	N	CLE	979	19
1898	N	CLE	972	13
1899	N	STL	1084	-22
1900	N	CHI	1212	20
1901	N	CHI	543	5
Total			9099	115

Other than Bill Dahlen, Childs is probably the most underrated player of the Dead Ball Era. We're missing his first two seasons in the National League (1891–92) and his one season in the American Association (1890). Assuming he was only average in the field those years, and adding his career offensive runs relative to his position, as estimated by Smith at baseballprojection.com, Cupid Childs was at least 40 wins above average over the course of his relatively short career, well above the normal Hall of Fame standard for career value. The blip in 1899 is easily explained: Childs contracted malaria, which not only severely affected his fielding, as seen above, but also his hitting.

Courtesy of Jimmy Keenan of SABR, we have this glimpse of Childs as he began his career in the minor leagues:

> Childs is the most curiously built man in the baseball business: he is about as wide as he is long …, yet there are few men in the league who can get over the ground faster than the 'dumpling'. … When he reported to the Kalamazoo club in the Tristate League in 1888 … he came in on a 'side-door Pullman' and presented himself to the management of the 'Celery Eaters' and asked for a trial. The manager thought he was joking after looking at his short length and broad girth, telling him he would make a better fat man in a side show than a ball player. Showing them he was anxious for a trial he was told to go to the grounds and practice with the rest of the team. A search was made for a uniform that would fit him, but none could be found, the only thing of that nature large enough for him being a pair of divided skirts, which he put on, cutting them off at the knees. His appearance with this costume on can be imagined and was so ludicrous that it threatened to break up the practice. However, as soon as he got out on the diamond and began to practice they began to open eyes and wonder. Such stops and throws were made as they never saw before and with such ease and grace that all were at once convinced he was a wonder. The management signed him on the spot and at a good salary, a move they never regretted, as his playing was the sensation of league all the season. Besides being one of the greatest ball players in the business, he is said to be one of the best humored, not a single instance of his ever losing his temper in a game being on record. *The Chicago Tribune*, March 25, 1900.

Childs has been underrated—no, worse than underrated, completely forgotten—because he played in the nineteenth century; because his real offensive skill was in drawing walks, which weren't even counted for batters when he was playing; because his defensive skill, though acknowledged by all who saw him play, was obscured by the statistical record he left behind, which shows him leading the league in errors more often than in any other category; and maybe also because he looked funny and had a silly-sounding name.

We close out the Dead Ball Era discussion with a brief look at part of the career of one of the second baseman with the greatest reputation (and most impressive fielding statistics) in the nineteenth century.

Bid McPhee

Year	L	Tm	IP	Runs
1893	N	CIN	1127	28
1894	N	CIN	1091	21
1895	N	CIN	1045	-7
1896	N	CIN	970	12
1897	N	CIN	705	8
1898	N	CIN	1136	-7
1899	N	CIN	885	4
Total			6958	59

Bid McPhee was the last man to play second without a glove. The table shows his performance only from the age of thirty-three onward; given his success as an older player, it is very easy to believe he saved another couple of hundred runs prior to 1893. That said, he played the first half of his career in the weaker, so-called major league, the American Association, which dissolved after the 1891 season. I believe that the level of competition was simply far too low to permit us to compare players from that time with players throughout the rest of major league history. Opinions on this point differ, however, and perhaps analysts will adapt DRA to periods before 1893.

Top Forty Second Basemen of All Time

MCS	First	Last	IP	Runs	Δ	TPAR
1928	Frankie	Frisch	15530	224		187
1944	Joe	Gordon	13453	191		162
1963	Bill	Mazeroski	18335	149		130
1984	Glenn	Hubbard	11206	137		129
1979	Bobby	Grich	15155	133		122
1984	Willie	Randolph	18675	118	Δ	109
1907	Nap	Lajoie	18043	147		99
2001	Pokey	Reese	4223	96	Δ	96
1986	Lou	Whitaker	19069	101	Δ	93
1909	Johnny	Evers	15246	136		90
1976	Rennie	Stennett	8922	101	Δ	88
1969	Dick	Green	9542	98		82
1994	Mark	Lemke	7674	82		79
1982	Julio	Cruz	9409	85	Δ	76
1982	Frank	White	17808	83	Δ	74
1989	Ryne	Sandberg	17233	79		74
1904	Hobe	Ferris	9063	123		73
1941	Lonny	Frey	8384	104		73

(continued)

Top Forty Second Basemen of All Time (*continued*)

MCS	First	Last	IP	Runs	Δ	TPAR
1967	Bobby	Knoop	9295	86		69
1990	Robby	Thompson	10720	69		64
1897	Cupid	Childs	9099	115		62
1980	Manny	Trillo	12798	72	Δ	62
2002	Craig	Counsell	4298	59		60
1989	Tony	Phillips	5844	66	Δ	60
1974	Ted	Sizemore	10832	71		58
1991	Mike	Gallego	4442	61		56
2004	M.	Grudzielanek	9271	52		54
1947	S.	Stirnweiss	6656	81		54
1929	Max	Bishop	10491	89		52
1898	Bobby	Lowe	11565	104		52
1999	Fernando	Vina	8733	51	Δ	51
1999	Rey	Sanchez	3724	50	Δ	49
1989	Harold	Reynolds	11279	54	Δ	48
1944	Bobby	Doerr	16405	74		45
1971	Tommy	Helms	9640	58		43
1991	Jose	Lind	8901	47	Δ	42
1978	Mike	Tyson	4678	53		42
1938	Billy	Herman	15978	74		42
2002	Tony	Graffanino	4100	40		41
1993	Jody	Reed	8870	45		41

During the Dead Ball Era, runs were so hard to come by that teams almost automatically sacrificed a runner at first to second, or tried a hit and run, or simply went for a stolen base, so double plays were relatively rare. When the live ball arrived, batting averages and walks went up and steals and sacrifices went down, setting up more double play opportunities. Sometime in the 1930s, teams came to expect their middle infielders, particularly second basemen, to be proficient at turning two, and second base became a much more demanding fielding position than it had been before.

One way to estimate this is by looking at the average *offensive* production of second basemen throughout history. The idea is that the more demanding the position, the smaller the pool of players with the skills to field it. With a smaller pool of players to draw from, compromises on offense become necessary to fill the position. The net differences in average offensive value indirectly reflect the difficulty of finding enough players to play the more difficult fielding positions, and thus, as a practical matter, how much more difficult the position is.

Michael Schell's book, *Baseball's All-Time Best Sluggers*, has a chart comparing the average offensive runs per 550 plate appearances for players at each of the positions. Second basemen were only five or so offensive runs below average during the Dead Ball Era and the 1920s. From 1931 through 1946, second basemen declined to −10 offensive runs, indirectly indicating that second base had become five runs 'more difficult' per season. If we apply this admittedly simplistic 'five-runs-per-season' discount to the top performers on the top forty chart who peaked before the 1930s (Frisch, Lajoie, and Evers), they all drop out of contention for a top ten spot. I think this is appropriate. Second base was a significantly less demanding position in those years.

One of the first second basemen to excel once the position had become more difficult was Lonny Frey.

Lonny Frey

Year	L	Tm	IP	Runs
1935	N	BRO	34	0
1936	N	BRO	230	-5
1937	N	CHI	83	2
1938	N	CIN	1084	6
1939	N	CIN	1141	16
1940	N	CIN	1365	36
1941	N	CIN	1294	4
1942	N	CIN	1227	15
1943	N	CIN	1292	13
1946	N	CIN	439	15
1947	N	CHI	59	0
1947	A	NY	71	0
1948	N	NY	66	0
Total			8384	104

Sometimes you just have to know when to give up. Frey struggled as a switch-hitting shortstop until 1939, when he traded down to second base, gave up switch hitting, and made the all-star team for the first of three times. Like his American League contemporary, Joe Gordon, he lost the 1944 and 1945 seasons to the War. Unlike Gordon, he wasn't able to get back into the lineup full-time again. Frey lived to be ninety-nine.

Though many fielders have inspired writers to wax poetic about the ballet-like grace of their fielding plays, only one fielder, so far as I know, has ever been nicknamed after a ballet star. Bobby "Nureyev" Knoop (pronounced kuh-NOPP) packed four Gold Glove quality seasons into his brief career (see next page).

Bobby Knoop

Year	L	Tm	IP	Runs	v-Tm
1964	A	LA	1359	21	5
1965	A	LA	1160	14	-2
1966	A	LA	1423	16	-2
1967	A	LA	1346	4	-1
1968	A	LA	1268	21	3
1969	A	LA	210	0	1
1969	A	CHI	873	10	6
1970	A	CHI	1030	3	2
1971	A	KC	398	-6	-3
1972	A	KC	228	2	3
Total			9295	86	12

Knopp struck out at a horrific rate, especially for someone who didn't walk or homer that much, but managed nevertheless to be a relatively effective offensive player during the second 'Dead Ball Era' of 1964–68. For whatever reason, his performance relative to the league dropped when offense returned to more normal levels in 1969 (thanks to rule changes that lowered the pitching mound and contracted the strike zone), and he played only part-time from 1970 through 1972.

Honorable Mention: Nap Lajoie

Year	L	Tm	IP	Runs
1898	N	PHI	1257	-30
1899	N	PHI	636	5
1900	N	PHI	948	14
1901	A	PHI	1061	-6
1902	A	PHI	11	0
1902	A	CLE	808	7
1903	A	CLE	1085	18
1904	A	CLE	774	-3
1905	A	CLE	551	1
1906	A	CLE	1173	26
1907	A	CLE	1130	48
1908	A	CLE	1409	46
1909	A	CLE	1047	26
1910	A	CLE	1302	0
1911	A	CLE	292	0
1912	A	CLE	838	2
1913	A	CLE	1076	17
1914	A	CLE	668	0
1915	A	PHI	1006	-14
1916	A	PHI	972	-10
Total			18043	147

As crazy as a couple of these numbers are, the career defensive runs estimate for Lajoie under DRA is (appropriately) about half of what has been reported for decades in baseball encyclopedias, mainly because DRA ignores infielder putouts, for reasons we've discussed. That said, and acknowledging that double plays were much less frequent in his time, LaJoie did in fact lead his league six times in double plays, including each year in his best four years of defensive runs ratings (1906–09). I think he owed part of his success to his size—at over six feet and two hundred pounds, he was considerably larger than the average player, and never felt intimidated by runners bearing down on him. He did, of course, get spiked from time to time. In 1905 he almost lost his leg because the blue dye in his socks had infected a spike wound. This led to a rule requiring players to wear sanitary white socks underneath their 'team color' socks.

Honorable Mention: Johnny Evers

Year	L	Tm	IP	Runs	Batting Runs	BB/ 655pa
1902	N	CHI	155	3	-5	20
1903	N	CHI	937	3	1	25
1904	N	CHI	1332	36	-6	31
1905	N	CHI	872	7	-2	45
1906	N	CHI	1373	22	-8	40
1907	N	CHI	1331	45	-6	44
1908	N	CHI	1128	-4	26	85
1909	N	CHI	1185	8	13	87
1910	N	CHI	1128	1	17	127
1911	N	CHI	277	0	-1	114
1912	N	CHI	1256	14	30	85
1913	N	CHI	1151	19	7	63
1914	N	BOS	1213	-4	14	93
1915	N	BOS	677	-3	5	15
1916	N	BOS	626	-14	-3	89
1917	N	BOS	197	0	-3	87
1917	N	PHI	398	4	-2	90
1922	A	CHI	9	0	0	n/a
1929	N	BOS	0	0	0	n/a
Total			15246	136	77	

People talk about the importance of clubhouse chemistry, but I hadn't seen much if any evidence that it really mattered until I reviewed Johnny Evers's defensive runs estimates. In 1907 he had a fight with his double play partner Joe Tinker, and the two literally didn't speak to each other for decades. For the next four years, Evers regressed sharply as a fielder. (In 1911 he missed most of the season to a nervous breakdown he attributed to losing his life's savings in a business deal.) His defensive runs went right back up in 1912—the first year after Tinker was traded—and remained strong the following year as well. It's possible, then, that the Tinker–Evers feud cost the Cubs about twenty runs a season on defense (Tinker's numbers remained relatively stable during that period).

There is yet another curious pattern to Evers's career that I have not seen discussed elsewhere. His offensive runs jumped up the same year his fielding fell off, almost entirely making up for the lost defensive runs. Virtually all of the improvement in Evers's offense came from doubling his walk rate from about forty to about eighty or more walks per full-time season—which happened all at once in 1908. To paraphrase a Little League mantra, in Evers's case, a walk was as good as a hit *prevented*.

Honorable Mention: Frankie Frisch

Year	L	Tm	IP	Runs
1919	N	NY	245	2
1921	N	NY	570	1
1922	N	NY	727	5
1923	N	NY	1166	4
1924	N	NY	1249	18
1925	N	NY	382	4
1926	N	NY	1111	26
1927	N	STL	1363	64
1928	N	STL	1283	22
1929	N	STL	1075	-7
1930	N	STL	1136	32
1931	N	STL	1131	19
1932	N	STL	692	9
1933	N	STL	1175	-4
1934	N	STL	958	17
1935	N	STL	727	12
1936	N	STL	502	-2
1937	N	STL	38	1
Total			15530	224

Frisch was yet another example of a very smart player (he earned a degree in chemistry from Fordham) who was a very effective fielder. The crazy number you see in 1927 reflects the fact that Frisch set the major league record for assists in a season, and there were no other contextual factors to discount the total—the team's ratios of ground outs to fly outs and left- and right-handed pitching were not particularly unusual. That doesn't mean that the defensive runs estimate above is correct. I do not believe that if the Cardinals had placed an average fielder at second that year they would have allowed sixty-four more runs. For some reason or another, there must have been an unusual number of ground balls hit near Frisch in 1927. Even if we cut the 1927 number in half, to equal his second best season, Frisch would still have had more career defensive runs than any other second baseman, and the second best TPAR.

The fact is, however, that second base was easier than third base when Frisch was in his prime, and Frisch himself demonstrated this nicely. During his second base career, with a mid-career season of 1928, Frisch averaged +21 defensive runs per 1450 innings; if you haircut his 1927 number by half, the career rate drops to +18 runs per 1450 innings played at second. During his third base career, with a mid-career season of 1924, Frisch averaged +10 defensive runs per 1450 innings at third. Yes, the older Frisch was about +8 defensive runs per season better at second base than the younger Frisch had been at third.

Number Ten: Mark Lemke

Year	L	Tm	IP	Runs	v-Tm
1988	N	ATL	152	-1	-1
1989	N	ATL	126	-1	0
1990	N	ATL	295	14	7
1991	N	ATL	605	7	3
1992	N	ATL	1065	0	-3
1993	N	ATL	1300	17	-1
1994	N	ATL	899	6	-1
1995	N	ATL	967	1	-5
1996	N	ATL	1166	21	-2
1997	N	ATL	850	23	0
1998	A	BOS	249	-4	-1
Total			7674	82	-3

Taking into account the increased competition from Latin American players since the 1980s, Lemke was probably the greatest fielding second baseman on a rate basis in history, excluding Pokey Reese. I was troubled slightly by his v-Tm runs, which show that after 1991 he did not appear to be better than his substitutes, but $Smith(R(t,s,d))$ has a similar career defensive runs total for him.

Number Nine: Frank White

Year	L	Tm	IP	Runs	v-Tm
1973	A	KC	95	3	3
1974	A	KC	253	-1	2
1975	A	KC	504	1	6
1976	A	KC	1025	17	13
1977	A	KC	1265	11	4
1978	A	KC	1194	9	1
1979	A	KC	1076	-4	-4
1980	A	KC	1285	0	1
1981	A	KC	824	-6	-1
1982	A	KC	1217	6	4
1983	A	KC	1241	12	-4
1984	A	KC	1109	23	6
1985	A	KC	1306	6	4
1986	A	KC	1265	-2	-2
1987	A	KC	1276	-4	3
1988	A	KC	1186	3	0
1989	A	KC	1057	13	0
1990	A	KC	628	-4	1
Total			17808	83	36

One of the more important simplifying assumptions used in DRA is that we can not only ignore errors for infielders, but also putouts, and concentrate on assists (and unassisted ground ball putouts for first basemen). For almost every rule there is an exception, and Frank White might be the exception to the rule that we shouldn't credit infielders (other than first basemen) for putouts. The Royals' most famous fan, Bill James, saw White play many times, and noticed that he was one of the first second basemen of the Astroturf era to figure out that it made sense to play very deep, because ground balls moved so fast on turf you could be confident they would reach you in time to make the throw. Because White was positioned so deep, James saw him catch a number of short flies that ordinarily would have dropped in as hits.

This is precisely the kind of contemporaneous, informed and specific subjective observation that is helpful in fielding evaluation. Note there is no evidence from the statistical record that White saved runs on putouts; his putout totals were within the norms for his position, and a handful of skill putouts per season would never be detectible in the random year-to-year variation in infielder putouts anyway. *The Fielding Bible* by John Dewan indicates, using batted ball data with an *appropriate* ball-hogging adjustment for fly outs recorded by infielders, that there was perhaps one second baseman (Orlando Hudson) in the 2003–05 period covered by the book with the consistent ability to save two, maybe three runs a season fielding fly balls. Given Bill James's informed observations and John Dewan's data, I think it is reasonable to credit White with a couple of runs per 1450 innings played for catching short fly balls that would otherwise drop in as hits, which would increase his career runs to +108 and his TPAR to +99, well within our top ten.

Number Eight: Pokey Reese

Year	L	Tm	IP	Runs	v-Tm
1997	N	CIN	49	3	3
1998	N	CIN	14	3	3
1999	N	CIN	1223	40	8
2000	N	CIN	1129	24	7
2001	N	CIN	407	2	6
2002	N	PIT	991	6	-2
2003	N	PIT	259	13	9
2004	A	BOS	152	5	6
Total			4223	96	41

The 1999 estimate is too high; *Smith(R(t,s,d))* reports +28 defensive runs. For the non-1999 seasons, DRA reports +56 defensive runs; the three different versions of Smith's system applicable in 1997–98, 2000–02, and 2003–04 collectively estimate about +30 defensive runs. As we'll see in the shortstop chapter, DRA probably slightly overrates defensive backups like Reese. DRA effectively treats each fielder playing the same position for a team as experiencing the same defensive context of relative fielding opportunities. But it's likely that teams put in defensive replacements when and where they are most needed—for example, Reese was probably put in at second in the late innings when ground ball right-handed pitchers (who would be more likely to face left-handed batters who would pull grounders to second) were on the mound. Smith's systems indirectly estimate batted ball distributions per plate appearance, so they can better estimate the particular defensive context faced by part-time defensive backups when they happen to be in the field.

Though DRA may have slightly overestimated Pokey Reese's defensive value, I find it intriguing that the most quantitatively sophisticated baseball organization in history, the post-2002 Boston Red Sox (owned by near-billionaire futures and foreign exchange trader John Henry), signed Reese as a free agent to be their defensive replacement at *shortstop* for the 2004 season. In a mere 508 innings, DRA estimates he had +13 defensive runs—an absolutely phenomenal rate of performance. $Fox(R(t),f,bh,bo)$ rates that year at +15 defensive runs and $Smith(R(t),f,bh,ph)$ at +17 defensive runs, so, even though it is a small sample size, I'm quite confident of the estimate. It would be an interesting project to document each of Pokey's most important fielding plays that year, including in the post-season, as he might have been just as important in helping Boston 'over the top' as Big Papi.

Number Seven: Lou Whitaker

Year	L	Tm	IP	Runs	v-Tm
1977	A	DET	74	-5	-4
1978	A	DET	1122	22	7
1979	A	DET	1017	16	8
1980	A	DET	1200	7	4
1981	A	DET	918	13	1
1982	A	DET	1283	18	1
1983	A	DET	1358	2	-7
1984	A	DET	1195	-4	4
1985	A	DET	1308	-12	0
1986	A	DET	1207	24	9
1987	A	DET	1267	5	0
1988	A	DET	904	2	0
1989	A	DET	1178	-7	-3
1990	A	DET	1037	20	0
1991	A	DET	1064	-3	-6
1992	A	DET	978	-15	-9
1993	A	DET	864	17	0
1994	A	DET	642	8	3
1995	A	DET	453	-6	0
Total			19069	101	7

Consistently excellent in his first few seasons but erratic (as a fielder) for most of the rest of his career, Lou Whitaker should have been elected to the Hall of Fame shortly after he became eligible, rather than getting dropped off the ballot in his first year. Whitaker is a classic example of a ballplayer who is above average at every element of his game, but not outstanding at any one in particular (other than fielding, which hasn't been measured well). Players like that garner less fame during their careers, so I suppose we shouldn't be surprised when they don't make the Hall of Fame.

Throughout this chapter we've been discussing how second base was originally an easier position but became harder sometime in the 1930s, as double plays became more important, and continued to become more difficult over the next few decades. The clearest indirect evidence for this is that offensive performance by second basemen, on average, declined steadily from the 1930s through the 1960s. Sometime between 1973 and 1981, the trend reversed. Based on Michael Schell's estimates of average offensive runs per position, mentioned earlier in this chapter, the average second baseman had −13 offensive runs per 550 plate appearances in 1963–72, −9 offensive runs in 1973–81, and −6 to −7 offensive runs from 1982 through 2003. Tom Tango has also recently done some careful studies of how well recent second basemen handle third and vice versa. Based on these studies, fielders who play both positions generally play them equally well or poorly, so it seems that second base has become 'easier' again.

Number Six: Willie Randolph

Year	L	Tm	IP	Runs	v-Tm
1975	N	PIT	114	3	0
1976	A	NY	1122	28	2
1977	A	NY	1271	20	1
1978	A	NY	1145	10	0
1979	A	NY	1336	5	-2
1980	A	NY	1215	-6	0
1981	A	NY	817	4	1
1982	A	NY	1235	-2	1
1983	A	NY	902	11	4
1984	A	NY	1249	6	4
1985	A	NY	1256	17	-3
1986	A	NY	1203	5	0
1987	A	NY	1040	6	0
1988	A	NY	962	12	4
1989	N	LA	1241	4	7
1990	N	LA	224	1	4
1990	A	OAK	695	6	-8
1991	A	MIL	997	3	-5
1992	N	NY	652	-16	-13
Total			18675	118	0

In the first game of the 1977 American League playoffs, Hal McRae broke up a double play by brutally up-ending Willie Randolph well outside the base path. Over the years, the rule permitting umpires to call the runner breaking up a double play out for interference had fallen into disuse. What McRae did to Randolph was so shocking that the rule began to get enforced again, now identified as the "McRae Rule." Though I haven't heard this idea proposed before, I believe the enforcement of the McRae Rule has made it easier to play second base, as well as short, thereby expanding the talent pool and making it easier to find good hitters.

In some sense, the difficulty of a position really has two separate components: the degree of skill required *and the extent of physical wear and tear.* Before the enforcement of the McRae Rule, being a middle infielder was almost as hazardous to your health as being a catcher. Presumably players who were exceptional hitters would shy away from playing short or second to limit the risk of injury. Once the position became safer, it was no longer so crazy to risk having your best hitter turning double plays. The seemingly miraculous appearance of all those slugging middle-infielders during the late 1990s and in this decade may be thanks in part to Hal McRae ... and Willie Randolph.

Number Five: Rennie Stennett

Year	L	Tm	IP	Runs	v-Tm
1971	N	PIT	265	4	5
1972	N	PIT	425	5	-1
1973	N	PIT	676	1	2
1974	N	PIT	1377	18	0
1975	N	PIT	1266	31	3
1976	N	PIT	1395	23	3
1977	N	PIT	1012	16	12
1978	N	PIT	655	3	0
1979	N	PIT	784	19	5
1980	N	SF	907	-13	-3
1981	N	SF	160	-7	-5
Total			8922	101	22

Stennett started playing at short, could also play the outfield, and beat out both Dave Cash and Willie Randolph for the Pirates' second base job in 1974. Unfortunately, Stennett broke his ankle in August 1977. He had forty-six stolen base attempts in the 116 games he played in 1977, but never more than eight in a season thereafter. Not a patient hitter, Stennett tended to hit more ground balls than fly balls, and presumably relied on his speed to leg out hits—his career batting average when he broke his ankle was .285, but he was only a .240 hitter after that. Had he not broken his ankle, I believe Stennett might have saved more runs at second than anyone in history.

Originally a shortstop, Grich established himself as a major league quality player two years before he got called up, but was blocked in the Orioles

Number Four: Bobby Grich

Year	L	Tm	IP	Runs	v-Tm
1970	A	BAL	82	4	3
1971	A	BAL	20	1	1
1972	A	BAL	376	3	-1
1973	A	BAL	1418	34	0
1974	A	BAL	1442	11	0
1975	A	BAL	1338	25	5
1976	A	BAL	1235	1	3
1978	A	LA	1238	6	-1
1979	A	LA	1297	5	0
1980	A	LA	1254	20	8
1981	A	LA	861	13	5
1982	A	LA	1223	-1	-4
1983	A	LA	1022	9	6
1984	A	LA	720	-9	-9
1985	A	LA	953	18	-5
1986	A	LA	677	-8	-8
Total			15155	133	3

organization by Belanger (which should also tell you something about Mark Belanger). Like Whitaker, Grich failed to impress the baseball writers who are Hall of Fame voters because he was good at everything but never outstanding at anything, other than fielding, which so far has only gotten people into the Hall who establish, rightly or wrongly, a decade of perceived dominance at their position. Grich missed a fair amount of time to injury. The one time he led the league in any high-profile statistical categories (home runs and slugging percentage) was the strike-shortened 1981 season.

Number Three: Glenn Hubbard

Year	L	Tm	IP	Runs	v-Tm
1978	N	ATL	389	3	5
1979	N	ATL	768	-9	-2
1980	N	ATL	1008	16	14
1981	N	ATL	872	2	3
1982	N	ATL	1271	17	-1
1983	N	ATL	1254	19	7
1984	N	ATL	1010	6	-7
1985	N	ATL	1142	34	10
1986	N	ATL	1178	7	6
1987	N	ATL	1186	19	8
1988	A	OAK	789	10	6
1989	A	OAK	340	12	3
Total			11206	137	52

Glenn Hubbard's 1985 season has generated controversy among baseball analysts since the first sabermetric baseball encyclopedias came out in the late 1980s. For many years, these encyclopedias credited Hubbard with something like +60 defensive runs in 1985, as well as very high estimates in other years, thus increasing his overall career rating far beyond what it should have been. The sixty-run estimate was driven by the fact that Hubbard's pitching teammates were all right-handed ground ball pitchers, who generated a historic number of ground ball and double play opportunities for him, and the baseball encyclopedia numbers made little or no adjustment for these facts, as DRA does. Though the 1985 defensive runs estimate is still probably too high, the DRA estimates for the other seasons appear reasonable and consistent. In addition, Hubbard fielded well when he changed teams and consistently and significantly outperformed his backups, based on his v-Tm runs.

Number Two: Bill Mazeroski

Year	L	Tm	IP	Runs	v-Tm
1956	N	PIT	671	7	5
1957	N	PIT	1238	9	6
1958	N	PIT	1344	26	-1
1959	N	PIT	1167	0	-3
1960	N	PIT	1341	3	3
1961	N	PIT	1333	12	1
1962	N	PIT	1410	13	0
1963	N	PIT	1229	30	12
1964	N	PIT	1439	17	0
1965	N	PIT	1132	10	-5
1966	N	PIT	1452	13	1
1967	N	PIT	1437	-10	1
1968	N	PIT	1256	9	0
1969	N	PIT	545	2	-2
1970	N	PIT	888	12	2
1971	N	PIT	345	-3	-2
1972	N	PIT	107	0	-1
Total			18335	149	15

The best systems available from the early 1950s through the late1980s, DRA and *Smith(pgor,bod)*, agree: Maz saved something like 150 runs in his career, not the 350 or 250 reported for many years in baseball encyclopedias. Mazeroski's defensive impact was overestimated in those encyclopedias for much the same reason that Hubbard's was: he played for teams with extreme ground ball pitchers. In addition, baseball encyclopedias over-credited each double play pivot, by giving the pivoting middle infielder credit for a putout (+.2 runs), an assist (+.4 runs), *and* the double play (+.4 runs), when the real value of getting the second out on a double play is closer to half that total.

For the last dozen years or so, analysts have been figuring out how many extra double plays teams record after taking into account how many times they had a runner on first and a ground out. (DRA uses essentially the same predictors to adjust for double play pivot assists.) These studies all confirm that Maz was indeed outstanding at turning the double play, even when you take into account that the pitchers on his teams generated ground balls at a very high rate. Long after Maz retired, a reporter asked Frank White who he thought had been the best at turning two. White said Maz. Trying to get more details, the reporter asked White when he had seen him play. White answered that he'd never actually seen him *play*—he'd only seen Mazeroski giving lessons at an instructional camp many years after retirement, and couldn't believe how quickly the old man sent the ball to first after getting the throw from short.

Number One: Joe "Flash" Gordon

Year	L	Tm	IP	Runs
1938	A	NY	1160	30
1939	A	NY	1331	35
1940	A	NY	1373	24
1941	A	NY	1165	17
1942	A	NY	1256	15
1943	A	NY	1393	30
1946	A	NY	946	21
1947	A	CLE	1367	14
1948	A	CLE	1262	9
1949	A	CLE	1274	2
1950	A	CLE	927	-7
Total			13453	191

Joe Gordon was the first outstanding fielder at second base after the position had clearly become defensively more demanding than third base, so it is reasonable to assume that Gordon's fielding competition was weaker than Mazeroski's, and for that reason, to consider dropping Flash behind Maz. However, Gordon lost two seasons to the War, which would have boosted his career defensive runs and TPAR by about another forty runs. That additional value puts so much space between the two men that I feel comfortable following where the numbers lead.

The situation is somewhat analogous to comparing Ruth on offense to later batting greats: by being first to master the trick of hitting home runs, Ruth was able to dominate his peers in offensive production to an extent that no one else ever would. And no matter how analysts try to adjust for his being the first true home run hitter, Ruth keeps coming out on top of the list of the greatest offensive players of all time (without taking talent pools into account). Similarly, by being the first truly to master the art of turning two, Gordon made himself into the 'Ruth of second base fielding', an oxymoron Gordon, who had a great sense of humor, might have chuckled over.

Shortstop

Contemporary Era

MCS	First	Last	IP	Runs	Δ
1998	Rey	Sanchez	7644	141	Δ
1995	Barry	Larkin	17555	112	Δ
1999	Jose	Valentin	10060	97	Δ
2001	Neifi	Perez	9169	79	Δ
2006	Adam	Everett	6528	66	
2005	Jack	Wilson	9960	65	
1996	Mike	Benjamin	2448	51	
2005	Rafael	Furcal	10798	51	Δ
1997	Kevin	Stocker	7156	47	
1999	Alex S.	Gonzalez	10942	44	
1997	Mike	Bordick	13357	42	
2005	Juan	Uribe	6859	39	Δ
2005	Cesar	Izturis	7477	36	Δ
1999	Royce	Clayton	17374	34	Δ
1997	Jose	Vizcaino	7250	33	Δ
2000	Jose	Hernandez	6379	33	Δ
2005	Craig	Counsell	3162	32	
1998	Benji	Gil	3438	31	Δ
2003	Alex	Cora	4247	31	Δ
1997	Tim	Bogar	3091	31	
2000	Deivi	Cruz	9317	21	Δ
2003	Miguel	Tejada	16098	15	Δ
1999	Rey	Ordonez	8017	12	Δ
2003	Juan	Castro	3559	12	Δ
2001	Rich	Aurilia	9044	11	
1994	Walt	Weiss	11932	8	
2000	Desi	Relaford	3782	8	Δ
2004	Orlando	Cabrera	14455	8	Δ
1993	Jay	Bell	12918	7	

(continued)

Contemporary Era *(continued)*

MCS	First	Last	IP	Runs	Δ
1995	John	Valentin	4941	4	
2004	Carlos	Guillen	7106	1	Δ
1993	Kevin	Elster	7224	-1	
1995	Gary	Disarcina	9304	-1	
1997	M.	Grudzielanek	5368	-3	
2004	Cristian	Guzman	10895	-4	Δ
1999	Alex	Rodriguez	10938	-7	Δ
1996	Pat	Meares	7388	-9	
2000	N.	Garciaparra	9157	-9	
1994	Andujar	Cedeno	4961	-9	Δ
2005	Angel	Berroa	5965	-10	Δ
2004	Julio	Lugo	9017	-12	Δ
1999	Omar	Vizquel	22755	-19	
2004	David	Eckstein	8302	-23	
2001	Tony	Womack	4280	-24	Δ
2003	Alex	Gonzalez	10320	-34	Δ
1994	Wil	Cordero	3266	-35	Δ
1999	Chris	Gomez	8650	-36	
1993	Jose	Offerman	5065	-38	Δ
2005	Felipe	Lopez	4994	-44	Δ
2002	Edgar	Renteria	16836	-56	Δ
2005	Jimmy	Rollins	12276	-64	Δ
1998	Ricky	Gutierrez	7049	-65	Δ
1994	Jeff	Blauser	8586	-84	
2002	Derek	Jeter	18440	-270	Δ

Remember shortstop "O" in chapter two? That was Omar Vizquel (see next page), who has received eleven Gold Gloves, more than any shortstop other than Ozzie Smith. Under DRA, he would appear to have been a worthy Gold Glove candidate in 1991 and 2007, but otherwise served as a more or less ordinary, though exceptionally durable, shortstop.

In 2007, at the age of forty, Vizquel turned in the best-documented late-career fielding season of all time, which yielded the following defensive runs estimates: +18 under DRA, +23 under $Smith(R(t),f,bh,ph)$, +29 under $Fox(R(t),f,bh,bo)$, and +20 under $MGL(B(t,s,d,v,bh))$. Vizquel actually did *not* win the Gold Glove that year.

On a career basis, the Smith and Fox systems assign over +120 defensive runs to Vizquel's career, but they also over credit error avoidance by between a quarter and a half a run. Vizquel has the highest career fielding percentage of any shortstop in history, at least for all shortstops with long careers, and has made about 150 fewer errors than he would have, given his total chances, if he had had an average fielding percentage. That would incorrectly boost Vizquel's career defensive runs under these systems by between forty and

Omar Vizquel

Year	L	Tm	IP	Runs	v-Tm
1989	A	SEA	1124	-1	9
1990	A	SEA	680	3	6
1991	A	SEA	1134	21	11
1992	A	SEA	1152	-5	-1
1993	A	SEA	1331	5	0
1994	A	CLE	613	-10	-4
1995	A	CLE	1187	0	2
1996	A	CLE	1312	-1	-2
1997	A	CLE	1307	-7	-2
1998	A	CLE	1316	-3	-1
1999	A	CLE	1214	-3	3
2000	A	CLE	1329	-19	-1
2001	A	CLE	1321	-7	-1
2002	A	CLE	1291	-5	1
2003	A	CLE	551	6	5
2004	A	CLE	1245	-8	-4
2005	N	SF	1292	1	-1
2006	N	SF	1281	-8	0
2007	N	SF	1219	18	3
2008	N	SF	658	-3	-5
2009	A	TEX	197	6	4
Total			22755	-19	21

eighty runs, thus suggesting an alternative defensive runs estimate of approximately +60 defensive runs over the course of his career—a good but not particularly outstanding total.

To me the best evidence of Vizquel's solid but unremarkable fielding comes from *Tango(p-wowy)*, which estimates that Vizquel made only twenty-three plays more than expected from 1993 through 2007. It is not clear how that should translate into defensive runs, but the *highest* estimate would be about +17 defensive runs. If you add the +18 defensive runs under DRA for Vizquel from 1989 through 1992, that yields a career rating of +35 defensive runs.

Even if we credit Vizquel about +60 defensive runs (basically the Smith and Fox evaluation, net of the likely effect of errors avoided), it is clear that Vizquel should not be in the Hall of Fame. He was an ordinary hitter and base runner, for a shortstop. In contrast, Ozzie Smith actually contributed about as much on offense as a league-average *player* (not just a league-average shortstop) because of his slightly above-average on-base percentage, outstanding bunting, and smart base stealing. At no time during Vizquel's career did he ever establish himself as clearly the best or among the best fielders at his position. In contrast, Smith had between five and ten seasons in which he was the best or among the best.

It's not my intention to be mean-spirited in this; Vizquel has had a wonderful two-decade career, has earned about $60 million in the process, and is giving back to his community. It is just that there are more than a hundred players throughout major league history who deserve this particular honor more than he does. I predict, however, that he will get in, because the writers will be impressed by *some* numbers (his record-setting total number of games played at shortstop, all-time record career fielding percentage, his nearly 2800 hits, and eleven Gold Gloves), and simply dismiss *other* numbers, independently compiled by Fox, Humphreys, Smith, and Tango, that collectively *demonstrate* that Vizquel did not help his teams win as many games as a Hall of Famer should.

Rey Ordonez's DRA evaluation is surprisingly modest as well.

Rey Ordonez

Year	Lg	Tm	IP	Runs	v-Tm
1996	N	NY	1262	12	2
1997	N	NY	956	6	0
1998	N	NY	1289	-7	2
1999	N	NY	1317	2	-1
2000	N	NY	355	-4	1
2001	N	NY	1226	0	-3
2002	N	NY	1165	2	-2
2003	A	TB	294	5	2
2004	N	CHI	153	-3	-3
Total			8017	12	-3

Ordonez began well in 1996 (+12 defensive runs), when he didn't win a Gold Glove. He was fielding even a little better as the 1997 season opened, but got hurt in June 1997, saw his assists rate drop, and missed over a third of the season. But he won his first Gold Glove. In the following year his DRA rating was negative, and yet he won his second Gold Glove. In 1999 $Smith(R(t,s,d))$ credits Ordonez with +37 defensive runs. $Smith(R(t,s,d))$ uses batted ball data, which is great, but also two computations (the "mixed method" for shared locations and the "error runs" calculation) that will predictably cause a shortstop to be overrated if he (i) plays next to a top third baseman and (ii) manages to avoid errors. In 1999, Ordonez's third base teammate was Robin Ventura, who clearly was an excellent third baseman and who is credited with +29 defensive runs under $Smith(R(t,s,d))$, and Ordonez made only four errors, only one more than the record low. DRA may be wrong about Ordonez' 1999, but I'm quite confident he did not save anywhere near forty runs in that year. Note also that despite being a perfect example of a poor-hitting defensive specialist who missed a lot of innings, he failed to outperform his substitutes over the course of his career, as indicated by his v-Tm numbers.

Up to know we've been discussing shortstops that DRA may rate lower than other systems; here are two shortstops who are probably overrated by DRA: Barry Larkin and Neifi Perez.

Barry Larkin

Year	Lg	Team	IP	Runs	v-Tm
1986	N	CIN	307	6	5
1987	N	CIN	1011	12	10
1988	N	CIN	1278	22	0
1989	N	CIN	691	20	15
1990	N	CIN	1344	24	4
1991	N	CIN	1032	21	6
1992	N	CIN	1208	13	4
1993	N	CIN	846	1	2
1994	N	CIN	960	4	1
1995	N	CIN	1091	-8	-6
1996	N	CIN	1243	2	1
1997	N	CIN	503	7	6
1998	N	CIN	1236	-5	4
1999	N	CIN	1373	9	0
2000	N	CIN	845	-3	-3
2001	N	CIN	341	-5	-2
2002	N	CIN	1092	-5	5
2003	N	CIN	470	-1	2
2004	N	CIN	684	-4	-3
Total			17555	112	50

The first thing one notices is that Larkin's best years all occurred before 1993, so in some sense he belongs more to the Modern Era than the Contemporary Era. However, he played so long that his mid-career season places him in the Contemporary Era.

If Barry Larkin really saved the number of runs reported above from 1987 through 1992, then he would have put together possibly the greatest six-year run of fielding performance, taking into account the increased amount of competition in more recent times, of any shortstop in history. However, *Smith(pgor,bod)* (1987–88), *Smith(R(t,s,d))* (1989–92), and *Fox(R(t),f,bh,bo)* (1988–92) would roughly cut the value of those seasons, in the aggregate, by at least half. The average of those systems for Larkin's truly full-time seasons during that period—1988, 1990, and 1992—would probably come in around something closer to +10 defensive runs than +20 defensive runs. In general, those three systems understate slightly the impact of good fielders, so perhaps Larkin was approaching a Gold Glove quality of +15 defensive runs when healthy and playing full time in those three seasons. But DRA also reports +41 defensive runs over the three-year period from 1989 through 1991, when Larkin was missing a lot of playing time and in fact played the equivalent of one and a quarter seasons. This needs to be questioned.

DRA first calculates a team rating at a position, and then allocates it among the players at that position. That allocation assumes that the contextual factors taken into account for that season (for example, the tendency of the team's pitchers to generate ground balls) remain constant throughout the season. That is probably approximately true in general, but not always, and a player who misses significant playing time due to injuries, as Larkin did throughout his career, might not experience the same 'context' of fielding opportunities during the portion of the season he played. Systems such as those developed by Smith and Fox do not assume a consistent team context throughout the season, and probably rate part-time seasons more accurately. Also, Larkin's v-Tm runs mean little, because the teammate he is compared against was Kurt Stillwell, the worst shortstop on our upcoming Modern Era list. I ultimately conclude, on the basis of the evidence provided by Smith and Fox, that Larkin was only fairly good, not great, when young.

Tango(p-wowy) and the Smith and Fox systems agree that Larkin declined to league-average performance after 1992. Larkin continued to steal bases at a good clip through 1999, so he did not seem to lose his speed. Perhaps he decided to field more conservatively to reduce the risk of injury, which, given his other skills and difficulty in staying healthy, would have been the smart thing to do, including for his team.

Larkin is probably overrated by DRA due to *random* fluctuations in his teams' context of fielding opportunities when he was in and out of the line-up due to injuries. But a certain set of fielders—defensive specialists—are probably *systematically* overrated by DRA because their teams *intentionally* put them into the game when their fielding skills are most needed by the particular pitcher on the mound, in a form of defensive platooning. Davey Johnson let the poor-fielding Howard Johnson play shortstop when extreme fly ball pitcher Sid Fernandez was pitching. Conversely, Neifi Perez probably

Neifi Perez

Year	L	Tm	IP	Runs	v-Tm
1996	N	COL	68	-3	-2
1997	N	COL	360	7	6
1998	N	COL	1386	12	3
1999	N	COL	1370	5	1
2000	N	COL	1403	14	1
2001	A	KC	396	1	-8
2001	N	COL	764	1	7
2002	A	KC	1210	-1	-3
2003	N	SF	311	14	13
2004	N	CHI	120	2	3
2004	N	SF	440	3	2
2005	N	CHI	1063	26	13
2006	A	DET	40	1	1
2006	N	CHI	132	-1	-2
2007	A	DET	108	-4	-3
Total			9169	79	31

took the field more frequently when his fielding skill was most needed, for example when left-handed ground ball pitchers were on the mound.

I do not believe that Neifi Perez saved fourteen runs for the Giants while playing 311 innings in 2003. *Smith (R(t),f,bh,ph)* and *Fox(R(t),f,bh,bo)* agree that Perez played well in 2005, but saved perhaps half the total above. None of the other systems report significant run-saving totals for 1998, 2000, or 2003. That said, *Tango(p-wowy)* places Perez among the top dozen or so shortstops based on fielding since 1993. Given the mixed evidence, Perez appears to have been one of the better shortstops of his era, but not among the very best.

Modern Era

MCS	First	Last	IP	Runs	Δ
1974	Mark	Belanger	15337	197	
1986	Ozzie	Smith	21786	151	Δ
1983	Garry	Templeton	16747	104	Δ
1978	Dave	Concepcion	18380	99	Δ
1972	Bert	Campaneris	17951	89	Δ
1991	Greg	Gagne	14455	88	
1969	Dal	Maxvill	9017	87	
1991	Ozzie	Guillen	15803	79	Δ
1978	Bill	Russell	14797	77	
1988	Jose	Uribe	8051	72	Δ
1977	Chris	Speier	15837	71	
1982	Craig	Reynolds	9767	63	
1985	Alan	Trammell	18270	60	
1969	Ed	Brinkman	15140	58	
1987	Dickie	Thon	9159	53	
1969	Hal	Lanier	5372	51	
1986	Scott	Fletcher	6541	50	
1989	Cal	Ripken	20232	47	
1977	Tim	Foli	12787	42	
1978	Rick	Burleson	10333	40	
1978	Bucky	Dent	11757	40	
1991	Alvaro	Espinoza	4681	32	Δ
1972	Bud	Harrelson	11510	31	
1985	Alfredo	Griffin	15835	29	Δ
1979	Robin	Yount	12945	18	
1975	Frank	Duffy	6861	16	
1988	Dick	Schofield	11410	14	
1989	Tony	Fernandez	13460	14	Δ
1980	Bill	Almon	4413	10	
1974	Toby	Harrah	6692	8	
1983	Dale	Berra	4913	6	
1978	Mario	Mendoza	3808	0	Δ
1990	Rafael	Belliard	5535	0	Δ
1988	Andres	Thomas	4608	-2	Δ

(continued)

Modern Era (*continued*)

MCS	First	Last	IP	Runs	Δ
1974	Darrel	Chaney	4482	-4	
1987	Rey	Quinones	3795	-8	Δ
1972	Hector	Torres	3254	-9	Δ
1975	Jim	Mason	4081	-10	
1973	Danny	Thompson	3885	-12	
1985	Julio	Franco	6172	-12	Δ
1989	Dale	Sveum	3530	-12	
1970	Jackie	Hernandez	3797	-12	Δ
1982	U L	Washington	5864	-14	Δ
1987	Dave	Anderson	3508	-14	
1991	Bill	Spiers	3420	-15	
1973	Enzo	Hernandez	5620	-15	Δ
1988	Mariano	Duncan	4250	-16	Δ
1992	Manuel	Lee	4054	-17	Δ
1979	Roy	Smalley III	8887	-17	
1990	Luis	Rivera	5416	-17	Δ
1978	Luis	Gomez	3193	-21	
1988	Spike	Owen	11397	-21	
1977	Mario	Guerrero	4599	-21	Δ
1986	Rafael	Santana	5184	-21	Δ
1979	Rob	Picciolo	3622	-22	
1980	Ivan	De Jesus	10809	-22	Δ
1977	Fred	Stanley	4175	-25	
1974	Rick	Auerbach	3168	-26	
1985	Bob	Meacham	3270	-27	Δ
1991	Shawon	Dunston	11276	-27	Δ
1971	Gene	Michael	6754	-28	
1975	Roger	Metzger	10001	-28	
1972	Marty	Perez	3678	-28	
1974	Freddie	Patek	13358	-29	
1986	Rafael	Ramirez	11567	-30	Δ
1987	Steve	Jeltz	4493	-31	Δ
1983	Glenn	Hoffman	4646	-32	
1986	Hubie	Brooks	3212	-35	Δ
1971	Don	Kessinger	16622	-41	
1981	Johnnie	LeMaster	7914	-43	
1991	Felix	Fermin	6592	-46	Δ
1978	Frank	Taveras	9005	-50	Δ
1977	Larry	Bowa	19058	-57	
1978	Tom	Veryzer	7362	-66	
1989	Kurt	Stillwell	5499	-84	

The table above generally looks about right, with just two major exceptions: Ozzie Smith is estimated to have 'only' about +150 defensive runs, and Cal Ripken 'only' about +50. Let's start with Ripken, because his case is more difficult to explain.

Here is how Ripken is evaluated under the best systems for that era. In addition to the standard DRA results (excluding v-Tm, because Ripken famously played every game except in his very last season), also shown are DRA ratings based on an alternative version of DRA that I developed using just 1977–2008 data. For Tango(*p-wowy*), I just pro-rated Ripken's aggregate 1993–97 ratings to each season.

Cal Ripken

Year	L	Tm	DRA 1977-08	DRA (pgor,bod)	Smith (R(t,s,d))	Smith (R(t),f,bh,bo)	Fox	Tango (p-wowy)
1981	A	BAL	-1	0	-1			
1982	A	BAL	5	6	3			
1983	A	BAL	13	17	11			
1984	A	BAL	30	30	23			
1985	A	BAL	0	4	0			
1986	A	BAL	5	7	16			
1987	A	BAL	-12	-12	0			
1988	A	BAL	-7	-7		-6	0	
1989	A	BAL	9	10		21	14	
1990	A	BAL	-2	0		22	17	
1991	A	BAL	10	8		23	19	
1992	A	BAL	-9	-11		12	11	
1993	A	BAL	-1	-3		11	11	8
1994	A	BAL	-1	1		17	16	6
1995	A	BAL	10	10		22	19	7
1996	A	BAL	0	1		2	-4	8
1997	A	BAL	-1	0		-3	0	0

The DRA and *Smith(pgor,bod)* assessments for the first part of Ripken's career (1981–1987) broadly agree that Ripken was sensational in 1983–84, solid in 1985–86, and sinking in 1987. The DRA, *Smith(R(t,s,d))*, and *Fox(R(t),f,bh,bo)* ratings suggests that his decline continued into 1988. His team apparently thought so as well, because in spring training of 1989 they experimented with sending Ripken back to his original position, third base, and trying out Juan Bell, the younger brother of George Bell, at short. At the end of spring training they sent Bell back to the minors, notwithstanding some brilliant plays and decent hitting, because he made six errors, some on routine plays, in only fourteen games. (Bell went on to play parts of a few seasons; his fielding percentage was far below league average, but DRA estimates he saved about five runs in fewer than a thousand innings played.) As *The Washington Post* reported, "The Orioles believe that with such a young pitching staff, the one thing they don't need is a shaky defense. One thing the Orioles know about Ripken is that he'll make almost all the routine plays."

Ripken got the message. He proceeded to cut his own error rate by half. In his first six full-time seasons, ending in 1988, he committed 25, 26, 26, 13, 20, and 21 errors. In the next five seasons of full-time play, ending before the 1994–95 strike, he committed only 8, 3, 11, 12, and 17 errors. As indicated many times elsewhere, all of the non-DRA systems above, except *Tango* (*p-wowy*), overrate sure-handed fielders. Although *Tango*(*p-wowy*) rates 1993–96 slightly higher than DRA (the table above just pro-rates the overall 1993–96 numbers by innings played), it also rates those years well below the Smith and Fox estimates.

Given the *Tango*(*p-wowy*) estimates, and the known biases of the other systems in favor of fielders who avoid errors, I am confident that the DRA assessment is about right or at worst only slightly too low: Ripken remained a solid shortstop for the rest of his career, relying on his experience, sure hands, and exceptionally strong and accurate arm to overcome his slow foot speed. He was not an all-time great fielder; nor was he even a consistently dominant fielder in his own time.

Ozzie Smith, of course, is without any question one of the greatest fielders of all time, even under the seemingly conservative estimate of career defensive runs under DRA. According to DRA, the Wizard of Oz had three phases in his career.

Ozzie Smith

Year	Lg	Tm	IP	DRA	v-Tm
1978	N	SD	1327	7	-3
1979	N	SD	1339	12	1
1980	N	SD	1398	28	1
1981	N	SD	986	18	-1
1982	N	STL	1249	19	0
1983	N	STL	1344	9	-2
1984	N	STL	1065	9	-1
1985	N	STL	1407	13	3
1986	N	STL	1287	3	3
1987	N	STL	1357	4	-4
1988	N	STL	1329	14	1
1989	N	STL	1336	4	2
1990	N	STL	1203	-12	-4
1991	N	STL	1253	-5	8
1992	N	STL	1156	14	10
1993	N	STL	1139	6	-2
1994	N	STL	822	-2	7
1995	N	STL	343	3	1
1996	N	STL	443	8	3
Total			21786	151	24

Sometime in July1985 Smith severely injured the rotator cuff on his throwing arm, which would have been a career-ending injury for a pitcher or an ordinary shortstop. Through 1985, Smith averaged about +16 defensive runs per 1450 innings played, an outstanding level of performance to maintain over an eight-year span. That rate might have been even a little higher if his 1981 season had not been shortened by the strike, if we look at only the portion of 1984 before he broke his wrist, and the portion of 1985 before he damaged his rotator cuff. In other words, when completely healthy, Smith probably saved his teams close to twenty runs per full-time season for several years. Smith refused to tell anyone about his rotator cuff injury, so opponents wouldn't try to take advantage of his weakened arm. It's difficult to get rotator cuff surgery without someone finding out; perhaps in order not to reveal his condition, or for whatever reason, Smith did not have surgery until 1995, and I do not believe it was for the rotator cuff. He simply played through the pain, avoided using his right arm in everyday life, and focused on improving his overall physical condition.

Between 1986 and 1989, Ozzie still ran great, so he still saved about seven runs per 1450 innings. In 1990, Ozzie was "hobbled by leg injuries for much of the season."[1] After these leg injuries, his DRA rating per 1450 innings played for the rest of his career was +3 defensive runs.

The other top systems available for much of Ozzie's career, $Smith(pgor,bod)$ (for 1978–1988), $Smith(R(t,s,d))$ (1989–1996), and $Fox(R(t),f,bh,bo)$ (1988–1996), broadly agree about his career value, once we back out an estimate of the number of runs by which they overrate Ozzie for avoiding errors, which would bring him to about +170 defensive runs, within hailing distance of the standard DRA estimate.

Sean Smith calculates double play runs separately from batted ball fielding runs (though all the numbers reported above for Ozzie include double play runs in the total for each season). Ozzie's double play runs under Smith's systems amount to a total of +5 defensive runs from 1978 through 1981, and from 1988 through 1996. In other words, essentially zero. The other twenty double play runs all occur between 1982 and 1987, with ratings of +4, +1, +4, +3, +4, and +4 defensive runs due to double plays. Sean Smith's systems split the credit for team performance in double play runs equally between the shortstop and the second baseman. DRA simply credits the player making the double play assist. Tommy Herr was Ozzie's double play partner from 1982 through 1988, and for no other seasons. I think those twenty double play runs belong to Herr. If we delete those runs from Ozzie's career total under Smith's systems, and also back out likely effect of over-crediting error avoidance, Smith's systems and DRA reach essentially the same career assessment for the Wizard of Oz: approximately +150 defensive runs.

Two final surprises before we leave the Modern Era: overrated multiple Gold Glove winners Tony Fernandez and Larry Bowa. Each performed at close to a true Gold Glove level very early in their careers, but quickly declined.

---

1. Claire Smith, "Smith Feeling Cardinals' Burdens," *The New York Times*, June 25, 1990.

Tony Fernandez

Year	Lg	Tm	IP	Runs	v-Tm
1983	A	TOR	79	-4	-3
1984	A	TOR	504	9	10
1985	A	TOR	1416	14	-1
1986	A	TOR	1443	-6	2
1987	A	TOR	1210	5	1
1988	A	TOR	1333	1	2
1989	A	TOR	1243	7	1
1990	A	TOR	1384	7	0
1991	N	SD	1263	2	7
1992	N	SD	1349	-20	-3
1993	A	TOR	820	2	0
1993	N	NY	414	0	0
1994	N	CIN	50	1	0
1995	A	NY	888	-5	-4
1997	A	CLE	66	2	2
Total			13460	14	14

Fernandez showed great promise as a fielder in 1984–85 (+17 defensive runs per 1450 innings played), but Gold Glove voters didn't notice him until he hit over .300 for the first time, in 1986. The next year he upped his batting average to .322, and was rewarded with a Gold Glove, even though he probably was no better than average as a fielder. The following year he faded a bit as a hitter, but still hit .287, a great rate in those days for a shortstop, and they gave him another Gold Glove. The next year his batting average dropped all the way down to .257, but his *fielding* average rose to a then record setting level for shortstops, and that garnered him his last Gold Glove.

Tony Fernandez was born in the Dominican Republic. Latin American middle infielders came to dominate the position sometime in the 1980s, and continue to dominate today. I've often wondered why Latin Americans primarily found their first and continuing success in the middle infield. Larry Bowa may be the answer. Well, part of the answer.

Bowa (see next page) fielded well in 1971 (+9 defensive runs) and 1972 (+11 defensive runs), and was not a bad choice for the Gold Glove in 1972. But in 1973 he spent thirty-seven days on the disabled list, and, perhaps only coincidentally, he never fielded well again. However, he did keep leading the league in fielding percentage and, it must be said, continued to steal his share of bases and with a solid success rate, so they kept him in the lineup.

Though clearly a dedicated and well-respected player, Bowa's career would have been half as long if batted ball data had been available to his teams because, unlike Jeter, he wasn't much of a hitter. Bowa did maintain an almost exactly league-average batting average, but rarely walked and had no power. But in his day that was all right, *for a shortstop*. Every major league roster in the 1970s had a few weak-hitting middle or utility infielders. And

Larry Bowa

Year	Lg	Tm	IP	Runs	v-Tm
1970	N	PHI	1244	2	4
1971	N	PHI	1410	9	0
1972	N	PHI	1308	11	-1
1973	N	PHI	1034	0	2
1974	N	PHI	1425	-15	2
1975	N	PHI	1196	-10	1
1976	N	PHI	1360	-3	2
1977	N	PHI	1346	-2	-1
1978	N	PHI	1351	2	-2
1979	N	PHI	1271	-10	1
1980	N	PHI	1293	-15	1
1981	N	PHI	844	-4	3
1982	N	CHI	1200	-19	0
1983	N	CHI	1193	-1	-1
1984	N	CHI	1032	0	3
1985	N	CHI	516	0	-5
1985	N	NY	34	-2	-2
Total			19058	-57	8

not only were they weak hitters—they weren't really all that great at fielding either. Weak-hitting, ordinary-fielding middle infielders constituted the segment of major league rosters most vulnerable to competition, because fielding, much more than hitting, can be improved with coaching and sheer effort. My hunch is that ambitious young players from the Caribbean and Central America figured out that by getting in great shape and practicing fielding all day, they'd have a decent shot at a major league career as middle-infielders, even if they didn't hit that well.

Transitional Era

MCS	First	Last	IP	Runs	Δ
1958	Roy	McMillan	16955	113	
1949	Phil	Rizzuto	13688	98	
1956	Johnny	Logan	12118	75	
1951	Granny	Hamner	8058	73	
1964	Ron	Hansen	9858	59	
1947	Buddy	Kerr	8943	56	
1961	Tony	Kubek	7566	54	
1968	Gene	Alley	8143	53	
1965	Maury	Wills	13400	51	Δ
1949	Pee Wee	Reese	17720	47	
1954	G.	Strickland	5522	43	
1954	Chico	Carrasquel	10543	41	Δ
1967	Bobby	Wine	8243	36	Δ
1947	Johnny	Pesky	5192	33	

(*continued*)

Transitional Era *(continued)*

MCS	First	Last	IP	Runs	Δ
1960	Dick	Groat	16308	33	
1956	Willie	Miranda	5344	30	
1964	Luis	Aparicio	22407	27	Δ
1961	Woodie	Held	4527	26	
1967	Ray	Oyler	3580	24	
1958	Rocky	Bridges	3154	22	
1964	Zoilo	Versalles	10853	21	Δ
1955	Billy	Hunter	4089	19	
1968	Rico	Petrocelli	6629	18	
1961	Joe	Koppe	3606	18	
1951	Ray	Boone	3833	17	
1957	Alex	Grammas	4353	17	
1957	Ernie	Banks	9953	13	Δ
1956	Joe	DeMaestri	8172	12	
1952	Solly	Hemus	3791	11	
1968	Woody	Woodward	3687	10	
1967	Jim	Fregosi	12113	9	
1967	Larry	Brown	6076	6	
1962	Eddie	Kasko	4282	2	
1950	Johnny	Lipon	6185	2	
1964	Ducky	Schofield	4975	0	
1964	Wayne	Causey	3417	-6	
1964	Dick	McAuliffe	5361	-7	
1963	Bob	Lillis	4088	-7	
1967	Leo	Cardenas	16005	-8	Δ
1952	Al	Dark	12306	-11	
1950	Sam	Dente	4401	-11	
1966	Tom	Tresh	3031	-12	
1949	Stan	Rojek	3719	-14	
1960	Chico	Fernandez	6705	-16	Δ
1967	Denis	Menke	6772	-16	
1957	Billy	Klaus	3215	-18	
1958	Daryl	Spencer	4630	-21	
1963	Ruben	Amaro	5287	-22	Δ
1962	Andre	Rodgers	5180	-22	Δ
1968	Roberto	Pena	3126	-25	
1953	Pete	Runnels	3860	-27	
1949	Virgil	Stallcup	4752	-29	
1947	Eddie	Joost	11206	-30	
1962	Eddie	Bressoud	8170	-31	
1963	Jose	Pagan	5396	-32	Δ
1968	Sonny	Jackson	5254	-32	Δ
1951	Roy	Smalley, Jr.	6644	-35	
1955	Harvey	Kuenn	6525	-44	
1959	Don	Buddin	5731	-50	
1963	Dick	Howser	4697	-56	

Possibly the one DRA career assessment at any position that worries me the most is Luis Aparicio's, so we'll jump right to the comparison with the best alternative system, *Smith(pgor,bod)*. We'll back out "Error Runs"—the estimated half run of excess credit per error avoided in *Smith(pgor,bod)*—so that we can isolate the real differences with DRA.

Luis Aparicio

Year	L	Team	IP	DRA	v-Tm	Smith(pgor,bod) – Error Runs (S-E)	DRA – (S-E)
1956	A	CHI	1300	7	-1	5	2
1957	A	CHI	1246	-10	-7	8	-18
1958	A	CHI	1266	14	0	15	0
1959	A	CHI	1339	-2	-1	4	-6
1960	A	CHI	1345	18	3	19	-2
1961	A	CHI	1331	10	2	7	3
1962	A	CHI	1281	7	1	8	-1
1963	A	BAL	1274	-7	-5	1	-8
1964	A	BAL	1272	10	6	10	0
1965	A	BAL	1270	13	4	12	1
1966	A	BAL	1366	3	-1	4	0
1967	A	BAL	1147	-10	-1	-2	-8
1968	A	CHI	1356	1	-2	6	-5
1969	A	CHI	1322	11	3	6	4
1970	A	CHI	1196	-5	1	-3	-1
1971	A	BOS	1057	-16	7	-9	-6
1972	A	BOS	936	-14	-2	-5	-9
1973	A	BOS	1105	-4	-2	10	-13
Total			22407	27	5	96	-67

On the basis of the number in the lower right corner, my best guess is that the true difference between *Smith(pgor,bod)* and DRA is sixty-seven runs. One of our goals here is to converge on estimates of career fielding value that are within twenty-five runs of each other.

Aparicio genuinely excelled in the first year he won a Gold Glove (1958; +14 defensive runs), but then so did Tony Kubek (+15 defensive runs). Aparicio won in 1958 and kept on winning because (i) the White Sox pitching staff generated huge numbers of ground balls that enabled Luis to lead the league in assists every year from 1956 through 1961, (ii) Luis led the league in fielding percentage eight times, (iii) he was flashy, and (iv) he led the league in stolen bases in each of his first nine seasons, thus 'proving' how quick he had to be as a fielder.

DRA and *Smith(pgor,bod)* (net of over-crediting for avoiding errors) are in rough agreement regarding Aparicio's prime from 1958 through 1962, when he was indeed a top flight fielder, though not necessarily any better than Tony Kubek (+56 defensive runs) over that time frame. I believe the *Smith(pgor,bod)* estimate is too high in 1957 because it gives each fielder credit for something close to a fixed percentage of team hits saved at all other positions, and the 1957 White Sox recorded the most outs on batted balls in play relative to the league rate. On the other hand, DRA is a few runs too low each of the three seasons Aparicio played in Fenway, because the Green Monster and the small foul territory suppress fly outs, which would cause expected plays at short and the infield to be too high, and net plays correspondingly too low.

Aparicio was only +5 defensive runs better than his backups over the course of his career. In comparison, Ozzie Smith was +26 defensive runs better than his. Now it is true that a fielder's career performance vis-à-vis his teammates at the same position is not a very reliable indicator of quality. For example, a dominant fielder who plays almost every inning in his prime *can't* have more than one or two v-Tm runs, because there isn't a large enough sample of teammate performance to outperform. During his 1958–62 prime, Aparicio played almost every inning of every game, so he could only accumulate +5 v-Tm runs over that span. After his prime, Aparicio usually missed about a hundred or a couple of hundred innings per season, which creates a large enough sample over eleven seasons to begin to feel more comfortable about the significance of *large* v-Tm numbers—but Aparicio was only +8 v-Tm runs after 1962.

My best guess is that Aparicio's true career defensive runs were higher than the +27 defensive runs reported by DRA, possibly by up to the additional +44 defensive runs by which *Smith(pgor,bod)* (as adjusted for errors) exceeds DRA in 1963, 1967, and 1971–73. That would certainly constitute a very good but not great fielding career: between +50 and +70 defensive runs.

It's a fair point to argue that seasons of negative defensive runs, particularly towards the end of a career, should not be considered when evaluating all-time great fielders—that only a fielder's prime years should count. For reasons discussed in the introduction to the player ratings, I've decided against that when compiling the lists, and subjectively back out negative defensive runs when it's important for evaluating an all-time great. Even if we construct an alternative career system that ranks fielders by their best three or five seasons, Aparicio would be nowhere near the top, though our next player might.

Pee Wee Reese (see next page) broke into the majors because of a reputation for great fielding, and nearly matched his cross-town rival Scooter Rizzuto until 1948, but faded thereafter. Back in the summer of 1952, Roger Kahn interviewed the then thirty-three-year-old Reese, who complained about being spiked by opponents trying to break up double plays ("[my] legs look like a road map"), and being too tired to warm up before day games following night games. Sounds like the summer he was having (–12 defensive runs, his worst ever). If you just concentrate on Pee Wee's peak, he would certainly be among the best shortstops of all time, but clearly not close to a top ten candidate.

Pee Wee Reese

Year	L	Tm	IP	Runs	v-Tm
1940	N	BRO	721	-3	
1941	N	BRO	1336	30	
1942	N	BRO	1353	30	
1946	N	BRO	1351	5	
1947	N	BRO	1230	11	
1948	N	BRO	1339	9	
1949	N	BRO	1396	2	
1950	N	BRO	1195	-1	
1951	N	BRO	1359	-8	
1952	N	BRO	1256	-12	3
1953	N	BRO	1171	3	6
1954	N	BRO	1253	1	1
1955	N	BRO	1249	-10	4
1956	N	BRO	1157	-6	0
1957	N	BRO	188	0	0
1958	N	LA	166	-3	-4
Total			17720	47	10

Live Ball Era

MCS	First	Last	IP	Runs	Δ
1922	Dave	Bancroft	16558	145	
1940	Luke	Appling	19479	141	
1944	Lou	Boudreau	13648	129	
1921	Rabbit	Maranville	19285	114	
1935	Joe	Cronin	16179	99	
1934	Billy	Rogell	10569	96	
1928	Travis	Jackson	11615	94	
1935	Dick	Bartell	14709	86	
1920	Everett	Scott	14349	84	
1928	Glenn	Wright	8948	83	
1945	Marty	Marion	13470	81	
1938	Billy	Jurges	13508	79	
1937	Arky	Vaughan	13076	57	
1938	Frankie	Crosetti	13203	52	
1929	Mark	Koenig	6211	47	
1924	Joe	Sewell	10787	46	
1920	Ernie	Johnson	3623	32	
1941	Skeeter	Newsome	7399	31	
1923	Wally	Gerber	12480	27	
1929	Tommy	Thevenow	7169	26	
1944	Eddie	Miller	12305	26	
1935	Rabbit	Warstler	6131	26	

(*continued*)

Live Ball Era *(continued)*

MCS	First	Last	IP	Runs	Δ
1932	Charlie	Gelbert	5734	24	
1927	Jackie	Tavener	5404	22	
1931	Woody	English	6840	17	
1938	Billy	Myers	6128	13	
1946	Vern	Stephens	11746	11	
1930	Hal	Rhyne	3739	9	
1943	Skeeter	Webb	3011	9	
1926	Jimmy	Cooney	3396	7	
1921	C.	Hollocher	6715	3	
1924	Topper	Rigney	5587	-2	
1939	Cecil	Travis	6165	-10	
1944	Lennie	Merullo	5021	-11	
1946	Dick	Culler	3274	-12	
1930	Bill	Cissell	3694	-14	
1935	Lonny	Frey	3634	-18	
1946	Eddie	Lake	5017	-21	
1935	B.	Knickerbocker	5592	-22	
1927	Hod	Ford	6921	-23	
1923	Ike	Caveney	3946	-25	
1941	Bobby	Bragan	3529	-29	
1934	Lyn	Lary	9736	-34	
1934	Leo	Durocher	12818	-43	
1934	Eric	McNair	5553	-44	
1929	Joe	Boley	4356	-46	
1934	Billy	Urbanski	5667	-53	
1944	John	Sullivan	4547	-58	
1932	Red	Kress	7093	-61	
1932	Jim	Levey	3829	-62	
1923	Chick	Galloway	8440	-85	
1925	Heinie	Sand	6430	-113	

I suppose the most surprising result is seeing Marty Marion eleventh on the list, rather than first, second, or third. Marion had a tremendous reputation as a fielder. He was tall, had long arms that seemed to catch everything (they called him the Octopus), and he led the league in fielding average in 1947–48.

Marion might be slightly underrated because we don't have reliable innings played data to calculate how much better he was than his backups, on the basis of their relative assists per nine innings. But he played very close to full seasons in 1941, 1942, and 1946, so it shouldn't make too much difference for those seasons, and though he certainly played at a level that would ordinarily lead the league, he didn't have any other outstanding seasons except during the Second World War, when the competition was obviously much weaker. A pretty good hitter for a shortstop at his peak, I think he was a genuine all-star quality player for five or six seasons, and would have been as well even if the War had not diluted the talent pool.

Marty Marion

Year	L	Tm	IP	Runs
1940	N	STL	1062	-11
1941	N	STL	1380	12
1942	N	STL	1314	14
1943	N	STL	1142	16
1944	N	STL	1265	27
1945	N	STL	1120	1
1946	N	STL	1275	17
1947	N	STL	1264	0
1948	N	STL	1225	3
1949	N	STL	1154	7
1950	N	STL	816	2
1952	A	STL	455	-6
			13470	81

Joe Cronin is another example of a fielder who had two very different careers at one position.

Joe Cronin

Year	L	Tm	IP	Runs
1926	N	PIT	21	0
1927	N	PIT	20	0
1928	A	WAS	563	2
1929	A	WAS	1269	14
1930	A	WAS	1353	45
1931	A	WAS	1375	24
1932	A	WAS	1260	15
1933	A	WAS	1366	26
1934	A	WAS	1146	23
1935	A	BOS	1259	-22
1936	A	BOS	561	-2
1937	A	BOS	1288	-26
1938	A	BOS	1226	10
1939	A	BOS	1240	-11
1940	A	BOS	1265	3
1941	A	BOS	960	-2
1942	A	BOS	6	0
Total			16179	99

Cronin led the league in errors in his first full-time season, with over sixty, but he also led the league in assists, and consistently excelled for the next five years. On September 4, 1934, Cronin broke his right wrist. During the off-season, Cronin's uncle by marriage, the owner of the Senators, thought the moment propitious to trade him to the Red Sox in exchange for a certain Lyn Lary and $225,000. As we discussed in evaluating Aparicio's defensive runs with the Red Sox, there is probably a Fenway Park effect that depresses DRA infielder estimates somewhat, but in no way by an amount to explain all of Cronin's abrupt decline, which probably resulted from the wrist injury as well as noticeable weight gain.

Rabbit Maranville's mid-career season falls within the Live Ball Era, because he managed to hang on for an extraordinarily long time past his peak.

Rabbit Maranville

Year	L	Tm	IP	Runs
1912	N	BOS	291	-6
1913	N	BOS	1287	10
1914	N	BOS	1409	49
1915	N	BOS	1337	11
1916	N	BOS	1378	22
1917	N	BOS	1272	9
1918	N	BOS	85	0
1919	N	BOS	1170	10
1920	N	BOS	1146	11
1921	N	PIT	1400	18
1922	N	PIT	1204	-4
1923	N	PIT	1297	-1
1925	N	CHI	702	-6
1926	N	BRO	508	-1
1927	N	STL	88	1
1928	N	STL	985	7
1929	N	BOS	1265	29
1930	N	BOS	1228	-14
1931	N	BOS	1235	-31
Total			19285	114

Rabbit was a key member of the Miracle Braves of 1914, when he had his best season: +49 defensive runs, which I hope is the second highest single season rating coughed up by the DRA system, other than the season Frankie Frisch set the record for assists at second. A bunch of those runs may be attributable to second baseman Johnny Evers, who joined the team that year and, I believe, somehow helped Rabbit record twenty more double plays than any other shortstop, and almost twenty more than any second baseman. The following season Evers played only part time, and Rabbit's double plays fell back towards the league-average rate. The seemingly crazy 1914 estimate is also, as we shall soon see, less crazy when compared to other shortstop defensive runs estimates during the Dead Ball era, and perfectly consistent with Rabbit's finishing second in MVP voting—while hitting .246 with no power, not even doubles power. The manager of that team, George Stallings, acclaimed Rabbit the greatest player since Ty Cobb.

Maranville never had another fielding season remotely as good, and was sometimes moved to second base, and once even demoted to the minors.

(However, like Omar Vizquel, he seems to have had one miraculous late-career fielding season.) Lacking a great arm, he compensated by studying the hitters and being the quickest at getting throws off.

Though Rabbit hung on too long, he literally went out with a bang *and* a whimper. And, true to his legendary showmanship, chronicled so well in *The Historical Abstract*, yet another bang. In his last game, at age forty-five, he came sliding hard into home plate. He broke his ankle so badly everyone in the infield could hear the bone crack, and everyone near the plate could see that the ankle was hideously twisted around. As recounted by Leo Durocher, Rabbit "rasped" to his teammate on deck, the 240-pound catcher Shanty Hogan, "'Don't just stand there, knock me out!' And just as quick as that, Hogan whacked [Rabbit] on the chin and knocked him out cold."[2]

Dead Ball Era

MCS	First	Last	IP	Runs	Δ
1907	Joe	Tinker	14298	283	
1916	Art	Fletcher	12693	275	
1901	Bill	Dahlen	18133	254	
1919	R.	Peckinpaugh	17630	140	
1906	Bobby	Wallace	16083	135	
1911	George	McBride	14554	100	
1909	Mickey	Doolan	11975	94	
1896	Hughie	Jennings	5831	92	
1898	Herman	Long	11259	89	
1900	Tommy	Corcoran	14726	81	
1909	Honus	Wagner	16932	81	
1902	George	Davis	11803	71	
1905	Freddy	Parent	10046	56	
1907	Lee	Tannehill	3275	50	
1898	Bones	Ely	10301	45	
1918	Doc	Lavan	9771	35	
1914	Buck	Herzog	4000	32	
1904	Kid	Elberfeld	8235	18	
1897	G.	DeMontreville	3280	18	
1917	Rogers	Hornsby	3134	13	
1910	Heinie	Wagner	7304	11	
1912	Jack	Barry	7756	11	
1915	Buck	Weaver	7383	9	
1907	Terry	Turner	6645	3	
1916	Ray	Chapman	8414	-4	
1900	Billy	Clingman	3281	-6	
1915	Donie	Bush	16710	-10	
1911	Arnold	Hauser	3348	-11	

(continued)

2. Leo Durocher with Ed Linn, *Nice Guys Finish Last* 35 (Simon & Schuster, 1975).

Dead Ball Era Shortstop (*continued*)

MCS	First	Last	IP	Runs	Δ
1919	Swede	Risberg	3482	-19	
1907	Charley	O'Leary	6299	-33	
1909	Al	Bridwell	8695	-45	
1914	Bob	Fisher	3434	-46	
1907	Phil	Lewis	4367	-60	
1905	Ed	Abbaticchio	3461	-68	
1901	Monte	Cross	14511	-89	
1919	Larry	Kopf	5929	-93	
1896	Ed	McKean	7206	-97	
1905	Rudy	Hulswitt	5218	-102	
1917	Ivy	Olson	9426	-125	

The numbers seem unbelievable. Could any shortstop, let alone three in one generation, really save between 250 and 300 runs? And is Honus Wagner only the eleventh best fielding shortstop of his own era?

When looking at these numbers, we need to imagine as vividly as possible the playing conditions of the Dead Ball Era, which were utterly different from any in living memory. The modern minor league farm system was not established until at least the middle 1920s, and Bill James has reported that at late as 1905, it was not uncommon to allow one or two amateur players just to show up and play in major league games. Presumably that day's amateurs were never entrusted to play the most important fielding position, and ball clubs tried their best to put their best fielders at the most important positions. But still it seems likely that there had to have been what would seem to us an almost pitiable variance in talent among major league shortstops in the Dead Ball Era.

In addition, there must also have been what today we would consider a monotonously high number of ground balls to shortstop. During the Dead Ball Era strikeout levels ranged from just above two per game to just under four, then just under three, so there were more total balls in play. It was accepted as incontrovertible fact that it was impossible to hit a lot of home runs, so players were coached to hit the ball on the ground to avoid hitting high fly balls that fielders could get under and catch. There were many fewer left-handed batters back then, so presumably a higher percentage of those ground balls were hit to the left side of the infield.

With total batted ball opportunities much higher and fielding ability varying more than we can imagine, the difference in plays made by the best and worst shortstops could only have been shockingly high.

It may be several years before any significant number of fans come to agree with me that Honus Wagner was only a solid-to-good, not great, fielder at shortstop.

Honus Wagner

Year	L	Tm	IP	Runs
1901	N	PIT	575	5
1902	N	PIT	380	4
1903	N	PIT	1041	8
1904	N	PIT	1020	-8
1905	N	PIT	1293	20
1906	N	PIT	1238	17
1907	N	PIT	1213	5
1908	N	PIT	1367	-2
1909	N	PIT	1213	12
1910	N	PIT	1209	2
1911	N	PIT	953	-2
1912	N	PIT	1325	28
1913	N	PIT	998	-5
1914	N	PIT	1161	8
1915	N	PIT	1140	2
1916	N	PIT	804	-11
1917	N	PIT	3	0
Total			16932	81

Perhaps in time the following arguments will persuade.

First, Honus padded his numbers with what were almost certainly a high number of discretionary high fly ball putouts. Over the course of his career as a shortstop, Honus averaged seventy-six putouts for every hundred assists. Joe Tinker, almost his exact contemporary, had only sixty-four putouts for every hundred assists. DRA does not give infielders credit for putouts. Per season, Honus probably had fifty extra putouts for which most other systems—Davenport Fielding Translations, Palmer Fielding Runs, and Bill James's Fielding Win Shares—would grant significant credit, about ten runs per season in the case of Palmer Fielding Runs, which would promote Honus to number four among Dead Ball Era shortstops. Honus began his career as an outfielder, and was for all intents and purposes the captain of his team. If he waved off his teammates at third, left, center, and second to catch those soft flies, nobody was going to argue.

Second, Wagner's contemporaries overrated him for something like the same reasons that Jeter is overrated. Nowadays, when many defensive metrics are available that didn't exist a hundred years ago, so-called informed baseball people still perceive the *worst* shortstop as the *best* shortstop, when such shortstop is a *good* hitter and *good* base runner and team leader who has made some visually spectacular fielding plays. Now imagine the corresponding halo effect for Honus Wagner, who was the *best* hitter and *best* base runner of his time, clearly capable of playing every position, the winner of some long-distance throwing competitions, and well known for having big hands, long arms, and using them to scoop up fistfuls of dirt while fielding ground balls, which for some reason seemed to impress people then. Honus *had* to be a great shortstop. But, to be clear—Honus was no Derek. He was clearly among the better-fielding shortstops of his time, just not an all-time great.

Third, Wagner regularly played through some truly extraordinary injuries, which may explain some of the inconsistency in his year-to-year ratings.

Honus had a doppelganger of sorts a few years later in the Junior Circuit.

Roger Peckinpaugh

Year	L	Tm	IP	Runs
1910	A	CLE	108	-2
1912	A	CLE	561	-2
1913	A	NY	850	-15
1914	A	NY	1397	12
1915	A	NY	1326	20
1916	A	NY	1318	12
1917	A	NY	1365	-4
1918	A	NY	1107	19
1919	A	NY	1106	32
1920	A	NY	1216	6
1921	A	NY	1314	-10
1922	A	WAS	1337	24
1923	A	WAS	1367	19
1924	A	WAS	1344	38
1925	A	WAS	1065	-3
1926	A	WAS	347	-4
1927	A	CHI	501	-2
Total			17630	140

BaseballLibrary.com reports that Peckinpaugh was "full-chested, and broad-shouldered, with big hands and bowed legs[;] he pursued the ball relentlessly and effectively, if not always gracefully." This matches every description of Honus Wagner. What does it tell you about the physical condition of players of the Dead Ball Era that two of its best shortstops (in terms of overall value) were conspicuously bow-legged? Of course some recent players have been a little bow-legged. But there is one photo of Wagner in *Dead Ball Stars of the National League* (a beautiful, must-have book for any fan of baseball history) in which a young Honus is walking straight towards the camera on a brilliantly sunny day, and he looks more bow-legged than any person I have ever seen.

Peckinpaugh's defensive runs estimates include three sharp single-season dips, but he was also extremely inconsistent year to year as a hitter, so perhaps his fielding performance really was very inconsistent from year to year. Over longer time frames he actually was fairly consistent—he had +14 defensive runs per 1450 estimated innings during his final three seasons with the Yankees and +22 defensive runs per 1450 estimated innings for the succeeding four seasons with the Senators.

Bobby Wallace was the first American League shortstop to be admitted to the Hall of Fame, and, according to William Curran, the first shortstop "credited with … field[ing] a grounder and throw[ing] in one motion." Scott Schul of SABR quotes Wallace as explaining his innovation as follows:

> As more speed afoot was constantly demanded for big league ball, I noticed the many infield bounders which the runner beat to first only by the thinnest fractions of a second. I also noted that the old-time three-phase movement, fielding a ball, coming erect for a toss and throwing to first wouldn't do on certain hits with fast men … it was plain that the stop and toss had to be combined into a continuous movement.[3]

As we've been trying to highlight throughout this section, fielding at short-stop in the Dead Ball Era was a lot different from what it is today.

Bobby Wallace

Year	L	Tm	IP	Runs
1899	N	STL	931	14
1900	N	STL	1115	-12
1901	N	STL	1214	39
1902	A	STL	1161	27
1903	A	STL	1194	13
1904	A	STL	1254	10
1905	A	STL	1385	-2
1906	A	STL	1230	15
1907	A	STL	1264	16
1908	A	STL	1257	28
1909	A	STL	773	-3
1910	A	STL	899	-9
1911	A	STL	1085	1
1912	A	STL	772	1
1913	A	STL	265	-2
1914	A	STL	142	-1
1915	A	STL	48	0
1916	A	STL	17	0
1917	N	STL	15	0
1918	N	STL	63	0
Total			16083	135

Wallace must have the longest final string of sub-par and part-time seasons of any Hall of Famer. I don't know what happened to him in 1909, but his hitting declined sharply as well.

3. http://bioproj.sabr.org/bioproj.cfm?a=v&v=l&bid=1780&pid=14761.

Herman Long holds a record that will never be broken: total errors in a career, at all positions. But he also holds the record for most chances per game at shortstop. His speed, range, and presumably acrobatic fielding inspired *The Boston Globe* to say he fielded his position "like a man on a flying trapeze." Though some say that fielder positioning was not that sophisticated until the 1940s, Long is reported to have positioned himself deeper and more to the right with left-handed hitters, leaving the third baseman to cover short slow grounders, and also to have positioned himself depending on the pitch called by the catcher.

Herman Long

Year	L	Tm	IP	Runs
1893	N	BOS	1112	23
1894	N	BOS	854	12
1895	N	BOS	1083	0
1896	N	BOS	1036	7
1897	N	BOS	889	7
1898	N	BOS	1250	22
1899	N	BOS	1258	-12
1900	N	BOS	1102	8
1901	N	BOS	1250	9
1902	N	BOS	953	14
1903	A	DET	305	-1
1903	A	NY	168	0
Total			11259	89

The numbers above do not include Long's first season, 1889, when he played for Kansas City in the American Association, or his first three years with the Boston Braves. Long racked up ninety-eight errors in 1893, but he did not lead the league in errors that season, or any season thereafter, though he did lead the American Association in shortstop errors, with over a hundred, in his first season.

Top Forty Shortstops of All Time

MCS	Frst	Lst	IP	Runs	Δ	TPAR
1916	Art	Fletcher	12693	275		179
1907	Joe	Tinker	14298	283		177
1974	Mark	Belanger	15337	197		167
1901	Bill	Dahlen	18133	254		141
1998	Rey	Sanchez	7644	141	Δ	138
1986	Ozzie	Smith	21786	151	Δ	135
1995	Barry	Larkin	17555	112	Δ	106
1999	Jose	Valentin	10060	97	Δ	95
1983	Garry	Templeton	16747	104	Δ	84

(continued)

Top Forty Shortstops of All Time *(continued)*

MCS	Frst	Lst	IP	Runs	Δ	TPAR
2001	Neifi	Perez	9169	79	Δ	80
1991	Greg	Gagne	14455	88		78
1978	Dave	Concepcion	18380	99	Δ	73
2006	Adam	Everett	6528	66		72
1940	Luke	Appling	19479	141		72
2005	Jack	Wilson	9960	65		70
1991	Ozzie	Guillen	15803	79	Δ	69
1944	Lou	Boudreau	13648	129		65
1958	Roy	McMillan	16955	113		65
1988	Jose	Uribe	8051	72	Δ	58
1972	Bert	Campaneris	17951	89	Δ	56
2005	Rafael	Furcal	10798	51	Δ	56
1922	Dave	Bancroft	16558	145		56
1978	Bill	Russell	14797	77		51
1969	Dal	Maxvill	9017	87		51
1919	R.	Peckinpaugh	17630	140		47
1996	Mike	Benjamin	2448	51		46
1977	Chris	Speier	15837	71		45
2005	Juan	Uribe	6859	39	Δ	44
1999	Alex S.	Gonzalez	10942	44		44
1985	Alan	Trammell	18270	60		43
1997	Kevin	Stocker	7156	47		43
2005	Cesar	Izturis	7477	36	Δ	42
1982	Craig	Reynolds	9767	63		42
1949	Phil	Rizzuto	13688	98		39
1997	Mike	Bordick	13357	42		38
1987	Dickie	Thon	9159	53		38
2005	Craig	Counsell	3162	32		37
2003	Alex	Cora	4247	31	Δ	35
1989	Cal	Ripken	20232	47		35
1986	Scott	Fletcher	6541	50		35

Taking into account talent pool concepts and the individual cases we've discussed already in this chapter, the top forty list is generally unremarkable, with one exception.

I cheated to get Mike Benjamin on our list—Benjamin had fewer than 3000 innings at short—because I don't know of a greater example in the history of the major leagues of sheer persistence and unrecognized excellence (leaving aside, of course, all of the Negro League ballplayers). Over the course of thirteen seasons at short, Benjamin consistently had +30 defensive runs per 1450 innings played. I am not aware of any similarly long stretch of proven excellence in the field.

Normally, defensive platooning results in misleadingly high v-Tm runs for defensive specialists. But in this case the numbers are legitimate indicators of extraordinary fielding ability, because of the high quality of the

Mike Benjamin

Year	L	Tm	IP	Runs	v-Tm
1989	N	SF	17	-1	-1
1990	N	SF	137	3	1
1991	N	SF	308	8	8
1992	N	SF	212	2	0
1993	N	SF	102	5	4
1994	N	SF	86	7	6
1995	N	SF	89	0	-1
1996	N	PHI	252	2	-1
1997	A	BOS	99	-2	-2
1998	A	BOS	163	3	2
1999	N	PIT	731	18	9
2000	N	PIT	163	6	5
2002	N	PIT	89	0	0
Total			2448	51	33

shortstops Benjamin substituted for. When Benjamin started out with the Giants, the starters at short were Jose Uribe (high on our top forty list) and Royce Clayton (a well above-average shortstop in those years). In Boston, Nomar Garciaparra, still very solid in the field, was the starting shortstop. Mike's next 'opportunity' was to play for the poor Pirates, and back up Jack Wilson (also high up on our top forty list). Benjamin played behind only one bad fielder (Kevin Stocker in 1996) and one mediocre fielder (Pat Meares in 2000). So, again, Benjamin's +33 v-Tm runs are about as meaningful and reliable as we've seen in this book. To stay in the lineup, Benjamin also played second and third, where he had +15 career defensive runs and +16 v-Tm runs in 2275 innings. That makes well over sixty runs of well-supported fielding value in only about 5000 innings. *Smith*($R(t,s,d)$), which is based on batted ball data, agrees almost perfectly with DRA.

It is very common for shortstops to have a career OPS+ of about 80 (meaning the sum of their on-base percentage and slugging average, adjusted for park effects, was about 80 percent of the league rate), and a few top fielders to get by with an OPS+ of about 70. Mike was down around 60, but he could have been a valuable regular, well above replacement level and possibly about average overall, if given the chance.

I believe that one powerful motivator keeping Benjamin's shoulder at the wheel was money. (And there is nothing wrong with that.) According to baseball-reference.com, he almost cracked the million dollar barrier in each of his last two seasons. One wonders whether a player before free agency with a similar mix of talents would have persisted as long as Benjamin did. Which is yet another reason I believe baseball is extraordinarily more competitive than ever.

We now come to a few "honorable mentions"—fielders for whom persuasive arguments could be made for placing them among the top ten.

Honorable Mention: Bill Dahlen

Year	L	Tm	Runs	v-Tm
1893	N	CHI	791	-5
1894	N	CHI	594	3
1895	N	CHI	1127	44
1896	N	CHI	1096	24
1897	N	CHI	684	5
1898	N	CHI	1245	22
1899	N	BRO	1003	0
1900	N	BRO	1154	19
1901	N	BRO	1143	12
1902	N	BRO	1217	12
1903	N	BRO	1196	28
1904	N	NY	1297	34
1905	N	NY	1312	26
1906	N	NY	1254	-11
1907	N	NY	1232	6
1908	N	BOS	1286	35
1909	N	BOS	485	0
1911	N	BRO	15	0
Total			18133	254

Bill Dahlen was the best shortstop of the high run-scoring portion of the Dead Ball Era, that is, the seasons before the two-strike foul rule, which the National League adopted in 1901 and the American League adopted in 1903. He is also the best player not in the Hall of Fame, and perhaps the most underrated player of all time at any position. If you apply the factors Bill James identified as most associated with being underrated (see *The Historical Abstract* essay on third baseman Darrell Evans), as well as the fact that Dahlen was most dominant before 1900, which also leads to being underrated (see *The Historical Abstract* discussion of Kid Nichols in the essay about the hundred greatest players of all time), one can readily see why Dahlen is not in the Hall of Fame.

However, the quality of fielding data from before 1920, and particularly before 1900, is poor—both limited and inconsistent—so we need to cast a cold eye on these numbers. I'm baffled by the 1908 rating, but we have at least one well-documented case in our times of a similar last hurrah (Omar Vizquel in 2007). If one smooths out the numbers across the years, it appears Dahlen was saving about twenty or twenty-five runs per 1450 innings played through 1905, and about ten runs per 1450 innings for the remainder of his career.

Honorable Mention: Dave Concepcion

Year	L	Tm	IP	Runs	v-Tm
1970	N	CIN	667	-1	-2
1971	N	CIN	778	3	4
1972	N	CIN	962	6	7
1973	N	CIN	764	7	-2
1974	N	CIN	1395	23	-2
1975	N	CIN	1115	16	-3
1976	N	CIN	1310	12	3
1977	N	CIN	1339	12	0
1978	N	CIN	1307	-1	-1
1979	N	CIN	1297	14	3
1980	N	CIN	1348	-7	0
1981	N	CIN	930	8	0
1982	N	CIN	1255	18	6
1983	N	CIN	1175	3	1
1984	N	CIN	838	-11	-4
1985	N	CIN	1298	-5	-4
1986	N	CIN	502	0	0
1987	N	CIN	19	0	0
1988	N	CIN	80	1	0
Total			18380	99	5

David Concepcion once said "Defense is a joy to me every day." But he didn't excel just because he loved his job—Concepcion was a true fielding innovator. After watching Brooks Robinson in the 1970 World Series improvise a few bouncing throws to first, Concepcion decided to apply the technique systematically on artificial turf, where the bounces were more reliable, the ball didn't lose as much speed, and the lower trajectory saved time.

Honorable Mention: Garry Templeton

Year	L	Tm	IP	Runs	v-Tm
1976	N	STL	443	4	4
1977	N	STL	1264	-6	0
1978	N	STL	1354	22	1
1979	N	STL	1315	19	-3
1980	N	STL	991	22	4
1981	N	STL	658	4	-2
1982	N	SD	1205	-4	4
1983	N	SD	1039	6	9
1984	N	SD	1227	6	4
1985	N	SD	1277	13	2
1986	N	SD	1190	-12	-6
1987	N	SD	1243	16	6
1988	N	SD	899	13	7
1989	N	SD	1193	2	3
1990	N	SD	1168	-3	5
1991	N	NY	279	4	2
1991	N	SD	4	-1	-1
Total			16747	104	40

I'm taking Garry Templeton (number nine by TPAR) out of contention for a top ten spot because we've already got so many shortstops from the Modern and Contemporary Eras, because *Smith(pgor,bod)* rates Templeton's 1978–80 peak much more modestly (though partly because it over-penalizes Templeton for his above-average error rates), and because Templeton was inconsistent. Still, I'm ambivalent about dropping him, because very few shortstops outperformed their back-ups more than Templeton did (+40 v-Tm runs).

Templeton led the league in triples his first three full-time seasons, and quickly established himself as a top fielder and all-around player. He was headed for Cooperstown until he broke his left thumb on July 23, 1980. *The Historical Abstract* reports that for some reason, even after his return from the disabled list, he "began to sit out games with minor and unknown injuries. Sometimes he didn't bother to run out ground balls." After he had made an obscene gesture to a heckling fan, his manager Whitey Herzog pulled him off the field and eventually had him traded for Ozzie Smith, who at that time was a much worse hitter and arguably not much better as a fielder.

Templeton got his act together again in San Diego, though he never regained the peaks in hitting and fielding performance he reached in St. Louis. After his playing days were over, the young man who had had trouble managing his own emotions eventually went on to manage teams of young men in two independent leagues and one AAA minor league.

Honorable Mention: Greg Gagne

Year	L	Tm	IP	Runs	v-Tm
1983	A	MIN	82	-6	-5
1985	A	MIN	786	7	5
1986	A	MIN	1287	-15	3
1987	A	MIN	1079	24	7
1988	A	MIN	1179	3	2
1989	A	MIN	1143	-4	3
1990	A	MIN	1074	2	3
1991	A	MIN	1068	5	5
1992	A	MIN	1146	17	-4
1993	A	KC	1331	10	2
1994	A	KC	922	6	-4
1995	A	KC	1008	16	-1
1996	N	LA	1127	21	7
1997	N	LA	1223	3	0
Total			14455	88	22

Greg Gagne had probably the weirdest career trajectory of any fielder at any position. In Minnesota, he was way down and up in his first two full seasons, then basically average until his last season there, in 1992, when he seems to have figured something out. Royals fan Bill James has admitted that he wasn't excited about Gagne coming to Kansas City, but eventually found him to be an outstanding shortstop who seemed to have uncanny judgment about taking fielding risks, such as whether to go for a lead runner or a sure out. Over a six-year period (1992–97) during which the position became insanely competitive from the influx of talent from abroad, Greg Gagne was saving about fifteen runs per 162 games for three different teams in two leagues.

Honorable Mention: Adam Everett

Year	L	Tm	IP	Runs	v-Tm
2001	N	HOU	7	0	0
2002	N	HOU	253	4	6
2003	N	HOU	1001	12	6
2004	N	HOU	842	6	4
2005	N	HOU	1292	3	-3
2006	N	HOU	1292	20	0
2007	N	HOU	535	6	7
2008	A	MIN	364	11	7
2009	A	DET	943	3	-2
Total			6528	66	25

We have many high-quality systems for evaluating the career of Adam Everett, all of which agree that Everett has been the best fielding major league shortstop since 2003, and probably somewhat better than the DRA estimate. Unfortunately for Everett, he's had some trouble hitting and staying healthy, and time may be running out to put up career numbers for a top ten slot. But in terms of proven peak skill, nobody's ever been better.

In finally settling upon our top ten, I've had to make some difficult choices, because of the great 'honorable mention' shortstops above. Part of the choices reflect the fact that the TPAR calculations can never be perfect, and we want to have all eras in baseball history reasonably represented in the top ten. Our final top ten at shortstop will feature two Contemporary, three Modern, one Transitional, two Live Ball, and two Dead Ball shortstops.

Luke Appling (see next page) must have had miraculous invisible range, because he was extraordinarily effective despite leading the league in errors five times, and without ever being perceived as particularly fast or rangy. Which is just the kind of fielder who has been underrated for the past century or so.

If we credit Phil Rizzuto (also on next page) with +20 defensive runs for each of the three seasons he lost to the War (he averaged +26 runs in 1941–42 and 1946) and the one season he was kept down in the minors when he was, in fact, vastly better than the Yankees' then-current shortstop, his TPAR would increase to +139, good for number five.

Number Ten: Luke Appling

Year	L	Tm	Runs	v-Tm
1930	A	CHI	52	-1
1931	A	CHI	673	-5
1932	A	CHI	785	-1
1933	A	CHI	1371	7
1934	A	CHI	924	-7
1935	A	CHI	1361	33
1936	A	CHI	1220	6
1937	A	CHI	1346	33
1938	A	CHI	677	9
1939	A	CHI	1272	11
1940	A	CHI	1332	11
1941	A	CHI	1384	11
1942	A	CHI	1207	7
1943	A	CHI	1386	7
1945	A	CHI	144	0
1946	A	CHI	1317	19
1947	A	CHI	1125	-3
1948	A	CHI	549	1
1949	A	CHI	1220	2
1950	A	CHI	134	2
Total			19479	141

Number Nine: Phil Rizzuto

Year	L	Tm	IP	Runs	v-Tm
1941	A	NY	1142	26	
1942	A	NY	1264	37	
1946	A	NY	1097	12	
1947	A	NY	1316	18	
1948	A	NY	1132	-12	
1949	A	NY	1323	9	
1950	A	NY	1355	8	
1951	A	NY	1239	4	
1952	A	NY	1312	1	1
1953	A	NY	1075	3	5
1954	A	NY	828	0	1
1955	A	NY	451	-8	-6
1956	A	NY	154	-1	0
Total			13688	98	0

We may still be not giving Phil Rizzuto enough credit. He was obviously good enough to play in the majors in 1940, when he was Minor League Player of the Year and hit .347, but probably also in 1939, when he was already twenty-two years old, playing in the same (AAA) league, and hit .316. So perhaps we should be adding not four, but five years to Rizzuto's fielding record. However, Rizzuto's ratings might also be slightly inflated because he had the good fortune to have Joe Gordon as his keystone partner. Bill James has identified the Rizzuto–Gordon double play combination as the best of all time, which means that Joe Gordon may have helped Rizzuto record more double-play assists by catching more ground balls on the right side and feeding them adroitly to Scooter. So I dropped Scooter down a few places.

Perhaps the simplest way of putting Rizzuto's career in perspective is to see him as the Ozzie Smith of his time: the best fielding shortstop in both leagues, someone with about a league-average on-base percentage (Ozzie's was three percent better; Scooter's one percent worse) and a below-average slugging percentage (Ozzie's was sixteen percent worse; Scooter's only eight percent worse), arguably the best bunter in both leagues, among the better base stealers (though base stealing was much more common in Ozzie's era), a leader of several highly successful teams, and a genuine MVP-quality player for at least one season (Ozzie deserved the MVP in 1987, but didn't get it; Scooter won it in 1950, and deserved to). If you took four or five of Ozzie's best seasons away from him, it would be easier to see all this. Possibly no Hall of Fame case was more contentious among well-informed baseball analysts than Scooter's. Fortunately, the Veterans Committee let him into the Hall while he was still alive. Now that we have a better handle on fielding evaluation, it seems, to me at least, that he belongs there.

Number Eight: Roy McMillan

Year	L	Tm	IP	Runs	v-Tm
1951	N	CIN	395	1	
1952	N	CIN	1356	11	0
1953	N	CIN	1348	19	2
1954	N	CIN	1332	3	-1
1955	N	CIN	1275	16	6
1956	N	CIN	1311	21	6
1957	N	CIN	1261	14	2
1958	N	CIN	1118	2	1
1959	N	CIN	621	-8	-6
1960	N	CIN	934	-1	2
1961	N	MIL	1352	19	1
1962	N	MIL	1101	10	9
1963	N	MIL	781	10	-3
1964	N	MIL	35	-2	-3
1964	N	NY	942	4	9
1965	N	NY	1243	-2	5
1966	N	NY	550	-5	-4
Total			16955	113	27

I bumped Roy McMillan above Rizzuto, whose TPAR is higher with War credit, because Roy played in a league that was at least somewhat integrated, and demonstrated high quality fielding with two different teams over a longer time frame. McMillan was on the disabled list for forty-four days in 1959 for a back injury, which presumably had some lingering effects the next year.

Number Seven: Ozzie Guillen

Year	L	Tm	IP	Runs	v-Tm
1985	A	CHI	1203	0	-2
1986	A	CHI	1322	23	4
1987	A	CHI	1291	21	1
1988	A	CHI	1360	28	-1
1989	A	CHI	1344	16	5
1990	A	CHI	1359	12	1
1991	A	CHI	1286	18	6
1992	A	CHI	107	0	1
1993	A	CHI	1133	-1	-4
1994	A	CHI	860	-6	-2
1995	A	CHI	968	-4	-9
1996	A	CHI	1197	-13	-2
1997	A	CHI	1191	-6	5
1998	A	BAL	29	0	0
1998	N	ATL	550	-9	-5
1999	N	ATL	421	1	3
2000	A	TB	181	1	-3
Total			15803	79	-3

Ozzie Guillen won only one Gold Glove, but he should have won a few more during the late 1980s that Tony Fernandez won with his bat and solid but unspectacular fielding. Guillen's fielding reputation was probably harmed by his fairly high error rates. *The Historical Abstract* has a wonderful essay about Ozzie's exciting brand of play, both as a fielder and a base runner. When you look at the table above, you'll see in dramatic fashion how Ozzie's outfield collision with Tim Raines in 1992, which, according to *The Historical Abstract*, cost Ozzie his speed, also destroyed his defensive value. But for that injury, Ozzie Guillen might have had as distinguished a career as a fielder as Ozzie Smith.

The numbers we showed earlier in this chapter for the peak years (1978–1985) of Ozzie I were no better than those above for Ozzie II in 1986–1991. Considering the massive inflow of talent from Latin America that began to arrive in the late 1980s, a case could be made that Ozzie II was, before he tore his knee ligaments in 1992, actually a better fielder than Ozzie I. In fact, the six-year prime of Ozzie II might have been the greatest ever. Having established all-time greatness, I didn't think it right to disestablish it just because he pulled his TPAR down by almost forty runs trying to continue pursuing his profession.

Number Six: Jose Valentin

Year	L	Tm	IP	Runs	v-Tm
1992	A	MIL	2	0	0
1993	A	MIL	156	0	-1
1994	A	MIL	697	20	3
1995	A	MIL	884	1	-2
1996	A	MIL	1291	17	5
1997	A	MIL	1150	7	3
1998	N	MIL	1060	-1	-2
1999	N	MIL	660	-6	5
2000	A	CHI	1212	19	0
2001	A	CHI	310	8	5
2002	A	CHI	409	-2	-4
2003	A	CHI	1200	17	-1
2004	A	CHI	1025	18	-1
2005	N	LA	2	1	1
Total			10060	97	11

Jose Valentin was shortstop X in chapter two, and, like Ozzie II, a perfect reminder of the still-forgotten wisdom of Branch Rickey that fielding percentages—in other words, errors—are worse than useless in fielding evaluation: they are deceptive. Valentin could even rank higher, for reasons explained below, but since I'm the only person who has even momentarily conceived of Jose Valentin as one of the best fifty, still less one of the best five fielding shortstops of all time, I decided to be a little conservative.

Valentin lost significant time to injuries, but recovered well from them and never had a meaningfully bad year. His first spell on the disabled list was in 1997, which saw his DRA rating fall by ten runs. The following year was merely okay. The year after that he spent sixty-six days on the disabled list and had his worst season (–6 defensive runs). When completely healthy in 2000, and playing for a new team, he delivered a great year. But management couldn't see that, presumably because he led the league in errors, and they shifted him to third when they acquired Royce Clayton. Clayton actually had quite a few good (though no great) years with the glove, before injuries took him down to league-average performance, well before he became Valentin's teammate. So the wrong guy got moved off short. That happens. Jeter should have moved to third (or second) when A-Rod joined the Yankees. Valentin reclaimed his spot in 2003, and had another two strong years before injuries forced him into a utility role.

If we treat the partial seasons 1992 through 1995 as one long season, Valentin had five seasons of between +15 and +20 defensive runs. If we conservatively pencil in +15 defensive runs in each of the two seasons, 2001 and 2002, when he was prevented from playing short because of his team's mistake, that gives Valentin seven seasons of true Gold Glove quality play during what was by far the most competitive era for shortstops. In 2006, at the age of thirty-six, he had a +22 net plays rating under John Dewan's Plus/Minus system as a second baseman for the Mets, which translates into about +17 defensive runs, and I can vouch that he seemed to cut off a lot of hits.

Number Five: Art Fletcher

Year	L	Tm	IP	Runs
1909	N	NY	152	0
1910	N	NY	113	-1
1911	N	NY	627	6
1912	N	NY	1172	13
1913	N	NY	1220	22
1914	N	NY	1197	13
1915	N	NY	1304	37
1916	N	NY	1191	32
1917	N	NY	1348	48
1918	N	NY	1100	37
1919	N	NY	1126	47
1920	N	NY	345	11
1920	N	PHI	912	9
1922	N	PHI	884	2
Total			12693	275

Fletcher, Tinker, and Dahlen still come out too high under the TPAR calculation I settled upon. There are many ways one could model the clear downward trend in career defensive runs of top shortstops over the past century, and some of those methods would result in TPARs significantly lower for Dead Ball Era shortstops. That is why I've demoted all three of the top Dead Ball Era shortstops to some degree or another.

I kept trying to think of reasons to knock Art Fletcher off the top ten list entirely, but couldn't think of any. He played well from the beginning and improved steadily. I thought there might be some weird relationship between Fletcher's outstanding fielding and the horrible fielding of his keystone partner Laughin' Larry Doyle, such as an extreme and consistent tendency on the part of the Giant pitchers to generate more ground balls to the left rather than the right side of the infield than other pitching staffs of their time. But Fletcher's numbers actually improved when Doyle was *not* playing full-time for the Giants (1916–19). The pitching staff had a normal turnover, so I can't see how there were unusual batted ball distributions over the ten years or so Fletcher excelled. And Fletcher's fielding success coincided with the success of the Giants, who won the pennant in 1912, 1913, and 1917, and finished second in 1914, 1918, and 1919. Finally, the Giant shortstop defensive runs estimates shortly before and after Fletcher's tenure were nothing unusual. Unlike our next honoree, Fletcher was forgotten because nobody wrote a catchy verse about him.

Number Four: Joe Tinker

Year	L	Tm	IP	Runs
1902	N	CHI	1128	15
1903	N	CHI	943	15
1904	N	CHI	1223	25
1905	N	CHI	1353	36
1906	N	CHI	1300	34
1907	N	CHI	1046	26
1908	N	CHI	1429	38
1909	N	CHI	1287	28
1910	N	CHI	1173	16
1911	N	CHI	1299	22
1912	N	CHI	1255	22
1913	N	CIN	841	7
1916	N	CHI	20	0
Total			14298	283

Here we have the linchpin of the team possessing, as Bill James first pointed out, the best one-year, two-year, three-year, four-year, five-year, six-year, seven-year, eight-year, nine-year, and ten-year won–lost records of all time. The ten-year run (1904–13) almost exactly coincided with Joe Tinker's entire career as the Cubs' starting shortstop. (Tinker played in the Federal League during the missing 1914–15 seasons.) In trying to understand how those Cubs teams could have been so successful, James eliminated several potential explanations: the pitching was good but not great; the outfield unexceptional; the hitting generally strong but not dominant. After this process of elimination, James ultimately concluded that the Cubs of 1904–1913 must have owed more of their success to infield defense than any team in history.

The quality of data we have for making DRA defensive runs estimates for seasons before 1920 is poor, but Tinker was so consistently outstanding, and his teams so successful due to defense, that I feel comfortable placing him this high. Of course, that's not to say that Joe Tinker, time-traveled to the present, and granted the best nutrition, training and medical treatment, would be a great shortstop in *our* time. Rather, his spot at number four acknowledges that, given the conditions of *his* time, he made perhaps the most important and currently underappreciated contribution to the success of the most dominant team of his or any era.

Number Three: Ozzie Smith
(See ratings on page 358.) above

Ozzie Smith should be commended for stoically adapting to a career-threatening injury and for steadily improving his offense, almost without anyone realizing it. He is exactly the kind of player who deserves the honor of election to the Hall of Fame. However, based on the evidence presented earlier in this chapter, I don't believe he was the greatest fielding shortstop of all time, though he probably would have been had it not been for the rotator cuff injury.

Number Two: Rey Sanchez

Year	L	Tm	IP	Runs	v-Tm
1991	N	CHI	65	-2	-2
1992	N	CHI	593	1	-1
1993	N	CHI	761	15	4
1994	N	CHI	189	8	7
1995	N	CHI	20	1	1
1996	N	CHI	768	21	13
1997	N	CHI	279	-1	0
1997	A	NY	24	0	1
1998	N	SF	505	7	5
1999	A	KC	1129	28	8
2000	A	KC	1198	23	5
2001	A	KC	851	25	5
2001	N	ATL	391	7	6
2002	A	BOS	71	1	1
2003	A	SEA	391	2	0
2003	N	NY	344	-1	-3
2005	A	NY	38	0	1
2004	A	TB	26	3	3
Total			7644	141	53

In a truly amazing coincidence, *Baseball's All-Time Best Sluggers* ranks Rey Sanchez the 1111th 'best' slugger of all time (out of 1140 players in major league history who had sufficient at-bats to be profiled), and our number one fielding shortstop … 1112th.

As bad a hitter as Sanchez was, his fielding was so valuable that he should have been allowed to play full-time for at least a decade, but instead could only put together two full-time seasons and those only for a losing, small-market team. Sanchez played virtually his entire career in the first half of the Contemporary Era. A-Rod, Jeter and Nomar had raised the expectations of what a shortstop should hit, but there still weren't widely published defensive runs estimates based on batted ball data that could clearly demonstrate the value of a player like Sanchez. I have little doubt that if Sanchez played now, when batted ball data is being used by most teams, or had played during the Modern Era for an Earl Weaver or Whitey Herzog, managers who both had an intuitive feel for how valuable defense could be, or even less enlightened Modern Era managers who were more forgiving of weak hitting in a good shortstop, Sanchez would have played far more and accumulated defensive numbers so impressive that he would have been acclaimed the greatest fielder of all time.

I decided not to give Sanchez full credit for time lost due to managerial ignorance. In every other case in which we have given credit for missing playing time to a player, the time credited has been a discrete, reasonably short period of time, so that we were merely filling in a gap. In the case of Sanchez, we would be imputing playing time over the course of ten or more seasons—in other words, essentially inventing a whole new career for him. Also, as noted first in the Neifi Perez comment above, a great fielding but weak hitting shortstop may be defensively platooned to play behind pitchers most in need of his services (low-strikeout left-handed ground ball pitchers) and warm the bench for others (high-strikeout right-handed fly ball pitchers). DRA doesn't take this into account, whereas systems developed by Fox and Smith can. DRA estimates +140 defensive runs for Sanchez at short, whereas the Smith and Fox estimates are closer to +110 defensive runs. Then again, as we saw in the preceding chapter, Sanchez also saved another bunch of runs when he was playing second base as a way of getting into the lineup, not because he couldn't play short. Though second is not as difficult as short, perhaps some of those runs should count towards his shortstop rating. In which case, he really might be the best ever.

Number One: Mark Belanger

Year	L	Tm	IP	Runs	v-Tm
1965	A	BAL	5	0	0
1966	A	BAL	44	3	3
1967	A	BAL	311	-1	1
1968	A	BAL	1234	26	8
1969	A	BAL	1294	9	1
1970	A	BAL	1150	17	6
1971	A	BAL	1278	1	-5
1972	A	BAL	768	8	2
1973	A	BAL	1309	22	3
1974	A	BAL	1375	16	1
1975	A	BAL	1262	33	1
1976	A	BAL	1329	25	4
1977	A	BAL	1089	14	-5
1978	A	BAL	985	26	3
1979	A	BAL	572	1	3
1980	A	BAL	730	-1	1
1981	A	BAL	436	1	-1
1982	N	LA	166	-1	-1
Total			15337	197	24

Belanger improved with age because he never stopped learning. Not blessed with great speed or agility, Belanger began by mastering the basics, and eventually transcended them. For example, he initially avoided backhanding the ball whenever possible, but after watching Aparicio (the Orioles shortstop when Belanger came up) he learned when it could be easier and more efficient than doing it the supposedly safer way. Likewise, the all-important first step in moving towards the ball is usually taken with the foot nearest to where the ball is expected to go. Over time, Belanger figured out that it was better to *pivot* off the lead foot. Belanger had a sore arm from time to time, but carefully maintained a consistent throwing motion, and actually improved his arm strength over the years. (Recall that what might have prevented Ozzie Smith from being the greatest shortstop of all time was the injury to his rotator cuff in mid-career.)

Alan Trammell said it best: "No one was ever smarter at the position."

There is a possible caveat: the Blade probably had better 'intelligence' at his disposal for anticipating batted ball distributions than any shortstop of his time. Earl Weaver, the only manager for whom Belanger played a full season, collected more and better data than anybody in baseball before the invention of the personal computer, with the possible exception of Branch Rickey's statistical analyst, Allan Roth. As revealed in *Weaver on Strategy*, the Orioles kept batted ball location charts on all the hitters. So maybe some of Belanger's numbers belong to the Earl of Baltimore.

Then again, maybe not. Belanger hit the disabled list for the first time in 1979, when he was thirty-five, and never played more than half a season thereafter. Here are Baltimore's team defensive runs estimates at shortstop after 1978 but before Ripken took over: −4, −3, +5, +1. Basically average. Without a healthy Belanger playing full-time, all of Earl's charts couldn't manufacture above-average fielding at shortstop.

Mark Belanger's hitting was something of a sad joke. But his fielding, ability to draw a decent number of walks, solid base-running, and bunting skill made him, on average and overall, a genuinely good player and, during his three best seasons with the bat, a true all-star.

14 | Conclusion

Baseball fans have always been obsessed with statistics—batting averages, runs batted in, home runs, won–lost records, earned run averages, strikeouts, stolen bases, and so on. Many very bright people, who've done many wonderful things in the real world, have admitted in public to spending many hours of their lives poring over baseball cards and baseball encyclopedias. What has changed in the last thirty years is that more and more fans have become interested in going beyond merely looking up and memorizing the traditional set of statistics—evocative and captivating though they have been—to developing, in the spirit of amateur scientists or social scientists, new statistics that pull everything together into a coherent estimate of overall value, denominated in terms of the bottom-line baseball currency: runs or wins.

The basic mathematical tools to combine all aspects of a player's offensive contributions into one estimate of runs created above or below the average level, what we've been calling "offensive runs," were all in place arguably about fifty years ago, and certainly forty years ago. There is not a single offensive statistic you will find in any baseball encyclopedia that introduces any basic mathematical idea or statistical technique that hasn't already been applied to baseball statistics for at least forty years. It's just taken the writing of Bill James, the personal computer, spreadsheet and database programs, and the internet to get these kinds of ideas out to the public.

In addition, by comparing how players at different positions perform on offense, many analysts have found reasonable methods to refine an initial offensive runs estimate of player value by taking into account the fact that he plays a more or less demanding fielding position, so that shortstops and left fielders are closer to being compared on a fairer scale. And, mainly thanks to

Bill James, analysts have come to appreciate the importance, especially when evaluating the overall value of everyday players, of taking into account not only their value above the league-average level at their position, but their value compared to a 'bench' or 'replacement level' player at that position. A player with an overall value (offense and defense) of 'zero' relative to the average level of play at his position is *not* worth zero, but is pragmatically worth what his team would lose if he were hurt and replaced by a backup bench player. And the difference between a bench and an average player is about the same as the difference between an average player and a border-line all star.

But, again, estimates of player value that take into account offensive value, the value of playing a more or less demanding position, and the important concept of replacement value have not required any new baseball statistics or mathematical modeling techniques.

The one last major piece in the valuation estimate puzzle has been to determine how much value a player contributes as a fielder relative to other players at that position. Considering how obsessed most fans have been about baseball statistics, it seems at first a little odd how little interest there has been in answering this question. For many years, some of the smartest baseball analysts kept re-answering the questions of offensive, positional, and replacement value again and again while essentially sweeping the fielding valuation question under the rug.

I think this partly related to the fact that traditional fielding statistics never caught fans' imaginations like traditional batting statistics did. I have never heard of anyone who ever memorized fielding statistics. Nobody ever rooted for their favorite player to reach a .980 fielding percentage, or record 450 putouts, or lead the league in double plays. There is not a single fielding statistic that has lodged itself into our collective consciousness like the numbers 60, 56, .406, 714, 3000, or 300.

The likely reason fans have never cared about fielding statistics is because they were so poorly designed that they never effectively conveyed value, or even components of value. Traditional offensive and pitching statistics left a lot to be desired, but you could still be pretty sure a batter with a .300 average, 30 homers, and 100 runs batted in was a good hitter, and a pitcher who won 20 games was a pretty good pitcher. No traditional fielding statistics ever acquired that meaning, probably because none was ever expressed in terms of 'hits saved', or runs, or wins.

Nor have any mathematical models been constructed to convert traditional fielding statistics into estimates of runs saved or allowed relative to the league-average rate, what we've been calling "defensive runs." Yes, there have been various ad hoc defensive formulas developed over the past thirty years, but none with the kind of robust mathematical structure that made the various methods of estimating offensive runs perfectly respectable statistical models from the perspective of any professional statistician. Nor did any of the creators of these ad hoc approaches ever test their defensive formulas as so many offensive ones have been tested, and, with one or maybe two exceptions, these ad hoc systems have never been fully disclosed.

The problem of generating good estimates of fielding value from the existing set of baseball statistics seemed more or less insoluble, and at any rate was unsolved. So analysts tried another approach. Rather than beat their heads trying to make sense of the fielding statistics bequeathed to us in 1876, they went out and *collected new statistics* that made more sense and were more reliable. For-profit companies were formed that hired stringers to go to games or watch games on video, and report where every batted ball was hit, and whether it was a grounder, line drive, fly ball, or pop up, and whether it was caught, and by whom. Since this data concerned the trajectory, location, and outcome of every batted ball, we've been calling this "batted ball data."

The basic idea, which we've been analyzing throughout this book, is that once the season was over, the data collector could say, "Of the 327 fly balls hit this year in the major leagues along the left field line, medium deep, 214, or 65 percent, were caught by major league left fielders." Based on this sample average, one would expect the average left fielder to catch 65 percent of the "fly balls, left field line, medium deep" that were hit when *he* was on the field. If, while Player X was playing left field that year, the stringers counted 10 "fly balls, left field line, medium deep," Player X's expected number of plays on those batted balls would be 6.5.

Then you would do the same type of calculation for every other trajectory and location combination for the position Player X fielded. The net sum across all trajectory and location 'buckets' would equal the number of plays Player X would be expected to make that year in all of his areas of the field combined, if he were *average*. Batted ball data systems would subtract this estimate of *expected plays* for Player X from the plays he *actually* made to arrive at his *net plays*.

Then, using records of what kinds of hits were allowed when left fielders did *not* successfully catch them, in other words, the proportion that were singles and doubles, one could estimate the average type of a hit allowed in left field. For each net play estimated by a left fielder, you would multiply it by the approximate value of the out created plus the hit prevented, which would usually come to something like .85 runs.

So, if Player X had +10 extra net plays throughout left field, and the average value of each left fielder play was .85 runs, batted ball data providers would credit Player X with +8.5, or +9, defensive runs.

There have been all sorts of implementation problems with batted ball data systems, mainly to do with faulty data collection and overly complex calculations that re-introduce biases. However, they potentially provide the most *direct* way to estimate the approximate runs saved by a fielder. All you do is take counts and averages. And it's great that we now have a couple of publicly reported estimates of defensive runs for players to look up on the internet.

What's not so great is that these on-line estimates are based on the same proprietary data set (except for one free collection of batted ball data from 1989 through 1999). I certainly understand why someone who has invested time and money collecting batted ball data would want to obtain a return on their investment, and for that to happen, it is probably necessary for that data to remain proprietary. But no scientist or social scientist would be taken seriously for too long if he reported results based on 'his' or 'her' data, without releasing the data for inspection and testing by other researchers. Perhaps, someday, data from prior seasons can be released and data providers can continue to earn the return on their investment by consulting teams on current player evaluation.

Of course, none of these batted ball systems can rate the all-time greats, because the data hasn't been around for the first hundred years or so of major league history. So the original problem of estimating defensive runs value based on traditional, publicly available, open-source baseball statistics throughout major league history has remained very much open and relevant to fans of baseball history.

This book has presented a system to solve this oldest and toughest puzzle in baseball statistics, perhaps the oldest well-known problem in all sports statistics. As mentioned before, the system applies to traditional, publicly available "defensive" statistics (including pitching and fielding statistics) the classic statistical technique of "regression analysis" to multiple seasons of major league data to estimate (i) expected plays each year for each team at each position, and (ii) the average value in runs of net plays at each position. When I first introduced the basic ideas of the system in an on-line article back in 2003, I called it Defensive Regression Analysis, or DRA, but it can be and is also called Defensive Runs Analysis, because it analyzes, or 'breaks down', defensive runs at each position, and the sum of estimated defensive runs at each position (including pitcher) adds up to an estimate of the number of runs the team 'should' have allowed vis-à-vis the average team in its league that year. Analysis and synthesis.

Batted ball data systems estimate expected plays for a player in a position by essentially counting the number of total batted balls hit in 'his' areas of the field, and multiplying that number by the average percentage of balls in the same locations that are converted into outs by all players throughout the league at that position. In contrast, DRA estimates expected plays for each player by identifying *other* defensive statistics of *his team* over the course of that season that help 'predict' how many more or fewer plays he should have made than the average number at his position that year.

To take a very simplified example, if 500 fly balls and line drives are allowed by a team's pitchers into the various areas of left field, and, based on league averages, 75 percent of fly balls and line drives hit to those areas of the field are caught by all the league's left fielders, batted ball systems estimate that the expected number of plays for that team's left fielders would be 75 percent of 500, or 375. For about a hundred years of major league history, we do not and will not ever have similar counts of all batted balls and their locations.

What DRA does is start with the league-average number of left fielder putouts that year as the base case expected number for the team, and then increases or decreases that base-case estimate depending upon a variety of team-level statistics that are statistically associated with more or fewer left field putouts. Based on the sample average of the league each season, we know there are x left field putouts (say, .08) per batted ball in play. So, for each extra batted ball in play allowed by the team's pitchers, we increase expected left field putouts by .08. Then, based on a "regression analysis" of large samples of team-level data over many seasons, we find that for each extra ground out recorded by the team above the league-average rate, given total balls in play (which we've already just taken into account), left field putouts, on average, decrease by y. For each extra ball in play allowed by a left-handed pitcher, taking into account total balls in play allowed by all the team's pitchers, left field putouts, on average, decrease by z. And so forth, for other factors that make sense from what we know about baseball and that have statistically reliable relationships with expected plays in left. At the end, you're left with an estimate of expected plays in left field.

Regression analysis is just the most common statistical technique for estimating an unknown random outcome (here, expected left field putouts), based on one or more predictors with statistically (and practically) significant association with that outcome.

You then go through a similar process at all the other positions. After subtracting *expected* plays for *each* team at *each* position from *actual* plays made by that team, you arrive at *net* plays per team at each position.

To find the average value of each play, we again turn to regression analysis to determine, on the basis of many team seasons of data over many years, the number of runs statistically associated with each net play at each position. We regress actual team runs below or above the league-average rate, given total innings played, onto each of our above-estimated net plays estimates. Regression reveals that for each net strikeout, expected runs allowed by the team, relative to the league average, should go down by about .3 runs. For each net home run allowed, expected runs allowed by the team should go up by 1.4 or 1.5 runs. For each net play, as estimated above, in left field, expected runs allowed should decrease by .5 or .6 runs, etc. (We explained the discrepancy between this estimate per left field play under DRA with the .85 estimate under batted ball data systems in chapter two.)

Finally, you multiply team net plays by the appropriate number of runs per play to get team defensive runs for that position, and allocate the team rating among the individual players pro rata based on playing time, then adjust up or down on the basis of their plays made above or below the team rate.

Why should anyone believe the resulting defensive runs estimates are correct? Well, the techniques used—though never before applied in this comprehensive way to defense—are fairly standard, of the kind one might learn in a second college statistics course. One or two aspects of the model might raise the eyebrow of a professional statistician, but I believe most would find it reasonably well constructed. The variables included make sense. The output generally looks reasonable. And the bottom line estimates of team runs allowed, based on team defensive statistics, are about as accurate as estimates of team runs *scored* under many decades-old *offensive* models.

I was never satisfied with those arguments. Ever since I developed the first version of DRA in 2003, I've been testing and publishing DRA output against output from batted ball data—the closest thing we have to 'objective truth'. We presented yet another series of tests in chapter three. And what I've continued to find is that DRA defensive runs estimates for recent players match with batted ball data defensive runs estimates either almost or just about as well as batted ball data estimates based on different data sets match with each other. By satisfying this most stringent test, DRA can reasonably be relied upon throughout history to give good, if imperfect and provisional, answers to the questions with which we opened this book.

Utley is much more valuable to the Phillies than Howard, and batted ball data systems are around to confirm this. Bonds's first ten seasons were more valuable than Griffey's first ten. Joe Morgan, great as he was, was not as great as Mike Schmidt. At his peak, however defined, Mays was, within any reasonable margin of error, as dominant as Mantle at his peak. Somewhere, The Thumper can gleefully retract his gracious acknowledgement many years ago that Joltin' Joe was a greater all-around player. Though Cobb still beats Speaker going strictly by the numbers, I say Speaker is close enough that you would have been better off, all things considered, having him on your team rather than Cobb. Wagner, traditionally viewed as the greatest Dead Ball Era all-around player, probably wasn't, even without our taking into account that he played in the weaker league. And the nineteenth century's greatest if ill-fated slugger, Ed Delahanty? Not nearly as valuable as that sharpie, Fred Clarke.

The very greatest recent fielders, such as Andruw Jones, probably saved about 200 runs, though generally the peak potential career defensive runs at most major league positions right now is about 150 or 175 runs. Going a little further back in time, we find that all-time greats such as Brooks Robinson, Willie Mays, and Roberto Clemente probably saved approximately 250 runs. A handful of Dead Ball Era fielders probably did as well, and in general the best fielders, going further back in time, 'saved' more runs.

This brought up the other age-old baseball stats question: how to compare players from different eras. Any system that concludes players are getting worse is wrong. We developed a new approach that puts the very top players from the one demographic group in history that has always been able to play baseball, white U.S. citizens, on approximately the same scale over time, taking into account population growth, and then rated other players on the same scale as their white U.S. peers. These "Talent Pool Adjusted Runs," or TPAR, were scaled so that the very best fielders at all positions would be shown to have saved approximately the same number of career runs as a top fielder whose career was centered on the year 2000.

TPAR brought many post-integration players to our attention, who might have otherwise been neglected, because it has been *so* much harder to stand out in fully integrated baseball: Rey Sanchez, Jose Valentin, Pokey Reese, Gary Pettis, Devon White, Brian Jordan, Jose Cruz, and Warren Cromartie, among many others.

Perhaps the toughest fielding evaluation challenge, which prior systems never really even attempted, was to measure the relative value of outfielders at each outfield position during seasons for which we lack separate putout and innings played data per outfield position. Actually, we never had that data officially. Retrosheet volunteers have gradually been compiling it from box scores and score sheets, but, as this was being prepared for publication, we lacked this data for the 1940s and all seasons before 1920.

An unavoidably more intricate version of DRA, what I call Dead Ball DRA, revealed the scale of fielding value of a whole slew of outfielders whose defensive contributions had been more or less totally invisible and forgotten for generations: Bobby Veach, Jimmy Sheckard, Kip Selbach, Harry Hooper, Mike Mitchell, Elmer Flick, Mike Griffin, Bill Lange, and Fielder Jones. And though the recent release of separate put out data from 1920 through 1940 has probably enabled certain popular systems to apply earlier published DRA outfielder formulas to generate and post on the internet good outfielder defensive runs estimates for those seasons, for the record, Mike Kreevich and Dom DiMaggio were the greatest fielding center fielders of Joe DiMaggio's time. And Sam Rice was one very fine outfielder.

You may have noticed, both in this chapter and throughout this book, the frequent insertions of the words "probably," "about," "approximately," and "perhaps." Would that more baseball analysts used these terms more freely.

The moment baseball fans decided to search for more *meaningful* statistics, they needed, whether they realized it or not, to abandon the idea of ever getting *exact* answers. One of the dangers of the 'magic numbers' derived from these new 'magic formulas' is that people forget that they are only *approximations*, only *estimates*. And what's worse, when they find out that some estimates differ or seem inconsistent, they just throw them out as useless. Which is just as bad as taking them too literally in the first place.

A batter's on-base percentage is a fact, or at any rate a fraction of yes/no facts. Once a batter comes to the plate, that plate appearance increases the denominator by one. After the outcome of that plate appearances is settled, if need be by an official scorer, either a zero or a one is added to the numerator. At the end of the season there is a fraction, usually expressed in decimal form to three decimals. An on-base percentage is in that sense a very precise, factual thing. And though, as Bill James said years ago, a non-pitcher's on-base percentage is the most important single fact you would want to know about him, it is only *one* fact. It is possible to have what would often be a league-leading on-base percentage and still be barely better than an average player in terms of overall value.

All-in-one offensive runs numbers, which have become commonplace over the past thirty years, are not facts, or at least shouldn't be viewed as facts. They are *approximations* of value based on different models of offense and different simplifying assumptions. They can't provide exact answers of how many more runs a team scored that year because Player X was on that team instead of Player Y, but they provide sensible estimates. Similarly, even batted ball data systems provide only approximations of defensive runs. It truly irritates me when I see fans criticize the defensive runs estimates developed by Mitchel Lichtman using batted ball data just because they go up and down for players from year to year. Of course they vary. Of course they may be 'wrong' to some extent. But incorporating those estimates into player evaluations is qualitatively better than ignoring defense or giving a thought, even for a moment, to a player's fielding percentage.

I've been very careful to emphasize that DRA numbers are also only approximations. This is why I have consulted estimates for more recent seasons derived by other analysts, and any other information that could guide the assessment of each player's fielding value.

But, in the meantime, DRA has generated the first set of defensive runs estimates throughout major league history that, I believe, *are* worth mulling over. That is why we've taken the trouble here to print out all those charts of defensive runs—to get people looking at and talking over these estimates, player by player, year by year, so that, over time, and with future improvements, these numbers become almost as meaningful and evocative as any others in baseball history.

We have one more set of runs estimates to look over before we wrap up.

These estimates look a good deal like defensive runs estimates. They're centered close to zero. They have about the same standard deviation (actually, slightly lower). But look at the low correlation between the year-to-year estimates. These numbers are indeed only weakly consistent from 2008 to 2009. Annual defensive runs estimates for full-time fielders under DRA and

Comparison of 2008 and 2009 Runs Estimates

First	Last	2008 Runs	2009 Runs
Lance	Berkman	14	-4
Michael	Bourn	-13	18
Ryan	Braun	0	15
Mike	Cameron	-3	-2
Jorge	Cantu	-9	-3
Stephen	Drew	9	-6
Adam	Dunn	-15	2
Yunel	Escobar	-7	-5
Andre	Ethier	8	-7
Prince	Fielder	-6	2
Jeff	Francoeur	-17	-5
Kosuke	Fukudome	-5	3
Adrian	Gonzalez	-5	-14
Cristian	Guzman	6	-1
Brad	Hawpe	6	17
Ryan	Howard	-8	6
Chipper	Jones	16	-11
Matt	Kemp	17	8
Jason	Kendall	-22	-18
Kevin	Kouzmanoff	-8	-10
Adam	LaRoche	1	7
Derrek	Lee	6	5
James	Loney	0	-13
Felipe	Lopez	2	14
Ryan	Ludwick	13	-9
Russell	Martin	-9	-18
Brian	McCann	-1	-4
Nate	McLouth	-7	-12
Bengie	Molina	-13	-17
Hunter	Pence	-5	-6
Brandon	Phillips	-15	-14
Albert	Pujols	11	-3
Hanley	Ramirez	4	23
Mark	Reynolds	4	6
Jimmy	Rollins	-7	-29
Cody	Ross	-1	-3
Aaron	Rowand	4	1

(*continued*)

Comparison of 2008 and 2009 Runs
Estimates (*continued*)

First	Last	2008 Runs	2009 Runs
Skip	Schumaker	-2	6
Alfonso	Soriano	-4	-11
Miguel	Tejada	-9	0
Ryan	Theriot	0	-4
Dan	Uggla	4	-14
Chase	Utley	-3	-7
Shane	Victorino	-2	3
Joey	Votto	3	17
Randy	Winn	9	-1
David	Wright	4	26
Chris	Young	0	-7
Avg		-1	-2
Std		9	11
Corr			0.26

batted ball data systems usually have year-to-year correlations of between .45 and .55. These estimates look inconsistent, unreliable, bad. Mitchel Lichtman's critics would say, "Toss 'em."

They're *offensive* runs estimates for all National League batters with 500 or more plate appearances in both 2008 and 2009, based on Pete Palmer's formula. Or rather, a special version of Pete's formula, excluding offensive runs attributable to striking out, walking, or hitting home runs. In other words, they are Pete Palmer-type estimates of offensive runs attributable to a batter's batted balls in play: singles, doubles, triples, and batting outs excluding strikeouts. What the above chart is suggesting is that a player's contribution when *hitting* a batted ball into the field of play is probably *less important* (because of the lower standard deviation) and *less predictable* (because of the lower year-to-year correlation) than his contribution when *fielding* a batted ball hit into the field of play.

Now this is just the first sample I took, and it is also the case that the so-called Three True Outcomes (strikeouts, walks, and home runs) have become much more important in recent years. So this pattern was surely less true thirty, sixty, or ninety years ago. But I'm fairly confident that future research will confirm that fielding, as measured by DRA and batted ball data systems for current and past players, can be a *more material and reliable* component of player evaluation than batting contributions when a batter is not walking, striking out, or hitting a home run. And just as offensive runs attributable to singles, doubles, triples, and non-strikeout batting outs have been included without question or comment in baseball encyclopedias for over thirty years, defensive runs should likewise be accepted as at least equally material and reliable.

Even if DRA and batted ball data defensive runs estimates are in some sense more accurate and reliable than truly comparable offensive runs estimates, they are, nevertheless, only approximations. Fortunately, however, DRA is not 'the answer' but a method, an overall approach that can be improved upon to provide *better* approximations. The key to DRA is to identify publicly available statistics that will provide the least biased, most accurate 'predictors' of estimated plays at each position. DRA can generate very good predictors using only a team's putouts and assists at each position, first base double plays, pitcher strikeouts and walks, and home runs allowed, player games at each position, as well as publicly available offensive statistics to estimate playing time for outfielders—in other words, the official set of baseball statistics that have been around since 1876.

But, as we've noted a few times, some of DRA's predictors are unavoidably biased. For example, using ground outs to 'predict' left field putouts is better than using fly outs (because otherwise you're using the left fielder's *actual* plays, which are included in the fly out total, to *predict* his *expected* plays). But if the team's infielders are genuinely good, they will record more ground outs than are accounted for solely by the ground ball versus fly ball tendency of the team's pitchers. So a good infield will make the team's pitchers 'look' more like ground ball pitchers, which will reduce the expected plays in left field, which will result in higher net plays estimates for the left fielders. In general, this is not a material problem, but it is a less-than-perfect approach that can be improved upon.

Due to the efforts of numerous volunteers at Retrosheet, an almost unimaginable amount of publicly available data from the original box scores and score sheets of major league baseball games has come on line. Though this data is not as rich as batted ball data, researchers Sean Smith and Dan Fox have identified some items of information that could potentially provide better, less-biased predictors of expected plays in a DRA-type model. And because DRA has now been fully disclosed, other researchers can make it even better; at least I will be trying to. We're at the end of this book, but really just at the beginning of historical fielder evaluation.

Index

Note: Page numbers followed by "f" and "t" denote figures and tables, respectively.